S.S.F. PUBLIC LIBRARY
West Orange
840 West Orange Avenue
South San Francisco, CA 94080

MAY 17

1 MAP

Northeast Milan
Pages 106–125

NORTHEAST
MILAN

Historic Centre
Pages 44–61

HISTORIC
CENTRE

SOUTHEAST
MILAN

| 0 metres | | 600 |
| 0 yards | | 600 |

Southeast Milan
Pages 94–105

EYEWITNESS TRAVEL

MILAN
& THE LAKES

EYEWITNESS TRAVEL

MILAN
& THE LAKES

DK

Produced by Fabio Ratti
Editoria Libraria e Multimediale, Milan, Italy

Project Editors Barbara Cacciani, Giovanni Francesio
Editors Emanuela Damiani, Mattia Goffetti,
Alessandra Lombardi, Marco Scapagnini
Designers Oriana Bianchetti, Silvia Tomasone

Dorling Kindersley Ltd
Project Editor Fiona Wild
Senior Art Editor Marisa Renzullo
DTP Designers Maite Lantaron, Samantha Borland, Sarah Meakin
Production Marie Ingledew

Contributor
Monica Torri

Illustrators
Giorgia Boli, Alberto Ipsilanti,
Daniela Veluti, Nadia Viganò

English Translation
Richard Pierce

Printed and bound in China

First American Edition, 2000
Published in the United States by DK Publishing,
345 Hudson Street, New York, New York 10014

16 17 18 19 10 9 8 7 6 5 4 3 2 1

**Reprinted with revisions 2003, 2005, 2007, 2009, 2011,
2013, 2015, 2017**

Copyright © 2000, 2017 Dorling Kindersley Limited, London
A Penguin Random House Company

All rights reserved. Without limiting the rights under copyright reserved
above, no part of this publication may be reproduced, stored in or introduced
into a retrieval system, or transmitted in any form, or by any means
(electronic, mechanical, photocopying, recording, or otherwise), without
the prior written permission of both the copyright owner and the above
publisher of this book.

Published in Great Britain by Dorling Kindersley Limited.

A catalog record for this book is available from the Library of Congress.

ISSN 1542-1554
ISBN 978-1-46545-742-4

Floors are referred to throughout in accordance with
European usage; ie the "first floor" is the floor above ground level.

MIX
Paper from
responsible sources
FSC FSC™ C018179
www.fsc.org

**The information in this
DK Eyewitness Travel Guide is checked regularly.**
Every effort has been made to ensure that this book is as up-to-date as possible
at the time of going to press. Some details, however, such as telephone numbers,
opening hours, prices, gallery hanging arrangements and travel information are
liable to change. The publishers cannot accept responsibility for any consequences
arising from the use of this book, nor for any material on third party websites, and
cannot guarantee that any website address in this book will be a suitable source of
travel information. We value the views and suggestions of our readers very highly.
Please write to: Publisher, DK Eyewitness Travel Guides, Dorling Kindersley,
80 Strand, London, WC2R 0RL, UK, or email: travelguides@dk.com.

Front cover main image: Ferry pier at Lake Como, Lombardy

◄ Looking over the Piazza Duomo from atop the Duomo

Contents

How to Use
this Guide 6

Sculpture by Fontana, Cimitero
Monumentale *(see p120)*

Introducing
Milan

Great Days in Milan
and the Lakes 10

Putting Milan on
the Map 14

The History
of Milan 18

Milan at
a Glance 30

Milan Through
the Year 38

Galleria Vittorio Emanuele II *(see p52)*,
inaugurated in 1867

Angel Musicians by Aurelio Luini (16th century), in the church of San Simpliciano *(see p115)*

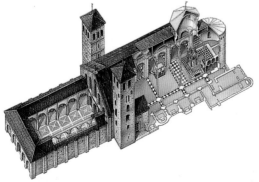

Sant'Ambrogio Basilica dating from the 4th century *(see pp86–9)*

HOW TO USE THIS GUIDE

This guide helps you to get the most out of your visit to Milan and the lakes of Northern Italy by providing detailed descriptions of sights, practical information and expert advice. *Introducing Milan,* the first chapter, sets the city in its geographical and historical context, and *Milan at a Glance* provides a brief overview of the architecture and cultural background. *Milan Area by Area* describes the main sightseeing areas in detail, with maps, illustrations and photographs. A special section is dedicated

to the lakes of Northern Italy, which are all within easy travelling distance of Milan's city centre. Information on hotels, restaurants, bars, cafés, shops, sports facilities and entertainment venues is covered in the chapter *Travellers' Needs,* and the *Survival Guide* section contains invaluable practical advice on everything from personal security to using the public transport system. The guide ends with a detailed Street Finder map and a map of the public transport network in Milan.

Finding Your Way Around the Sightseeing Section

The city of Milan is divided into five sightseeing areas, each with its own colour-coded thumb tab. Each area has its own chapter, which opens with a numbered list of the sights described. The lakes of

Northern Italy are covered in a separate chapter, also colour coded. The chapter on the lakes opens with a road map of the region. The major sights are numbered for easy reference.

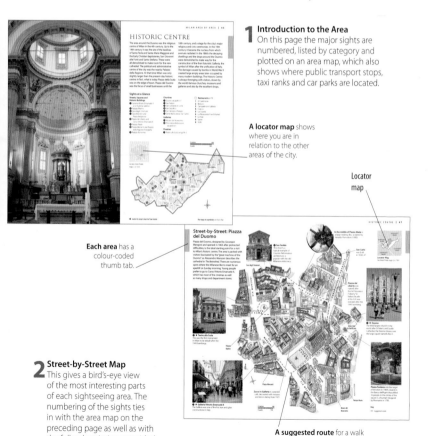

1 Introduction to the Area
On this page the major sights are numbered, listed by category and plotted on an area map, which also shows where public transport stops, taxi ranks and car parks are located.

A locator map shows where you are in relation to the other areas of the city.

Each area has a colour-coded thumb tab.

Locator map

2 Street-by-Street Map
This gives a bird's-eye view of the most interesting parts of each sightseeing area. The numbering of the sights ties in with the area map on the preceding page as well as with the fuller descriptions provided on the pages that follow.

A suggested route for a walk covers the most interesting streets in the area.

Milan Area by Area

The five coloured areas shown on this map (see pp16–17) correspond to the main sightseeing areas of Milan – each of which is covered by a full chapter in the Milan Area by Area section (see pp42–125). These areas are also highlighted on other maps, for example in the section Milan at a Glance (see pp30–37). The colours on the margins of each area correspond to those on the colour-coded thumb tabs.

Numbers refer to each sight's position on the area map and its place in the chapter.

Practical information provides everything you need to know to visit the sights, including map references to the *Street Finder* (see pp222–35).

3 Detailed Information on Each Sight

All the most important monuments and other sights are described individually. They are listed in order, following the numbering on the area map. The key to the symbols used is shown on the back flap for easy reference.

The story boxes discuss interesting aspects of the places described.

Stars indicate the features you should not miss.

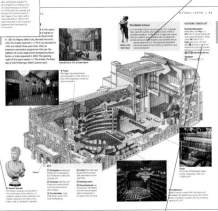

4 The Top Sights

All the most important sights are described individually in two or more pages. Historic buildings and churches are dissected to reveal their interiors. and museums and galleries have colour-coded floorplans to help you locate the major works on display.

The Visitors' Checklist provides all the practical information needed to plan your visit.

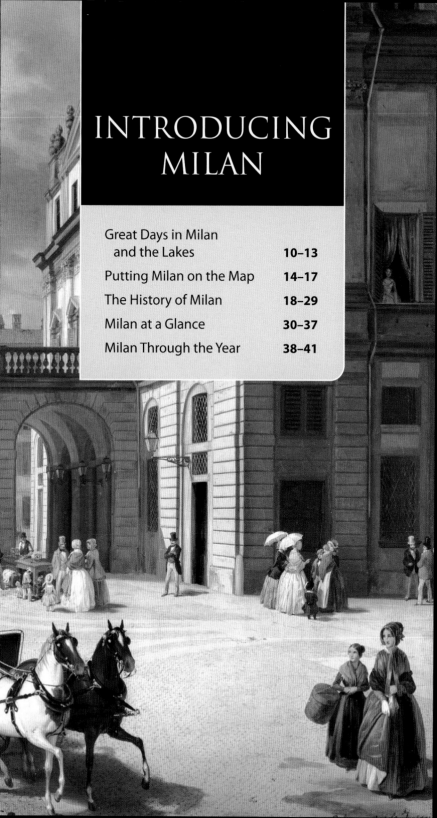

INTRODUCING MILAN

GREAT DAYS IN MILAN AND THE LAKES

Milan is a city packed with a variety of great things to see and do – from cultural riches such as da Vinci's *Last Supper*, the Duomo and the Brera art gallery to top fashion boutiques and an exuberant nightlife. The following itineraries are designed to provide a flavour of life in this vibrant city. Some of the best attractions are arranged first thematically and then by duration of stay. Costs given include travel, food and admission for two adults, or in the case of the "Family Day" itinerary, for a family of four.

Art and Shopping in Central Milan

Two adults allow at least €99

- Galleries of Old Masters
- Fashion boutiques
- View from the Duomo
- Opera at Teatro alla Scala

Morning

Start the day with the Old Masters – da Vinci, Raphael, Caravaggio – in the **Pinacoteca Ambrosiana** *(pp58–61)*. Then, walk east to Via Torino and the **Piazza del Duomo** *(pp46–7)*. Enjoy spectacular views of the city from the roof of Italy's second-largest cathedral, the **Duomo** *(pp48–51)*. Stop over for lunch at one of the cafés, and then browse around Milan's splendid 19th-century shopping mall, **Galleria Vittorio Emanuele II** *(p52)*.

Afternoon

After lunch, head for Piazza della Scala, which is flanked by the world-renowned **Teatro alla Scala** opera house *(pp54–5)* and its Museo Teatrale, devoted to luminaries such as Verdi and Toscanini. The season runs year-round; check their website *(p199)* for booking details.

Nearby is the Quadrilatero d'Oro, a "Golden Rectangle" (bounded by Via Manzoni, Via Montenapoleone, Via Sant'Andrea and Via della Spiga) of boutiques by the likes of Dolce & Gabbana, Gucci and Ferragamo. Art lovers have two excellent museums in the area, **Poldi Pezzoli** *(p110)* and **Bagatti Valsecchi** *(p111)*, showcasing the private collections of Milan's 19th-century elite. Round off the day at the **Pinacoteca di Brera** *(pp116–19)* in the Brera district, then pop in to one of the lively bars for a drink.

The fountain in front of the Castello Sforzesco

Medieval and Renaissance Milan

Two adults allow at least €83

- da Vinci's *Last Supper*
- Ancient churches
- Roman remains
- Trendy Navigli district

Morning

Begin the day at the **Castello Sforzesco** *(pp66–9)* exploring the collections of sculpture, including Michelangelo's *Rondanini Pietà*, and Renaissance paintings. Then, walk into the **Museo Archeologico** *(pp76–7)* to ponder over Milan's early history while awaiting the scheduled noon entry time (reserve at least six weeks in advance) to da Vinci's *Last Supper* *(pp74–5)* in **Santa Maria delle Grazie** *(p73)*. For lunch, double back along Corso Magenta to the corner with Via Carducci to the Art Nouveau **Bar Magenta** *(p184)*.

Gothic spires of the Duomo, the second-largest cathedral in Italy

◄ *Teatro alla Scala in 1852, by Angelo Inganni*

Afternoon
Visit the 4th-century church of **Sant'Ambrogio** *(pp86–9)*, then go to the **Museo della Scienza e della Tecnologia Leonardo da Vinci** *(p90)*, which holds replicas of some of Leonardo's inventions. Walk along the Parco delle Basiliche to see another 4th-century church, **San Lorenzo alle Colonne** *(pp82–3)* preceded by a row of Roman columns. Further down the street lies the **Museo Diocesano** *(p92)*, a repository for art from church treasuries across Lombardy. A short distance away is **Sant'Eustorgio** *(p92)*, a church filled with Renaissance frescoes. Finally, unwind in the nearby Navigli area, home to numerous bars and restaurants.

Lake Maggiore, surrounded by snow-capped mountains

A Family Day on Lake Maggiore

Family of 4 allow at least €116

- Island-hop by ferry
- Glorious gardens
- Lunch by the lakeside
- Breathtaking panoramas

Morning
The best way to enjoy Lake Maggiore is by flitting between its three tiny **Borromean Islands** *(p139)*. Start island-hopping at the lakeside town of **Stresa** *(p139)*. Spend the morning at Isola Bella and Isola Madre, where peacocks wander the exotic gardens and the palace rooms are filled with quirky exhibits, including marionette stages and liveried mannequins. Then head to the village on Isola dei Pescatori for a leisurely lunch by the lake.

Afternoon
Hop off the ferry heading to Stresa at the Mottarone stop and take a cable car (open daily) to the top of Monte Mottarone to admire spectacular views. It is a 3-hour trek back down, so consider buying a return ticket. Stresa's cafés are a 20-minute walk along a lakeside path lined with crumbling villas.

Later, stop outside the town of **Arona** *(p138)* to climb the 35-m- (115-ft-) high statue of San Carlo Borromeo. Kids (only those over 8 years old allowed) love to clamber up the spiral staircase inside the statue to the head, and peer out of the eyes or nostrils at a lake panorama.

A Day on Elegant Lake Como

Two adults allow at least €48

- Lavishly decorated Duomo
- Ornate gardens
- Lakeside strolls
- Palatial villas

Morning
Begin the day at **Como** *(p144)*, on the southwest arm of the lake. Wander along the lakeside promenade, browse the silk outlets, and visit the impressive Duomo and the museum of notable scientist Alessandro Volta. Then, travel up to the lovely resort town of **Bellagio** *(p147)*. The tip of Bellagio's promontory is occupied by the grounds of Villa Serbelloni, which you can visit only by guided tour (sign up at the tourist office).

Afternoon
Take a ferry to **Varenna** *(p146)*, on the eastern shore, and stop for lunch. Next, tour the formal gardens at Villa Cipressi and Villa Monastero, or hike up to the ruins of medieval Castello di Vezio for stunning lake views. Afterwards, cross by ferry to the western shore and the town of **Tremezzo** *(p145)*, home to the 18th-century Villa Carlotta, with its terraced gardens and works by Canova and Hayez. Return to Bellagio for a leisurely evening stroll through its pretty alleyways.

Villa Monastero, one of many elegant lakeside villas on Lake Como

The landmark Teatro alla Scala overlooking the monument to Leonardo da Vinci

2 Days in Milan

- Admire the stained-glass windows in the Duomo
- Enjoy an evening at the Teatro alla Scala
- See Leonardo da Vinci's *Last Supper* in the Santa Maria delle Grazie

Day 1

Morning Start the day at the historic centre of Milan, which is dominated by the **Piazza del Duomo** *(pp46–7)* and its picturesque Duomo. Don't miss the stained-glass windows of the **Duomo** *(pp48–51)*, especially the fifth in the right-hand aisle, which dates from about 1470. Nearby stands the magnificent **Galleria Vittorio Emanuele II** *(p52)*; pause to admire its architecture over a cappuccino in one of the trendy cafés here.

Afternoon From the piazza take Via Mercanti to the **Piazza Mercanti** *(p56–7)*. The medieval Palazzo della Ragione is one of the oldest buildings in Milan. Reserve plenty of time to walk around **Pinacoteca Ambrosiana** *(pp58–61)*, which houses classic works, including the *Portrait of a Musician* by Leonardo da Vinci. Spend the evening at the **Teatro alla Scala** *(pp54–5)*.

Day 2

Morning The basilica of **Sant'Ambrogio** *(pp86–9)* with its golden altar and elaborate decoration, makes for a nice visit before **Santa Maria delle Grazie** *(pp73–5)*, and Leonardo da Vinci's *Last Supper*.

Afternoon The **Castello Sforzesco** *(pp66–9)* is a charming castle with the **Parco Sempione** *(p70)* as its backdrop. Spend a couple of hours in this picturesque park, and then make way east, past the Gothic church of **Santa Maria del Carmine** *(p114)*, to reach the **Pinacoteca di Brera** *(pp116–19)*. The highlights here include a portrait of Christ by Mantegna. End the day at a waterside trattoria in the Navigli area.

3 Days in Milan

- See fabulous paintings by Picasso in the Palazzo Reale
- Mingle with locals under the glass canopy of the Galleria Vittorio Emanuele II
- Enjoy one of Brera's lively trattorias

Day 1

Morning Dedicate the morning to exploring Milan's historic centre. In addition to spending a couple of hours at the **Duomo** *(pp48–51)*, with its high Gothic spires, take time to visit the **Museo del Novecento** *(p56)* and the **Palazzo Reale** *(p56)*, two excellent museums that house splendid collections of contemporary art and paintings, as well as fascinating temporary exhibitions.

Afternoon Spend an hour or more in the **Pinacoteca Ambrosiana** *(pp58–61)* before moving on to the church of **San Sepolcro** *(p57)*, dating, in part, from 1030, and the historic churches of **San Giorgio al Palazzo** *(p57)* as well as **Santa Maria presso San Satiro** *(p57)*. There is some great medieval architecture to admire along the way. Return to the **Duomo** *(pp48–51)* in the evening to see it gorgeously floodlit.

Day 2

Morning Join locals under the elegant glass canopy of the **Galleria Vittorio Emanuele II** *(p52)*, before heading to the nearby **Teatro alla Scala** *(pp54–5)* for a tour. See the opera house's splendid wooden auditorium, a vision of red velvet and gilded stuccowork.

Afternoon Take Via Alessandros Manzoni past **Casa Manzoni** *(p53)*, the late Italian novelist Alessandro Manzoni's house, and the **Museo Poldi Pezzoli** *(p110)* to reach the fashion quarter in **Brera** *(pp112–13)*. Here, see the premises of celebrated designers such as Dolce & Gabbana and Valentino. Reserve time to visit the **Pinacoteca di Brera** *(pp116–19)*.

Day 3

Morning Start the day by exploring the beautiful **San Lorenzo alle Colonne** *(pp82–3)*, a Milan landmark. Allow about an hour to see its Roman columns and the 5th-century Cappella di Sant'Aquilino. Then, make your way from Piazza della Vetra along

Traditional Lombard terracotta decoration on the façade of Casa Manzoni

Via Lanzone to **Sant'Ambrogio** *(pp86–9)*, where nine kings of Italy were crowned from the 9th to the 15th century.

Afternoon After lunch, visit the **Santa Maria delle Grazie** *(pp73–5)* to see Leonardo da Vinci's *Last Supper*. From here, it's a short walk to the **Castello Sforzesco** *(pp66–9)*. Take a tour of this impressive fortress that has protected the city for centuries.

5 Days in Milan

- Take a trip on the Naviglio Grande canal
- Get a panoramic view of Milan from the roof terrace of the Duomo
- Enjoy the tranquility of the Abbazia di Chiaravalle

Day 1

Morning Begin the day at the historic **Piazza del Duomo** *(pp46–47)*. Climb to the top of the **Duomo** *(pp48–51)* and enjoy a panoramic view of the city from the roof terrace. Explore the area, taking in the church of **San Fedele** *(p52)*, past the **Casa degli Omenoni** *(p53)* studio to the grand **Palazzo Marino** *(p52)*, said to have once been home to Marianna de Leyva, the famous nun of Monza.

Afternoon Spend time touring the **Teatro alla Scala** *(see pp54–5)* and seeing the impressive **Galleria Vittorio Emanuele II** *(p52)*. Afterwards, explore the **Pinacoteca Ambrosiana** *(pp58–61)*, which houses one of Raphael's breathtaking paintings, the *Cartoon for the School of Athens*.

Day 2

Morning Arrive at the bustling **Brera** *(pp112–13)* quarter to explore the **Pinacoteca di Brera** *(pp116–19)*, which holds some of Italy's finest works. A short walk north lie the splendid churches of **Santa Maria del Carmine** *(p114)* and **San Marco** *(p114)*, as well as the 4th-century **San Simpliciano** *(p115)*.

A fresco depicting the Crucifixion of Christ, San Marco

Afternoon Eat lunch in one of Brera's restaurants, before heading to the adjoining area where Milan's top fashion designers congregate. Its main thoroughfare, **Via Manzoni** *(p110)*, is a wide boulevard lined with palazzi showrooms. Check out **Museo Poldi Pezzoli** *(p110)* and the **Museo Bagatti Valsecchi** *(p111)*, two former residences that have their owners' priceless possessions as exhibits. The nearby **Palazzo Morando – Costume Moda Immagine** *(p111)* is a must visit for fashion enthusiasts.

Day 3

Morning Start the day at the splendid **Sant'Ambrogio** *(pp86–9)*; don't miss the enchanting Apse Mosaic that dates from the 4th century. A detour to the redeveloped Zona Tortona quarter to visit **Armani/ Silos** *(p93)* is worth the time. This exhibition space celebrates the iconic work of the fashion designer Giorgio Armani.

Afternoon Take a leisurely trip along the **Naviglio Grande** *(p91)* from Piazza XXIV Maggio. Stop over at **San Lorenzo alle Colonne** *(pp82–3)* on the way to the square. End the day with dinner at a waterside trattoria.

Day 4

Morning Take a stroll from the **Castello Sforzesco** *(pp66–9)* through the picturesque **Parco Sempione** *(p70)*. The nearby **Acquario Civico**, the 19th-century **Arena Civica** *(p70)* and the **Arco della Pace** *(p71)* triumphal arch are must-sees.

Afternoon After lunch in the **Triennale Design Museum's** *(p71)* Michelin-starred DesignCafe, view the museum's extraordinary design exhibits. Then, go to **San Maria delle Grazie** *(pp73–5)* to see *The Last Supper*.

Day 5

Morning Drive out of the city to the peaceful abbey of **Abbazia di Chiaravalle** *(pp104–5)*. See its intricate frescoes, cloisters and bell tower. Spend time relaxing in its garden, before heading back to the bustle of the city centre.

Afternoon After lunch, go to the towering **Torre Velasca** *(p98)* that dominates the Piazza San Nazaro area. Next, visit the **San Nazaro Maggiore** *(p98)* and the elegant **Ca'Granda** *(p99)*. Unwind in Milan's oldest park, the **Giardino della Guastalla** *(p100)*, before attending an opera at the famous **Teatro alla Scala** *(pp54–5)*.

Exquisite frescoes decorating the interior walls of the Abbazia di Chiaravalle

ing Milan on the Map

Milan is the capital of Lombardy (Lombardia), the most densely populated and economically developed region in Italy. The population of Milan is over 1,300,000 (second only to Rome). This figure does not include the many people who live in the suburbs – which have spread outwards over the years – who depend on the city both for work (there are large numbers of commuters) and entertainment. The city lies in the middle of the Po river valley (Valle Padana) and has always been a key commercial centre. Today it forms part of an industrial triangle with the cities of Turin and Genoa. Milan's position makes it an ideal starting point for visits to the Alpine lakes. Lake Maggiore and Lake Como are close to Milan, whereas Lake Garda is further east, with the western shore part of Lombardy, the eastern shore part of the Veneto.

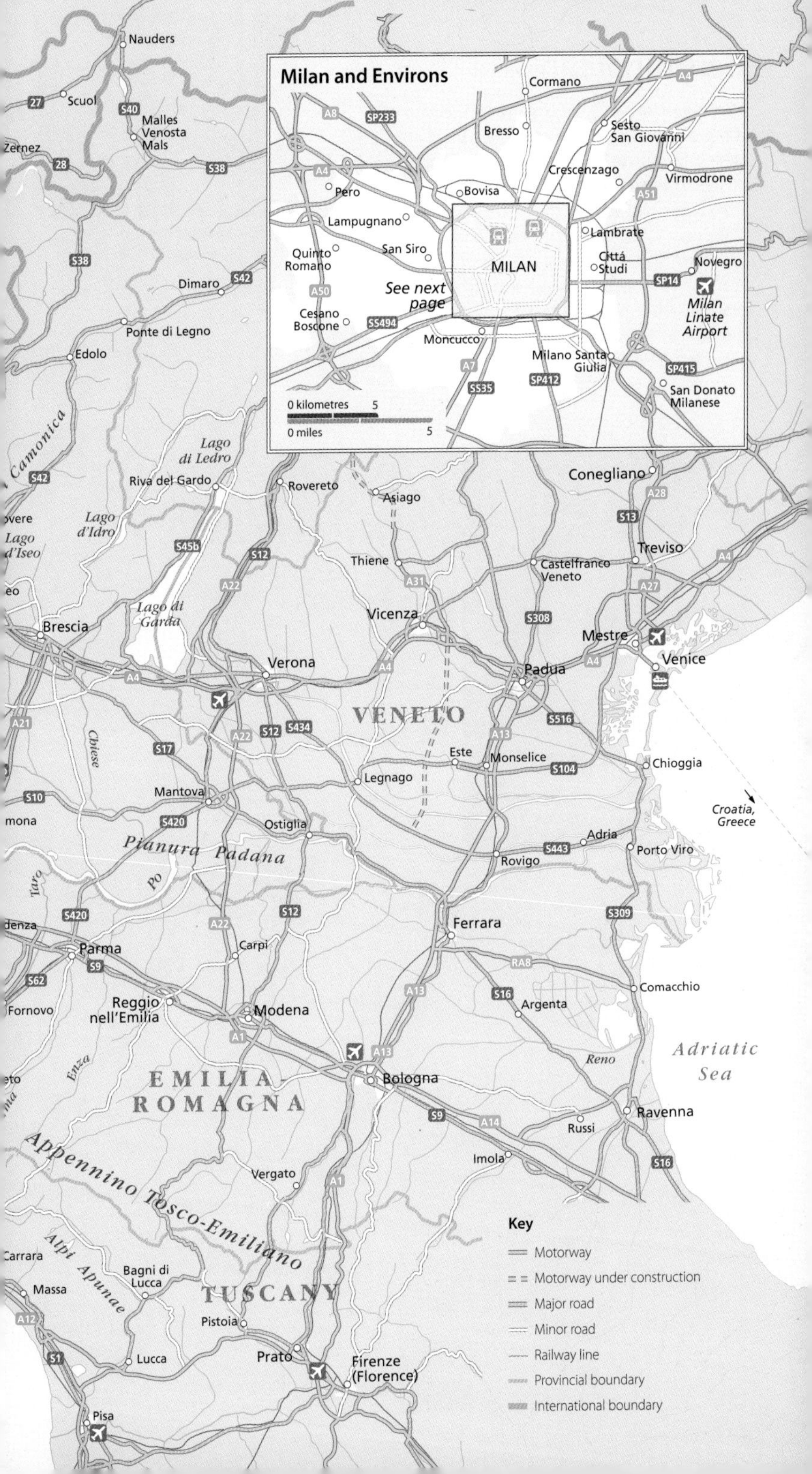

Milan and Environs

Cormano
Bresso
Sesto
San Giovanni
Crescenzago
Virmodrone
SP233
A8
A4
Pero
Bovisa
Lampugnano
A51
Lambrate
San Siro
Quinto
Romano
Città
Studi
MILAN
Novegro
SP14
A50
Milan
Linate
Airport
Cesano
Boscone
See next page
SS494
Moncucco
Milano Santa
Giulia
SS35
SP412
SP415
San Donato
Milanese

0 kilometres 5
0 miles 5

Nauders
27 Scuol
S40
Malles
Venosta
Mals
Zernez
28
S38
S42
S38
Dimaro
Ponte di Legno
Edolo
Camonica
S42
Lago
di Ledro
Riva del Garda
Rovereto
Asiago
Conegliano
Lago
d'Idro
S45b
S12
Thiene
Castelfranco
Veneto
A28
S13
Treviso
A22
A31
eo
Lago di
Garda
Vicenza
S308
Mestre
A4
Venice
Brescia
Verona
A4
A27
A4
A21
A22
S12 S434
VENETO
S13
S516
Padua
Chiese
S17
Este
Monselice
S104
Chioggia
S10
Mantova
Legnano
*Croatia,
Greece*
mona
S420
Ostiglia
Adria
Porto Viro
Pianura Padana
Po
Rovigo
S443
Taro
S420
S12
Ferrara
S309
denza
Parma
A22
Carpi
RA8
S62
Reggio
nell'Emilia
A13
S16
Argenta
Comacchio
Fornovo
Modena
Reno
*Adriatic
Sea*
EMILIA
ROMAGNA
A1
Bologna
A13
Ravenna
Enza
S9
A14
Russi
S16
Appennino Tosco-Emiliano
Vergato
Imola
A1
Alpi Apunae
Carrara
Bagni di
Lucca
TUSCANY
Massa
Pistoia
A12
S1
Lucca
Prato
Firenze
(Florence)
Pisa

Key

═══ Motorway
═ ═ Motorway under construction
─── Major road
─── Minor road
─── Railway line
─── Provincial boundary
─── International boundary

Central Milan

Although Milan is a major city in all respects, it is comparatively small. The city has been divided into five areas in this guide. The historic centre, which you can visit on foot, takes in the Duomo and Teatro alla Scala; in the northwestern district are the Castello Sforzesco and Santa Maria delle Grazie, whose refectory houses Leonardo da Vinci's famous *Last Supper*. Sant'Ambrogio and San Lorenzo lie in the southwest; the southeast boasts the Ca' Granda, now the university. The large northeastern district includes the Brera quarter, with its famous art gallery, Corso Venezia and the so-called Quadrilateral, with its designer shops.

Via Montenapoleone
This is the most famous street in the area known as the "Quadrilateral", where the leading fashion designers are located (*see pp108–9*).

Castello Sforzesco
The Visconti built this fortress in 1368 and it was later rebuilt by the Sforza dynasty, creating one of Europe's most elegant Renaissance residences (*see pp66–9*).

| 0 metres | | 600 |
| 0 yards | | 600 |

San Lorenzo alle Colonne
This church is one of the Early Christian basilicas built for Sant'Ambrogio (St Ambrose) in the 4th century. It is the only one that still preserves some of its original parts (*see pp82–3*).

Duomo
Milan's Lombard-Gothic cathedral is the third largest church in the world and took four centuries to finish. On top is the Madonnina, a statue of the Madonna that has become a symbol of the city *(see pp48–51)*.

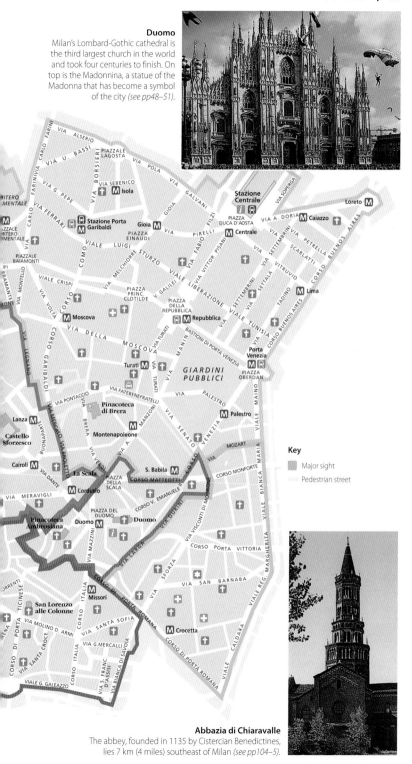

Key

Major sight

Pedestrian street

Abbazia di Chiaravalle
The abbey, founded in 1135 by Cistercian Benedictines, lies 7 km (4 miles) southeast of Milan *(see pp104–5)*.

THE HISTORY OF MILAN

According to the words of a 17th-century ambassador, "Milan never fails to be a great city, and when it declines it soon becomes great again". The sentiments encapsulate one of the characteristics of the city – its ability to rise from the ruins of wars, epidemics, sieges and bombings suffered over the centuries, and to regain dynamism and prosperity once more.

The Prehistoric and Roman City

In the 3rd–2nd millennium BC, the area covered by Milan today was inhabited by the Ligurians. It was later settled by Indo-European populations and then, in the 5th century BC, by the Etruscans. Around the lakes, archaeologists have unearthed fascinating pre-Roman objects that reveal the presence of a Celtic civilization in the 9th–6th centuries BC. Milan itself was founded in the early 4th century BC when the Gallic Insubre tribes settled there.

The origins of the city are somewhat obscure, as is its name, which most scholars say derives from *Midland* (or "middle of the plain"), while others say it derives from *scrofa semilanuta* (half-woolly boar), the city emblem in ancient times. In 222 BC the Romans, led by the consuls Gnaeus Cornelius Scipio Calvus and Claudius Marcellus, defeated the Celts and conquered the Po river valley and its cities. Milan soon became a flourishing commercial centre and in the Imperial era attained political and administrative independence. In AD 286 it became the capital of the Western Roman Empire (until 402) and was the residence of Emperor Maximian. By the late Imperial era Milan was the most important city in the West after Rome and it became a leading religious centre after Constantine's Edict of Milan in 313, which officially recognized Christianity as a religion. Sant'Ambrogio (Ambrose) exerted great influence at this time. He was the first great figure in Milan's history: a Doctor of the Church, he built four basilicas (San Simpliciano, Sant'Ambrogio, San Lorenzo, San Nazaro) and was a leading opponent of the Arian heresy (which denied the divinity of Christ). Sant'Ambrogio was the first in a long series of bishops who ran the city's affairs in the early Middle Ages.

Roman Milan was a substantial size: the Republican walls, enlarged to the northeast during the Imperial Age, defined an area that was roughly the same size as the present-day city centre. The few traces of public buildings that remain, such as the Colonne di San Lorenzo and the remains in Via Circo, attest to the importance of Milan's role at the time.

14th–3rd century BC	2nd–1st century BC	1st–2nd century AD	3rd–4th century AD

4th century BC Foundation of *Mediolanum* by Gallic Insubres	**191 BC** Through an alliance, Milan becomes an integral part of Roman world	**89 BC** Milan becomes Latin colony	**15 BC** Milan capital of IX Augustan region	*Sant'Ambrogio*
			AD 286 Maximian makes Milan Imperial capital	
222 BC Gnaeus Cornelius Scipio Calvus conquers Milan	**55–50 BC** Virgil attends School of Rhetoric in Milan	**49 BC** *Lex Roscia* confers Roman citizenship on Milan	**AD 313** With the Edict of Milan, Constantine grants Christians religious freedom	**AD 374** Sant'Ambrogio (340–397) is made Bishop of Milan

Virgil

◀ The *Sforzesca Altarpiece* (1494), now in the Brera art gallery, with portraits of Beatrice d'Este and Lodovico il Moro

The Early Middle Ages and the Commune of Milan

The 5th and 6th centuries marked a period of decline for Milan. In 402 it lost its status as Imperial capital, was sacked by Attila's Huns in 452, conquered by the Germanic Eruli in 476 and then by Ostrogoths in 489. During the war between the Greek Byzantines and Goths, the city, allies of the former, was attacked by the Goths and utterly destroyed. Reconstruction began in 568, when the city was reconquered by the Byzantine general Narses, who was forced to cede it to the Lombards in the following year. Milan was then ruled by the city of Pavia. The few remaining citizens, led by their bishop Honorius, fled to Liguria: what had been one of the most prosperous cities in the Western Roman Empire was reduced to ruins in the 6th and 7th centuries. The Edict of Rothari of 643 describes in detail Lombard administrative structures of the time.

In 774, the Franks defeated the Lombards and conquered Northern Italy. The archbishops regained power and there was a revival of the economy with the rise of an artisan and merchant class, which in the 11th century led to the birth of the commune. After centuries in which Monza and Pavia had been the focal points of Lombardy, Milan was once again the political centre of the region. The aristocrats and mercantile classes struggled for power in the 11th century, but then joined forces to defend the city against the

Emperor Frederick Barbarossa at the Battle of Legnano (1176) in a 1308 miniature

King Rothari proclaims his edict (643), miniature, Codex Legum Longobardorum

emperor. Once again the city was led by a series of archbishops, some of whom, such as Ariberto d'Intimiano (1018–45), were both bishops and generals. In 1042 the free commune of Milan was founded and a new city wall built. It was demolished in 1162 when, after a siege, the Milanese were forced to open their gates to Frederick Barbarossa: for the second time the city was burned to the ground. Milan and other northern communes together formed the Lombard League, which defeated Barbarossa's troops at Legnano in 1176. Seven years later the Treaty of Constance sanctioned the freedom of these communes.

---

c.491 Invasion of Burgundians

569 Invasion of Alboin's Lombards

570 Entire Po river valley under Lombard dominion

616 Theodolinda, wife of Authari and then of Agilulf, heads regency

Agilulf and Theodolinda

| 400 | 500 | 600 | 700 | 800 | 900 |

452 Milan is sacked by Attila

539 The Goths exterminate the local population

591 Agilulf is elected King of Italy in the Roman circus

643 Edict of Rothari

824 Milan becomes powerful under its bishops who, defying the Church of Rome, defend the Ambrosian rite

In the 13th century, Milan created a formidable canal network, the Navigli, which linked the city to Ticino in Switzerland. However, power struggles among the leading families sapped the strength of the entire city and foreshadowed its decline.

The Great Dynasties

In 1277 at Desio, the Visconti, under Archbishop Ottone, overthrew the Torriani family. The Visconti then summoned the leading artists of the time, including Giotto, to Milan to embellish the city and its palazzi, and they commissioned new buildings such as the Castello and the Duomo (see pp48–51). The height of Visconti power was achieved under Gian Galeazzo, who became duke in 1395 and undertook an ambitious policy of expansion. Milan soon ruled most of Northern Italy and even controlled some cities in Tuscany, but the duke's dream of a united Italy

Coat of arms of the Visconti family

under his lead came to an end with his death in 1402. The Visconti dynasty died out in 1447 and for three years the city enjoyed self-government under the Ambrosian Republic. In 1450 the condottiere Francesco Sforza initiated what was perhaps the most felicitous period in the history of Milan: he abandoned the Visconti expansionist policy and secured lasting peace for the city, which flourished and grew to a population of 100,000. The Visconti castle was rebuilt and became the Castello Sforzesco (see pp66–9), while architects such as Guiniforte Solari and Filarete began work on the Ospedale Maggiore, better known as Ca' Granda (see p99). However, Milan's cultural golden age came with Lodovico Sforza, known as "il Moro" (1479–1508). He was an undisciplined politician but a great patron of the arts. His policy of alliances and strategic decisions marked the end of freedom for Milan, which in 1499 fell under French dominion, yet during his rule Milanese arts and culture were second only to Medici Florence. From 1480 on, great men such as Bramante and Leonardo da Vinci were active in Milan. The former restored numerous churches and designed Santa Maria delle Grazie (see p73), in whose refectory Leonardo painted The Last Supper (see pp74–5), one of his many masterpieces. Leonardo also worked on major city projects such as the Navigli network of canals.

Milan in a 15th-century print

1000	1100	1200	1300	1400	1500
1038 Archbishop Ariberto d'Intimiano leads Milanese against Corrado II and uses *Carroccio* cart with city banner as symbol of Milan	**1158** Barbarossa lays siege to Milan. In 1162 the city is destroyed by Imperial troops	**1277** Rise of the Visconti	**1447–50** Ambrosian Republic		**1482–99** Leonardo da Vinci in Milan
			1395 Gian Galeazzo Visconti becomes duke		**1499** Lodovico cedes duchy to Louis XII
1057 Rise of the Pataria movement against abuses of the clergy	**1154** Frederick Barbarossa suppresses commune at Roncaglia	**1176** Lombard League defeats Barbarossa at Legnano	**1450** Rise of the Sforza **1494** Lodovico il Moro rules	*Frederick Barbarossa*	**1525** Sforza return to power **1535** Charles V takes over duchy

The Visconti and Sforza

The period of the Signorie, or family lordships, from the late 13th to the early 16th century, was one of the most successful in the history of Milan. The Visconti dynasty succeeded – especially during Gian Galeazzo's rule – in expanding the city's territories, albeit for a brief span of time. The Sforza dukedom is best known for the cultural and artistic splendour commissioned by Lodovico il Moro, who invited the leading artists and architects of the time to his court.

Gian Galeazzo imprisoned his uncle Bernabò in 1385 and became sole ruler of Milan. He was made a duke by Emperor Wenceslaus ten years later.

Ottone
Archbishop of Milan in 1262, he was recognized lord of the city in 1277, after the battle of Desio.

Visconti

After defeating the Della Torre (Torriani) family in 1277, the Visconti ruled Milan until 1447, and from 1395 were dukes of the city. Their policy centred around systematic territorial expansion. Under Gian Galeazzo the duchy reached its maximum extent, even conquering Perugia and Siena in central Italy.

Umberto
† before 1248

OTTONE
Archbishop of Milan
Lord of Milan
(1277–8, 1282–5)
† 1295

Obizzo

Andreotto

Tebaldo
† 1276

MATTEO
Lord of Milan (1291–1302, 1311–22)
† 1322

Marco
† 1329

GIOVANNI
Archbishop of Milan
Lord of Milan (1339)
† 1354

Stefano
Lord of Arona
† 1327

GALEAZZO I
Lord of Piacenza
Lord of Milan
(1322–27)
† 1328

LUCHINO
Lord of Milan
(1339)
† 1349

BERNABÒ
Lord of Milan
(1354–85)

GALEAZZO II
Lord of Milan
(1354)
† 1378

MATTEO II
Lord of Milan
(1354)

AZZONE
Lord of Milan
(1329–39)

Caterina
Wife of Gian Galeazzo
† 1404

GIAN GALEAZZO
Count of Virtue
Lord of Milan (1378)
Duke of Milan (1395–1402)
Married Caterina di Bernabò

GIAN MARIA
Duke of Milan
(1402–12)

FILIPPO MARIA
Duke of Milan
(1412–47)

Bianca Maria
Wife of Francesco Sforza
Duke of Milan
(1450–66)

Bianca Maria Visconti and Francesco Sforza
The sole heir to the duchy, Bianca Maria married Francesco Sforza in 1441 and then helped her husband to take over power in Milan.

† indicates year of death

Francesco I

This great warrior had fought for Filippo Maria Visconti, and married his daughter Bianca Maria. In 1454 he began expanding the duchy through peaceful means until it included Genoa and Corsica.

Sforza

After the three-year Ambrosian Republic, the city had a new duke in 1450, Francesco Sforza, the condottiere son of Muzio Attendolo, known as "Sforza". The 50 years of Sforza family rule were the most prosperous and splendid Milan had ever enjoyed. Art and commerce flourished, particularly under Lodovico il Moro. However, his unscrupulous foreign policy led to the fall of the dukedom and the end of freedom in Milan.

Muzio Attendolo
Count of Cotignola
† 1424

FRANCESCO I
Natural son of Lucia Terzani,
married Bianca Maria Visconti
Duke of Milan from 1450
† 1466

GALEAZZO MARIA
Duke of Milan from 1466
† 1476

LODOVICO called IL MORO
Duke of Milan from 1494
† 1508

Ascanio
Became cardinal in 1484
† 1505

GIAN GALEAZZO MARIA
Duke of Milan from 1476
† 1494

Bianca Maria
wife of Emperor Maximilian
of Habsburg
† 1510

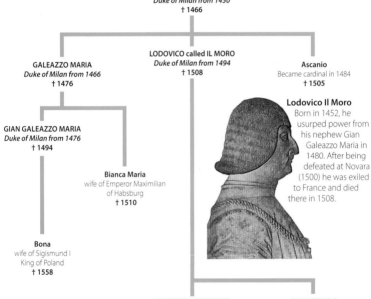

Lodovico Il Moro

Born in 1452, he usurped power from his nephew Gian Galeazzo Maria in 1480. After being defeated at Novara (1500) he was exiled to France and died there in 1508.

Bona
wife of Sigismund I
King of Poland
† 1558

ERCOLE MASSIMILIANO
Duke of Milan (1512–15)
† 1530

FRANCESCO II
Duke of Milan
(1521–24; 1525; 1529–35) † 1535

The Castello Sforzesco is one of the symbols of the Signoria period in Milan.

Where to See Visconti and Sforza Milan

The Milan of the Visconti family is basically Gothic. The main monuments either started or completed under Visconti rule are the Duomo (*see pp48–51*), San Gottardo (*see p56*) and San Marco (though it has been radically altered: *see p114*). Under the Sforza family there was a transition from Gothic to Renaissance architecture, as can be seen in San Pietro in Gessate (*see p101*) and especially in Santa Maria delle Grazie, where Leonardo painted *The Last Supper* (*see pp73–5*). The Ospedale Maggiore, or Ca' Granda (*see p99*), was designed by Filarete for Francesco Sforza, and the Castello Sforzesco (*see pp66–9*) was built by the Visconti but enlarged and embellished by the Sforza, hence the name.

France and Spain

The Renaissance petered out in the 16th century and was followed by a long period of decline. Milan was greatly affected by the loss of political and military importance on the part of the Italian states, now battlefields for other European powers, and because of its wealth and strategic position the city was a key target. The presence of foreign troops was so common that it gave rise to a bitterly sarcastic proverb: "Franza o Spagna purché se magna" (France or Spain, it doesn't matter, as long as we have something on our platter). When Francesco Sforza died in 1535, Emperor Charles V appointed a governor for Milan and the city thus officially became an Imperial province. However, the city nonetheless continued to thrive and the population grew to 130,000. Its territory

Charles V in a portrait by Titian (1532–3)

expanded and from 1548 to 1560 new city walls were built (called the Spanish walls) corresponding to today's inner ring road. The walls were the most important public works undertaken during Spanish rule. All that is left now is Porta Romana arch, though not in its original position. Many Baroque buildings, such as Palazzo Durini and those facing Corso di Porta Romana, were also built in this period. Among the leading figures in Spanish Milan was San Carlo Borromeo (1538–84), cardinal and archbishop of Milan, patron of the arts and benefactor, who rebuilt many churches and was one of the leading figures in the Counter Reformation. His nephew Federico (1564–1631) was also later archbishop of Milan and was immortalized in Manzoni's novel *I Promessi Sposi (The Betrothed)*, a wide-ranging portrait of Milan under Spanish rule. Economic and social decline reached its lowest point with the 1630 plague, which brought the city's population down to 60,000.

Enlightenment Milan

Spanish rule ended in 1706, when during the War of Spanish Succession Austrian troops occupied the city. Milan remained part of the Austro-Hungarian Empire

Alessandro Manzoni's The Betrothed

Considered one of the greatest novels in Italian literature and a masterpiece of 19th-century European narrative, *The Betrothed (I Promessi Sposi)* is also a splendid portrait of Milan under Spanish rule in the 1600s. Manzoni rewrote it several times and had three different editions published (1820, with the title *Fermo e Lucia*, 1827 and 1840). The novel is set in 1628–31 and portrays different phases of Milanese life. In chapter 12 the hero Renzo is involved in the bread riots (in Corso Vittorio Emanuele, a plaque marks the site of the bakery), while from chapter 31 onwards there are vivid descriptions of the city devastated by the plague of 1630.

Title page of a rare 1827 edition of Manzoni's novel

1548 Construction of the Spanish walls begins

1576–7 The so-called San Carlo plague spreads

1609 Foundation of the Biblioteca Ambrosiana

Original nucleus of the Biblioteca Ambrosiana

1706 Eugen Savoy drives last Spa gove

1550	1575	1600	1625	1650	1675

1560 Carlo Borromeo Archbishop of Milan

1595 Federico Borromeo Archbishop of Milan

San Carlo Borromeo

1631 Death of Cardinal Federico Borromeo

1629–31 The so-called Manzonian plague strikes the city. The Lazzaretto (leper-house), built by Lodovico il Moro in 1480, is reopened

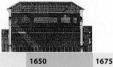

French troops at the city walls

until 1859, except for the Napoleonic period and the Cinque Giornate rebellion (see pp26–7). Economic and, in particular, cultural revival marked the 18th century. Milan was one of the capitals of the Enlightenment, encouraged by Maria Theresa's wise administration (1740–80). From June 1764 to May 1766 a group of Milanese intellectuals, including Cesare Beccaria and the Verri brothers, published the periodical *Il Caffè*, influencing Italian cultural life by propounding the ideas of the French "Encyclopedists". The leading architect of the time was Giuseppe

Piermarini, who designed the Teatro alla Scala (see pp54–5), rebuilt Palazzo Reale in a Neo-Classical style, planned the urban renewal of the historic centre and designed the Corso Venezia gardens. The city's flourishing cultural life did not diminish even when the Austrians had to flee from Napoleon's troops in 1796. As the capital of the short-lived Cisalpine Republic, Milan was the setting for Napoleon's coronation in the Cathedral (1804) and witnessed the construction of various new building projects, including the Foro Bonaparte, the Arena and the Arco della Pace. After Napoleon's defeat, the Congress of Vienna handed Milan back to the Habsburgs, whose government, however, was quite different from the one under Maria Theresa.

Maria Theresa of Austria (1717–80)

There were many abortive revolts, and Milan became one of the focal points of Romanticism and the struggle for Italian independence and unity as propounded in the local periodical *Il Conciliatore*. The publication was repressed by censors and its main exponents (Pellico, Confalonieri and Maroncelli) were imprisoned. The independence movement continued to grow, with the help of the operas of Verdi, and reached its peak with the revolt known as the *Cinque Giornate di Milano*, when the Milanese succeeded, albeit briefly, in driving the Austrian troops out of the city.

Abbé Longo, Alessandro Verri, Giovanni Battista Biffi and Cesare Beccaria, the founders of *Il Caffè*

	1725	1750	1775	1800	1825	1850
Above line		**1740** Beginning of Maria Theresa's rule in Milan	**1778** Inauguration of La Scala opera house	**1796** French troops enter Milan — **1805** Italic Kingdom proclaimed / **1820** Pellico imprisoned by Austrians		**1848** Cinque Giornate revolt / **1848** Radetzky occupies Milan
Below line	**1714** Treaty of Utrecht: Lombardy ceded to Austria	*Cesare Beccaria*	**1764–66** Pietro Verri publishes *Il Caffè* / **1764** Cesare Beccaria publishes *On Crimes and Punishment*	**1818** *Il Conciliatore* published / **1797** Cisalpine Republic	**1839** Cattaneo founds *Il Politecnico* / **1849** Austria-Piedmont peace treaty	**1859** Milan liberated by French-Piedmontese troops

The Cinque Giornate Revolt

This historic event was preceded by the "smoking strike", held during the first three days of 1848, when the Milanese refused to buy tobacco as a protest against Austrian taxation. The "Five Days" revolt began on 18 March 1848. Clashes broke out after a demonstration and continued in a disorderly fashion for two days, during which the Austrians, led by Field Marshal Radetzky, were initially besieged inside the Castello Sforzesco. After the formation of a War Council and a Provisional Government on 22 March at Porta Tosa, the Imperial troops were defeated and driven out of Milan.

Carlo Cattaneo (1801–69)
Cattaneo was one of the leaders in the Cinque Giornate, and later went into exile in Switzerland.

Carlo Alberto's Proclamation
With this declaration, Carlo Alberto, king of Sardinia, put himself at the head of the revolt. Yet when the opportune occasion arose he failed to attack the Austrians and in August 1848 he was forced to cede Milan to the Austrian Radetzky.

Behind the barricades
were people from all social classes, demonstrating the unity of the Milanese in the battle for independence.

The Austrian Army
Field Marshal Radetzky had some 74,000 men (about a third of them Italians) at his disposal, divided into two army corps. The first and larger one was stationed in Milan.

Porta Tosa
This painting by Carlo Canella, now in the Museo di Milano, represents the Battle at Porta Tosa, when the Milanese dealt the final blow to the Austrian troops on 22 March. After this historic event, the city gate, which is situated in the eastern part of the city, was renamed Porta Vittoria (Victory Gate).

Pasquale Sottocorno
Despite being crippled, this 26-year-old shoemaker managed to set fire to the military engineers' building where the enemy troops were barracked, and capture the hospital of San Marco, which was another Austrian stronghold.

The Austrians Return
After he had defeated King Carlo Alberto at Custoza (25 July), Radetzky returned to Lombardy, as announced in this proclamation of 27 July. He recaptured Milan on 6 August.

The Austrians, forced into retreat

Over 1,600 barricades were set up throughout the city during the insurrection.

The Soldier's Widow
In Italy the struggle for independence was closely linked to Romanticism, as can be seen in works dating from this period, such as this 1851 sculpture by Giovanni Pandiani.

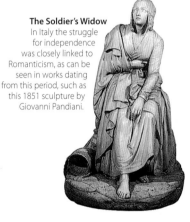

The Cinque Giornate Revolt

Radetzky

The revolt spreads throughout the city and barricades are built everywhere

Radetzky proposes an armistice but is rejected

18 March	**19 March**	**20 March**	**21 March**	**22 March**

Demonstration in the Monforte district for freedom of the press and the establishment of a Civil Guard. Radetzky is besieged in the Castello Sforzesco

Formation of the War Council and Provisional Government

Guardia Nobile helmet

The Imperial troops suffer defeat in the last battle at Porta Tosa (renamed Porta Vittoria) and abandon Milan

Milan After Italy's Unification

In 1861 the population of Milan was 240,000, which shows how much the city had grown under Austrian rule. However, the real demographic explosion was yet to come. Although Milan did not become the political capital after the unification of Italy, it became the economic and cultural capital of the country. Infrastructure created by the Austrians was exploited to the full and by 1920 the city had developed into a thriving industrial metropolis. Business was booming, *Corriere della Sera*, the leading Italian daily newspaper, was founded, the city increased in size and the population exploded (there were 850,000 inhabitants in 1923). This over-rapid growth inevitably brought major social consequences: the first trade union centre was founded, and socialist groups grew in strength.

A *Corriere della Sera* poster

Demonstrations and strikes became more and more frequent, and social tensions exploded in 1898, when a protest against the high cost of living was violently repressed by cannon fire, on the orders of General Bava Beccaris. The early 20th century witnessed the rise of an important avant-garde movement in Milan (the second in the city after the Scapigliatura movement of the second

The 1898 demonstration quelled by Bava Beccaris

half of the 19th century): Futurism, which was founded by Filippo Tommaso Marinetti (a plaque in Corso Venezia commemorates the event). The Futurists were not only important from an artistic standpoint, but also because their ideas and actions fitted in perfectly with the cultural temper of the times, characterized by the pro-intervention attitude regarding World War I and then the rise of Fascism. In fact, Fascism and Mussolini had a very close relationship with Milan. The original nucleus of the movement was founded in Milan in 1919. In 1943, after the fall of the regime and the foundation of the Repubblica Sociale puppet government, Milan – severely damaged by bombing raids – was the last large Italian city to remain under the control of the remaining Fascists and the Germans. On 26 April 1945, the story of Mussolini and Italian Fascism played out its final moments in Milan: the corpses of il Duce, his mistress Claretta Petacci and some party officials were put on display in Piazzale Loreto, exactly the same place where some partisans had been executed a few weeks earlier.

Milan after the 1943 bombings

1860	1870	1880	1890	1900	1910	1920	1930	1

1866–7 Mengoni builds the Galleria Vittorio Emanuele II

1876 Foundation of *Corriere della Sera*

1900 Umberto I assassinated by Gaetano Bresci

1906 Falck firm founded

1919 Fascists meet in Piazza San Sepolcro

1943 The city is heavily bombed

1873 Alessandro Manzoni dies

1872 Pirelli company founded

1898 Insurrection thwarted by Bava Beccaris

1901 Verdi dies at the Grand Hotel et de Milan

1920 Fiera di Milano founded

1946 Toscanini conducts opening concert at the restored La Scala

Fiera poster

The Postwar Period

On 11 May 1946, Arturo Toscanini conducted a concert celebrating the re-opening of the Teatro alla Scala, which had been destroyed by bombs during the war. This historic event demonstrated the desire for recovery and reconstruction that characterized postwar Milan. The linchpin of an industrial triangle with Turin and Genoa, Milan now had 1,800,000 inhabitants. This period of secure growth, disturbed only by student protests in 1968, ended on 12 December 1969, when the explosion of a terrorist bomb in a bank in Piazza Fontana, causing a massacre, began a long, grim period of terrorist activity. The 1980s saw the development of the fashion industry that has made Milan one of the world leaders in this field. The most significant event in the city's recent history was the 1992 anti-corruption investigations which forced many members of the ruling parties to step down from power.

Logo of Teatro alla Scala

Present-Day Milan

Thanks to the dynamism, productivity and inventiveness of its people, today's Milan is a leading European city, but it still has a number of problems: the decline in population, now 1.33 million, is proof of a growing dissatisfaction with a city that is considered, for example, unsuitable for children. The rapid increase in commuter traffic has not been matched by adequate long-distance public transport, which is why the city is frequently blocked by heavy traffic. Last, although Milan is probably the most multicultural city in Italy, clandestine immigration causes its own social problems. Despite this, Milan is an avant-garde city by all standards, a financial, professional and cultural leader in Italian life.

The Growth of Milan

This map shows the growth of Milan from the original Roman city to the present-day metropolis.

Key

- The Roman city
- The Medieval city
- Up to the 18th century
- The 19th century
- The early 20th century
- Present-day Milan

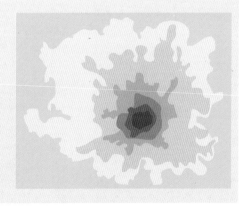

The Pirelli Building

1950 Creation of Metanopoli, satellite city of San Donato Milanese

1955–60 The Pirelli Building is constructed

1973 Telemilano (later Canale 5) first private TV station in Italy

1973 Bomb in Via Fatebenefratelli

1969 Bomb at Piazza Fontana

1992 Outbreak of political corruption scandal

1997 Dario Fo, actor and playwright, wins Nobel Prize for Literature

2004 Teatro alla Scala re-opens after extensive restoration

2000 "Needle, Thread and Knot" sculpture erected in Piazza Cadorna

2015 EXPO 2015 World Fair held in Milan

1950	1960	1970	1980	1990	2000	2010	2020

MILAN AT A GLANCE

One of the many clichés about Milan is that it is a practical, industrious, even drab city, wholly dedicated to work and the world of commercial gain. In fact, besides being a leading metropolis in Europe from a financial standpoint and in terms of productivity, it is also rich in history and culture, architecture and art. The historic centre has no single dominating architectural style, and the buildings are perhaps more varied than any other city centre in Italy. The museums and galleries are among the finest in Northern Italy, and many of the leading figures in the fields of Italian art, design, culture and politics were either born in Milan or achieved success here. The following eight pages will provide brief descriptions of some of the major aspects of the city, while below is a selection of top attractions that no visitor to Milan should miss.

Milan's Top Ten Attractions

Sant'Ambrogio
See pp86–9

Teatro alla Scala
See pp54–5

Pinacoteca Ambrosiana
See pp58–61

Ca' Granda
See p99

San Lorenzo alle Colonne
See pp82–3

Abbazia di Chiaravalle
See pp104–5

Duomo
See pp48–51

Castello Sforzesco
See pp66–9

Pinacoteca di Brera
See pp116–19

The Last Supper
See pp74–5

◀ Ornate interior of the Gothic-style Duomo

Famous Residents and Visitors

Many leading figures in Italian cultural life are connected in some way with Milan, from intellectuals, journalists and politicians to composers, writers and poets. The Italian novelist Alessandro Manzoni was born in Milan, and many other artists have been drawn here, hoping to make their fortune (an illustrious example is Giuseppe Verdi) or, more simply, to find work. One of the most widespread, and perhaps most accurate, sayings about Milan is that it is an open, receptive city ready to give strangers and foreigners a sincere, if brusque, welcome.

Carlo Emilio Gadda (1893–1973)
Milanese by birth, Gadda was one of the great 20th-century authors. One of his major works, *L'Adalgisa*, celebrates the lives of middle-class Milanese and ends with the hero cleaning the tombs in the Monumental Cemetery.

NORTHWEST
(See pp62–77)

CORSO SEMPIONE

VIA LEGNANO

VIA VINCENZO MONTI

VIA MARIO PAGANO

CORSO MAGENTA

CORSO GENOVA

CORSO DI PORTA TICINESE

RIPA DI PORTA TICINESE

Giorgio Strehler (1921–97)
In 1947 the great Trieste-born director founded the Piccolo Teatro della Città di Milano with Paolo Grassi. It was the first permanent theatre in Italy.

Leonardo da Vinci (1452–1519)
In 1482 Lodovico il Moro invited Leonardo da Vinci to his court in Milan, where he remained for almost 20 years. He left a number of works, including the *Codex Atlanticus*, now in the Biblioteca Ambrosiana and *The Last Supper*, in Santa Maria delle Grazie *(see pp74–5)*.

| 0 metres | | 700 |
| 0 yards | | 700 |

Benito Mussolini (1883–1945)
In 1919, in Milan's Piazza San Sepolcro, Mussolini founded the Fasci Nazionali di Combattimento, the nucleus of the future Fascist movement. On 16 December 1944 Mussolini gave his last speech at the Teatro Lirico in Milan. A few months later, on 26 April 1945, his corpse was hung upside down in Piazzale Loreto.

Giuseppe Verdi (1813–1901)
Born in Busseto, in the province of Parma, Verdi moved to Milan at a very early age. His third opera, *Nabucco* (1842), brought him fame. He died at the Grand Hotel et de Milan, which he had made his home.

Alessandro Manzoni (1785–1873)
Manzoni wrote what is considered the greatest Italian novel, *The Betrothed*, as well as plays and poetry. His house in Piazza Belgioioso *(see p53)* is open to the public.

NORTHEAST
(See pp106–125)

VIA MELCHIORRE GIOJA

VIALE TUNISIA

VIALE VITTORIO VENETO

CORSO BUENOS AIRES

VIALE VENEZIA

VIALE PIAVE

CORSO VENEZIA

VIALE PREMUDA

VIA A. MANZONI

Cesare Beccaria (1738–94)
A leading exponent of the Enlightenment movement in Milan, Beccaria wrote its most representative work, *On Crimes and Punishment*. In the square named after him is a monument in his honour.

HISTORIC CENTRE
(see pp44–61)

SOUTHEAST
(See pp94–105)

VIALE MONTE NERO

SOUTHWEST
pp78–93

The Verri Brothers
Pietro (1728–97) and Alessandro (1741–1816) Verri met other noted Enlightenment figures at the Caffè Greco, opposite the Duomo, where they conceived the influential periodical *Il Caffè*.

Carlo Porta (1775–1821)
A poet who wrote in Milanese dialect, Porta offered a vivacious description of the society of his time in his satirical poems. There is a monument in his honour in Piazza Santo Stefano, which was the setting for one of his best-known works, *Ninetta del Verzee*.

Milan's Best: Churches and Basilicas

The churches of Milan are built in two basic architectural styles: Lombard Romanesque, which can be seen elsewhere in the region, and the Counter-Reformation Mannerism of Milan under the Borromeos. The only exception is the Duomo, a splendid example of Lombard Gothic. There are very few examples of older styles. This is partly the result of destructive invasions and time, but is mostly due to the fact that the city is built just above the water table, and older buildings had to be demolished to make way for new ones.

Santa Maria delle Grazie
Besides being home to Leonardo's *Last Supper*, this church, designed by Solari and Bramante, is a marvellous example of Renaissance architecture *(see pp73–5)*.

Basilica of Sant'Ambrogio
The famous church founded by Sant'Ambrogio has a long architectural history, culminating in the restoration carried out to repair damage caused by the bombs of World War II *(see pp86–9)*.

NORTHWEST
(See pp62–77)

CORSO SEMPIONE
VIA V. MONTI
VIA LEGNANO
VIA MARIO PAGANO
CORSO MAGENTA
CORSO GENOVA

Basilica of San Lorenzo
This late 4th-century basilica still has some original architectural elements, such as the columns that surround the courtyard *(see pp82–3)*.

Basilica of Sant'Eustorgio
Inside this 9th-century basilica are several aristocratic chapels, including the Cappella Portinari, one of the great examples of Renaissance architecture in Milan *(see p92)*.

San Marco
The basic structure is 13th-century Romanesque, while the Neo-Gothic façade was restored in 1871. The three statues depicting San Marco between Sant'Ambrogio and Sant'Agostino *(above)* are works of the Campionese school *(see p114).*

San Fedele
This typical example of Counter-Reformation architecture was begun in 1569. Pellegrini's original design was completed by Bassi, who built the façade, and by Richini *(see p52).*

NORTHEAST
(See pp106–125)

HISTORIC
CENTRE
(See pp44–61)

SOUTHEAST
(See pp94–105)

SOUTHWEST
(See pp78–93)

Duomo
Milan's cathedral is the third largest church in the world *(see pp48–51).* It was begun by the Visconti family in 1386 and finished by Napoleon in 1805 – more than four centuries later.

| 0 metres | 700 |
| 0 yards | 700 |

Basilica of San Nazaro Maggiore
Founded by Sant'Ambrogio towards the end of the 4th century, the basilica has been altered many times, but restoration work has revived its original austere beauty. Do not miss the Trivulzio Chapel *(see p98).*

Milan's Best: Museums and Galleries

Besides housing priceless works of art, the museums and art galleries of Milan also reflect the history of the city. The Pinacoteca di Brera was founded at the height of the Enlightenment period and the Ambrosiana is the result of the patronage of religious art by the Borromeo family. The Castello Sforzesco collections date from the period of the *Signorie*, while the Galleria d'Arte Moderna and the Museo dell'Ottocento are a sign of civic commitment to fine arts. The Museo Bagatti Valsecchi and Poldi Pezzoli, private collections, are typical manifestations of the Milanese love of art.

Pinacoteca di Brera
One of Northern Italy's largest art galleries has works from the 14th to the 19th century. Above, *Pietà* by Giovanni Bellini *(see pp116–19)*.

Musei del Castello
The Castello Sforzesco museums are rich in sculpture, furniture and applied arts and also include a gallery with works by great artists, such as this *Madonna and Child with the Infant St John the Baptist* by Correggio *(see pp66–9)*.

Museo Nazionale della Scienza e della Tecnologia Leonardo da Vinci
The Science and Technology Museum has wooden models of Leonardo's inventions and a section given over to clocks, computers and means of communication and transport *(see p90)*.

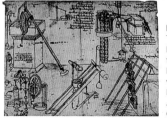

Pinacoteca Ambrosiana
This art gallery was founded by Cardinal Federico Borromeo in the 17th century to provide models for the students at the Fine Arts Academy. The collections include works by artists such as Caravaggio and Raphael *(see pp58–61)*, while the Biblioteca Ambrosiana (library) contains the precious *Codex Atlanticus* by Leonardo da Vinci.

NORTHWEST
(See pp62–77)

CORSO MAGENTA

SOUTHWES
(See pp78–93)

Museo Poldi Pezzoli
Together with the many works by Italian artists in this splendid residence-cum-museum *(see p110)* is Lucas Cranach's *Portrait of Martin Luther.*

Galleria d'Arte Moderna
Villa Belgiojoso – Galleria d'Arte Moderna *(see p123)* houses important 19th-century Italian art collections, the Vismara Collection and the Grassi Collection. Right, *Matilda Juva Branca* (1851) by Francesco Hayez.

Museo Bagatti Valsecchi
This marvellous example of a 19th-century private residence contains 16th-century handicrafts, furniture, arms, ivory pieces, paintings and ceramics *(see p111).*

Museo Teatrale alla Scala
The Museo Teatrale was founded in 1913 and tells the story of the opera house. It holds a vast collection of musical instruments, portraits and documents dedicated to the greatest musicians, from Giuseppe Verdi to Arturo Toscanini *(see p54).*

NORTHEAST
(See pp106–125)

VIA M. GIOIA

VIALE TUNISIA

VIALE VITTORIO VENETO

CORSO BUENOS AIRES

VIALE PIAVE

CORSO VENEZIA

VIALE PREMUDA

HISTORIC CENTRE
(p44–61)

SOUTHEAST
(See pp94–105)

CORSO DI PTA ROMANA

VIALE MONTE NERO

Palazzo Reale
The former royal palace has a long and distinguished history that can be divided into four historic phases: Neo-Classical, Napoleonic, Restoration and the Unification of Italy. The sumptuous interiors create a grand backdrop for the art exhibitions that take place here *(see p56).*

| 0 metres | 700 |
| 0 yards | 700 |

MILAN THROUGH THE YEAR

Milan offers a range of different events and attractions during different seasons of the year, from traditional to commercial. The city's citizens are still attached to traditional religious celebrations such as the Carnevale Ambrosiano (Milanese Carnival) and the festivities that take place around 7 December, the Festival of Sant'Ambrogio, the city's patron saint. This is also the date of opening night at La Scala, the world-famous opera house. Such traditional and characteristic festivities alternate with other events that are perhaps more in keeping with the image of a modern, industrial city. Among these are Fashion Week, one of the world's top fashion shows, held twice a year, and SMAU, an important international multimedia and communications technology trade show.

Private courtyards in Milan, open to the public in the spring

Spring

After the long Milanese winter, local inhabitants welcome the arrival of spring with a sigh of relief. The pleasant spring breezes clear the air of the notorious Milanese smog and the city seems to take on different colours. On very clear days, if you look northwards you will see the peaks of the Alps, which are still covered with snow – one of the finest views the city affords at this time of year.

Towards the end of spring, the clear weather may very well give way to showers and even violent storms, which may blow up in the space of just a few hours, causing problems with city traffic.

This is the season when tourist activity resumes at the lakes. Boat services start up again and the water becomes a major weekend attraction for the Milanese once more.

March
Cartoomics *(three days mid-Mar)*. Fieramilanocity, an event for fans of comics and animation, also features areas dedicated to science fiction and the *Star Wars* films. It has plenty of activities for kids.
Oggi Aperto *(third weekend)*. Monuments and historic buildings that are usually closed to the public are opened up for the weekend.
Stramilano *(end Mar)*. This celebrated marathon is for professionals and amateurs alike and attracts an average of 50,000 competitors every year.

April
Fiera dei Fiori *(Mon after Easter)*. In and around Via Moscova, near the Sant'Angelo Franciscan convent, is this fair devoted mainly to flower growing.
Barclays Milano City Marathon *(early Apr)*. This relay marathon for teams of four runners starts at Fiera di Rho, takes in many of the city's famous sights, and ends at Piazza Castello.

MIA Photo Fair *(late Apr–early May)*. Entirely dedicated to photography, this fair sees events and conferences with key figures from the Italian and international art scene.

May
Milano Cortili Aperti.
The courtyards of the city's private residences are open to the public.
Pittori sul Naviglio. Outdoor art display along the Alzaia Naviglio Grande canal *(see p91)*.
Estate all'Idroscalo. Near Linate airport, the Milan seaplane airport inaugurates its summer season with sports events, water entertainment and concerts.
Sagra del Carroccio. At Legnano, 30 km (19 miles) from Milan, there is a commemoration of the battle of 1176, when the Lombard League defeated Emperor Frederick Barbarossa. There are costume parades, folk festivities and events.
Orticola Flower growing and garden furnishings show and market in the Porta Venezia Giardini Pubblici *(see p122)*.

Well-stocked comic stand at Cartoomics

Average daily hours of sunshine

Sunshine Hours
The hours of sunshine in Milan are in line with the Mediterranean average. However, in autumn and winter the weather can be very foggy, which is a typical feature of the climate in the Po river valley, exacerbated by city pollution. The lakes, surrounded by the Alps, are more shaded in the morning and evening.

Pavilions at Fotoshow

Summer

June is one of the most pleasant months to visit Milan because the climate is mild and the programme of cultural and sports events is truly packed. In July the torrid, muggy summer heat (the temperature may be as high as 40° C/104° F), together with the heavy traffic, can make sightseeing quite uncomfortable.

In August, most of the factories and offices close for the summer holidays and the empty city is an unusual and, in some respects, quite pleasant sight. The same streets that were crowded a week earlier are now quiet, even restful.

Despite the exodus, many events, both cultural and recreational, are held in Milan during the summer.

This is the busiest season for visiting the lakes of Northern Italy, but also the sunniest. Even at the peak of the summer heat, the water can have a cooling effect.

June

Milano–San Remo. Part of the city centre hosts the start of this prestigious international bicycle race.

Festa del Naviglio *(first Sun)*. You can find everything under the sun at this festival, held in the atmospheric setting of the illuminated Navigli canals: street artists and performers, concerts, sports, an antiques market, handicrafts, regional cooking.

Milano d'Estate *(Jun–Aug)*. This marks the beginning of summer entertainment in the city (concerts, exhibits, various cultural events), which takes place in the Parco Sempione.

Arianteo *(Jun–mid-Sep)*. The Anteo motion-picture theatre organizes a series of outdoor showings at various venues around the city. The programme includes all the most important films featured in Milan's cinemas and theatres during the year.

Sagra di San Cristoforo *(third Sun)*. The patron saint of travellers, St Christopher, is celebrated along the Naviglio, in the square facing the church. In the evening decorated barges glide along the canals.

Estate all'Umanitaria. The Humanitarian Association organizes a festival of cinema, dance, music, theatre and cartoons and shows for children.

Fotoshow *(odd years)*. An interesting video, photography and optics show in the Fiera (Exhibition Centre) pavilions.

Sagra di San Giovanni. At Monza, a few miles north of Milan, the patron saint's feast day is celebrated with sports and cultural events, some of which are held at a splendid venue – the park at the Villa Reale.

July and August

Festival Latino-Americano. The Forum di Assago hosts this lively festival of Latin-American music, handicrafts and cuisine.

The Milan–San Remo race, opening the Italian cycling season

Average monthly rainfall

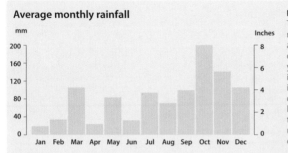

Rainfall

The average monthly rainfall in the Milan area can vary quite considerably during the year. The wettest season is certainly autumn, when it may rain for several days without a break. In late spring and summer the average rainfall level may increase because of unexpected storms.

Autumn

September in Milan really gives you the impression of life beginning anew. In general, by the last week of August the Milanese have returned from holiday, but it is only in September that things get back into full swing. As far as the weather is concerned, fog and rain alternate with lovely clear days with that typical "Lombard sky" which Alessandro Manzoni, in *The Betrothed*, described as being "so beautiful when it is beautiful, so blue, so serene".

A Ferrari at the Gran Premio di Monza

September

Premier League Football (soccer). By September the Italian football season is under way (the opening match takes place on the last Sunday in August). The football season is of great importance to the city, which is home to two of Italy's top teams, Inter and AC Milan.

Panoramica di Venezia (*early Sep*). Milan cinemas show films from the Venice Film Festival as they are being screened there.

Gran Premio di Monza. Held at one of the top motor racing circuits, the Grand Prix of Italy is often crucial to the outcome of the Formula One competition.

Mi Milano Prêt-à-Porter (*last weekend*). A major fashion show for leading Italian and international fashion designers.

October

Fiera Di Chiaravalle (*first Mon*). This famous fair is held in the shade of the *ciribi-ciaccola* (as the Milanese call the bell tower of the Chiaravalle Cistercian abbey, (*see pp104–5*). The fair features music, dancing and an art exhibition.

SMAU (*first week*). International multimedia show held in the

The Fiera, host to both SMAU and fashion shows

Fiera Exhibition Centre: IT, encompassing everything from computers for offices to Virtual Reality and 3D printers.

Bagutta-Pittori all'Aria Aperta (*mid-Oct*). The famous Via Bagutta plays host to a fascinating outdoor exhibition of artists' work.

November

Premio Bagutta Milan's most important literary prize is awarded.

Public Holidays

New Year's Day (1 Jan)

Epiphany (6 Jan)

Easter Sunday & Monday

Liberation Day (25 Apr)

Labour Day (1 May)

Festa della Repubblica (2 June)

Ferragosto (15 Aug)

All Saints' Day (1 Nov)

Sant'Ambrogio (7 Dec)

Immaculate Conception (8 Dec)

Christmas (25 Dec)

Santo Stefano (26 Dec)

San Siro stadium, packed with fans at the beginning of the season

Average monthly temperature

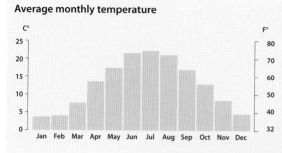

Temperature

Milan is inland and there are big differences in temperature between winter and summer. The winters can be very cold, particularly in December and January, typical of continental Europe, while there may be torrid heat in summer. The climate is always very humid.

Winter

Characterized by severe cold (heavy snowfall is not rare), the Milanese winter is "warmed up" by a rich and fascinating programme of cultural events, major holidays and special occasions. The city becomes especially lively around the feast day of Sant'Ambrogio (St Ambrose), the local patron saint, and then for Christmas, which is preceded by the usual shopping sprees in the city-centre shops. On the cultural side, the theatres of Milan present a high-quality theatre season, headed by the world-famous Piccolo Teatro.

Typical antiques stalls at the Oh bej Oh bej fair

Christmas decorations in the Galleria Vittorio Emanuele II

December

Festa di Sant'Ambrogio (*7 Dec*). This is the feast day of the patron saint of Milan, just before Immaculate Conception (*8 Dec*). Sant'Ambrogio is celebrated with many events: the jam-packed **Fiera degli Oh bej Oh bej**, a vast street fair featuring antiques as well as other articles. It is held in the streets around the basilica of Sant'Ambrogio (*see pp86–9*).

La Scala. The season at the world-famous opera house (*see pp54–5*) starts on 7 December. The opening night is a major cultural event, and an important occasion in the Milanese social calendar.

January

Corteo dei Re Magi (*6 Jan*). A traditional procession with a *tableau vivant* of the Nativity goes from the Duomo to Sant'Eustorgio.

Fiera di Sinigaglia (*every Sat all year long*). Along the Naviglio Grande, where the canal meets Via Valenza, is a colourful market offering ethnic handicrafts, records and bicycles.

Mercato dell'Antiquariato di Brera (*third Sat of month, all year*). Stalls with antiques, books, postcards, jewellery.

February

Carnevale Ambrosiano The longest carnival in the world ends on the first Saturday of Lent. Floats and Milanese characters, such as Meneghin, take part in a parade to Piazza del Duomo.

BIT (*mid-Feb*). The Fiera (Milan's Exhibition Centre) hosts an international tourist trade show.

Mi Milano Prêt-à-Porter (*late Feb*). The autumn-winter collections of the leading international and Italian fashion designers go on show.

Taking part in the Carnevale Ambrosiano in Piazza del Duomo

Panoramic view of the city of Milan ▶

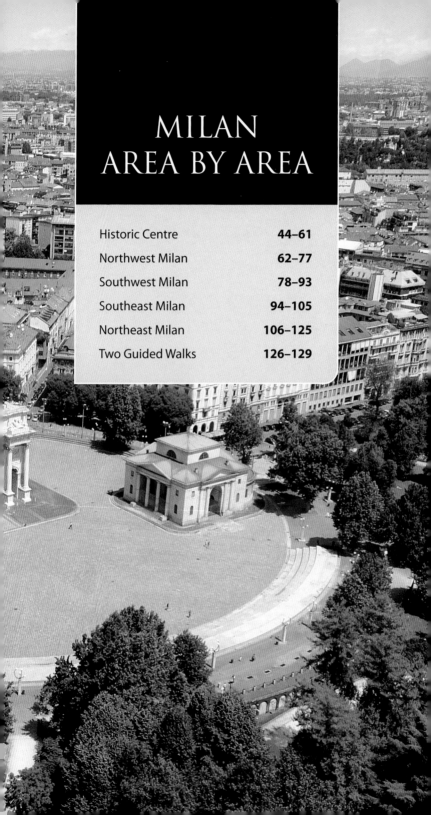

MILAN
AREA BY AREA

HISTORIC CENTRE

The area around the Duomo was the religious centre of Milan in the 4th century. Up to the 14th century it was the site of the basilicas of Santa Tecla and Santa Maria Maggiore and the Early Christian baptisteries, San Giovanni alle Fonti and Santo Stefano. These were all demolished to make room for the new cathedral. The political and administrative centre of the city was the nearby Palazzo della Ragione. At that time Milan was only slightly larger than the present-day historic centre; in fact, what is today Piazza della Scala was on the edge of town. Piazza del Duomo was the focus of small businesses until the 18th century, and a stage for the city's major religious and civic ceremonies. In the 19th century it became the nucleus from which avenues radiated. In the 1860s the decaying dwellings and the shops around the Duomo were demolished to make way for the construction of the then futuristic Galleria, the symbol of Milan after the unification of Italy. The damage caused by bombs in World War II created large empty areas later occupied by many modern buildings. The Historic Centre is always thronging with visitors, drawn by the world-famous churches, museums and galleries and also by the excellent shops.

Sights at a Glance

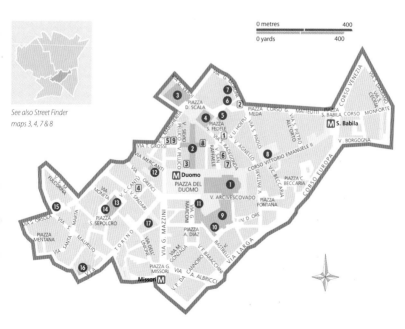

See also Street Finder maps 3, 4, 7 & 8

0 metres 400
0 yards 400

For keys to symbols see back flap

Street-by-Street: Piazza del Duomo

Piazza del Duomo, designed by Giuseppe Mengoni and opened in 1865 after protracted difficulties, is the ideal starting point for a visit to Milan's historic centre. The area is packed with visitors fascinated by the "great machine of the Duomo", as Alessandro Manzoni describes the cathedral in *The Betrothed*. There are numerous spots where the Milanese like to meet for an aperitif on Sunday morning. Young people prefer to go to Corso Vittorio Emanuele II, which has most of the cinemas as well as many shops and department stores.

5 San Fedele
This church, a typical example of Counter-Reformation architecture, is popular with the old Milanese aristocracy.

Casa degli Omenoni

VIA MANZONI

PIAZ MED

PIAZZA SCALA

PIAZZA SAN FEDELE

3 ★ Teatro alla Scala
This was the first monument in Milan to be rebuilt after the 1943 bombings.

Palazzo Marino

VIA MENGONI

VIA GROSS

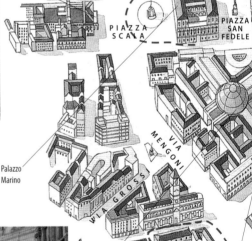

Piazza Mercanti and Palazzo della Ragione Fotografia

Zucca in Galleria is a popular café, decorated with mosaics and decor dating from 1921.

2 ★ Galleria Vittorio Emanuele II
The Galleria was one of the first iron and glass constructions in Italy.

0 metres	100
0 yards	100

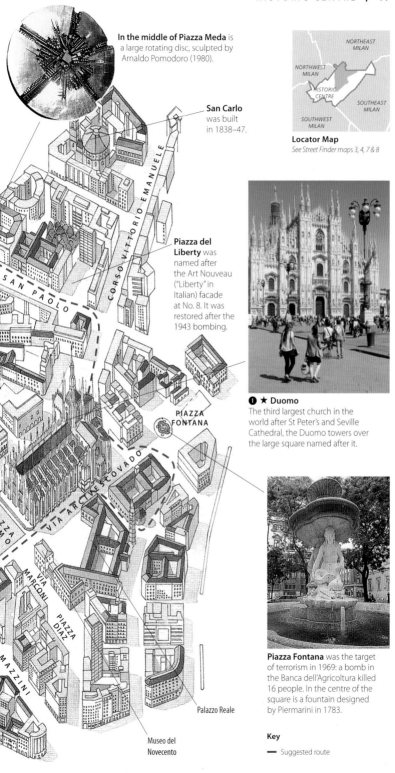

In the middle of Piazza Meda is a large rotating disc, sculpted by Arnaldo Pomodoro (1980).

San Carlo was built in 1838–47.

Piazza del Liberty was named after the Art Nouveau ("Liberty" in Italian) facade at No. 8. It was restored after the 1943 bombing.

CORSO VITTORIO EMANUELE

SAN PAOLO

PIAZZA FONTANA

VIA ARCIVESCOVADO

VIA MARCONI

PIAZZA DIAZZA

MAZZINI

Palazzo Reale

Museo del Novecento

Locator Map
See Street Finder maps 3, 4, 7 & 8

NORTHEAST MILAN
NORTHWEST MILAN
HISTORIC CENTRE
SOUTHEAST MILAN
SOUTHWEST MILAN

❶ ★ Duomo
The third largest church in the world after St Peter's and Seville Cathedral, the Duomo towers over the large square named after it.

Piazza Fontana was the target of terrorism in 1969: a bomb in the Banca dell'Agricoltura killed 16 people. In the centre of the square is a fountain designed by Piermarini in 1783.

Key

— Suggested route

❶ Duomo

The construction of the Duomo began in 1386, with the city's bishop, Antonio da Saluzzo, as its patron. Duke Gian Galeazzo Visconti invited Lombard, German and French architects to supervise the works and insisted they use Candoglia marble, which was transported along the Navigli canals. The official seal AUF (*ad usum fabricae*), stamped on the slabs, exempted them from customs duty. The cathedral was consecrated in 1418, yet remained unfinished until the 19th century, when Napoleon, who was crowned King of Italy here, had the façade completed.

La Madonnina
The 4.16-m (14-ft) gilded statue of the Madonna was sculpted by Giuseppe Bini in 1774.

★ Stained-glass Windows
Most of the windows depict scenes from the Bible, and date from the 19th century. The oldest one – the fifth in the right-hand aisle – dates back to 1470–75 and depicts the life of Christ, while the newest one (the seventh) dates from 1988.

The Building of Milan Cathedral

1386 The first stone of the Duomo is laid

1418 Pope Martin V consecrates the high altar

1567 Pellegrino Tibaldi ("il Pellegrino") redesigns the presbytery

1500 Central spire inaugurated

Martin V

1656 Carlo Buzzi continues façade in Gothic style

1617 Francesco Maria Richini begins work on the façade

1774 The Madonnina is placed on the tallest spire

1838–65 The Bertinis make the apse windows

1813 Façade completed with Gothic spires

1981–4 Presbytery piers restored

| 1300 | 1400 | 1500 | 1600 | 1700 | 1800 | 1900 |

★ Roof Terraces
The view of the city from the roof terraces is simply unforgettable. You can also have a close-up look at the central spire. The roof bristles with spires, the oldest of which dates from 1404.

VISITORS' CHECKLIST

Practical Information
Piazza Duomo. **Map** 7 C1.
Tel 02-72 02 26 56.
Open 8am–7pm daily. 🏛 🏛
Museum: **Open** 10am–6pm
Thu–Tue (till 10pm Thu & Sat).
🏛 🏛 Baptistery/Digs: **Open**
9am–6pm daily. 🏛 🏛 Roof
Terraces: **Open** 9am–7pm daily
(till 10pm May–mid-Sep). 🏛 ♿

Transport
Ⓜ 1, 3 Duomo. 🚋 1, 2, 3, 12, 14,
15, 16, 24, 27.

The Interior
The 5 aisles in the nave are separated by 52 piers, whose capitals are decorated with statues.

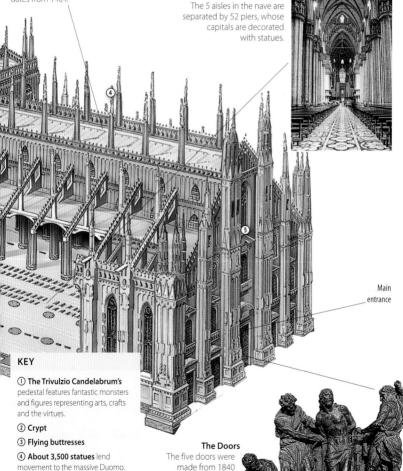

Main
entrance

KEY

① **The Trivulzio Candelabrum's**
pedestal features fantastic monsters and figures representing arts, crafts and the virtues.

② **Crypt**

③ **Flying buttresses**

④ **About 3,500 statues** lend movement to the massive Duomo. They are typically medieval, representing saints, animals and monsters.

⑤ **A plaque** confirms that the Duomo is dedicated to Maria Nascente.

The Doors
The five doors were made from 1840 to 1965. Right, *The Flagellation* by Ludovico Pogliaghi, a bronze relief in the central door.

Exploring the Duomo

So that the Duomo could be built, a great Jubilee was proclaimed in 1390 in order to urge the Milanese to contribute money and manual labour to carry out the work. The initial plan was to build it in fired bricks, as the excavations in the northern sacristy have revealed, but in 1387 Duke Gian Galeazzo Visconti, who wanted the cathedral to be seen as a great symbol of his power, demanded that marble should be used instead and that the architectural style should be International Gothic. Building continued over five centuries, resulting in the obvious mixture of styles that characterizes the cathedral.

The presbytery, with the small ciborium dome in the foreground

The Façade

Up to the first level of windows the façade is Baroque. It was completed in the 19th century with Neo-Gothic ogival windows and spires, revealing the difficulties entailed in building the Duomo.

The Interior

Tall cross vaults cover the interior and the 5 aisles in the nave are separated by 52 piers (for the 52 weeks of the year). The capitals on the piers are decorated with statues of saints. Behind the façade, embedded in the floor, is a meridian ①, installed in 1786 by the Brera astronomers. It marked astronomical noon, thanks to a ray of sunlight that enters from the first bay of the south aisle on the right-hand side.

This is a good starting point for a visit to the Duomo. To the right is the sarcophagus of Archbishop Ariberto d'Intimiano ②, bearing a copy of the crucifix that he donated to the San Dionigi monastery (the original is in the Museo del Duomo). Next to this, on the left, is a plaque with the date of the foundation of the cathedral. The corresponding stained-glass window, executed in the old mosaic technique, relates the *Life of St John the Evangelist* (1473–7). The stained-glass windows in the next three bays, showing episodes from the Old Testament, date from the 16th century. In the fifth bay there is a stained-glass window executed between 1470 and 1475 that illustrates the *Life of Christ* ③. Compare this with the other window in the seventh bay – it was made in 1988 and is dedicated to

Stained-glass window, detail

Cardinals Schuster and Ferrari ④. The presbytery ⑤ is constructed in the style imposed in 1567 by Pellegrini who, at the request of San Carlo Borromeo, made this part of the Duomo the Lombard model of a typical Counter-Reformation church. In the middle, under the ciborium behind the altar, is the Tabernacle ⑥, donated by Pius IV to his nephew San Carlo (St Charles). In front of them are two 16th-century gilded copper pulpits ⑦ with episodes from the Old and New Testaments, surmounted by the organs painted by Giovanni Ambrogio Figino, Camillo Procaccini and Giuseppe Meda.

Behind the altar is an extraordinary wooden choir with the

Floor Plan

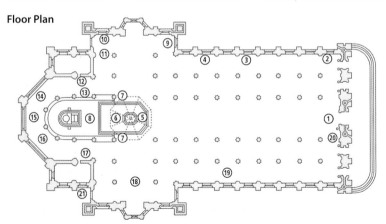

The Holy Nail of the Cross

Tabernacle of the Nail of the Cross

In the vault above the choir, a red light marks the location of the niche where a nail from Christ's Cross has been kept since 1461. The nail, which was once kept in the early medieval Santa Maria Maggiore, is in the shape of a horseshoe and was found by St Helena and later given to her son, Emperor Constantine. It was later donated to Sant'Ambrogio and carried by San Carlo in procession during the 1576 plague.

It is shown to the public every 14 September, when the Bishop of Milan is raised up to the level of the niche which holds the nail in a kind of decorated balcony, drawn by invisible pulleys.

Life of Sant'Ambrogio ⑧, carved in 1572–1620. In the right-hand transept is the funerary monument of Gian Giacomo Medici ⑨, the brother of Pope Pius IV, which was once attributed to Michelangelo but is in fact the work of Leone Leoni (1560–63). Past the chapel dedicated to St John the Good, Bishop of Milan in the 7th century, above the side entrance is the splendid stained-glass window of St Catherine of Alexandria ⑩, designed by the Arcimboldi brothers in 1556. A little further on is the strange statue of the flayed St Bartholomew ⑪, signed and dated 1562 by Marco d'Agrate.

At the beginning of the ambulatory there is a *Deposition* on the southern door of the sacristy ⑫ (1393), dedicated to the "Mysteries of the Virgin Mary". Steps ⑬ lead to the crypt (1606), where San Carlo Borromeo is buried, the Duomo Treasury, with its exceptional collection of church vestments and objects, and the Coro Jemale, a small 16th-century room decorated with fine stuccowork (check out the relief sculpture cycle of the *Life of the Virgin Mary*, a 17th-century masterpiece). The apse is illuminated by the three huge 19th-century stained-glass windows by the Bertini brothers with episodes from the Old ⑯ and New ⑭ Testaments and the Apocalypse ⑮. The ambulatory

Chalice in the Duomo Treasury

ends at the northern portal of the sacristy ⑰, with *Christ the Lord and Judge* (1389). The left-hand transept is dominated by the 5-m (16-ft) bronze Trivulzio Candelabrum ⑱, a 12th-century masterpiece by the goldsmith Nicola da Verdun. The candelabrum carries scenes from the Old Testament and the Three Wise Men riding towards the enthroned Virgin. Going down the north aisle, you will see the Chapel of the Crucifix ⑲ carried by San Carlo in procession during the 1576 plague. Behind this is a window with a depiction of the *Discovery of the True Cross by St Helena* (1570–77). To the left of the entrance, steps lead down to the remains of an Early Christian apse of Santa Tecla and an octagonal baptistery ⑳

where, according to tradition, Sant'Ambrogio (St Ambrose) baptized St Augustine in AD 387. From San Carlo's feast day to Epiphany, the *Quadroni di San Carlo* go on display in the nave. These paintings, the work of leading 17th-century Lombard artists, depict the story of the life and miracles of San Carlo.

Roof Terraces

On the way to the lift ㉑ which goes up to the roof, you should go to the apse to admire the central stained-glass window, designed by Filippino degli Organi in 1402. From the roof there is a magnificent view of the city and the mountains to the north, as well as the Duomo spires and statues and even the buttresses below.

Museo del Duomo

The Cathedral museum, founded in 1953, is at No. 15 Via Arcivescovado. It houses paintings, sculptures, religious objects and stained-glass windows from the Duomo. Among the best works are *St Paul the Hermit*, Tintoretto's *Christ among the Doctors* (1530) and a wooden model of the Duomo, begun in 1519. It focuses on both the historical and artistic elements of the Duomo, and also documents the restoration of the four central piers (1981–4).

The right side of the presbytery of the Milan Duomo

❷ Galleria Vittorio Emanuele II and Highline Galleria

Piazza della Scala, Piazza del Duomo.
Map 7 C1. Ⓜ 1, 3 Duomo. Highline
Galleria ticket office: Via Silvio Pellico 2
(4th Floor). **Tel** 02-45 39 76 56.
Open 10am–9pm daily (summer:
10am–11pm daily). **Closed** 1 Jan,
1 May, 2 Jun, 25 & 26 Dec.
Ⓦ highlinegalleria.com

The Galleria is an elegant
arcade lined with cafés, shops
and a famous restaurant, Savini
(see p170). Work began in 1865,
overseen by the architect
Giuseppe Mengoni, and it
was opened two years later by
the king, Vittorio Emanuele II,
after whom it was named.
The gallery was designed to
connect Piazza del Duomo
and Piazza della Scala, and
formed part of an ambitious
urban renewal project. On
the floor in the central
octagonal area, directly under
the 47-m- (154-ft-) high glass
dome, is the heraldic symbol
of the Savoy family, a white
cross on a red ground. Around
it are the arms of four major
Italian cities: the bull of Turin,
the wolf of Rome, the lily of
Florence and the red cross
on a white ground (Milan). On
the vault are mosaics of Asia,
Africa, Europe and America.

It is now possible to access
the walkways on the roofs
around the Galleria and
experience this historical
monument from a unique and
fascinating perspective. The
Highline Galleria also offers
stunning views of the Duomo
spires and the Milan skyline.
Guided walks run from morning

San Fedele church overlooking Piazza San Fedele

till late in the evening all year
round and can be booked from
the office in Via Silvio Pellico.

❸ Teatro alla Scala

See pp54–5.

❹ Palazzo Marino

Piazza della Scala. **Map** 3 C5.
Ⓜ 1, 3 Duomo. **Closed** to the public.

This palazzo was designed in
1558 by Galeazzo Alessi for
the banker Tommaso Marino,
but remained unfinished until
1892, when Luca Beltrami
completed the façade. From
Via Marino on the right you
can see the richly decorated,
porticoed courtyard of honour.

According to tradition the
palazzo, home of the Milan
Town Hall since 1860, was
the birthplace of Marianna
de Leyva, the famous nun
of Monza described by
Alessandro Manzoni in *The
Betrothed* as the "Signora".

❺ San Fedele

Piazza San Fedele. **Map** 3 C5. **Tel** 02-86
35 22 15. Ⓜ 1, 3 Duomo. 🚋 1. 🚌
61. **Open** 7:30am–1:15pm, 4:30–6pm
Mon–Fri. 🕆 7:50am, 12:45pm Mon–
Fri; 6:30pm Sat; 11am, 7pm Sun.

This church is the Milanese
seat of the Jesuit Order,
commissioned by San Carlo
Borromeo from Pellegrino Tibaldi
in 1569. The work was continued
by Martino Bassi and the dome,
crypt and choir were designed
by Francesco Maria Richini
(1633–52). With its austere
architecture and nave without
aisles, this is a typical Counter-
Reformation church. The façade
is being restored, but the interior
has three interesting paintings.
By the first altar on the right is
St Ignatius's Vision by Giovan
Battista Crespi, known as "il
Cerano" (c.1622). A *Transfig-
uration* by Bernardino Campi
(1565) is in the atrium after the
second altar on the left; Campi
also painted the *Blessed Virgin
and Child,* by the second altar
(left). These last two works came
from Santa Maria della Scala,
which was demolished to make
room for La Scala opera house
(see pp54–5).

The wooden furniture is also
worth a closer look: the confes-
sionals (1596) have scenes from
the life of Christ carved by
Giovanni Taurini, and the
cupboards in Richini's sacristy
(1624–28) are by Daniele Ferrari
(1639). A statue of writer
Alessandro Manzoni, whose
death certificate is kept in San
Fedele, stands in the square.

Looking across at the Duomo from the Highline

❻ Casa degli Omenoni

Via Omenoni 3. **Map** 3 C5. Ⓜ 1, 3 Duomo. 🚃 1. **Open** to the public.

Eight telamones, which the Milanese call *omenoni* ("large men"), are the most striking feature of this house-cum-studio, built by the sculptor Leone Leoni in 1565. The artist collected many works of art, including paintings by Titian and Correggio and Leonardo da Vinci's famous *Codex Atlanticus (see p61).*

A reference to Leoni can be seen in the relief under the cornice, in which Calumny is torn up by lions *(leoni)*.

The entrance to the Casa degli Omenoni

❼ Casa Manzoni and Piazza Belgioioso

Via Morone 1. **Map** 4 D5. **Tel** 02-86 46 04 03. Ⓜ 3 Montenapoleone. 🚃 1. **Open** 10am–6pm Tue–Fri, 2–6pm Sat (guided tours only). **Closed** public hols. ♿

This is the house where Italian author Alessandro Manzoni lived from 1814 until his death

Part of the façade of Palazzo Liberty, at No. 8 Piazza del Liberty

in 1873 after a fall on the steps of San Fedele. The perfectly preserved interior includes Manzoni's studio on the ground floor, where he received Garibaldi in 1862 and Verdi in 1868. Next to this is the room where poet and author Tommaso Grossi had his notary office, while on the first floor is Manzoni's bedroom. The house is now the seat of the National Centre for Manzoni Studies, which was founded in 1937. It includes a library with works by Manzoni and critical studies of his oeuvre, as well as the Lombard Historical Society Library with over 40,000 volumes. The brick façade overlooks Piazza Belgioioso, named after the palazzo at No. 2 (closed to the public). This monumental palazzo was designed by Piermarini in 1777–81 for Prince Alberico XII di Belgioioso d'Este. The façade bears heraldic emblems. In the interior a fresco by Martin Knoller represents the apotheosis of Prince Alberico.

❽ Piazza del Liberty and Corso Vittorio Emanuele II

Map 8 D1. Ⓜ 1, 3 Duomo, 1 San Babila. 🚃 15, 23. 🚌 60, 61, 73.

Once past the arch at the end of Piazza Belgioioso, go through Piazza Meda (1926) and past Corso Matteotti, which was built in 1934 to link Piazza della Scala with Piazza San Babila, and then go down Via San Paolo, which will take you to Piazza del Liberty. This small square owes its name to the Art Nouveau (Liberty) façade on No. 8, restored by Giovanni and Lorenzo Muzio in 1963 with architectural elements from the Trianon café-concert, a building dating from 1905 which was moved from Corso Vittorio Emanuele II. Go along Via San Paolo to reach Corso Vittorio Emanuele II. This is Milan's main commercial street, and was once called "Corsia dei Servi" (Servants' Lane). It follows the course of an ancient Roman street and in 1628 was the scene of bread riots, described by Manzoni in *The Betrothed*. Near San Carlo al Corso, at No. 13 is the *Omm de preja* (local dialect for *uomo di pietra* or "man of stone") statue, a copy of an ancient Roman work. It is also called "Sciur Carera", a misspelling of the first word of a Latin inscription under the statue *(carere debet omni vitio qui in alterum dicere paratus est).*

The *Omm de preja* statue

Casa Manzoni, now home to the National Centre for Manzoni Studies

❸ Teatro alla Scala

Built by Giuseppe Piermarini in 1776-8, this opera house owes its name to the fact that it stands on the site of Santa Maria della Scala, a church built in 1381 for Regina della Scala, Bernabò Visconti's wife. The theatre opened in 1778; it was bombed in 1943 and rebuilt three years later. After an extensive restoration programme that saw the addition of a new stage tower designed by Mario Botta, La Scala reopened in 2004. The opening night of the opera season is 7 December, the feast day of Sant'Ambrogio, Milan's patron saint.

Teatro alla Scala in 1852, by Angelo Inganni

★ Foyer
This large, mirror-lined salon was renovated in 1936. There is a bust of the legendary conductor Arturo Toscanini.

Entrance

★ Museo Teatrale
The theatre museum was founded in 1913 and boasts a fine collection of sculpture, original scores, paintings and ceramics related to the history of La Scala as well as of theatre in general.

KEY

① **The façade** was designed by Piermarini so that passers-by in Via Manzoni could catch a glimpse of it.

② **The boxes** were like small living rooms where romantic trysts and parlour games were arranged.

③ **The chandelier**, made of Bohemian crystal (1923), holds 383 lightbulbs.

④ **A tank**, filled with water, placed over the wooden vault, was ready for use in case of fire.

⑤ **Dressing rooms**

⑥ **The orchestra pit** was introduced in 1907. Before then the orchestra played behind a balustrade on the same level as the stalls.

The Ballet School

La Scala's Ballet School was founded in 1813. Originally there were 48 students who studied dance, mime or specialist disciplines. At the end of an eight-year course, the best students were awarded merits of distinction and became part of the theatre's *corps de ballet* with an annual stipend of €1.5. This rigorously disciplined school has produced such artists as Carla Fracci and Luciana Savignano.

Students at the Ballet School

VISITORS' CHECKLIST

Practical Information
Piazza della Scala. **Map** 3 C5.
Tel 02-88 791. Museo Teatrale alla Scala: Largo Ghiringhelli 1 (Piazza Scala). **Tel** 02-88 79 74 73.
Open 9am–noon, 1:30–5pm daily. (includes a look at the theatre from a balcony, provided there are no rehearsals or shows).
teatroallascala.org

Transport
1, 3 Duomo. 1, 61.

Stage
This is one of the largest stages in Italy, measuring 1,200 sq m (13,000 sq ft).

★ Auditorium
Made of wood covered with red velvet and decorated with gilded stuccowork, the interior boasts marvellous acoustics and has a seating capacity of 2,015.

The entrance to the church of San Gottardo in Corte

❾ San Gottardo in Corte

Via Pecorari 2. **Map** 8 D1. **Tel** 02-86 46 45 00. Ⓜ 1, 3 Duomo. 🚊 3, 12, 15, 16, 24, 27. 🚌 54. **Open** 8am–noon, 2–6pm Mon–Fri (to 5:30pm Fri), 2–4pm Sat, 8am–noon Sun.

Azzone Visconti, lord of Milan, ordered the construction of this church in 1336 as the ducal chapel in the Broletto Vecchio (Courthouse) courtyard. The interior was rebuilt in Neo-Classical style by Piermarini. On the left-hand wall is a *Crucifixion* by the school of Giotto.

Azzone Visconti's funerary monument, by Giovanni di Balduccio, is in the apse: the reclining statue of Visconti is flanked by the figures of two women. The octagonal brick bell tower with small stone arches and columns is by Francesco Pecorari (c.1335).

❿ Palazzo Reale

Piazza del Duomo. **Map** 7 C1. **Tel** 02-88 46 52 30. Ⓜ 1, 3 Duomo. 🚊 1, 2, 3, 12, 24, 27. 🚌 54, 60. **Open** 9:30am–7:30pm daily (from 2:30pm Mon, to 10:30pm Thu & Sat).

The seat of the commune administration in the 11th century, this building was drastically rebuilt by Azzone Visconti in 1330–36. At the height of its importance, it was the headquarters of the lords of Milan. Galeazzo Maria Sforza's decision to move the palace began the decline of the Palazzo Reale. In 1598 it housed the first permanent theatre in Milan. Made of wood, it was rebuilt in 1737 and Mozart played here as a child. In 1776 it was destroyed by a fire.

The present Neo-Classical appearance dates from 1778, when Giuseppe Piermarini made it into a residence for Archduke Ferdinand of Austria. In 1920 Vittorio Emanuele III granted the place temporarily to the city of Milan, and in 1965 the city purchased it to use as offices and museums and for important temporary exhibitions by sculptors and painters such as Claude Monet and Pablo Picasso.

⓫ Museo del Novecento

Palazzo dell'Arengario, Piazza del Duomo. **Map** 7 C1. **Tel** 02-88 44 40 72. Ⓜ 1, 3 Duomo. 🚊 1, 2, 3, 12, 14, 24, 27. 🚌 54, 60. **Open** 2:30–7:30pm Mon, 9:30am–7:30pm Tue, Wed, Fri & Sun, 9:30am–10:30pm Thu & Sat.

Construction of the Arengario, designed by architect Piero Portaluppi and others, began in the late 1930s as part of a modernisation plan for the city. The name *arengario* refers to the place where medieval town councils were held.

The building now houses the Museo del Novecento (Museum of 20th-Century Art). Architect Italo Rota's design includes an exterior steel and glass bridge to connect the building to the Palazzo Reale, creating an important museum complex. The museum traces the history of 20th-century Italian art, with sections devoted to movements like Futurism, Metaphysical Art, Arte Povera and Abstractionism.

Unique forms of Continuity in Space (1913) by Umberto Boccioni

Works by 20th-century Milanese artists are also featured.

⓬ Piazza Mercanti and Palazzo della Ragione Fotografia

Map 7 C1. Ⓜ 1 Cordusio, 1 & 3 Duomo. 🚊 1, 2, 3, 12, 14, 16, 24, 27. 🚌 54. Palazzo della Ragione Fotografia: **Tel** 02-43 35 35 35. **Open** 9:30am–8:30pm Tue–Sun (to 10:30pm Thu & Sat). ♿ 🖥 palazzo dellaragionefotografia.it

This corner of medieval Milan was the seat of public and civic activities and also housed the prison. Palazzo della Ragione was built in 1233 by the chief magistrate (and virtual ruler) Oldrado da Tresseno, who is portrayed in a relief by Antelami on the side facing the square.

Palazzo Reale, now used as a venue for temporary exhibitions

The well in Piazza Mercanti and, on the left, Palazzo delle Scuole Palatine

This courthouse is also known as "Broletto Nuovo" to distinguish it from the older Broletto Vecchio near Palazzo Reale. Markets were held under the porticoes, while the Salone dei Giudici on the first floor was used as the law court. In 1773 another storey was added to house the notarial archive. On one side of the square is the Loggia degli Osii, built by Matteo Visconti in 1316. The façade is decorated with the arms of the districts of Milan and statues of the Virgin Mary and saints (1330). Next is the Palazzo delle Scuole Palatine (1645), the façade of which bears statues of St Augustine and the Latin poet Ausonius. The Palazzo dei Panigarola (to the right), which was rebuilt in the 15th century, was used to register public documents.

In a secluded corner of the square, which has at its centre a 16th-century well, the Palazzo della Ragione Fotografia occupies a historic 13th-century building. The space, now restored, hosts some of the city's best photography exhibitions.

In Via Mercanti is the Palazzo dei Giureconsulti, dominated by the Torre del Comune, built by Napo Torriani in 1272. At the foot of this tower is a statue of Sant'Ambrogio.

⑱ Pinacoteca Ambrosiana

See pp58–61.

⑭ San Sepolcro

Piazza San Sepolcro. **Map** 7 B1. **M** 1, 3 Duomo. 🚋 1, 2, 14. **Open** noon–2pm Mon–Fri. 🕆 5pm pre-hols; noon (winter), 5pm hols. ✉

San Sepolcro was founded in 1030 in the area of the ancient Roman Forum and rebuilt in 1100 at the time of the second Crusade. The Neo-Romanesque façade was built in 1897, while the interior is basically Baroque. There are two terracotta groups by Agostino De Fondutis (16th century): *Christ Washing His Disciples' Feet* and *The Flagellation of Christ with Caiaphas and St Peter.* The only extant part of the 1030 church is the Romanesque crypt, with a sculpture group of the *Deposition* by the De Fondutis school in the apse. The lower part of the church, the Chiesa Inferiore San Sepolcro, reopened in 2016 after being closed for more than 50 years.

⑮ Palazzo Borromeo

Piazza Borromeo 7. **Map** 4 D4. **M** 1 Cordusio. 🚋 1, 2, 3, 14, 16, 27. **Open** courtyard only.

This prestigious early 15th-century residence was badly damaged by the 1943 bombings and the only remaining original architectural element is the ogival portal, with leaf decoration and the coat of arms of the Borromeo family. The partly rebuilt second courtyard has porticoes on three sides and on the fourth, between the brick windows, is the original decoration with the family motto *Humilitas.* This courtyard leads to the 15th-century Sala dei Giochi, which is decorated with frescoes of the games played by the aristocracy of the time, including the *Game of Tarot.* The red background developed as the result of a chemical reaction which changed the original blue of the sky.

⑯ San Giorgio al Palazzo

Piazza San Giorgio 2. **Map** 7 B1. **Tel** 02-805 71 48. 🚋 2, 14. **Open** 7:30am–noon, 3:30–6pm daily. 🕆 8am Mon–Fri; 6pm pre-hols; 11am hols.

Founded in 750, this church was named after an ancient Roman *palatium* which stood here. It was radically changed in 1623 and 1800–21 by the architects Richini and Cagnola respectively, and little remains of the original or Romanesque (1129) structures. The third chapel in the right-hand aisle contains paintings by Bernardino Luini (1516) with scenes from the Passion. On the vault there is a fresco of the Crucifixion.

⑰ Santa Maria presso San Satiro

Via Speronari 3. **Map** 7 C1. **Tel** 02-87 46 83. **M** 1, 3 Duomo. 🚋 1, 2, 3, 14, 16, 24, 27. 🚌 54. **Open** 7:30–11:30am, 3:30–6:30pm Mon–Fri, 9am–noon, 3:30–7pm Sat & Sun. 🕆 7:45am, 6pm Mon–Sat, 11am, 6pm Sun.

Santa Maria presso San Satiro

The original nucleus of this church, founded by archbishop Ansperto da Biassono, dates from 876. The only remnant is the Sacello della Pietà (chapel of pity), which was altered by Bramante in the 15th century, and the Lombard Romanesque bell tower. In 1478 Bramante was asked to rebuild the church to salvage a 13th-century fresco on the façade, which was said to have miraculous powers. Bramante set it on the high altar, solving the problem of lack of space by creating a sort of *trompe l'oeil* apse of only 97 cm (38 in) with stuccowork and frescoes. The transept leads to the Chapel of San Satiro with a terracotta *Pietà* (c.1482). In the right-hand aisle is the octagonal baptismal font decorated by De Fondutis.

⓭ Pinacoteca Ambrosiana

The Ambrosiana art gallery was founded in 1618 by Cardinal Federico Borromeo, the cousin of San Carlo and his successor in charge of the archdiocese of Milan. A true art connoisseur, Borromeo planned the gallery as part of a vast cultural project which included the Ambrosiana Library, opened in 1609, and the Accademia del Disegno (1620) for the training of young Counter-Reformation artists. The gallery, founded to provide inspiration for emerging artists, held 172 paintings – some of which already belonged to Borromeo, while others were purchased later after painstaking research by the cardinal.The collection was then enlarged thanks to private donations.

★ **Madonna del Padiglione**
The restoration of this work by Botticelli has revealed its masterful and elegant brushwork.

Adoration of the Magi
Cardinal Borromeo considered this painting by Titian (purchased in 1558) a treasure trove for painters "for the multitude of things therein".

The library is on the ground floor.

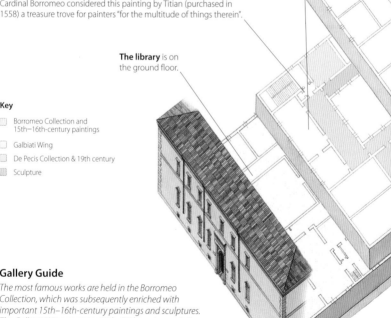

Key

- Borromeo Collection and 15th–16th-century paintings
- Galbiati Wing
- De Pecis Collection & 19th century
- Sculpture

Gallery Guide

The most famous works are held in the Borromeo Collection, which was subsequently enriched with important 15th–16th-century paintings and sculptures. The Galbiati Wing contains 16th–20th-century paintings, a collection of objects, the Sinigaglia Collection of miniature portraits and scientific instruments.

★ Basket of Fruit
Caravaggio painted this extraordinarily realistic work around 1594. The fruit alludes to the symbolism of the Passion of Christ.

VISITORS' CHECKLIST

Practical Information
Piazza Pio XI 2. **Map** 7 B1
Tel 02-80 69 21. **Open** 10am–6pm Tue–Sun (last adm: 5:30pm).
   partial.
w ambrosiana.eu

Transport
M 1, 3 Duomo, 1 Cordusio.
1, 2, 14, 16, 27.

Nicolò da Bologna Room

San Sepolcro was annexed to the gallery in 1932.

Centrepiece with Fishing Scene
This is part of the prestigious collection of Neo-Classical gilded bronze objects donated to the Ambrosiana by Edoardo De Pecis in 1827.

★ Portrait of a Musician
This is the only Milanese wood panel painting by Leonardo da Vinci. The subject is Franchino Gaffurio, the Sforza court composer.

★ Cartoon for the School of Athens
This was a preparation for the painting now in the Vatican. Raphael used the faces of contemporary artists – Leonardo, for instance, appears in the guise of Aristotle.

Exploring the Pinacoteca Ambrosiana

After seven years of painstaking restoration work, the Pinacoteca was reopened in October 1997. It is housed in a palazzo originally designed by Fabio Mangone in 1611. It was enlarged in the 19th century and again in 1932, when San Sepolcro was added. The new rooms were inaugurated on the third centenary of the death of Federico Borromeo, when about 700 paintings were exhibited, arranged in rows or set on easels. Today the Pinacoteca, whose collections are even larger thanks to donations, has 24 rooms and is one of Milan's finest museums.

Portrait of a Young Man, attributed to Giorgione

The Borromeo Collection, 15th–16th-Century Paintings

The visit begins in the atrium, which has plaster casts of Trajan's Column, narrating the emperor's victories against the Dacians; on the staircase there are other casts of the *Laocoön* and Michelangelo's *Pietà*. Rooms 1, 4, 5, 6 and 7 house the Borromeo Collection, which boasts many of the best-known works in the gallery. Room 1, which features Venetian and Leonardo-esque painting, opens with the *Holy Family with St Anne and the Young St John the Baptist* by Bernardino Luini (c.1520). Next to this is Titian's *Adoration of the Magi* (1559–60), which is still in its original frame bearing the carved initials of Henry II of France and his wife, who commissioned the work. The main scene is at the far left, while animals and minor figures fill the right-hand half of this original composition. On the opposite wall is a series of portraits, including *Profile of a Lady* by Ambrogio De Predis, and those of *The Young Jesus with Lamb* and *Benedictory Christ* by Luini, ending with Titian's *Man in Armour*. Rooms 2 and 3 have works acquired after 1618. They include Botticelli's *Madonna del Padiglione*, with its many symbols of the Virgin Mary, and *Sacred Conversation* by Bergognone (c.1485). Another unmissable work is *Adoration of the Child*, by the workshop of Domenico

Adoration of the Child, Domenico Ghirlandaio's workshop

Ghirlandaio. Room 3 features 15th–16th-century Leonardo-esque and Lombard paintings, among which is Salaino's *St John the Baptist*, whose finger pointing upwards alludes to the coming of Christ. Next to this are three works by Bartolomeo Suardi, known as "il Bramantino". In his *Madonna of the Towers* (which may have had an anti-heretic function), next to the Virgin are St Ambrose and St Michael Archangel

Holy Family with St Anne and the Young St John the Baptist by Bernardino Luini

kneeling and offering a soul to the Christ Child. Room 4 has copies from Titian and Giorgione and the *Rest on the Flight into Egypt*, traditionally attributed to Jacopo Bassano (c.1547). In room 5 is a Raphael study for *The School of Athens*, the only great Renaissance cartoon that has come down to us. It was purchased by Cardinal Borromeo in 1626. Raphael executed the cartoon in 1510 as a study for his marvellous fresco in the Vatican. The fresco's architectonic setting and figure of Heraclitus (portrayed with Michelangelo's face) are not seen in the cartoon because Raphael only added them when, halfway through painting, he got a glimpse of the Sistine Chapel and was deeply impressed.

The large body of Flemish paintings in the Borromeo Collection is on display in room 7, where you can compare the works of Paul Bril and Jan Brueghel. *Landscape with St Paul* is the most dramatic of the several Bril works on display. Bril worked with the early 17th-century's most popular sacred scenes, but set them in his beloved, intricately executed landscape form. Interesting works by Brueghel include *The Mouse with Roses* and *Allegories of Water and Fire*, which Napoleon removed and took back to France. They were later returned.

The room known as Aula Leonardi is home to one of the most famous works in the museum, *Basket of Fruit*, painted by Caravaggio in the late 1500s on a used canvas. In the same room hangs Leonardo's *Portrait of a Musician*, with its innovative three-quarter profile position and intense expression. It was probably painted in early 1485.

The Galbiati Wing

The Sala Della Medusa and the Sala delle Colonne feature Renaissance paintings and a collection of objects, the most curious of which are Lucrezia Borgia's blonde hair and Napoleon's gloves.

A short passageway leads to the Spiriti Magni courtyard, decorated with statues of illustrious artists. The three rooms that follow feature 16th-century Italian and Venetian paintings, including an *Annunciation* by Bedoli (room 11), the *Portrait of Michel de l'Hospital* by Giovan Battista Moroni (1554) and Moretto's altarpiece, *Martyrdom of St Peter of Verona* (c.1535, room 12). This latter room, known as the "exedra room", is decorated with a mosaic reproducing a miniature by Simone Martini from the volume of Virgil annotated by Petrarch in the Biblioteca Ambrosiana.

Italian and Flemish painting of the 16th and 17th centuries is on display in the Sala Nicolò da Bologna, on the upper floor, along with an unfinished *Penitent Magdalen* (1640–42) by Guido Reni. Seventeenth-century Lombard paintings are on display in rooms 14, 15 and 16. Among the interesting works are *Still Life with Musical Instruments* by Evaristo Baschenis (room 14) and Morazzone's *Adoration of the Magi* (room 15), while the

following room has works by Francesco Cairo and Daniele Crespi, as well as *Magdalen* by Giulio Cesare Procaccini. Paintings by Magnasco, Magatti, Fra Galgario and Londonio represent 18th-century Italian art in room 17, but the jewels are two works by Tiepolo on the wall near the entrance.

Lucrezia Borgia's hair

De Pecis Collection and 19th Century

Rooms 18 and 19 form the largest section of the Pinacoteca Ambrosiana, donated by Giovanni Edoardo De Pecis in 1827. This collection consists mostly of Italian and Flemish paintings and includes a series of small Neo-Classical bronze pieces and a *Self Portrait* by

Funerary monument by il Bambaia

sculptor Antonio Canova, inspired by Roman portraiture. The exhibition in this wing ends with a selection of 19th- and early 20th-century canvases, including works by Andrea Appiani *(Portrait of Napoleon)*, Mosé Bianchi and Francesco Hayez. Emilio Longoni is represented with his masterpiece *Locked out of School* (1888). Room 21 has 15th–17th-century German and Flemish art as well as the *Dantesque Stained Glass* by Giuseppe Bertini, the Duomo master glassblower. It was executed in 1865 and depicts the author of the *Divine Comedy* surrounded by his characters and with the Virgin Mary above him.

Sculpture

Room 22 is given over to sculpture. There are ancient Roman, Romanesque and Renaissance pieces as well as the highly elegant bas-reliefs by Agostino Busti – known as "il Bambaia" – sculpted for the tomb of Gaston de Foix around 1516.

Biblioteca Ambrosiana

Virgil illuminated by Simone Martini

This was one of the first libraries open to the public. It boasts over 750,000 printed volumes, 2,500 of which are incunabula (early printed works), and 36,000 manuscripts. Among them is the 5th-century *Ilias Picta*, a copy of Virgil's book annotated by Petrarch and illuminated by Simone Martini; a volume of Aristotle with annotations by Boccaccio; as well as Arab, Syrian, Greek and Latin texts. The Ambrosian Library also has over 1,000 pages of Leonardo da Vinci's *Codex Atlanticus*, purchased in 1637, removed by Napoleon in 1796 and only partly returned in 1815. The Library opened in 1609, already equipped with shelves and wooden footstools to protect readers from the cold floors.

NORTHWEST MILAN

In the 14th century, when the construction of the Castello Sforzesco began, this district stood outside the city walls and was covered in woods. After the demolition of the Spanish walls around the Castello in the early 19th century, a new plan for the area was drawn up (but only partly realized). The aim was to transform the zone into a monumental quarter by building the Arco della Pace and a number of elegant buildings, which were to be used as offices, luxury residences, markets and theatres. By the end of the century, Via Dante, which leads to the Castello and is lined with fine buildings, was complete, as was the Corso Magenta residential district around Santa Maria delle Grazie. Northwest Milan also hosts two historic theatres: Dal Verme (1872) and the Piccolo Teatro (now called Teatro Grassi), founded in 1947.

Sights at a Glance

Parks and Gardens
❷ Parco Sempione

Streets, Squares and Historic Buildings
❶ Castello Sforzesco see pp66–9
❹ Arena Civica
❺ Arco della Pace
❼ Corso Sempione
❿ Certosa di Garegnano
⓫ Casa degli Atellani and Vigna di Leonardo
⓭ Corso Magenta
⓮ Palazzo Litta
⓱ Via Brisa

⓲ Piazza Cordusio
⓳ Piazza Affari

Public Buildings
❸ Acquario Civico
❽ Fieramilanocity
❾ Meazza (San Siro) Stadium

Churches
⓬ Santa Maria delle Grazie see pp73–5
⓰ San Maurizio

Museums
❻ Triennale Design Museum
⓯ Civico Museo Archeologico

☐ Restaurants pp170–71
1 B-Floor
2 La Felicita
3 Primo Novecento
4 Quattro Mori
5 Shockolat
6 Tagiura
7 Tara
8 Taverna della Trisa
9 Tondo
10 Trussardi alla Scala
11 Trussardi Café

See also Street Finder maps 2, 3, 6 & 7

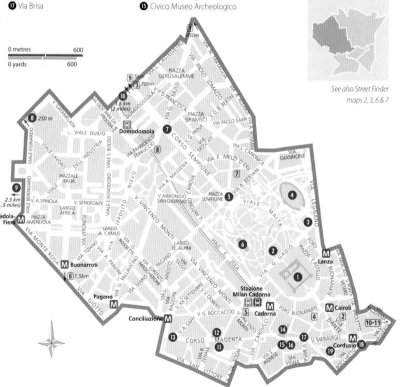

◀ Detail from the bas-relief on Arco della Pace

For keys to symbols see back flap

Street-by-Street: Around the Castello Sforzesco

The Castello Sforzesco and Parco Sempione today are the result of late 19th-century landscaping and restoration. Architect Luca Beltrami managed to thwart attempts to demolish the castle by converting it into a museum centre. He restored many of its original elements. In the early 1800s, the Arco della Pace and the Arena were built in the Parco Sempione, which was landscaped as an "English" garden by Emilio Alemagna. To mark the 1906 opening of the Galleria del Sempione, an International Exposition was held, featuring new products that later became household names in Italy.

❸ **Acquario Civico**
The Civic Aquarium was built in 1906 as an exhibition and educational centre. The building still has its original decoration of tiles and reliefs.

❹ **Arena Civica**
This amphitheatre, built in 1806, was used for boating displays, when it was filled with water from the Naviglio canals.

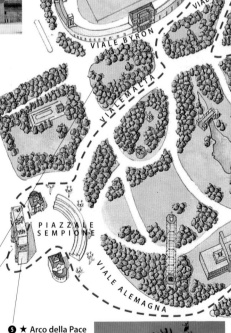

❷ ★ **Parco Sempione**
The 47-hectare (116-acre) English-style garden was designed by Emilio Alemagna in 1893. It contains a number of historic buildings and monuments.

❺ ★ **Arco della Pace**
Modelled on the triumphal arch of Septimius Severus, the Arch of Peace was built to celebrate Napoleon's victories. However, it was inaugurated by Francis I in memory of the peace declared in 1815.

❼ **Corso Sempione**
Napoleon built this avenue leading to the Castello, modelling it on the Champs-Elysées in Paris.

Via Dante, one of the city's most elegant streets, is a pedestrian precinct, and one of the few in Milan where you can sit and have a drink outdoors.

Locator Map
See Street Finder maps 2 & 3

The Foro Buonaparte is a semicircular boulevard lined with imposing late 19th-century buildings.

Key

— Suggested route

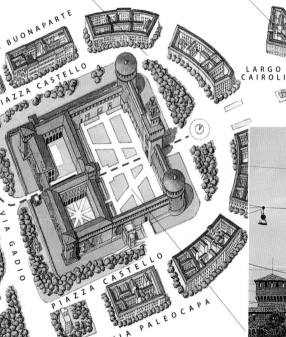

FORO BUONAPARTE

PIAZZA CASTELLO

LARGO CAIROLI

VIA DANTE

VIA GADIO

PIAZZA CASTELLO

VIA PALEOCAPA

❶ ★ **Castello Sforzesco**
The castle, a symbol of Milan, was initially the palace of the Visconti, who built it in 1368 and named it Castello di Porta Giovia, and then of the Sforza, who embellished it, turning it into a magnificent Renaissance residence.

❻ **Triennale Design Museum**
The Palazzo dell'Arte is home to the Triennale Design Museum, which features decorative art, fashion and handicrafts.

0 metres	100
0 yards	100

❶ Castello Sforzesco

Built in 1368 by Galeazzo II Visconti as a fortress, the Sforza castle was enlarged in the 14th century by Gian Galeazzo and then by Filippo Maria, who transformed it into a splendid ducal palace. It was partly demolished in 1447 during the Ambrosian Republic. Francesco Sforza, who became lord of Milan in 1450, and his son Lodovico il Moro made the castle the home of one of the most magnificent courts in Renaissance Italy, graced by Bramante and Leonardo da Vinci. Under Spanish and Austrian domination, the Castello went into gradual decline, as it resumed its original military function. It was saved from demolition by the architect Luca Beltrami, who from 1893 to 1904 restored it and converted it into an important museum centre.

★ Trivulzio Tapestries
The 12 tapestries designed by Bramantino, depicting the months and signs of the zodiac, are masterpieces of Italian textile art.

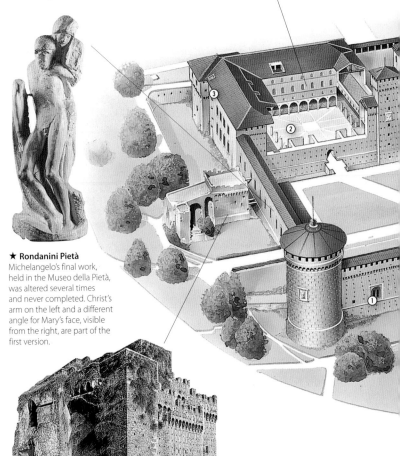

★ Rondanini Pietà
Michelangelo's final work, held in the Museo della Pietà, was altered several times and never completed. Christ's arm on the left and a different angle for Mary's face, visible from the right, are part of the first version.

Porta Vercellina
Only ruins remain of the great fortified structure that once protected the gate of Santo Spirito.

Cappella Ducale

The Ducal chapel still has the original frescoes painted in 1472 by Stefano de Fedeli and Bonifacio Bembo for Galeazzo Maria Sforza. On the vault is a *Resurrection* and on the wall to the left of the entrance is an *Annunciation* with saints looking on.

VISITORS' CHECKLIST

Practical Information
Piazza Castello. **Map** 3 B5.
Tel 02-88 46 37 00.
Castello: **Open** 7am–6pm daily (to 7pm in summer).
Musei Civici: **Tel** 02-88 46 37 03.
Open 9am–5:30pm Tue–Sun (last adm: 5pm). **Closed** 1 Jan, Easter, Easter Mon, 1 May, 25 Dec.
w milanocastello.it

Transport
M 1 Cairoli–Cadorna, 2 Lanza–Cadorna. 1, 4. 50, 57, 61, 94.

★ Sala delle Asse

This pergola, painted to look like an open air space, was the work of Leonardo (1498). The room owes its name to the planks (asse) once thought to cover the walls.

The Filarete Tower collapsed in 1521 when the gunpowder kept there exploded. It was rebuilt in 1905 by Luca Beltrami, who worked from drawings from the period.

KEY

① **The holes** in the castle walls, now used by pigeons, were made to anchor the scaffolding used for maintenance work.

② **The Cortile della Rocchetta** was the last refuge in the event of a siege. Its three porticoes, formerly frescoed, were designed by Ferrini and Bramante. The oldest wing (1456–66), opposite the entrance to the Corte Ducale, was the apartment of Lodovico and his wife before he became duke.

③ **The Torre Castellana** was where Lodovico il Moro kept his treasury. It was "guarded" by a figure of Argus, in a fresco by Bramantino at the Sala del Tesoro entrance.

④ **Ducal court**

Exploring the Civic Museums in the Castello Sforzesco

Since 1896, the Castello Sforzesco has housed the Civic Museums with one of the largest collections of art in Milan. The Corte Ducale is home to the Raccolte di Arte Antica and the art and sculpture gallery, as well as the furniture collection, while the Rocchetta holds decorative arts (ceramics, musical instruments and gold) and the Trivulzio Tapestries. In addition, the photography archive and the Achille Bertarelli Collection, featuring about 700,000 prints, books and photographs from the 19th century, are here. Major institutions, such as the Art Library and the Trivulziana Library can also be found within the same building.

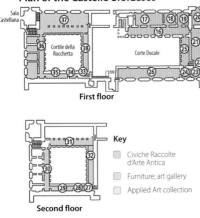

Relief of the Three Magi, School of Antelami (12th century)

Civiche Raccolte d'Arte Antica

The displays making up the collections of Ancient Art are arranged in chronological order (except for Room 6) in rooms facing the Corte Ducale, where the 14th-century Pusterla dei Fabbri postern, rebuilt after being demolished in 1900, has 4th–6th-century sculpture. In room 1 ① is the Sarcophagus of Lambrate (late 4th century) and a bust of the Empress Theodora (6th century). Room 2 ② features Romanesque and Campionese sculpture, with a fine early 12th-century telamon. The relief of the Three Magi is by the school of Benedetto Antelami, the great 12th-century sculptor and architect. The main attraction, however, is the *Mausoleum of Bernabò Visconti*, sculpted by Bonino da Campione in 1363 for the lord of Milan. He is portrayed on horseback between Wisdom and Fortitude, while on the sarcophagus are *Scenes from the Passion*. Room 3

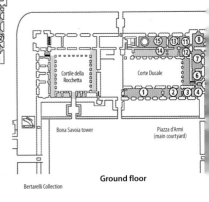

The *Mausoleum of Bernabò Visconti*

③ has a window with a 14th-century Tuscan *Benedictory Christ*. Room 4 ④ is given over to Giovanni di Balduccio, with fragments from the façade of Santa Maria di Brera (14th century). A passage leads to the Cappelletta ⑤, dominated by a 14th-century wooden Crucifix.

Room 6 ⑥ features reliefs from the Porta Romana (1171) narrating the *Return of the Milanese after Being Driven out of Town by Barbarossa* and *St Ambrose Expelling the Arians*. In room 7 ⑦ is the *Gonfalone* (Standard) of Milan designed by Giuseppe Meda in 1566, with scenes from Sant'Ambrogio's life. On the walls are 17th-century Flemish tapestries. The Sala delle Asse ⑧ is known for its fine fresco decoration on the vault, designed by Leonardo in 1498, which, despite its poor condition, is a good example of Sforza decoration. From here you go to the bridge over the moat ⑨ ⑩, with important small sculptures by Agostino Busti (Il Bambaia). Next is the Sala dei Ducali ⑪, named after the arms of Galeazzo Maria Sforza, with Lodovico's set above. Here the early 15th-century sculpture is dominated by Agostino di Duccio's relief of

Plan of the Castello Sforzesco

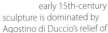

First floor

Second floor

Key

- Civiche Raccolte d'Arte Antica
- Furniture; art gallery
- Applied Art collection

Sala Castellana
Cortile della Rocchetta
Corte Ducale

Bona Savoia tower
Cortile della Rocchetta
Corte Ducale
Piazza d'Armi (main courtyard)

Ground floor

Bertarelli Collection

The armour collection in the Sala Verde

St Sigismund on a Journey from the Malatesta Temple in Rimini. Left, is the door to the Cappella Ducale ⑫, with a braided Virgin, *Madonna del Coazzone*, a 15th-century work attributed to Pietro Antonio Solari. On the vault is a *Resurrection* painted around 1472 by Bonifacio Bembo and Stefano de' Fedeli. Late 15th-century sculpture is featured in the Sala delle Colombine ⑬, with the Visconti coat of arms and motto, *A Bon Droit*. One of the finest works here is Antonio Mantegazza's *Kneeling Apostles*. The 1463 Portale del Banco Mediceo (portal) in the Sala Verde ⑭ is attributed to Filarete. This room also has some fine armour.

The last room, the Sala degli Scarlioni ⑮, boasts a world-famous sculpture: Gaston de Foix's funerary monument with marvellous reliefs. Sculpted by Agostino Busti, known as "Il Bambaia", it commemorates the death on the battlefield of the young captain of the French troops in 1512. The exit route goes through the Cortile della Fontana, where the only original window left in the castle can be seen. It was used by Beltrami as a model in his restoration of the Castello.

In the Ospedale Spagnolo is the Museo della Pietà Rondanini, created to house Michelangelo's masterpiece, the *Rondanini Pietà*. The artist was working on this until a few days before his death in 1564 (he had begun it in 1552–3): the standing Mother of Christ supports the heavy body of her Son.

Furniture Collection and Pinacoteca

Showcasing the traditions from which Milanese furniture design has grown, "From the Sforza to Design" is the name given to the furniture collection ⑯, ⑰, ⑱, ⑲, housing pieces from the 15th to the 20th centuries. Beginning with Court and Church furniture from the 15th to the 16th centuries and Baroque inlaid furniture, as well as collections from aristocratic Milanese families, the collection ends with 20th-century pieces by important Milanese designers such as Giò Ponti and Ettore Sottsass.

Madonna in Glory and Saints, by Andrea Mantegna

The art gallery houses works in chronological order from the mid-15th to the 18th centuries. It begins in room 20, the former Falconry Tower ⑳, with 14th–15th-century Italian paintings, while rooms 21 ㉑ and 22 ㉒ contain works by Milanese artists such as Vincenzo Foppa. Room 23 ㉓ contains major works such as Mantegna's *Madonna in Glory and Saint John* (1497), Antonello da Messina's *Saint Benedict* (c. 1470–73), Lorenzo Veneziano's *Resurrection* (1371), Giovanni Bellini's *Madonna and Child* (c. 1460–65) and *Madonna of Humility* by Filippo Lippi (1430). Room 24 ㉔ features Correggio's *Portrait of a Man Reading* along with examples of Cremonese Mannerism, an Italian art movement founded during the Renaissance period. In room 25 ㉕ Venetian paintings are displayed, boasting examples by Titian and Tintoretto, which contrast with pieces from the 16th-century schools of Brescia and Bergamo. Room 26 ㉖, the former Salone della Cancellaria, houses works by "plague painters" such as Morazzone and Il Cerano (Crespi), finishing with two views of Venice by Canaletto.

Applied Art Collection

Return to the entrance for access to the first floor to see the collection of old musical instruments ㊱ ㊳, which includes a Flemish double virginal with ottavino. Between these two rooms is the large Sala della Balla (ballroom) ㊲, with Bramantino's splendid Trivulzio Tapestries representing the 12 months (1503–09). On the second floor (rooms 28–32) is a large collection of fine Italian and European glass, ceramics, majolica and porcelain, ivory works, gold medieval jewellery and scientific instruments.

Lastly, in the basement of the Corte Ducale, are a Prehistoric and an Egyptian section with funerary cult objects, including a tomb from c.640 BC.

❷ Parco Sempione

Piazza Castello–Piazza Sempione
(Eight entrances around perimeter).
Map 2 F3–4, 3 A3–4. Ⓜ 1 Cadorna,
Cairoli, 2 Lanza, Cadorna. 🚆 Ferrovie
Nord, Cadorna. 🚌 1, 4, 12, 14,
19, 27. 🚋 18, 43, 57, 58, 61, 94.
Open Mar–Apr: 6:30am–9pm;
May: 6:30am–10pm; Jun–Sep:
6:30am–11:30pm; Oct: 6:30am–9pm;
Nov–Feb: 6:30am–8pm.

Although it covers an area of
about 47 ha (116 acres), this
park occupies only a part of
the old Visconti ducal garden,
enlarged by the Sforza in the
15th century to make a 300-ha
(740-acre) hunting reserve.
The area was partly abandoned
during Spanish rule, and in the
early 1800s part of it was used
to create a parade ground
extending as far as the Arco
della Pace. The present-day
layout was the work of Emilio
Alemagna, who in 1890–93
designed it along the lines of an
English garden. In World War II
the park was used to cultivate
wheat, but after the reconstruction period it returned to its
former splendour as a locals'
haunt, especially in spring and
summer, when it plays host
to many entertainment events.
Walking through the park
after dark is not advisable.
 Standing among the trees are
the monuments to Napoleon III
(designed by Francesco
Barzaghi), De Chirico's
Metaphysical construction
Mysterious Baths, the sulphur
water fountain near the Arena
and the Torre del Parco, a
108-m (354-ft) tower made
of steel tubes in 1932 after
a design by Giò Ponti.

❸ Acquario Civico

Viale Gadio 2. **Map** 3 B4. **Tel** 02-88
46 57 50. Ⓜ 2 Lanza. 🚌 2, 4, 12, 14.
🚋 57. **Open** 9am–1pm, 2–5:30pm
Tue–Sun. 🌐 **acquariocivico
milano.eu**

The Civic Aquarium was built by
Sebastiano Locati for the 1906
National Exposition, and it is the
only remaining building.
Its 36 tanks house
about 100 species
(fish, crustaceans,
molluscs and
echinoderms)
typical of the
Mediterranean
sea and Italian
freshwater fauna.
There are also rare
kinds of tropical
fish on display.The
aquarium museum
is also home to the
Hydrobiological Station, which
has a library specializing in the
subject. The aquarium building
itself (1906) is a fine example of
Art Nouveau architecture and is
decorated with Richard-Ginori
ceramic tiles and statues of
aquatic animals, dominated by
Oreste Labò's statue of Neptune.

Sea creature decorating the
façade of the Aquarium

❹ Arena Civica

Via Legnano, Viale Elvezia.
Map 3 A-B3. Ⓜ 2 Lanza. 🚌 2, 4,
12, 14. 🚋 57. **Open** for exhibitions
and events only.

This impressive Neo-Classical
amphitheatre, designed in
1806 by Luigi Canonica, was –
together with the Arco della
Pace, Caselli Daziari and Foro
Buonaparte – part of the
project to transform the
Castello Sforzesco area into
a monumental civic centre.
Napoleon was present at
the Arena inaugura-
tion, and it was the
venue for various
cultural and
sports events,
from horse and
mock Roman
chariot races
to hot-air balloon
launchings, mock
naval battles and
festivities. With a
seating capacity
of 30,000, it has also been
a football stadium, but San
Siro *(see p72)* is now the more
important ground. The Arena
is mainly a venue for athletics
(it has a 500-m, 1,640-ft track),
concerts and civil weddings.

The Parco Sempione: in the foreground, the artificial lake and in the background, the Castello Sforzesco

❺ Arco della Pace

Piazza Sempione. **Map** 2 F3. 1, 19.
43, 57, 61.

Work on Milan's major Neo-Classical monument was begun by Luigi Cagnola in 1807 to celebrate Napoleon's victories. It was originally called the Arch of Victories, but building was interrupted and not resumed until 1826 by Francis I of Austria, who had the subjects of the bas-reliefs changed to commemorate the peace of 1815 instead. The Arch of Peace was inaugurated on 10 September 1838 on the occasion of Ferdinand I's coronation as ruler of the Lombardy–Veneto kingdom. The arch is dressed in Crevola marble and decorated with bas-reliefs depicting episodes of the restoration after Napoleon's fall. On the upper level are personifications of the rivers in the Lombardy–Veneto kingdom: the Po, Ticino, Adda and Tagliamento.

At the top of the monument stands the huge bronze Chariot of Peace, by Abbondio Sangiorgio, surrounded by four Victories on horseback. The chariot originally faced France. However, when Milan was ceded to Austria in 1815, it was turned to face the centre of the city, and was the site of the triumphal entrance into Milan of Vittorio Emanuele II, first king of Italy upon unification in 1861.

Tree-lined Corso Sempione

❻ Triennale Design Museum

Viale Alemagna 6. **Map** 3 A4. **Tel** 02-72 43 41. 1–2 Cadorna. 61.
Open 10:30am–8:30pm Tue–Sun (last adm: 7:25pm). **triennale.org**

The Palazzo dell'Arte, southwest of Parco Sempione, was built by Giovanni Muzio in 1932–3 as a permanent site for the International Exhibition of Decorative Arts. The Triennale show was founded in 1923 to foster the development of Italian arts and always played a primary role in promoting architectural development. The building now houses the Triennale Design Museum, offering both a permanent collection and temporary exhibitions showcasing Milan as a centre for cutting-edge design. The museum includes an excellent decorative arts bookstore as well as a research library with specialized and often rare research resources in the fields of architecture, art and fashion. The DesignCafé is worth a visit to take in the surroundings and Michelin-starred cuisine. Next to the museum is the Teatro dell'Arte, redesigned in 1960.

Obelisk in front of the Palzzo dell'Arte

❼ Corso Sempione

Map 2 D1, E2, F3. 1, 19.
37, 43, 57.

Modelled on the grand boulevards of Paris, Corso Sempione was the first stage of a road built by Napoleon to link the city with Lake Maggiore, Switzerland and France via the Simplon Pass.

The first section, starting at the Arco della Pace, is pedestrianized. The Corso is lined with late 19th-century and early 20th-century houses and is now the main thoroughfare in a vast quarter. The initial stretch (towards the park) is considered an elegant area, with good shops, bars and restaurants, the headquarters of Milanese banks and Italian State Radio and TV, RAI (at No. 27). Opposite, at No. 36, is a residence designed by Giuseppe Terragni and Pietro Lingeri in 1935, one of the first examples of Rationalist architecture in Milan.

The semicircular Via Canova and Via Melzi d'Eril cross the Corso, every angle of which offers a different view of the Arco della Pace.

The horses on the Arco della Pace, each cast in one piece

❽ Fieramilanocity

Largo Domodossola 1. **Map** 1 C2.
Tel 02-499 71. Fax: 02-49 97 76 05.
Ⓜ 1–5 Lotto FieraMilanoCity, 5
Portello. 🚋 27. 🚌 37, 48, 68, 78.
Shuttle from Linate airport. ATM
circle line buses (free). **Open** for
exhibitions only. 🅿️ ♿ 📷 🏪
Ⓦ fieramilano.it

The fiera Campionaria, or
Trade Fair, was founded in
1920 to stimulate the
domestic market in postwar
Italy. It was originally located
near Porta Venezia and in
1923 was moved to the
ground behind the Castello
Sforzesco. It was fitted out
with permanent pavilions
and buildings, many of which
were damaged or destroyed
in World War II. Some original
Art Nouveau buildings have
survived at the entrance in
Via Domodossola and the
Palazzo dello Sport (sports
arena). The old main entrance
to the Fiera is in Piazza Giulio
Cesare, which is dominated
by a Four Seasons fountain,
placed there in 1927.

One of the leading exhibition
centres in Europe, the Fiera di
Milano has become a symbol
of Milanese industriousness.
It hosts 78 specialist
international shows attracting
2.5 million visitors every year.

Rho, a town located just
outside Milan, now holds
most trade fairs at an
innovative centre known
as Fieramilano.

San Siro Stadium, now named after footballer Giuseppe Meazza

❾ Meazza (San Siro) Stadium

Piazzale A. Moratti. **Map** 1 A2. **Tel**
02-48 79 82 01. Ⓜ 5 San Siro Stadio.
🚋 16. 🚌 49. San Siro Museum:
Entrance gate 14. **Open** 9:30am–6pm
daily. 🅿️ 📷 Ⓦ sansiro.net

Named after Giuseppe Meazza,
the famous footballer who
played for the local teams,
Inter and AC Milan, Italy's
top stadium is commonly
known as San Siro, after the
surrounding district. It was
built in 1926, rebuilt in the
1950s with a capacity of
85,000, and then renovated
in 1990, when another ring
of tiers and a roof were
added (see pp200–201).
The stadium and changing
rooms can be visited on the
museum tour.

❿ Certosa di Garegnano

Via Garegnano 28. **Tel** 02-38 00 63 01.
🚋 14. 🚌 40. **Open** 9:30am–noon,
3:30–5:30pm daily (closed Thu am).
✝️ 7:30am & 6pm Mon–Fri pre-hols;
8:30, 10 & 11:30am & 6pm.

The church that
forms the heart
of this important
Carthusian
monastery,
dedicated to
Our Lady of the
Assumption, was
founded in 1349
by Archbishop
Giovanni Visconti.
Sadly, the Certosa
is well-known
because the main
cloister was ruined
by the construction
of the A4 motorway.
The courtyard is of
impressive size, with

the monks' houses, each
with a kitchen garden, around
the sides. The rules imposed
by the semi-closed order
required each monk to live
independently. The complex
was rebuilt in late Renaissance
style in 1562; the façade,
completed in 1608, was
decorated with obelisks and
statues, crowned by a statue
of Our Lady. A porticoed
atrium with an exedra-
shaped vestibule provides
a harmonious introduction
to the complex.

Vincenzo Seregni designed
the interior in the 1500s. The
aisleless nave is crowned by
a barrel vault flanked by blind
arcades. The church is famous
for the frescoes by Daniele
Crespi, a leading 17th-century
Lombard artist. He reputedly
painted the entire cycle (The
Legend of the Foundation of the
Order) to thank the Carthusian
monks for offering refuge after
he had been charged with
murder. The cycle begins by the
first arch on the right, continues
on the wall behind the façade,
designed by Simone Peterzano,
and is resumed on the vault,
where there are four medallions.
In the first bay on the left Crespi
included a self-portrait of
himself as a servant blowing a
horn and added the date (1629)
and his signature in a scroll.

Simone Peterzano painted
the frescoes in the presbytery
and apse (1578), with scenes
from the life of Mary. The
chapel on the right has two
macabre 17th-century paintings
informing novices of the various
forms of torture they might
encounter while spreading
Christianity. On leaving, look
at the 14th-century cloister
on the right, the only surviving
part of the original monastery.

Façade of the Certosa di Garegnano (1608)

⓫ Casa degli Atellani and Vigna di Leonardo

Corso Magenta 65. **Map** 6 F1.
Tel 02-48 16 150. Ⓜ 1, 2 Cadorna,
1 Conciliazione. 🚊 16, 19.
Open 9am–6pm daily. **Closed** 1 Jan,
1 May, 2 Jun, 25 & 26 Dec. &
🆆 vignadileonardo.com

Ludovico il Moro Sforza,
Duke of Milan, wanted
to create a residential
neighbourhood where he
could establish his most
loyal followers. In 1490, he
gave houses to the Atellani
family of Sforza courtiers and
to Leonardo da Vinci. In 1498,
he also gave Leonardo a
vineyard. Casa degli Atellani
is one of the few traces left
of Ludovico's Renaissance
dream. Over the course of
the 20th century, it was
transformed by Piero
Portaluppi, a major Milanese
architect, while still retaining
its grandeur. Both the house
and the vineyard in the garden
are open to the public.

⓬ Santa Maria delle Grazie

Piazza Santa Maria delle Grazie.
Map 2 F5. **Tel** 02-46 76 111. Ⓜ 1, 2
Cadorna, 1 Conciliazione. 🚊 16.
Open 7am–noon, 3–7pm Mon–Sat,
7:30am–12:15pm, 3:30–8:15pm Sun.
✝ 7:30, 8 (except Jul–mid-Sep);
8:30 & 9:30am, 6:30pm Mon–Sat;
6:30pm pre-hols; 7, 9:30, 10:30 &
11:30am, 6:30 & 8pm (except Jul &
Aug) hols.

Construction of this church
designed by Guiniforte
Solari, began in 1463 and

The façade of Santa Maria delle Grazie,
designed by Guiniforte Solari

was completed in 1490.
Two years later Lodovico il
Moro asked Bramante to
change the church into the
family mausoleum: Solari's
apse section was demolished
and replaced by a Renaissance
apse. After il Moro lost power
in 1500, the Dominicans
continued to decorate the
church, later assisted by the
court of Inquisition, which
had moved here in 1558.
Restoration was undertaken
only in the late 19th century.
In 1943 a bomb destroyed
the main cloister, but the
apse and the room containing
Leonardo's *Last Supper* were
miraculously left intact;
restoration work has continued
since then. On the exterior,
Solari's wide brick façade is
worthy of note. The doorway
was designed by Bramante;
it is preceded by a porch
supported by Corinthian
columns and the lunette
has a painting by Leonardo
da Vinci with the Madonna
between Lodovico and his
wife, Beatrice d'Este. The
sides and polygonal apse
are also of interest. As you
enter the church you notice
the difference between
Solari's nave, which echoes
Lombard Gothic architecture –
entirely covered with frescoes
and with ogival arches – and
Bramante's design for the
apse, which is larger, better
lit and is almost bare of
decoration. The two parts of
the church reflect Bramante's
impact on Milanese culture;
he introduced the Renaissance
style that dominated Tuscany
and Umbria in the early 15th
century. The all-pervasive
painting decoration of the
aisle walls is by Bernardino
Butinone and Donato
Montorfano (1482–6). The
Della Torre chapel is the first
one in the right-hand aisle:
the altar has a 15th-century
fresco and to the left is the
tomb of Giacomo Della Torre,
with bas-relief sculpture by
the Cazzaniga brothers (1483).
The fourth chapel, dedicated
to Santa Corona, has frescoes
by Gaudenzio Ferrari. In the

The ogival arches in the nave of Santa
Maria delle Grazie

next chapel is a *Crucifixion*
by Giovanni Demìo (1542).

The apse, decorated only
with graffiti to maintain the
purity of the architectural
volumes, is a perfect cube
crowned by a hemisphere.
It was built to house the
tomb of Lodovico il Moro
and Beatrice d'Este, but the
work never reached Santa
Maria delle Grazie (it is now
in the Charterhouse of Pavia).
The decoration of the dome
is rich in Marian symbols,
while the Doctors of the
Church appear in the roundels
in the pendentives. The carved
and inlaid wooden stalls of the
choir are lovely.

A door on the right leads
to the small cloister known as
Chiostrino delle Rane because
of the frogs *(rane)* in the central
basin. The cloister leads to the
old sacristy, with its painted
wardrobes, one of which
conceals a secret underground
passageway, used by Lodovico
to come from the Castello on
horseback. Back in the church,
the chapels in the north aisle
begin with the Madonna delle
Grazie chapel, with Cerano's
*Madonna Freeing Milan of the
Plague* (1631) on the entrance
archway. The altarpiece,
Madonna delle Grazie, dates
from the 15th century. The
sixth chapel has a *Holy
Family with St Catherine* by
Paris Bordone, and the first
chapel contains the cloak of
St Catherine of Siena.

Leonardo da Vinci's *Last Supper*

This masterpiece was painted for Lodovico il Moro in the refectory of Santa Maria delle Grazie in 1495–7. Leonardo depicts the moment just after Christ has uttered the words, "One of you will betray me". The artist captures their amazement in facial expressions and body language in a remarkably realistic and vivid *Last Supper*. It is not a true fresco, but was painted in tempera, allowing Leonardo more time to achieve the subtle nuances typical of his work. The room was used as a stable in the Napoleonic era and was badly damaged by bombs in 1943. Fortunately, the work was saved because it was protected by sandbags.

Jesus Christ
The isolated, serene figure of Christ contrasts with the agitated Apostles. Half-closed lips show he has just spoken.

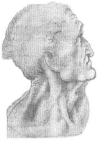

Judas
Unable to find a truly evil face for Judas, Leonardo drew inspiration from that of the prior in the convent, who kept on asking when the work would be finished.

The Last Supper
is famous for the gesturing hands of the Apostles, which are so harmonious and expressive that critics have said they "speak".

The Apostle Andrew, with his arms upraised, expresses his horror at Christ's words.

The Crucifixion by Montorfano
The Dominicans asked Donato Montorfano to paint a fresco of the Crucifixion on the opposite wall to depict Christ's sacrifice. In this dense composition the despairing Magdalen hugs the cross while the soldiers on the right throw dice for Christ's robe. On either side of the work, under the cross, Leonardo added the portraits – now almost invisible – of Lodovico il Moro, his wife Beatrice and their children, signed and dated (1495).

The Restoration

It was not the humidity but the method used by Leonardo, *tempera forte*, that caused the immediate deterioration of *The Last Supper*. As early as 1550 the art historian Vasari called it "a dazzling blotch" and regarded it as a lost work. There have

been many attempts to restore *The Last Supper*, beginning in 1726, but in retouching the picture further damage was done. The seventh restoration ended in spring 1999: although it lacks the splendour of the original, it is at least authentic.

Material used for restoration

VISITORS' CHECKLIST

Practical Information
Piazza Santa Maria delle Grazie 2.
Map 2 F5. **Tel** Compulsory
advance booking: 02-92 80 03 60,
🆆 vivaticket.it. **Open** 8:15am–
6:45pm Tue–Sun. **Closed** pub
hols, 1 May, 15 Aug. 🅿 ♿ ✉
📷 🆆 **cenacolovinciano.org**

Transport
Ⓜ 1, 2 Cadorna. 🚋 16. 🚌 18.

The tablecloth, plates and bowls were probably copied from those in the convent to give the impression that Christ was at a table with monks.

Sketches of the Apostles

Leonardo used to wander around Milan in search of faces to use for the Apostles. Of his many sketches, this one for St James is now in the Royal Library in Windsor, England.

Christ and the Apostles

1 Christ
2 Thomas
3 James the Greater
4 Philip
5 Matthew
6 Thaddaeus
7 Simon

8 John
9 Peter
10 Judas
11 Andrew
12 James the Lesser
13 Bartholomew

⓭ Corso Magenta

Map 3 A5. Ⓜ 1 Conciliazione, 1, 2 Cadorna. 🚊 16, 27. 🚌 18.

This street is fascinating, with its elegant shops and historic buildings making it one of the loveliest and most elegant quarters in Milan. At No. 65, just past Santa Maria delle Grazie, is a building incorporating the remains of the Atellani residence, decorated by Luini, where

Leonardo da Vinci stayed while working on *The Last Supper*. Piero Portaluppi carried out the work on No. 65 in 1919. In the garden at the back there are some vines, said to be the remains

Pastry shop sign in Corso Magenta

of the vineyard that Lodovico il Moro gave to the great artist. The next building (No. 61), Palazzo delle Stelline, originally a girls' orphanage, is now a convention centre and houses the Fondazione Stelline, which holds art exhibitions. The Fondazione also has a garden, created from the land given to Leonardo. At the corner of Via Carducci, which was built over the original course of the Naviglio canal, is Bar Magenta (*see p184*). The medieval city gate, the Porta Vercellina, once stood at this junction.

⓮ Palazzo Litta

Corso Magenta 24. **Map** 3 A5. Ⓜ 1, 2 Cadorna. 🚊 16, 27. 🚌 18, 50, 58, 94. **Open** during cultural events only.

Considered one of the most beautiful examples of 18th-century Lombard architecture, this palazzo was first built in 1648 for Count Bartolomeo Arese by Francesco Maria Richini. At the end of the century the interior was embellished and in 1763 the pink façade was built at the request of the heirs, the Litta Visconti Arese. The façade, by Bartolomeo Bolli, is late

The Sala Rossa in Palazzo Litta, with mementos of Napoleon's visit here

Baroque, the door flanked by large telamones. Since 1905 the building has housed the State Railway offices.

Inside is a number of sumptuous rooms looking onto a 17th-century courtyard. The broad staircase, designed by Carlo Giuseppe Merlo in 1740 and decorated with precious marble and the family coat of arms (a black and white check), has a double central flight. It leads up to the *piano nobile*, where one of the rooms is named the Sala Rossa (Red Room) after the colour of its wallpaper (a copy of the original). Set in the floor is a pearl, there to commemorate a tear said to have been shed during a meeting between the Duchess Litta and Napoleon.

The next room is the Salone degli Specchi, which seems to be enlarged to infinity by the large mirrors (*specchi*) on the walls. The vault decoration is by Martin Knoller. The Salotto della Duchessa is the only room in the palazzo which still has its original 18th-century wallpaper. The Teatro Litta stands to the left of the palazzo, the oldest theatre in the city.

⓯ Civico Museo Archeologico

Corso Magenta 15. **Map** 7 A1. **Tel** 02-88 44 52 08. Ⓜ 1, 2 Cadorna. 🚊 16, 27. 🚌 18, 50, 58, 94. **Open** 9am–5:30pm Tue–Sun. 🅿 🛆 *(phone ahead)*. ✉

The Archaeological Museum is well worth a visit for the finds and to see the only remaining part of the city's Roman walls. At the entrance, graphic reconstructions illustrate urban planning and architecture in Milan from the 1st to the 4th century AD. The visit begins in a hall on the right, with clay objects, including a collection of oil lamps. This is followed by Roman sculpture. One of the most interesting pieces in the series of portraits dating from Caesar's era to late antiquity (1st–4th century AD), is the *Portrait of Maximian* (mid-3rd century AD). At the end of this room is a huge fragment of

Roman sarcophagus of a lawyer, on display in the Civico Museo Archeologico

a torso of Hercules from the Milanese thermae, dating from the first half of the 2nd century AD. Behind this are some 3rd-century AD floor mosaics found in Milanese houses.

By the window are two of the most important works in the museum: the Parabiago Patera and the Diatreta Cup. The Patera is a gilded silver plate with a relief of the triumph of the goddess Cybele, mother of the gods, on a chariot pulled by lions and surrounded by the Sun and Moon and sea and Zodiac divinities (mid-4th century AD). The marvellous Diatreta Cup, also dating from the 4th century AD, comes from Novara and consists of a single piece of coloured glass, with finely wrought, intricate decoration. Winding around the cup is the inscription *Bibe vivas multis annis* ("Drink and you will live many years"). The entrance hall leads to a courtyard, where you will see the Torre di Ansperto, a Roman tower, from the ancient Maximianian walls. Leading from the courtyard is a three-storey exhibition space displaying early medieval, Etruscan and Greek collections. The basement houses art from Gandhar and Caesaera (Israel), as well as Roman and Mediolanum flooring.

Stela with portraits, Museo Archeologico

🔟 San Maurizio

Corso Magenta 13.
Map 7 A1. **Tel** 02-86 66 60 (Santa Maria alla Porta).
Ⓜ 1, 2 Cadorna. 🚋 16, 27.
🚌 50, 58, 94. **Open** 9:30am–5:30pm Tue–Sat. ✝ 6pm Mon–Fri, 10:15am (Greek–Albanian) Sun.

The Roman ruins in Via Brisa

In 1503 Gian Giacomo Dolcebuono began construction of this church, which was intended for the most powerful closed order of Benedictine nuns in Milan, with one hall for the public and another for the nuns. In the first hall, to the right of the altar, is the opening through which the nuns receive the Body of Christ. Most of the decoration was done by Bernardino Luini. He painted the frescoes in the first hall, including the *Life of St Catherine* (third chapel to the right) and those on the middle wall. The second chapel on the right was decorated by Callisto Piazza, the chapels to the left by pupils of Luini. On the altar is an *Adoration of the Magi* by Antonio Campi. The middle wall of the second hall, occupied by the choir, has frescoes by Foppa, Piazza, an *Annunciation* attributed to Bramantino and *Episodes of the Passion*. Concerts are held here in the winter.

🔟 Via Brisa

Map 7 B1. Ⓜ 1, 2 Cadorna. 🚋 16, 27. 🚌 50, 58.

Excavations carried out after the 1943 bombing of this street revealed Roman ruins which were probably part of Maximian's imperial palace: the foundation of a round hall surrounded by apsidal halls and preceded by a narthex. Note the columns that raised the pavement to allow warm air to pass into the palace.

🔟 Piazza Cordusio

Map 7 C1. Ⓜ 1 Cordusio. 🚋 1, 2, 3, 12, 14, 16, 27.

This oval-shaped piazza was named after the *Curtis Ducis*, the main seat of the Lombard duchy. The area, Milan's financial district, was laid out from 1889 to 1901. Buildings include Luca Beltrami's Assicurazioni Generali building, Casa Dario, and the main offices of UniCredit, designed by Luigi Broggi.

🔟 Piazza Affari

Map 7 B1 (9 B3). Ⓜ 1 Cordusio. 🚋 3, 16, 27.

The heart of the financial district, this square was laid out in 1928–40 to house the city's markets (especially farm produce). The Borsa Valori, Italy's most important Stock Exchange, stands here. Founded in 1808, it is housed in a building designed by Paolo Mezzanotte in 1931. Ruins of a 1st-century BC Roman theatre were found in the basement area.

The Milan Stock Exchange in Piazza Affari, built in 1931

SOUTHWEST MILAN

Religious complexes once covered this district, preventing further building until the early 19th century. The suppression of the monasteries in the late 18th century paved the way for the urbanization of the area between the medieval and Spanish walls, crossed by two large avenues, Corso Italia and Corso di Porta Ticinese. Beyond Porta Ticinese, which leads to the southern part of Milan, is Corso San Gottardo. The area is bordered by the inner ring road, which follows the course of the medieval walls, and the outer ring road, which replaced the Spanish walls. Further on is the Naviglio canals quarter, with the Naviglio Grande and the Pavese, the last vestiges of what was once a major network for communications and commerce. Barges used the Naviglio Grande to transport the Candoglia marble used to build the Duomo and, in the 1950s, the material for postwar reconstruction.

Sights at a Glance

Streets, Squares and Historic Buildings

❷ Piazza della Vetra and medieval Porta Ticinese
❸ Largo Carrobbio and Via Torino
❹ Via Circo

Churches

❶ San Lorenzo alle Colonne see pp82–3
❺ San Bernardino alle Monache
❻ Sant'Ambrogio see pp86–9
❽ San Vittore al Corpo
❿ Sant'Eustorgio

⓫ Santa Maria dei Miracoli presso San Celso
⓬ Sant'Alessandro

Museums and Galleries

❼ Museo Nazionale della Scienza e della Tecnologia Leonardo da Vinci
❾ Museo Diocesano
⓭ Armani/Silos

☐ **Restaurants** pp171–2
1 Al Pont de Ferr
2 Al Porto
3 Alla Collina Pistoiese
4 Dal Bolognese
5 L'Oca Giuliva
6 Osteria dei Binari
7 Osteria Porta Cicca
8 Osteria di Via Pre
9 Pizzeria Tradizionale con Cucina di Pesce
10 Premiata Pizzeria
11 Trattoria Aurora
12 L'Ulmet

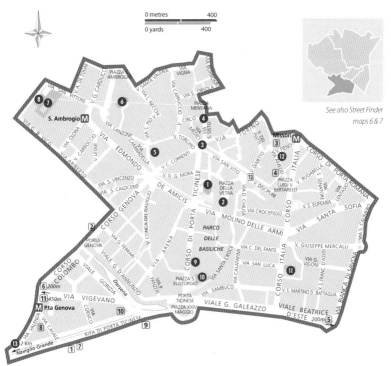

See also Street Finder maps 6 & 7

◀ Magnificent golden ceiling in the basilica of Sant'Ambrogio

For keys to symbols see back flap

Street-by-Street: From Sant'Ambrogio to San Lorenzo

Situated just outside the Roman walls, this area was occupied by Early Christian cemeteries and Imperial Age buildings such as the Arena and Circus. Though little remains of this ancient heritage, it is significant, particularly the columns of the triumphal entrance to the basilica of San Lorenzo. Nine kings of Italy were crowned in Sant'Ambrogio in the 9th–15th centuries with four buried here. Napoleon came here in 1805, and Ferdinand of Austria in 1838, after their respective coronations in the Duomo. On the feast day of Sant'Ambrogio, 7 December, the ("how beautiful" in Milanese dialect) fair is held in the streets.

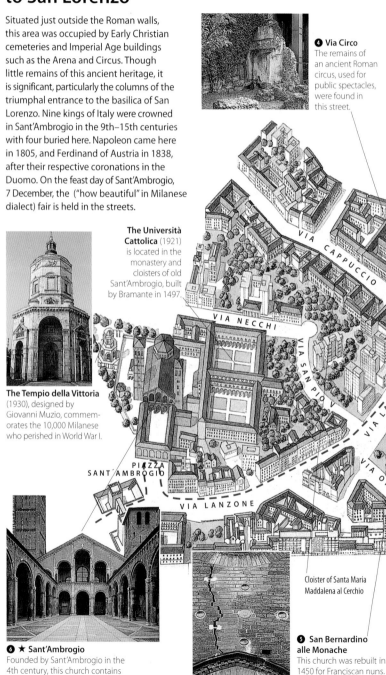

❹ Via Circo
The remains of an ancient Roman circus, used for public spectacles, were found in this street.

The Università Cattolica (1921) is located in the monastery and cloisters of old Sant'Ambrogio, built by Bramante in 1497.

The Tempio della Vittoria (1930), designed by Giovanni Muzio, commemorates the 10,000 Milanese who perished in World War I.

PIAZZA
SANT'AMBROGIO

Cloister of Santa Maria Maddalena al Cerchio

❻ ★ Sant'Ambrogio
Founded by Sant'Ambrogio in the 4th century, this church contains masterpieces such as the San Vittore mosaics and the Golden Altar.

❺ San Bernardino alle Monache
This church was rebuilt in 1450 for Franciscan nuns. The façade is decorated with majolica bowls.

❸ Largo Carrobbio
The name of the crossroads at the end of Via Torino may derive from Quadrivium, meaning a place where four streets converge.

Locator Map
See Street Finder map 7

A tower from the Roman Porta Ticinese is hidden in the courtyard of a building between Via del Torchio and Via Medici.

In Largo Carrobbio
the small deconsecrated church of San Sisto houses the Museo Messina.

❷ Piazza della Vetra
From this square there are spectacular views of the apses of San Lorenzo and Sant'Eustorgio. Until 1840 the piazza was the scene of executions.

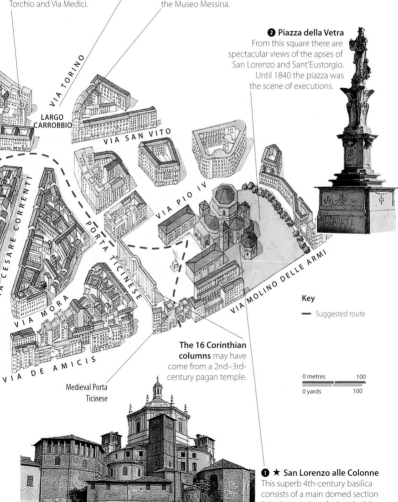

VIA TORINO

LARGO CARROBBIO

VIA SAN VITO

VIA CESARE CORRENTI

VIA PIO IV

PORTA TICINESE

VIA MORA

VIA MOLINO DELLE ARMI

VIA DE AMICIS

Key
— Suggested route

0 metres 100
0 yards 100

The 16 Corinthian columns may have come from a 2nd–3rd-century pagan temple.

Medieval Porta Ticinese

❶ ★ San Lorenzo alle Colonne
This superb 4th-century basilica consists of a main domed section linked to a series of minor buildings, dating from different periods.

❶ San Lorenzo alle Colonne

Dating from the 4th century, San Lorenzo is one of the oldest round churches in Western Christendom and may have been the ancient Imperial palatine chapel. The church was built utilizing materials from a nearby Roman amphitheatre. The plan, with exedrae and women's galleries, is unlike Lombard architecture and reveals the hand of Roman architects and masons. Some art historians also see the influence of Byzantine art in the unusual plan. After several fires the church was reconstructed in the 11th and 12th centuries and was again rebuilt after the dome collapsed in 1573, but the original quatrefoil plan has been preserved. The chapel of Sant'Aquilino contains some of the best mosaics in Northern Italy.

Cappella di San Sisto
This chapel was frescoed by Gian Cristoforo Storer in the 17th century.

Main entrance

★ Roman Columns
The 16 Corinthian columns, from the 2nd–3rd century, were part of an unidentified temple and were placed in their present location in the 4th century.

Statue of Constantine
This bronze work is a copy of a Roman statue of the emperor who issued the Edict of Milan in AD 313, bringing persecution of Christians to an end.

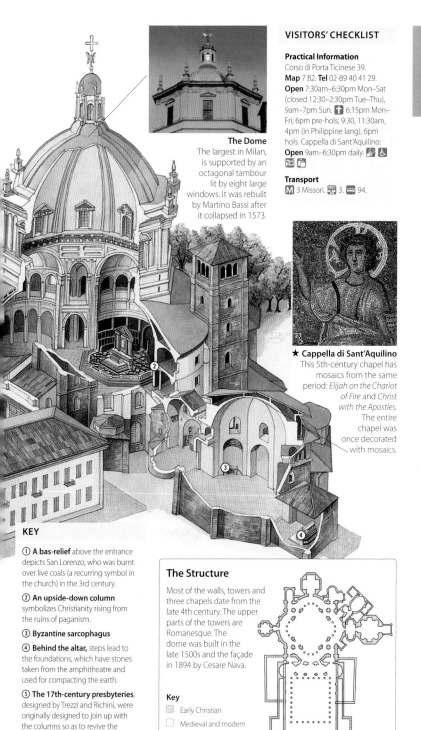

The Dome
The largest in Milan, is supported by an octagonal tambour lit by eight large windows. It was rebuilt by Martino Bassi after it collapsed in 1573.

VISITORS' CHECKLIST

Practical Information
Corso di Porta Ticinese 39.
Map 7 B2. **Tel** 02-89 40 41 29.
Open 7:30am–6:30pm Mon–Sat (closed 12:30–2:30pm Tue–Thu), 9am–7pm Sun. 🕇 6:15pm Mon–Fri; 6pm pre-hols; 9:30, 11:30am, 4pm (in Philippine lang), 6pm hols. Cappella di Sant'Aquilino: **Open** 9am–6:30pm daily. 🅿 ♿ 📷 🏠

Transport
Ⓜ 3 Missori. 🚊 3. 🚌 94.

★ **Cappella di Sant'Aquilino**
This 5th-century chapel has mosaics from the same period: *Elijah on the Chariot of Fire* and *Christ with the Apostles*. The entire chapel was once decorated with mosaics.

KEY

① **A bas-relief** above the entrance depicts San Lorenzo, who was burnt over live coals (a recurring symbol in the church) in the 3rd century.

② **An upside-down column** symbolizes Christianity rising from the ruins of paganism.

③ **Byzantine sarcophagus**

④ **Behind the altar,** steps lead to the foundations, which have stones taken from the amphitheatre and used for compacting the earth.

⑤ **The 17th-century presbyteries,** designed by Trezzi and Richini, were originally designed to join up with the columns so as to revive the pattern of the ancient quadriporticus.

The Structure

Most of the walls, towers and three chapels date from the late 4th century. The upper parts of the towers are Romanesque. The dome was built in the late 1500s and the façade in 1894 by Cesare Nava.

Key
⬛ Early Christian
⬜ Medieval and modern
⬜ Romanesque

The busy Via Torino, bustling with people

❷ Piazza della Vetra and medieval Porta Ticinese

Map 7 B2. 🚋 2, 3, 14, 15. 🚌 94.

The vast area of greenery dominated by a column bearing the statue of San Lazzaro (1728) is also called Parco delle Basiliche, because it lies between the basilicas of San Lorenzo and Sant'Eustorgio. The name "Vetra" seems to derive from the Latin *castra vetera*, which probably alluded to the Roman military camps positioned here to defend the nearby imperial palace. The name was also given to a canal that was once on the northern side of the square and was lined with tanners' workshops (the tanners were called *vetraschi*).

Until 1840 the square was used for the public hangings of condemned commoners, while nobles were decapitated in front of the law court, the Broletto *(see p56)*.

During the Roman era there was a small port here, at the point where the Seveso and Nirone rivers converged in the navigable Vettabbia canal.

This square is worth visiting just for the magnificent view of the apses of the basilicas. In the 12th century, when the city walls were enlarged to include San Lorenzo, the Roman gate at present-day Largo Carrobbio was replaced by the "new" medieval Porta Ticinese. A moat ran around the new walls and along present-day Via Molino delle Armi, which was named after the water mills *(molini)* used mostly to forge weapons. Porta Ticinese was remodelled after 1329 by Azzone Visconti and decorated with a tabernacle of the *Madonna and Child with St Ambrose Proffering the Model of the City* by the workshop of Giovanni di Balduccio (14th century). This city gate – the only one, along with Porta Nuova on Via Manzoni, still standing – was fortified with two towers in 1865.

Detail of the tabernacle of Porta Ticinese: *Madonna and Child with St Ambrose* by Giovanni di Balduccio's workshop

❸ Largo Carrobbio and Via Torino

Map 7 B2. 🚋 2, 3, 14. Museo Messina: Via San Sisto 4. **Tel** 02-86 45 30 05. **Open** 10am–7pm Tue–Sat. **Closed** 1 Jan, Easter, 1 May, 15 Aug, 25 Dec. 🚫 ♿

The vast Carrobbio square, which connects Via Torino and Corso di Porta Ticinese, was either named after the *quadrivium*, a crossroads of four streets, or after *carrubium*, a road reserved for carts. One of the towers flanking the Roman Porta Ticinese still stands at the corner of Via Medici and Via del Torchio. The name of the gate derived from the fact that it opened onto the road for Pavia, which in ancient times was called *Ticinum*. At the junction with Via San Sisto is the deconsecrated 17th-century church of San Sisto. In 1976 it became the museum-studio of sculptor Francesco Messina (who died in 1990) and now houses a

Female nude by Francesco Messina (1967)

collection of his bronze and coloured plaster sculpture pieces and graphic art.

Largo Carrobbio is at one end of Via Torino, a major commercial street that developed after the merger of the old city districts, which were filled with the workshops of oil merchants, silk weavers, hatters and famous armourers – as is reflected in the names of some streets.

The 16th-century Palazzo Stampa, built by Massimiliano Stampa, stands in Via Soncino. When the Sforza dynasty died out in 1535, Stampa introduced Spanish dominion to the city by hoisting the flag of Charles V on the Castello Sforzesco in exchange for land and privileges. The imperial eagle still stands on the palazzo tower, over the bronze globe representing the dominions of Charles V.

The cloister at Santa Maria Maddalena al Cerchio

❹ Via Circo

Map 7 B1. 🚋 2, 3, 14. 🚌 50, 58.

The area extending from Largo Carrobbio to Corso Magenta is very rich in 3rd- and 4th-century ruins, particularly mosaics and masonry, much of it now part of private homes. This was the period when the Roman emperor Maximian lived in Milan: his splendid palace was near Via Brisa. In order to create a proper imperial capital, he built many civic edifices to gain the favour of the Milanese: the Arena, the thermae and the huge Circus used for two-horse chariot races. The Circus, 505 m

(1,656 ft) long, was one of the largest constructions in the Roman Empire. The only remaining parts are the end curve, visible at the junction of Via Cappuccio and Via Circo, and one of the entrance towers, which became the bell tower of San Maurizio in Corso Magenta.

The Circus, active long after the fall of the Roman Empire, was the venue of the coronation of the Lombard king Adaloaldo in 615, while in the Carolingian period it became a vineyard, as the place name of nearby Via Vigna indicates. At No. 7 Via Cappuccio, the 18th-century Palazzo Litta Biumi has incorporated, to the left of the central courtyard, the delightful 15th-century nuns' convent Santa Maria Maddalena al Cerchio, which has been partly rebuilt. Its name, a corruption of the Latin *ad circulum*, refers to the Circus over which it was built. The hood of the nuns' habit *(cappuccio)* is probably the origin of the name of the street where the convent is located. Further along, at No. 13, is Palazzo Radice Fossati (a private house), of medieval origin, with a 13th-century portal and 18th-century frescoes inside.

On Via Sant'Orsola you come to Via Morigi, named after a famous Milanese family who once lived here; all that remains of their residence is a 14th-century tower with a small loggia. The nearby square is dominated by the 14th-century Torre dei Gorani, another tower crowned by a loggia with small stone columns.

Fifteenth-century frescoes by the school of Vincenzo Foppa

❺ San Bernardino alle Monache

Via Lanzone 13. Map 7 A1.
Tel 02-86 45 08 95. 🚋 2, 3, 14. 🚌 94.
Open 4–6pm Fri, 10am–noon Sun.

The church is the only remaining building in a Franciscan nuns' convent dating from the mid-15th century and attributed to the Lombard architect Pietro Antonio Solari. The church was named after the preacher Bernardino da Siena, whose relics are kept here. It was partly rebuilt in 1922. The narrow, elegant brick façade is decorated with majolica bowls and a fine elaborate cornice with small arches.

The interior houses fine 15th-century frescoes painted by the school of Vincenzo Foppa, and others dating from the early 16th century. Of note is *Madonna and Child with Saint Agnes*.

Part of the curve of the Circus built by the Roman emperor Maximian in the late 3rd century AD

❻ Sant'Ambrogio

The basilica was built by Bishop Ambrogio (Ambrose) in AD 379–86 on an Early Christian burial ground as part of a programme to reorganize the Christian face of Milan. The church was dedicated to Ambrogio, a defender of Christianity against Arianism, after his burial here. The Benedictines began to enlarge it in the 8th century, then in the following century Archbishop Anspert built the atrium, which was rebuilt in the 12th century. In the 11th century, reconstruction of the entire church began. The dome collapsed in 1196, and the vaults and pulpit were rebuilt. In 1492 the Sforza family asked Bramante to restructure the rectory and the Benedictine monastery. Sadly, the basilica was badly damaged by bombs in 1943.

The Capitals
The columns are enlivened by Bible stories and fantastic animals symbolizing the struggle between Good and Evil. Some date from the 11th century.

The Interior
The solemn proportions typical of Lombard-Romanesque style characterize the interior. The nave is covered by ribbed cross vaulting supported by massive piers.

Apse Mosaic
The mosaic dates from the 4th–8th centuries and was partially restored after the 1943 bombings. It depicts the enthroned Christ and scenes from Sant'Ambrogio's life.

VISITORS' CHECKLIST

Practical Information
Piazza Sant'Ambrogio 15.
Map 7 A1. **Tel** 02-86 45 08 95.
Open 7:30am–12:30pm, 2:30–7pm daily (not during services).
🕙 6:30pm pre-hols; 8, 10 & 11am (in Latin), 12:15, 6 & 7pm hols; 8 & 9am, 6:30pm Mon–Fri. 🏛
Museo della Basilica: **Tel** 02-86 45 08 95. Enter via presbytery.
Open 9am–12:30pm, 2:30–6pm Mon–Sat; 10am–1pm, 3–5pm Sun. **Closed** am pre-hols and hols. 🎟 🏛 Chapel of San Vittore in Ciel d'Oro: 🎟

Transport
Ⓜ 2 Sant'Ambrogio. 🚌 50, 58, 94.

★ Chapel of San Vittore in Ciel d'Oro
The chapel was named after the gold (oro) mosaics on the vault. Sant'Ambrogio is depicted in one of the 5th-century panels.

Museum entrance

★ Golden Altar
This golden altar was made by Volvinius (9th century) for the remains of Sant'Ambrogio. The reliefs depict the lives of Christ (front) and Ambrogio (to the rear).

★ Sarcophagus of Stilicho
Situated under the pulpit, this 4th-century masterpiece has a wealth of relief figures with religious significance. It is traditionally referred to as the tomb of the Roman general Stilicho, but probably contained the remains of the emperor Gratian.

KEY

① **Anspert's Atrium** (11th century) was used by local people as a refuge from danger before the city walls were built.

② **The Canons' bell tower** was erected in 1124 to surpass in height and beauty the campanile of the nearby Benedictines.

③ **Apse**

④ **The ciborium** is the small 10th-century baldachin that protects the Golden Altar. It is supported by four Roman porphyry columns and decorated with stuccowork.

Exploring Sant'Ambrogio

The fact that the church of Sant'Ambrogio houses the remains of the city's patron saint, the church's founder, makes it a special place for the Milanese. Most of its present-day appearance is the result of rebuilding in the 10th and 12th centuries by the Benedictines from the nearby monastery, who made it a model of Lombard Romanesque religious architecture. All that remains of the 4th-century basilica are the triumphal arch and its columns, which became part of the apse. In 1937–40 and in the postwar period the Romanesque structure and delicate colours were restored. From the Pusterla (gate) there is a marvellous view of the church, with its two bell towers and atrium, flanked by the rectory and museum.

Pusterla di Sant'Ambrogio

The Pusterla di Sant'Ambrogio, one of the minor gates on the medieval walls, is a good starting point for a visit to the church. Rebuilt in 1939, it houses a museum with old weapons and instruments of torture.

A decorated capital in the atrium

Anspert's Atrium

Just before the atrium, to the left, is the isolated Roman Colonna del Diavolo (Devil's Column), with two holes halfway up which, according to tradition, were made by the Devil's horns while he was tempting Sant'Ambrogio. The present-day atrium, with its blind arches, dates from the 12th century and replaced one built by Archbishop Anspert in the 9th century.

This large courtyard acts as an entrance foyer for the church proper and sets off the façade. A row of piers (some Roman) with sculpted capitals continues into the basilica. The rhythmic pattern of the arches, half-columns and small suspended arches, as well as the proportions, match those in the church, creating a harmonious continuity between exterior and interior. The atrium houses finds and tombstones from this area, which was once an Early Christian cemetery.

The fourth side of the atrium, or narthex, has five bays and is part of the façade, which has an upper loggia with five arches. In the narthex is the main portal (8th–10th centuries), with small columns with figures of animals and the Mystic Lamb, while its wooden wings (1750) have reliefs of the *Life of David*.

The atrium, with finds and tombstones from the surrounding area

The Interior

The nave provides the best view of the interior, revealing the basilica in all its splendour. The nave has two side aisles divided by arcades supporting the women's galleries with piers with carved capitals. At the beginning of the nave is the Serpent's Column, said to have been erected by Moses in the desert. Beside it, to the left, excavations show the level of the original 4th-century floor.

The pulpit (or ambo) is made of pieces saved when the dome collapsed in 1196. This magnificent monument is decorated with an eagle and a seated man, symbols of the evangelists John and Matthew. Underneath is the sarcophagus of Stilicho (4th century) with reliefs representing (going clockwise) *Christ Giving the Law to St Peter*, four scenes from the Old Testament, *Christ among the Apostles* and the *Sacrifice of Isaac*. Under the octagonal cupola is the ciborium (10th century), the heart of the basilica, supported by columns taken from the 4th-century ciborium. Its painted stucco sides depict various episodes: on the front is *Christ Giving the Keys to St Peter and the Law to St Paul*. The ciborium acts as a baldachin for the Golden Altar, an embossed work that Archbishop Angilberto commissioned from Volvinius in the 9th century. On the back, a silver relief narrates the *Life of Sant'Ambrogio* and has the artist's signature. On the same side, two small doors allowed the faithful to worship the body of St Ambrose, once kept under the altar. The front is made of gold and jewels, and narrates the *Life of Christ*. Behind the ciborium is the wooden choir with the *Life of Sant'Ambrogio* (15th century) and, in the middle, the bishop's throne (4th and 9th centuries), also used by

The Serpent's Column, at the beginning of the nave

the kings of Italy crowned here. Part of the large mosaic in the apse dates from the 6th and 8th centuries. The scene on the left, a *Benedictory Christ*, is of the same period, while the one on the right is the result of 18th-century and postwar reconstruction. Next to the presbytery is the stairway to the crypt, decorated with stucco (c.1740). Under the Golden Altar, an urn (1897) has the remains of Saints Ambrogio, Gervasio and Protasio. Back upstairs, at the end of the south aisle is the stunning San Vittore in Ciel d'Oro Sacellum, the 4th-century funerary chapel of the martyr, which was later incorporated into the basilica. The 5th-century mosaics on the walls show various saints, including Saints Ambrogio, Gervasio and Protasio.

The Risen Christ by Bergognone (c.1491)

The South Aisle

Returning to the entrance in the south aisle, you will see the monks' chapels, built in different eras. St George's chapel – sixth from the entrance – houses an altarpiece of the *Madonna and Child with the Infant St John the Baptist* by Bernardo Lanino, who frescoed the *Legend of St George* on the sides (1546). The Baroque chapel of the Holy Sacrament, the fifth, contains the frescoes *The Death of St Benedict* by Carlo Preda and *St Bernard* by Filippo Abbiati (17th and 18th century respectively). In St Bartholomew's chapel (the second) are the *Legends of Saints Vittore and Satiro* (1737) by Tiepolo, detached from the San Vittore Sacellum; they demonstrate the cultural openness of the Cistercians, who commissioned the work. The altarpiece in the second chapel, *The Virgin Mary with St Bartholomew and St John the Baptist*, is attributed to Gaudenzio Ferrari, as is the 1545 *Deposition* in the next chapel, which also has frescoes by Luini on the pillars.

The North Aisle

Go up this aisle from the baptistery (first chapel), which has a porphyry font by Franco Lombardi with the *Conversion of St Augustine* (1940), the saint baptized by

Sant'Ambrogio in Milan. It is dominated symbolically by Bergognone's *The Risen Christ* (c.1491).

In the third chapel is an interesting painting by Luini, a *Madonna with Saints Jerome and Rocco*.

Museo della Basilica

At the end of the north aisle you come out into the Portico della Canonica, the presbytery portico, which was left unfinished by Bramante (1492–4) and rebuilt after World War II. The columns of the central arch, sculpted to resemble tree trunks, are unusual. The entrance to the Basilica Museum, with six rooms featuring objects and works of art from the church, is here. Among the most interesting pieces are a 12th-century multicoloured tondo of St Ambrose; a cast of Stilicho's sarcophagus; St Ambrose's bed; fragments of the apse mosaics and four wooden panels from the 4th-century portal. The museum also has a *Triptych* by Bernardo Zenale (15th century) and *Christ among the Doctors* by Bergognone. In the garden opposite is St Sigismund's oratory, already famous by 1096, with 15th-century frescoes and Roman columns.

Plaque of the Università Cattolica del Sacro Cuore

Università Cattolica del Sacro Cuore

On the right-hand side of the church (entrance at No. 1 Largo Gemelli), in the former Benedictine monastery, is the university founded by padre Agostino Gemelli in 1921. Its two cloisters, with Ionic and Doric columns, were two of the four Bramante had designed in 1497. In the refectory is *The Marriage at Cana* by Callisto Piazza (1545).

Old motion picture camera, the Science and Technology Museum

❼ Museo Nazionale della Scienza e della Tecnologia Leonardo da Vinci

Via San Vittore 21. **Map** 6 F1.
Tel 02-48 55 51. Ⓜ 2 Sant'Ambrogio.
🚌 50, 58, 94. **Open** 9:30am–5pm
Tue–Fri; 9.30am–6:30pm Sat, Sun &
hols. ▨ ♿ 🅿 🚫 🎦 (book at
Ufficio Didattico). Library, lecture
rooms. 🆆 **museoscienza.org**

The Science and Technology
Museum is housed in the
former Olivetan monastery of
San Vittore (16th century) –
partly designed by Vincenzo
Seregni – which became a
military hospital and then
a barracks after monasteries
were suppressed in 1804. In
1947 it became the home of the
museum. In the two courtyards
surrounded by the old section
of the museum, you can see
part of the foundation of the
San Vittore fortress and that
of the octagonal mausoleum
of Emperor Valentinian II, both
ancient Roman.

The museum boasts one
of the world's leading science
and technology collections.
The vast exhibition space is
housed in different buildings.
The former monastery contains
the technological sections
on metallurgy, casting and
transport, as well as science
sections featuring physics,
optics, acoustics and astronomy.
Another section shows the
development of calculation,
from the first mechanical
calculating machine, invented

by Pascal in 1642, to IBM
computers. There is also a
section on time measurement,
with a reconstruction of a 1750
watchmaker's workshop. The
printing section shows the
1810 automatic inking method
by which 800 sheets an hour
could be printed, and also
has the father of the modern
typewriter (1855).

The cinema photography
section shows how the claw
device, used to make motion-
picture film move, grew out
of a sewing machine needle
conceived by Singer in 1851.
In the rooms given over to
telephones and television, there
is a reconstruction of the 1856
pantelegraph, the ancestor
of the fax machine.

The history of trains begins
with the first locomotive in Italy,
used for the Naples-Portici line
in 1839, and ends with 1970s
models. A pavilion in Via
Olona houses
the air and sea
transport
section,
featuring two
historic pieces:
the bridge
of the trans-
atlantic liner *Conte
Biancamano* and a
naval training ship.

The Leonardo da Vinci Gallery
has fascinating wooden models
of the machines and apparatus
invented by the genius, shown
together with his drawings.
Some, like the rotating crane
and the helical airscrew, which
demonstrate principles of
physics and applied mechanics,
can be operated by the public.

❽ San Vittore al Corpo

Via San Vittore 25. **Map** 6 F1. **Tel** 02-
48 00 53 51. Ⓜ 2 Sant'Ambrogio.
🚌 50, 58, 94. **Open** 7:30am–noon,
3:30–6pm daily. 🕆 8am, 6pm Mon–
Fri; 8:30am, 10:30am, noon, 6pm, 9pm
Sun; 10am & 6pm hols. 🚫 available
for groups (book in advance).

The original basilica on this site
was founded in the 4th century,
next to the mausoleum of
Emperor Valentinian II, who died
in 392. The church was rebuilt in
the 11th and 12th centuries by
Benedictine monks, and again
altered in 1560 by the Olivetans,
who replaced the monks.
The architect (either Alessi or
Seregni) reversed the orientation
and made it one of Milan's most
sumptuous churches, with
splendid late 16th-century
paintings. The Baroque Arese
Chapel (1668), designed by
Gerolamo Quadrio, and
the right-hand
apse, with
scenes from
the life of
St Gregory
by Camillo
Procaccini
(1602), are
of particular
interest. Moncalvo

Façade detail, San Vittore
al Corpo

frescoed the angel
musicians on the cupola in
1619. The wooden choir stalls,
with carvings of episodes from
St Benedict's life, date from
1583; above them are three
canvases on the same subject
by Giovanni Ambrogio Figino.
Last, the chapel of Sant'Antonio
Abate was entirely frescoed
in 1619 by Daniele Crespi.

The façade of San Vittore al Corpo

Along the Naviglio Grande

Now one of the liveliest quarters in Milan, the Navigli area formed the city's port district until the 19th century. Work on the Naviglio Grande canal first began in 1177, followed by the Pavia, Bereguardo, Martesana and Paderno canals. A system of locks allowed boats to travel along the canals on different levels (Candoglia marble was taken to the Duomo of Milan in the 14th century in this way).

Lodovico il Moro improved this network of canals with the help of Leonardo da Vinci in the 15th century. Barges arrived laden with coal and salt and departed with handmade goods and textiles. Some sections of the canals, which once extended for 150 km (93 miles), were filled in during the 1930s and navigation ceased altogether in 1979. Thanks to the Navigli canals, in 1953 Milan was ranked the 13th port in Italy despite being landlocked.

Typical houses
Along the Naviglio there are typical blocks of flats in "Milan yellow", built with running balconies around courtyards.

San Cristoforo al Naviglio
The church of the patron saint of boatmen is two buildings in one (12th and 14th century).

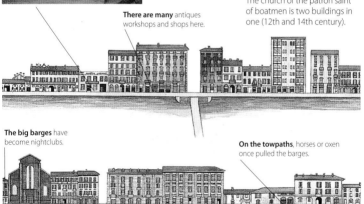

There are many antiques workshops and shops here.

The big barges have become nightclubs.

On the towpaths, horses or oxen once pulled the barges.

The church of Santa Maria delle Grazie al Naviglio faces the water.

Mercatone dell'Antiquariato
On the fourth Sunday of the month, from September to June, 400 antique dealers take part in this lively market on the Naviglio Grande.

Vicolo dei Lavandai
On the towpath you can still see the old washing troughs, sheltered by wooden roofs, where women washed clothes in the canal water.

A stucco of Sant'Ambrogio kept at the Museo Diocesano

The Relics of the Magi

Emperor Constantine donated the relics in around 315 and they were taken to Milan by Bishop Eustorgius. Legend has it that the sarcophagus was so heavy the cart had to stop at the city gates, where the original Sant'Eustorgio basilica was founded and the Apostle Barnabas baptised the first Milanese Christians. Barbarossa moved the relics to Cologne in 1164. Some were returned in 1903, an event still celebrated at Epiphany with a procession.

Tabernacle with the relics of the Magi

❾ Museo Diocesano

Corso di Porta Ticinese 95. **Map** 7 B3.
Tel 02-89 42 00 19. 🚋 3, 9. 🚌 94.
Open 10am–6pm Tue–Sun. 🚫
📅 Jul–Sep: 7pm–midnight Tue–Sat (to book, call 02-89 42 00 19). ♿
🌐 museodiocesano.it

The mission of the Museo Diocesano is to recover and highlight the artistic heritage of the Milan diocese, which extends as far north as the towns of Varese and Lecco.

This museum of religious art is housed in the cloisters of Sant'Eustorgio, next to the basilica. It features about 320 works of art dating from the 6th to the 19th centuries, from paintings from the private collections of past Milanese archbishops to items rescued from tiny village churches. Two of the highlights are the frescoes of the Stations of the Cross by late 19th-century artist Gaetano Previati and the section devoted to Milan's patron saint, Sant'Ambrogio.

❿ Sant'Eustorgio

Piazza Sant'Eustorgio 1. **Map** 7 B3.
Tel 02-58 10 15 83. 🚋 3, 9, 15, 29, 30. 🚌 94. **Open** 7:30am–noon, 3:30–6:30pm. ✝ 7:45am & 5pm pre-hols; 9:30am, 11am, 12:30pm (in Portinari Chapel), 5pm hols.
Portinari Chapel: **Tel** 02-89 40 26 71.
Open 10am–6pm daily.

In the 11th century work began on building a basilica over one founded by St Eustorgius in the 4th century, to house the relics of the Magi. The main body of the present-day church was built in the 1300s. On the right-hand side of the façade, which was rebuilt in 1865, there are several chapels dating from the 13th–15th centuries. The Brivio chapel houses Tommaso Cazzaniga's tomb of Giovanni Stefano

Sculpture on the façade of Sant'Eustorgio

Brivio (1486). The middle bas-relief depicts the *Adoration of the Magi*, and the altarpiece is a triptych by Bergognone. In the Baroque Crotta-Caimi chapel is a fine sarcophagus by 15th-century sculptor Protaso Caimi, and a *St Ambrose on Horseback*. The Visconti chapel has beautiful 14th-century frescoes: on the vault are the Evangelists; below left, a *St George and the Dragon*; and right, the *Triumph of St Thomas*. The Torriani chapel is frescoed with symbols of the Evangelists.

In the south transept is the large late-Roman sarcophagus that once housed the relics of the Magi, and on the altar is a Campionese-school marble triptych of the journey of the Magi (1347). The Magi are also the subject of the fresco on the left, attributed to Luini. The high altar houses the remains of St Eustorgius and bears a marble altar-front depicting an unfinished Passion of Christ.

Behind the altar, a passage-way leads to the Portinari chapel, commissioned by banker Pigello Portinari as his tomb, and to house the body of St Peter Martyr. The first example of a 15th-century central-plan church in Milan, it exemplifies the clarity of Bramante's vision and features typical Lombard decoration attributed to Vincenzo Foppa. Under the dome is the tomb of St Peter Martyr (1339) by Giovanni di Balduccio, held

The Neo-Romanesque façade of Sant'Eustorgio, built in 1865

up by the eight Virtues and showing scenes of his ministry. The small chapel on the left has an urn containing the saint's skull.

⓫ Santa Maria dei Miracoli presso San Celso

Corso Italia 37. **Map** 7 C3. **Tel** 02-58 31 31 87. 🚊 15. 🚌 94. **Open** 7am–noon, 4–6:30pm daily. 🕙 7:30am, 9am, 6pm daily (except Jul & Aug); 6pm pre-hols; 9 & 11am, noon (except Jul & Aug), 7pm hols. San Celso: ask sacristan.

In 1493 construction began on a sanctuary dedicated to Santa Maria dei Miracoli. It was first designed by Gian Giacomo Dolcebuono and subsequently by Vincenzo Seregni and Alessi. The late 16th-century façade is enlivened by sculptures by Stoldo Lorenzi and Annibale Fontana – more of their work can be seen on the pillars inside. The late Renaissance interior, constructed and redesigned throughout the 16th century, features a pavement by Martino Bassi and was frescoed by Cerano and Procaccini. Under the cupola with terracotta Evangelists by De Fondutis and paintings by Appiani (1795) is the high altar (16th century) in semi-precious stones. The wooden choir is from 1570. On the Altar of the Madonna is Fontana's *Our Lady of the Assumption*. Below, a 4th-century fresco lies under two embossed silver doors.

There are major works of art in the various chapels: a painting (1606) by Procaccini; the *Holy Family with St Jerome* altarpiece (1548) by Paris Bordone; Antonio Campi's *Resurrection* (1560); *Baptism of Jesus* by Gaudenzio Ferrari; Moretto da Brescia's *Conversion of St Paul* (1539–40); *Martyrdom of St Catherine* by Cerano (1603); and an altarpiece by Bergognone.

By the right-hand transept is the entrance to **San Celso**, a Romanesque church built in the 11th century over the remains of a 4th century church. It was originally

The cupola of Sant'Alessandro, seen from Corso di Porta Romana

founded to mark the spot where St Ambrose discovered the remains of the martyrs Celso and Nazaro. The church is decorated with 11th–15th-century frescoes and columns with carved capitals.

⓬ Sant'Alessandro

Piazza Sant'Alessandro. **Map** 7 C2. **Tel** 02-86 45 30 65. Ⓜ 3 Missori. 🚊 2, 3, 12, 15, 24, 27. **Open** 7:30am–noon, 4–7pm daily. 🕙 11:30am, 6pm Mon–Sat; 6:30pm pre-hols; 7:30am (winter), 10:30am, noon, 6:30pm Sun.

Lorenzo Binago built this church in 1601 for the Barnabiti family. The interior has lavish Baroque furnishings and decoration; the frescoes were painted by Moncalvo and Daniele Crespi. In the presbytery is the *Life of St Alexander* by Filippo Abbiati and Federico Bianchi. The high altar (1741) is decorated with semi-precious stones.

Next to the church are the Scuole Arcimbolde, schools for the poor founded in 1609 by the Barnabiti family. Opposite is Palazzo Trivulzio, rebuilt by Ruggeri in 1713, with the family coat of arms on the middle window. This family founded the Biblioteca Trivulziana, the library now in the Castello Sforzesco. Nearby Via Palla leads to the Tempio Civico di San Sebastiano, begun by Pellegrino Tibaldi in 1577 and completed in the 1700s. Its interior has works by Legnanino, Montalto and Federico Bianchi.

⓭ Armani/Silos

Via Bergognone 40. **Map** 6 E4. **Tel** 02-91 63 00 10. Ⓜ 2 Porta Genova. 🚊 2, 9, 14, 19. 🚌 68, 90, 91. **Open** 11am–7pm Wed–Sun (to 9pm Thu & Sat). ♿ 🌐 armanisilos.com

This large and stark former industrial building – built in 1950 for the preservation of cereals – opened to the public in 2015. Here, visitors can enjoy a selection of garments created between the 1980s and the present day by the fashion designer Giorgio Armani. The collection, showcased over four floors, explores and illustrates the aesthetics of the famous stylist and is divided not chronologically but into the themes that have inspired his creative work, including the lure of the exotic and colour. This permanent collection confirms the role of Milan as one of the world's premier fashion capitals.

Iconic fashions on display at Armani/Silos

SOUTHEAST MILAN

The area between Corso Monforte and Corso di Porta Romana was a typical suburb up to the early 19th century, characterized by aristocratic residences, monasteries and more modest houses typical of the artisans' and commercial districts of Milan. Development of the area began in the 17th century with the construction of Palazzo Durini, one of the most important civic buildings of its time. At the end of the 18th century Corso di Porta Romana and the adjacent streets were changed in keeping with the vast street network renewal plans

encouraged by Maria Theresa of Austria. When the empress ordered the suppression of many monasteries, the land where they had stood was purchased by rich nobles. Other areas became available when the Spanish ramparts were demolished. The old atmosphere of Southeast Milan survives above all around the Ca' Granda (now the University), which for almost 500 years was the city hospital, and in the first stretch of Corso di Porta Romana. However, the only vestige of the Verziere, the old vegetable market in Largo Augusto, is the place name.

Sights at a Glance

Streets, Squares and Historic Buildings

1. Corso di Porta Romana
2. Torre Velasca
4. Ca' Granda
7. Largo Augusto and Via Durini
9. Palazzo di Giustizia
11. Rotonda di Via Besana
12. Conservatorio di Musica Giuseppe Verdi
14. Palazzo Isimbardi

Churches and Abbeys

3. San Nazaro Maggiore
6. Santo Stefano Maggiore and San Bernardino alle Ossa
10. San Pietro in Gessate
13. Santa Maria della Passione
16. Abbazia di Chiaravalle see pp104–105

Parks and Gardens

5. Giardino della Guastalla

Libraries

8. Palazzo Sormani Andreani

Museums

15. Fondazione Prada

Restaurants pp172–3

1. I Chiostri Di San Barnaba
2. Da Giacomo
3. Dongio
4. Globe Restaurant Lounge Bar
5. Mauro
6. Raw Fish Café Centro Ittico
7. La Rena Ristorante
8. That's Vapore
9. Trattoria del Pescatore

See also Street Finder maps 4, 7 & 8

0 metres   400
0 yards   400

◀ The cloister at the Abbazia di Chiaravalle   **For keys to symbols** *see back flap*

Street-by-Street: San Nazaro to Largo Augusto

There are many interesting old buildings in this area, which includes the university quarter, with cafés and specialist bookshops, as well as crafts shops on Via Festa del Perdono. Architectural styles range from the 4th-century San Nazaro, founded by St Ambrose, to the Ca' Granda, the old hospital, a marvellous sight when viewed from Largo Richini because of its sheer size and the beauty of its 15th-century arcade. More changes of style come with the palazzi in Corso di Porta Romana and Via Sant'Antonio, and the modern Torre Velasca. The quarter's hospital tradition can be seen in the votive columns at the crossroads, where mass for the sick was celebrated, and the San Bernardino alle Ossa chapel, decorated with the bones of those who died in the hospital.

Sant'Antonio Aba was rebuilt in 1582. It houses paintings by Bernardino Campi, Moncalvo and Ludovico Carracci and is a sort of gallery of early 17th-century painting in Milan.

❷ Torre Velasca
The symbol of modern Milan was built in 1956–8. The tower, 106 m (348 ft) high, houses both offices and flats and is often compared to medieval towers because of the shape of the upper section.

Duomo

❶ Corso di Porta Romana
Palazzi with magnificent gardens line this avenue. It follows the route of the ancient Roman road which led from Porta Romana all the way to Rome.

❸ ★ San Nazaro Maggiore
One of four basilicas founded by Sant'Ambrogio, this church still has some of the original 4th-century masonry. It is preceded by the Trivulzio Chapel, the only Milanese architectural work by Bramantino (1512–50). The view of the back of the church is very striking.

Key

 Suggested route

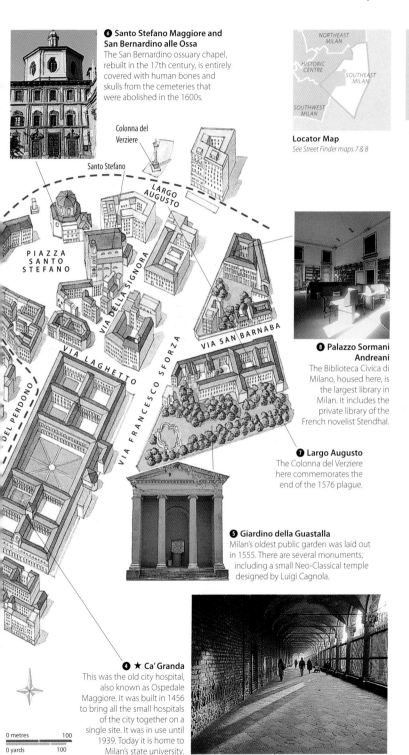

❻ Santo Stefano Maggiore and San Bernardino alle Ossa
The San Bernardino ossuary chapel, rebuilt in the 17th century, is entirely covered with human bones and skulls from the cemeteries that were abolished in the 1600s.

Colonna del Verziere

Santo Stefano

LARGO AUGUSTO

Locator Map
See Street Finder maps 7 & 8

NORTHEAST MILAN

HISTORIC CENTRE

SOUTHEAST MILAN

SOUTHWEST MILAN

PIAZZA SANTO STEFANO

VIA DELLA SIGNORA

VIA SAN BARNABA

VIA FRANCESCO SFORZA

VIA LAGHETTO

DEL PERDONO

❽ Palazzo Sormani Andreani
The Biblioteca Civica di Milano, housed here, is the largest library in Milan. It includes the private library of the French novelist Stendhal.

❼ Largo Augusto
The Colonna del Verziere here commemorates the end of the 1576 plague.

❺ Giardino della Guastalla
Milan's oldest public garden was laid out in 1555. There are several monuments, including a small Neo-Classical temple designed by Luigi Cagnola.

❹ ★ Ca' Granda
This was the old city hospital, also known as Ospedale Maggiore. It was built in 1456 to bring all the small hospitals of the city together on a single site. It was in use until 1939. Today it is home to Milan's state university.

0 metres 100
0 yards 100

Entrance to the Teatro Carcano, in Corso di Porta Romana

❶ Corso di Porta Romana

Map 7 C2. **Ⓜ** 3 Missori, Crocetta. 🚋 12, 15, 16, 24, 27. 🚌 77, 94.

This avenue was laid out over a porticoed stretch of the ancient Roman road outside the city walls (2nd–3rd century AD) that led to Rome. It ran from Porta Romana – then just beyond present-day Piazza Missori – to a triumphal arch (near the widening in the road known as Crocetta), transformed by Barbarossa into a fortified gate in the walls in 1162. The new gate (1171), further back, was demolished in 1793.

The Corso is lined with many noble palazzi. The 17th-century Palazzo Acerbi at No. 3; Palazzo Annoni at No. 6, designed by Francesco Maria Richini (1631), famous for its art collection which includes works by Rubens and Van Dyck; Palazzo Mellerio at No. 13 and Casa Bettoni (1865) at No. 20, with statues of Bersaglieri flanking the door. Via Santa Sofia crosses the Corso, and goes over the Naviglio canal close to the Crocetta, whose name derives from a votive cross set there during the 1576 plague.

Opposite is the Teatro Carcano (1803), where the great Italian actress Eleonora Duse performed. The Corso ends at the Porta Romana (in Piazzale Medaglie d'Oro), built in 1598. To the right you can see a fragment of the Spanish walls built by Ferrante Gonzaga (1545); they ran for 11 km (7 miles) and were demolished in 1889.

❷ Torre Velasca

Piazza Velasca 5. **Map** 7 C2. **Ⓜ** 3 Missori. 🚋 12, 15, 16, 24, 27. 🚌 94.

This tower, built in the late 1950s by architects Belgioioso, Nathan Rogers and Peressutti, is one of the best-known monuments in modern-day Milan. The over-hang of the upper part of the building and its red colour are reminiscent of Italian medieval towers, but the shape actually grew out of the need to create more office space in a limited area.

Cappella Trivulzio, in San Nazaro Maggiore (16th century)

❸ San Nazaro Maggiore

Piazza San Nazaro. **Map** 8 D2. **Tel** 02-58 30 77 19. **Ⓜ** 3 Missori, Crocetta. 🚋 16, 24. 🚌 77, 94. **Open** 8:45am–noon, 3:30–5:30pm. 🕂 8am, 6pm pre-hols (except Jul & Aug); 10, 11:30am, 6pm hols. 📷 ♿

The original basilica was built by Sant'Ambrogio in AD 382–6 to house the remains of the Apostles Andrew, John and Thomas, which is why it was known as the *Basilica Apostolorum*. It was dedicated to San Nazaro when his remains – found by Sant'Ambrogio near the basilica – were buried here in 396. The church was built outside the walls in an Early Christian burial ground – as can be seen by the sarcophagi outside and the epitaph in the right-hand transept – and looked onto an ancient Roman porticoed street. It was rebuilt after a fire in 1075 reusing much original material.

The church is preceded by the octagonal Trivulzio Chapel, begun in Renaissance style in 1512 by Bramantino and continued by Cristoforo Lombardo. It houses the tomb of Gian Giacomo Trivulzio and his family.

The nave of the church has a cross vault. Either side of the entrance you will see the remains of the Romanesque doorway covered by the Trivulzio Chapel. On the walls, among fresco fragments, are parts of the original masonry. In the crossing, the dome is supported by the 4th-century piers; two altars in the choir contain the remains of the Apostles and San Nazaro. Left of the altar is the small cruciform chapel of San Lino, with traces of 10th–15th-century frescoes. In the transepts are a fine *Last Supper* by Bernardino Lanino (right) and *Passion of Jesus* by Luini (left). The Chapel of St Catherine (1540) has Lanino's *Martyrdom of St Catherine* and a 16th-century stained-glass window depicting the *Life of St Catherine*.

The remains of San Nazaro, found by Sant'Ambrogio in AD 396

❹ Ca' Granda

The "Casa Grande", or Ospedale Maggiore, was built for Francesco Sforza from 1456 on with the aim of uniting the city's 30 hospitals. The "large house" was designed by Filarete, who built only part of it, and was finished in stages in the 17th and 18th centuries. In 1939 the hospital moved to a new site, and since 1952 the Ca' Granda has housed the liberal arts faculties of the Università Statale, Milan's university. The hospital was modern for its time: there were separate wings for men and women – each with a central infirmary – and a large courtyard between them.

VISITORS' CHECKLIST

Practical Information
Via Festa del Perdono 5.
Map 8 D2. **Tel** 02-55 031.
Open 7:30am–7:30pm Mon–Fri;
8am–noon Sat (first 3 weeks of
Aug: 7:30am–3:30pm Mon–Fri).
Closed Sun & hols (open in
morning pre-hols). ♿ ✉
Chiesa dell'Annunciata: **Tel** 02-58
30 77 19. **Open** 8am–7pm (when
University is open).

Transport
Ⓜ 3 Missori. 🚊 12, 15, 16, 24,
27. 🚌 54, 77, 94.

The church of the Annunciata (17th-century) contains a 1639 canvas by Guercino.

The Neo-Classical Macchio Wing, seat of the Faculty of Letters, Philosophy and Jurisprudence, housed the benefactors' art gallery, with portraits by leading artists.

★ Fifteenth-century Façade
The brick façade has round arches and is richly decorated. There were workshops and warehouses at ground level.

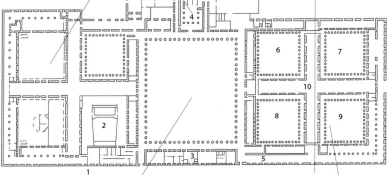

★ Cortile Maggiore
Francesco Maria Richini designed the courtyard with a Renaissance arcade and Baroque loggia, adding busts in yellow-pink-grey stone.

★ Fifteenth-century Courtyards
These housed the women's bathrooms, the ice-house and the woodshed. The Spezieria is the oldest courtyard.

Key

- ▨ 15th-century section
- ▨ 17th-century section
- ▨ 18th–19th-century section
- **1** Entrance to the Faculties of Liberal Arts, Philosophy and Jurisprudence
- **2** Aula Magna
- **3** Courtyard entrance
- **4** Chiesa dell'Annunciata
- **5** Porticoes, 15th-century wing
- **6–9** Courtyards, 15th-century wing
- **10** Crociera, formerly the infirmary

The fish pond in the Giardino della Guastalla, near Via Sforza

❺ Giardino della Guastalla

Via Francesco Sforza, Via S Barnaba, Via Guastalla. **Map** 8 D2. 🚊 12, 23, 27. 🚌 60, 73, 77, 84, 94. **Open** daily. Mar: 7am–8pm; Apr & Oct: 7am–9pm; May–Sep: 7am–10pm; Nov–Feb: 7am–7pm.

This garden – Milan's oldest – was laid out in 1555 by Countess Ludovica Torelli della Guastalla, next to the college of the same name for the daughters of impoverished aristocrats. In the early 1600s it was transformed into an Italian-style garden, and a goldfish pond on two communicating terraces was added. There is also a 17th-century shrine representing Mary Magdalen attended by angels and a Neo-Classical temple by Luigi Cagnola. In 1939 the garden was separated from the adjacent Sormani park and opened to the public. At the Via Guastalla exit (No. 19) you can visit the Synagogue, designed by Luca Beltrami (1890–92) and, at the corner of Via San Barnaba, the church of Santi Barnaba e Paolo, which is part of the nearby Chierici Regolari di San Paolo college. It is a prototype of 16th-century Lombard churches, founded in 1558 and then modified by Galeazzo Alessi. Inside are paintings by Aurelio Luini, son of Bernardino, Camillo Procaccini and Moncalvo.

❻ Santo Stefano Maggiore and San Bernardino alle Ossa

Piazza Santo Stefano. **Map** 8 D1. Ⓜ 1, 3 Duomo. 🚊 12, 23, 27. 🚌 54, 60, 73, 77. Archivio Storico Diocesano: Via San Calimero 13. **Map** 8 D2. **Tel** 02-58 49 98 01. **Open** 9:15am–12:15pm Mon–Fri. **Closed** Aug. San Bernardino alle Ossa: **Open** 8am–noon, 1:30–6pm Mon–Fri; 9:30am–12:30pm Sat & Sun. ✝ 8:30am Mon–Sat (in Italian Fri), 11am Sun (Korean). ✉ ♿

Santo Stefano dates back to the 5th century. It was rebuilt in 1075 after being destroyed by a fire and was rebuilt in its present form in 1584 by Giuseppe Meda. The Baroque bell tower was built in 1643–74 by Carlo Buzzi: the pilaster at the base is all that remains of the quadriporticus that once faced the medieval basilica. The church was used as the Diocesan Archive, which has now moved. Next door are San Bernardino alle Ossa, originally medieval but since rebuilt many times, and the ossuary chapel (with a concave façade) built in 1210 and altered in 1695. The latter is small and covered with human bones and skulls. The dim light and dark walls contrast with the bright colours of the fresco on the vault by Sebastiano Ricci (1695): *The Triumph of Souls among Angels.*

Statue on the façade of San Bernardino alle Ossa

❼ Largo Augusto and Via Durini

Map 8 D1, E1. Ⓜ 1, 3 Duomo. 🚊 12, 15, 23, 27. 🚌 54, 60, 61, 73, 77, 84, 94.

The Verziere Column, commissioned by Carlo Borromeo to celebrate the end of the 1576 plague, has stood in Largo Augusto since 1580. It is one of the few votive columns to survive the late 18th century. Many were lost after the suppression of the monastic orders that owned them, or sacrificed to make room for new buildings. This square marks the beginning of Via Durini, which is dominated by the concave façade of Santa Maria della Sanità (1708). No. 20 is Casa Toscanini, the great conductor's house, and No. 24 is Palazzo Durini, built in 1648 by Francesco Maria Richini and now the headquarters for Inter Milan. On nearby Corso Europa is 16th-century Palazzo Litta Modignani, where a Roman mosaic was found.

❽ Palazzo Sormani Andreani

Corso di Porta Vittoria 6. **Map** 8 E1. **Tel** 02-88 46 33 97. 🚊 12, 23, 27. 🚌 54, 60, 73, 77, 84, 94. **Open** 9am–7:30pm Mon–Sat. **Closed** public hols, Aug.

The palazzo, constructed in the 18th century, was enlarged in 1736 by Francesco Croce, who made it into one of the most lavish residences

Façade of Palazzo Sormani, the Municipal Library since 1956

of the time. Croce also designed the characteristic late Baroque curved façade. Reconstructed after World War II, the palazzo became the home of the Municipal (or Sormani Andreani) Library, the largest in Milan. It has over 580,000 works, including Stendhal's private library, a newspaper library with about 19,500 Italian and foreign publications, and a record and CD collection. A catalogue of all the Milan libraries is also here, as is the regional periodicals catalogue.

The Neo-Classical back opens onto a garden, part of the larger original one, which is used for small exhibitions. Nearby, at No. 2 Via Visconti di Modrone, is one of Milan's excellent traditional *pasticcerie*, the Taveggia pastry shop *(see p185)*.

⑨ Palazzo di Giustizia

Corso di Porta Vittoria. **Map** 8 E1.
🚊 12, 23, 27. 🚌 60, 73, 77, 84.

The centre of attention in the early 1990s because of the Mani Pulite (clean hands) corruption inquests and trials that changed much of the face of Italian politics, the Milan Law Courts were designed in typical Fascist style (1932–40) by Marcello Piacentini. The building also houses the Notarial Acts Archive, formerly in the Palazzo della Ragione *(see p56)*. The Palazzo has 1,200 rooms and 65 law courts with works by contemporary artists, including Mario Sironi's fresco in the Assize Court.

The Palazzo di Giustizia (1932–40), a typical example of Fascist architecture

Detail from the fresco *The Legend of the Virgin*, San Pietro in Gessate

⑩ San Pietro in Gessate

Piazza San Pietro in Gessate. **Map** 8 E1.
Tel 02-54 10 74 24. 🚊 12, 23, 27.
🚌 60, 73, 77, 84. **Open** Jul–mid-Sep: 8am–noon Mon–Fri, 8:30am–noon, 5–8pm Sat & Sun; mid-Sep–Jun: 7:30am–6pm Mon–Fri, 7:30am–noon, 2:30–6pm Sat & Sun. ✝ 1:15pm Mon & Fri, 8am Tue & Thu, 8:30am Wed, 7pm Sat, 9am, noon, 7pm Sun.

This church was built in 1447–75 by the Solari school and financed by the banker Pigello Portinari, whose emblem is on the outer wall of the apse. In the middle of the façade, rebuilt in 1912, is a portal with an effigy of St Peter, which was added in the 1600s. The Gothic interior has a three-aisle nave with ribbed vaulting and pointed arches and has preserved some original painting. The

church was damaged during World War II, in particular the right-hand chapels, where there are traces of frescoes by Antonio Campi, Moncalvo and Bergognone (whose *Funeral of St Martin* is in the fifth chapel). The third and fifth chapels on the left have fine frescoes by Montorfano: *Life of St John the Baptist* (1484) and *The Legend of St Anthony Abbot*. The eight choir stalls were rebuilt with the remains of the 1640 ones by Carlo Garavaglia, damaged in 1943 and partly used as firewood during the war. The left-hand transept has frescoes of the *Life of Sant'Ambrogio* (1490) commissioned by the Sforza senator Ambrogio Grifi from Bernardino Butinone and Bernardino Zenale. In the lunettes under the vault, next to *Sant'Ambrogio on Horseback*, you can see the figure of a hanged man whose rope "drops" into the scene below, down to the hangman. These frescoes were discovered in 1862.

View of the arcade in the Rotonda di Via Besana

⓫ Rotonda di Via Besana

Via San Barnaba, corner of Via Besana. **Map** 8 F2. **Tel** 02-43 98 04 02. 🚊 9. 🚌 77, 84. **Open** for exhibitions and summer cultural events only. Museo dei Bambini: **Open** 9:30am–6pm Tue–Fri, 10am–7pm Sat, Sun & hols. 🅿 🆆 muba.it

The Rotonda was the cemetery of the nearby Ca' Granda Hospital, designed in 1695 by Francesco Raffagno on present-day Viale Regina Margherita. When it was closed in 1783, viceroy Eugène de Beauharnais tried to change it into the Pantheon of the Regno Italico (1809), but the project fell through and the round brick building first housed patients with infectious diseases and then, up to 1940, was the hospital laundry. It is now used for temporary exhibitions and as an outdoor cinema in summer.

The Rotonda is also home to the Museo dei Bambini, an eductional museum for kids that holds specially concep-tualised laboratory activities and several interactive exhibits.

In the middle is the decon-secrated San Michele ai Nuovi Sepolcri, built in 1713. It has a Greek cross plan with a central altar, visible from all sides. The small skulls sculpted on the capitals are a reminder of the original function of this complex.

On Via San Barnaba is Santa Maria della Pace, designed by Pietro Antonio Solari in 1466, the property of the Order of Knights of the Holy Sepulchre. In 1805 the church was suppressed and the paintings removed (some are now in the Brera), but some 17th-century frescoes by Tanzio da Varallo remain.

The nearby monastery is the home of the Società Umanitaria, founded in 1893 to educate and aid the poor. It has a library devoted to labour problems. The only remaining part of the monastery is the refectory, with a *Crucifixion* by Marco d'Oggiono. Returning to Corso di Porta Vittoria, you come to Piazza Cinque Giornate, with a monument by Giuseppe Grandi (1895) commemorating the anti-Austrian insurrection of 1848 *(see p26)*. The female figures symbolize the Five Days, whose dead are buried in the crypt below.

⓬ Conservatorio di Musica Giuseppe Verdi

Via Conservatorio 12. **Map** 8 E1. **Tel** 02-762 11 01. 🚊 12, 23, 27. 🚌 54, 61, 77. **Open** for concerts only. Library: **Tel** 02-762 110 219. **Open** 8am–8pm Mon–Fri, 8am–2pm Sat.

Milan's Conservatory was founded by viceroy Eugène de Beauharnais in 1808. Important musicians and composers have studied here – though, despite the institution's name, the young Verdi was refused admission. There is a chamber music hall and a large auditorium for symphonic music. The library boasts over 35,000 books and 460,000 pieces of written music and scores, including works by Mozart, Rossini, Donizetti, Bellini and Verdi. A small museum showcases precious stringed instruments.

⓭ Santa Maria della Passione

Via Conservatorio 14. **Map** 8 E-F1. **Tel** 02-76 02 13 70. 🚊 12, 23, 27. 🚌 54, 61, 77, 94. **Open** 7:45am–noon, 3:30–6:15pm Mon–Fri; 9am–12:30pm, 3:30–6:30pm Sat & Sun. 🕇 8:15am, 5:30pm Mon–Fri; 5:30pm pre-hols; 10am, 11:15am, 5:30pm hols.

The second largest church in Milan, after the Duomo, was built under the patronage of the prelate Daniele Birago, who had donated the land to the Lateran Canons. Work began in 1486 to a design by Giovanni Battagio. Originally the church had a Greek cross plan but it was lengthened with a nave and six semi-circular chapels on each side in 1573 by Martino Bassi. The façade of the church – and the nearby convent, now the home of the Conservatory – was added in 1692 by Giuseppe Rusnati, who kept it low so that visitors could appreciate the majestic octagonal covering of the dome designed by Cristoforo Lombardo (1530). To enhance this view and link the church with the Naviglio, Abbot Gadio had the Via della Passione laid out in front of the entrance in 1540. The interior, with a frescoed barrel vault, is very atmospheric. Fourteen early 17th-century portraits of the saints of the Lateran Order, attributed to Daniele Crespi and his school, are on the piers. In the right-hand chapels, two works worth seeing are *Christ at the Pillar*

The Giuseppe Verdi Conservatory, housed in a former monastery

The octagonal dome of Santa Maria della Passione (17th century)

by Giulio Cesare Procaccini, on the altar of the third chapel, and the *Madonna di Caravaggio*, a fresco attributed to Bramantino, in the sixth chapel. The presbytery still has its original Greek cross structure. The paintings hanging from the piers, mostly the work of Crespi, narrate the Passion and include *Christ Nailed to the Cross*. Behind the Baroque high altar is a wooden choir (16th-century) with mother-of-pearl inlay. The church became a place of intense musical activity in the 16th and 17th centuries, when two organs were built opposite each other, on either side of the choir. The instrument on the right was created by the famous Antegnati, and the one on the left by Cristoforo Valvassori, who was involved in building the organ in the Duomo. The doors of the latter instrument have scenes from the Passion painted by Crespi. Frequent classical music concerts for organs pieces composed for four hands are still held here.

There are remarkable Cinquecento paintings in the transepts: the artwork on the right-hand side has a *Deposition* altarpiece by Bernardino Ferrari (after 1514) with the *Legend of the Cross* in the predella; and on the altar to the left is Gaudenzio Ferrari's *Last Supper* (1543), with a *Crucifixion* by Giulio Campi (1560) alongside.

The chapels on the left-hand side of the nave contain fine works by Camillo Procaccini, Vermiglio and Duchino. The first chapel is noteworthy because of the impressive realism of Crespi's *St Charles Fasting*, and the vault fres-coed by Giulio Campi (1558) is also impressive. The 15th-century Chapter House was designed and painted by Bergognone: saints and doctors are in a false peristyle.

On the right-hand wall is *Christ with the Apostles*. In Via Bellini you can see the left side of the church and the dome. At No. 11 is the Art Nouveau Casa Campanini (1904), with wrought iron work by Alessandro Mazzucotelli.

⓮ Palazzo Isimbardi

Corso Monforte 35. **Map** 4 E5. **Tel** 02-774 01 (Lombardy Province PR Office). Ⓜ 1 San Babila. 🚋 9, 23. 🚌 54, 61, 94. **Open** apply to IAT *(see p207)*.

The seat of the Milan provincial government since 1935, this palazzo dates from the 15th century but was enlarged by the noble families who lived in it, among whom were the Isimbardi, who purchased it in 1775. The 18th-century façade on Corso Monforte leads to the porticoed court of honour (16th century), which still has its original herringbone pattern paving. The garden behind this boasts an admirable Neo-Classical façade designed by Giacomo Tazzini (1826).

The 18th-century façade of Palazzo Isimbardi, in Corso Monforte

The palazzo is open to the public and features many interestingly decorated rooms and fine works of art, such as the wooden 17th-century globe by Giovanni Jacopo de Rossi. The most important room is the Giunta (Council Chamber), which in 1954 became the home of Tiepolo's masterful *Triumph of Doge Morosini*, which came from Palazzo Morosini in Venice. The Sala dell'Antegiunta has a lovely 18th-century Murano glass chandelier, while the Sala degli Affreschi boasts 17th-century frescoes taken from the villa of Cardinal Monti at Vaprio d'Adda. The Studio del Presidente is decorated with a Neo-Classical ceiling, partly in fine gold. In 1940 the Province of Milan enlarged the palazzo. The new façade on Via Vivaio was decorated with bas-reliefs sculpted by Salvatore Saponaro depicting the activities of the Milanese. At No. 31 Corso Monforte is the Palazzo della Prefettura, rebuilt in its present state in 1782. It has frescoes by Andrea Appiani. It is not open to the public.

⓯ Fondazione Prada

Largo Isarco 2. **Map** 8 E5. **Tel** 02-56 66 26 11. Ⓜ 3 Lodi TIBB. 🚌 65. **Open** 10am–7pm Mon, Wed & Thu; 10am–9pm Fri–Sun. **Closed** 1 Jan, 25 Dec. ♿ ▣ Ⓦ **fondazioneprada.org**

The brainchild of fashion designer Miuccia Prada and her husband Patrizio Bertelli, the Fondazione Prada is an institution dedicated to contemporary art, cinema and culture. As well as organizing exhibitions by international artists, the Fondazione promotes activities such as film festivals, multidisciplinary and philo-sophical conferences, and events related to architecture and design.

The venue itself, an early 20th-century distillery attract-ively redesigned by the Dutch architect Rem Koolhaas, is worth the visit alone.

⑯ Abbazia di Chiaravalle

French Cistercian monks began constructing this church in 1150–60 and it was dedicated to the Virgin Mary in 1221. The complex is a combination of French Gothic and Lombard Romanesque, resulting in a delightful example of Cistercian architecture. The bell tower was added in 1349. The entrance is in the 16th-century tower flanked by two small churches. In 1798 Napoleon suppressed the monastic order, the monks were forced to leave and the abbey deteriorated so much that in 1861 Bramante's 15th-century cloister was demolished to make room for a railway line. Restored and given back to the monks, the abbey has regained its former splendour and is again an oasis of peace.

★ Frescoes
The 14th-century frescoes on the dome narrate *The Legend of the Virgin*. Those in the transept (above), represent among other things the genealogical tree of the Benedictine monks.

★ Wooden Choir
The 44 stalls have carvings of the *Life of St Bernard* by Carlo Garavaglia (1645), who according to legend took refuge in the abbey to expiate the murder of his brother.

Entrance

The Monks' Land Reclamation

The Cistercian monasteries were based on the rule of *ora et labora* – prayer and labour – and played a crucial role in reclaiming the marshy Milanese terrain, which thanks to the monks became extremely fertile. They used the new water meadow technique, which consisted in flooding the meadows with water from an adjoining stream (kept at a constant temperature of 12° C/54° F) so that the grass would grow quickly and could be harvested even in winter.

A Cistercian monk at work in the garden

★ Bell Tower
(ciribiciaccola) Eighty small marble columns adorn the bell tower designed by Francesco Pecorari in 1329–40. Called *ciribiciaccola* (clever contraption) by the Milanese, its bells accompanied the farmers' and monks' working day. The tower bell rope still hangs in the church.

VISITORS' CHECKLIST

Practical Information
Via Sant'Arialdo 102, Chiaravalle Milanese. **Tel** 02-57 40 34 04.
Open 9am–noon, 2:30–5:30pm Tue–Sat; 2:30–5pm Sun.
🕭 8, 9:15 (Gregorian chant) & 11am, 5:30pm hols; 8am, 5:30pm Mon–Sat. 🚹 📷 (no flash).
🔲 📷 4pm Sun.

Transport
Ⓜ 3 Corvetto, then bus 77.
🚌 77.

Madonna della Buonanotte
Painted in 1512 by Bernardino Luini at the top of the steps leading to the dormitory, this picture is known as the *Madonna della Buonanotte* because she "said goodnight" to the monks going to bed.

KEY

① **The top of the façade**, made of brick, is what remains of the original. The porch was added in 1625. The 16th-century main portal has figures of Cistercian saints, including St Bernard with the church in his hand.

② **The interior** had no paintings because this would have distracted the monks from their prayers. The 17th-century frescoes tell the story of the order.

③ **The many windows** (double, triple and quadruple lancet) lend movement to the tower structure.

④ **The chapter house**, designed in the late 15th century by Bramante, has three graffiti from that period depicting Santa Maria delle Grazie, the Duomo and Castello Sforzesco.

⑤ **Refectory**

★ Cloister
Rebuilt in 1952 by using the one surviving side as a model, the cloister has a plaque commemorating the founding of the church, next to which is a stork, the symbol of Chiaravalle.

NORTHEAST MILAN

Elegant Via Manzoni is the heart of a vast area stretching from the Brera quarter to Via Montenapoleone and Corso Venezia. Brera is known for its characteristic winding streets, some of which still have their 18th-century paving. The fashion district around Via Montenapoleone is the domain of the designer shops. Starting from Piazza San Babila and continuing through Corso Venezia,

with its many aristocratic palazzi, you will come to the Giardini Pubblici and the Villa Reale, home of the Modern Art Gallery. The area extending beyond the ramparts, which was undeveloped up to the early 19th century, includes the Cimitero Monumentale, the Stazione Centrale (main railway station) and the Pirelli building, Milan's tallest.

Sights at a Glance

Churches
6 San Marco
10 Santa Maria del Carmine
11 San Simpliciano
12 Sant'Angelo
13 Santa Maria Incoronata

Streets, Squares and Historic Buildings
1 Via Manzoni
5 Archi di Porta Nuova
9 Palazzo Cusani
16 Pirelli Building
17 Stazione Centrale
18 Bastioni di Porta Venezia
23 Corso Venezia see pp124–5

Museums and Galleries
2 Museo Poldi Pezzoli
3 Museo Bagatti Valsecchi
4 Palazzo Morando – Costume Moda Immagine

7 Pinacoteca di Brera see pp116–19
15 Hangar Bicocca
19 Planetarium
20 Museo di Storia Naturale
22 Villa Belgiojoso Galleria d'Arte Moderna

Gardens and Cemeteries
8 Orto Botanico
14 Cimitero Monumentale
21 Giardini Pubblici

☐ Restaurants pp173–5
1 10 Corso Como
2 Akropolis
3 Alla Cucina delle Langhe
4 Il Baretto al Baglioni
5 Bulgari
6 Café Verdi di Rosso Maria
7 Il Coriandolo
8 Da Giannino

9 Da Ilia
10 Giglio Rosso
11 Hong Kong
12 Joia
13 Lon Fon
14 Malavoglia
15 Nobu Armani
16 Obikà
17 Osteria La Piola
18 Osteria del Treno
19 Piccola Cucina
20 Princi
21 Rigolo
22 Serendib
23 Il Teatro
24 Tomoyoshi Endo
25 Trattoria Al Matarel

| 0 metres | 600 |
| 0 yards | 600 |

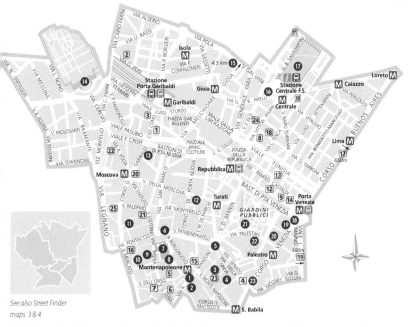

See also Street Finder maps 3 & 4

◄ *Napoleon as Mars the Peacemaker* in the courtyard of Pinacoteca di Brera

For keys to symbols *see back flap*

Street-by-Street: the Fashion District

Via Montenapoleone represents the elegant heart of Milan and is one of the four sides of the so-called *quadrilatero* or fashion district (the other three sides are Via Manzoni, Via Sant'Andrea and Via della Spiga). When strolling through this district, besides the shops of some of the top Italian and international fashion designers, you will see grand Neo-Classical aristocratic residences such as Palazzo Melzi di Cusano, at No. 18 Via Montenapoleone, built in 1830. Via Bigli, on the other hand, is lined with 16th- and 17th-century palazzi with porticoed courtyards.

⑤ Archi di Porta Nuova
This city gate, once part of the medieval walls, is decorated with copies of 1st-century AD Roman tombstones. Left, a stele representing a family.

VALENTINO

GIORGIO ARMANI

❶ Via Manzoni
This broad street is lined with aristocratic palazzi.

Grand Hotel et de Milan

Under the Portico del Lattèe (milk-man's arcade) is the wall of the demolished church of San Donnino alla Mazza.

❷ ★ Museo Poldi Pezzoli
The Portrait of a Young Lady (15th century), attributed to Antonio Pollaiolo, is the symbol of this museum created by Gian Giacomo Poldi Pezzoli. Besides paintings by Mantegna, Piero della Francesca and Bellini, it has rugs, armour and precious ceramics.

0 metres   50
0 yards   50

❸ ★ Museo Bagatti Valsecchi

This Neo-Renaissance palazzo was built as the family residence by the Bagatti Valsecchi brothers. It still has 16 rooms with their original 19th-century furnishings and many works of art belonging to the owners, who were art collectors.

Locator Map
See Street Finder, map 3 & 4

DOLCE & GABBANA

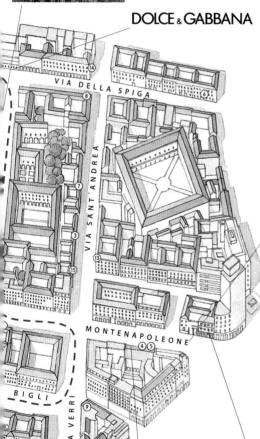

VIA DELLA SPIGA

VIA SANT'ANDREA

MONTENAPOLEONE

BIGLI

VIA VERRI

VERSACE

GUCCI

A Renaissance portal with a bas-relief *Annunciation* leads to the courtyard of Palazzo Bigli, decorated with frescoes by the school of Luini.

Via Montenapoleone
Following the course of the ancient Roman walls, it gets its name from a bank that once stood here called "Monte Napoleone". Designer shops line the street.

Key

━ Suggested route

Top Fashion Designers

① **A Ferretti** Via Montenapoleone 18.
② **Byblos** Via della Spiga 33.
③ **Chanel** Via Sant'Andrea 10.
④ **Etro** Via Montenapoleone 5.
⑤ **Fendi** Via Montenapoleone 3.
⑥ **Gio Moretti** Via della Spiga 30.
⑦ **Gianfranco Ferrè** Via Sant'Andrea 15.
⑧ **Hermès** Via Sant'Andrea 21.
⑨ **Jil Sander** Via P Verri 6.
⑩ **Krizia** Via della Spiga 23.
⑪ **Laura Biagiotti** Via Borgospesso 19.
⑫ **Marni** Via della Spiga 50.
⑬ **Missoni** Via Sant'Andrea 2B.
⑭ **Prada** Via Sant'Andrea 21.
⑮ **Trussardi** Via Sant'Andrea 5.

Fountain in the inner garden of a palazzo in Via Manzoni

❶ Via Manzoni

Map 4 D4. **M** 1 Duomo, 3 Montenapoleone. 🚃 1. 🚌 61, 94. Palazzi not open to visitors.

Once known as "Corsia del Giardino" (Garden Lane) because of its many parks, this street acquired its present name in 1865, when the great Italian novelist Manzoni died. Its aristocratic appearance is created by the patrician palazzi and Teatro alla Scala *(see pp54–5)*, which stimulated the opening of chic cafés attracting a smart clientele. At No. 6 is 19th-century Palazzo Brentani, decorated with medallions with busts of illustrious persons, and No. 10 is Palazzo Anguissola (1775–8), which now houses the historic archive of the Banca Commerciale Italiana. No. 12, another 19th-century building, is the home of the famous Museo Poldi Pezzoli, and No. 29 is the Grand Hotel et de Milan (1865), where Giuseppe Verdi died in 1901.

Near the end of Via Montenapoleone stands Aldo Rossi's monument to former Italian President Sandro Pertini (1990) and, next to this, Palazzo Gallarati Scotti (No. 30), built in the early 1700s. Opposite, Via Pisoni takes you to the remains of the 15th-century cloister of the Umiliate di Sant'Erasmo monastery, now part of a modern building. In the last stretch is 18th-century Palazzo Borromeo d'Adda, which was a haunt for literati and artists, including Stendhal.

❷ Museo Poldi Pezzoli

Via Manzoni 12. **Map** 4 D5. **Tel** 02-79 48 89. **M** 3 Montenapoleone. 🚃 1. 🚌 61, 94. **Open** 10am–6pm Wed–Mon (last adm: 5:30pm). **Closed** 1 Jan, Easter, 25 Apr, 1 May, 15 Aug, 1 Nov, 8, 25 & 26 Dec. 📷 (no flash). 🚻 Lecture hall, Library. 📷
W museopoldipezzoli.it

This private museum was established by nobleman Gian Giacomo Poldi Pezzoli and opened to the public in 1881. The museum, a singular example of a late 19th-century aristocratic Milanese residence, contains Poldi Pezzoli's fine collection of paintings, sculpture, rugs, armour, glass, watches and textiles. The ground floor houses arms and armour from the 14th to the 19th century in a setting designed by artist Arnaldo Pomodoro. The Fresco Room, named after *The Apotheosis of Bartolomeo Colleoni* frescoed by Carlo Innocenzo Carloni, boasts a Tabriz carpet with hunting scenes (Persia, 1542–3). In the adjoining room is the museum's collection of lace.

Poldi Pezzoli Museum logo

The staircase, decorated with landscapes by Magnasco, leads to the first floor. In the Lombard Rooms is 15th–16th-century Lombard painting, with works by Bergognone, Luini, the Leonardoesque painters, a *Polyptych* by Cristoforo Moretti, and Vincenzo Foppa's *Portrait of Giovanni Francesco Brivio*. The portraits of Martin Luther and his wife by Lucas Cranach (1529) are in the Foreign Artists Room. A showcase of precious porcelain separates the next room from the Golden Room, where masterpieces are on display. These include *St Nicholas of Tolentino* by Piero della Francesca, Botticelli's *Madonna and Child* and *Lamentation*, a *Madonna and Child* by Andrea Mantegna, Giovanni Bellini's *Pietà* and the *Portrait of a Young Woman* attributed to Piero del Pollaiolo. Three small rooms house the Visconti Venosta collection, the portraits by Fra Galgario, including *The Gentleman with the Tricorn* and a very important collection of clocks from the 16th to the 19th century. The Murano Glass Room has fine specimens of Venetian glasswork, and the Dante Study features two stained-glass windows celebrating Dante's life. The last rooms house paintings by Tiepolo, Guardia, Canaletto and 14th-century panels. Lastly, the Jewellery Room hosts a collection of precious jewellery and goldsmithery from antiquity to the 19th century.

On some Wednesdays the museum organizes a "happy hour" between 6 and 9pm. The €9 fee includes admission to the museum and a drink to enjoy while taking in the exhibits. Check the museum website for further details.

Botticelli's *Pietà* (1495), Museo Poldi Pezzoli

A cradle from the Camera Rossa in the Museo Bagatti Valsecchi

❸ Museo Bagatti Valsecchi

Via Gesù 5. **Map** 4 D5. **Tel** 02-76 00 61 32. **M** 3 Montenapoleone. ⬚ 1. 🚌 61, 94. **Open** 1–5:45pm Tue–Sun. **Closed** 1 & 6 Jan, Easter, 25 Apr, 1 May, 2 Jun, 15 Aug, 7, 8, 25 & 26 Dec. 🅿️ 🚪 ground floor only. 🎧 by appt. 📷 **W** **museobagattivalsecchi.org**

Opened in 1994 in the prestigious late 19th-century residence of the two Bagatti Valsecchi brothers, Fausto and Giuseppe, this fascinating museum is an important record of art collectors' taste in that period. The building was designed in Neo-Renaissance style, with an elegant façade and two well proportioned courtyards, and was furnished with works of art and imitation Renaissance furniture. It was seen as a private house and not a museum, and was furnished with every possible comfort. The rooms feature tapestries, ivory work, ceramics and arms, as well as important paintings such as the elegant *Santa Giustina* by Giovanni Bellini (c.1475; kept in what was Giuseppe Bagatti Valsecchi's bedroom), Bernardo Zenale's panels and a *Polyptych* by Giampietrino. The library, with its valuable 15th-century parchments and a series of 16th–17th-century porcelain pharmacy vases, is also worth a look.

The intriguing Valtellinese bedroom has a magnificent 16th-century bed with Christ ascending Calvary and scenes from the Old Testament carved in the bedstead. The Sala della Stufa Valtellinese is also interesting, with its marvellous 16th-century wood panelling with an elegant sculpted frieze and a piece of furniture ingeniously concealing a piano. The Camera Rossa contains a delightful small collection of 15th–17th-century furniture for children that includes a high chair, a baby walker and a cradle. The dining room has a collection of kitchenware, tapestries and sideboards.

❹ Palazzo Morando – Costume Moda Immagine

Via Sant'Andrea 6. **Map** 4 D5. **Tel** 02-88 46 59 33. **M** 1 San Babila, 3 Montenapoleone. ⬚ 1, 2. 🚌 94. **Open** 9am–1pm, 2–5:30pm Tue–Sun. **Closed** 1 Jan, 1 May, 25 Dec. **W** **costumemodaimmagine.it**

Appropriately located in the Fashion District (Quadrilatero della Moda), Milan's Museum of Costume can be found in an 18th-century aristocratic townhouse that displays the elegant style of the time with its original furnishings.

The collection illustrates the history of Milanese fashion from the 18th to the 20th century, combining the costumes and accessories of the Municipal Collections of Applied Arts, (which used to be stored at the Castello Sforzesco) with the contents of the former Museum of Milan. The paintings and artifacts displayed alongside the costumes on the first floor reveal the extensive heritage of the city's art in its various forms.

On the ground floor are temporary exhibits connected with the history of Milan's fashion. Documentaries are screened at the museum, and concerts are also held here.

❺ Archi di Porta Nuova

Map 4 D4. **M** 3 Montenapoleone. ⬚ 1. 🚌 61, 94.

This city gate, restored in 1861, is one of two that survive forming part of the medieval wall system. Construction began in 1171, and the gate was probably modelled on the corresponding Porta Romana, some of whose building materials it used. The inner side on Via Manzoni is decorated with copies of 1st-century AD Roman tombstones, while the outside facing Piazza Cavour bears a tabernacle decorated with a *Madonna and Child with Saints Ambrose, Gervase and Protasius* (1330–39).

Facing the piazza is Palazzo dei Giornali (No. 2), built in 1942 as the main office of the newspaper *Il Popolo d'Italia* and decorated with bas-reliefs by Mario Sironi. The square is framed by the Giardini Pubblici, in front of which is a monument to Cavour by Odoardo Tabacchi (1865).

The Porta Nuova arches seen from Via Manzoni

Street-by-Street: the Brera Quarter

The name of Milan's traditional Bohemian quarter derives from the Germanic word *braida*, which denoted a grassy area. The presence of art students at the Accademia di Belle Arti and the world-famous Brera art gallery has contributed to the lively feel of this quarter, which is reinforced by the many cafés, restaurants, galleries, antique shops and night-clubs established here. In summer the narrow streets are enlivened even more by street stalls and fortune tellers. An antiques market is held on the third Saturday of each month in Via Brera.

❻ ★ San Marco
The façade of this church, founded in 1254, was rebuilt in 1871 in Neo-Gothic style. The only remaining part of the original is the stone doorway, which has a relief of Christ between two saints and among symbols of the Evangelists.

```
0 metres        100
0 yards         100
```

Key

— Suggested route

The Museo Minguzzi
has 100 pieces by the Bolognese sculptor.

❿ ★ San Simpliciano
This church was one of the four basilicas founded by Sant'Ambrogio and has preserved most of its original Early Christian architecture.

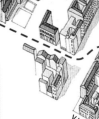

Inside the Jamaica café, in Via Brera

Café Life in the Brera

The cafés and bars of the Brera quarter are lively and atmospheric, many with live music. The Tombon de San Marc (Via San Marco) was once the haunt of the stevedores from the nearby Naviglio and now welcomes customers of all kinds. The famous Jamaica café (Via Brera) has jazz sessions on Mondays. Another atmospheric spot is Sans Égal, in the pedestrian precinct of Via Fiori Chiari, which turns into a sports pub on Sundays (*see pp184–5*).

Locator Map
See Street Finder maps 3, 4

❼ ★ Pinacoteca di Brera
The nucleus of one of Italy's top art galleries consists of works taken from churches that were suppressed in the late 1700s. The Brera boasts masterpieces by great artists such as Piero della Francesca, Mantegna, Raphael and Caravaggio.

The Civico Museo del Risorgimento, opened in 1896, is in Neo-Classical Palazzo Moriggia.

Orto Botanico
The Botanical Gardens have been part of the Brera Astronomical Museum since 1774. Founded under Empress Maria Theresa of Austria, they include two ginkgo biloba trees, among the oldest in Europe, plus a 40-m- (131-ft-) high linden tree and a Caucasian walnut.

VIA FATE BENE FRATELLI

VIA BORGONUOVO

VIA BRERA

VIA SOLFERINO

VIA MADONNINA

VIA PONTE VETERO

VIA DELL' ORSO

❽ Palazzo Cusani
This building with a late Baroque façade (1719) is the headquarters of the Third Army Corps. On the first floor is the Officers' Club.

❾ Santa Maria del Carmine
The 15th-century church was built with material taken from the nearby Castello Sforzesco when it was partly demolished.

The lunette over the entrance to San Marco

❻ San Marco

Piazza San Marco 2. **Map** 3 C4.
Tel 02-29 00 25 98. 🚌 43, 61, 94.
Open 7am–noon, 4–7pm daily.
✝ 7:45, 9:30am, 6:30pm Mon–Fri;
6:30pm pre-hols; 9:30am, noon,
6:30pm hols.

This church was begun in
1254 by the Augustine monk
Lanfranco Settala. It was built
on the site of an older church,
dedicated by the Milanese
to St Mark, patron saint of
Venice, to thank the Venetians
for help in the struggle
against Emperor Frederick
Barbarossa. In 1871 Carlo
Maciachini built a new, Neo-
Gothic façade around the
Campionese school ogival
portal and tabernacle.
    The church has a Latin
cross plan and nine patrician
chapels, which were added
to the right-hand aisle in the
14th– 19th century. They
contain 16th–17th-century
paintings, including some
by Paolo Lomazzo. In the
right-hand transept is the
*Foundation of the Augustine
Order* by the Fiammenghino
brothers, Settala's sarcophagus
by Giovanni Balduccio (1317–
49), and fragments of late
Gothic frescoes found during
the 1956 restoration. The
presbytery is decorated with
large canvases by Camillo
Procaccini and Cerano
depicting the Legend
of St Augustine, and the
Genealogical Tree of the Order
by Genovesino (17th century),
who also painted the *Angels'
Backs* on the cupola. The left-
hand transept leads to the
Chapel of the Pietà, with

The Ascent to Calvary by
Ercole Procaccini. The left-
hand aisle has canvases by
Camillo and Giulio Cesare
Procaccini and Palma il
Giovane, and a Leonardoesque
fresco found in 1975. From
outside the Romanesque
transept the 13th-century
bell tower is visible.

❼ Pinacoteca di Brera

See pp116–19.

❽ Orto Botanico

Via Brera 28 and Via Fratelli Gabba 10.
Map 3 C4. **Tel** 02-50 31 46 80.
Ⓜ 1/3 Duomo, 2 Lanza. 🚊 1, 4,
12, 14, 27. 🚌 61. **Open** Apr–Oct:
10am–6pm Mon–Sat; Nov–Mar:
9:30am–4:30pm Mon–Sat. **Closed**
1 Jan, 1 May, 2 Jun, 25 & 26 Dec. ♿
🌐 brera.unimi.it

At a mere 5,000 sq m (53,820
sq ft), the Orto Botanico di
Brera is probably one of the
tiniest botanical gardens on
earth. It forms part of a large
cultural compound housed in
the nearby Brera Palace, which
includes the Pinacoteca di Brera
art gallery *(see pp116–19)*, the
Astronomical Observatory, the
Biblioteca Braidense library and
the Academy of Fine Arts. The
secluded and peaceful gardens
make for a welcome change
amid Milan's bustle.
    Founded in 1774 under
the Austrian Empress Maria
Theresa of Austria, the
gardens include a collection
of medicinal plants, salvias
and decorative trees.

❾ Palazzo Cusani

Via Brera 15. **Map** 3 C4. Ⓜ 2 Lanza.
🚊 2, 12, 14. 🚌 61. **Closed** to
the public.

Originally built in the 1500s,
this palazzo was rebuilt in 1719
by Giovanni Ruggeri, who
designed the late Baroque
façade with its ornate windows
and balconies, while the Neo-
Classical façade facing the
garden was designed by
Piermarini. Tradition has it that
the Cusani brothers ordered
twin entrances so that each
could have independent yet
equal access. In the drawing
room is an allegorical Tiepolo-
like fresco (1740). The palazzo
was the seat of the Ministry of
War in the 19th century.

The ornate late Baroque façade of
Palazzo Cusani

❿ Santa Maria del Carmine

Piazza del Carmine 2. **Map** 3 C4.
Tel 02-86 46 33 65. 🚊 1, 2, 12, 14.
🚌 57, 61. **Open** 7:15–11:30am,
3:30–7pm daily. ✝ 8am (except Sat),
9:30am, 6:30pm Mon–Sat; 5pm (Eng)
Thu; 8:30am (Eng and Tagalog),
10:30am (Eng), 11:30am, 4:30pm &
6:30pm (Eng and Tagalog) Sun.

Santa Maria del Carmine was
built in Gothic style in 1447 over
a Romanesque church and was
then rebuilt in the Baroque
period, while the present-day
façade was designed by Carlo
Maciachini in 1880. The spacious

Angel Musicians by Aurelio Luini (16th century), in the church of San Simpliciano

interior has a three-aisle nave covered by cross vaulting. The inclination of the first piers is due to the absence of a façade for a long period and the subsequent gradual settling of the building.

The right-hand transept contains part of the tomb of the Ducal Councillor Angelo Simonetta, above which are two paintings by Carlo Francesco Nuvolone and Fiammenghino; the opposite transept is decorated with a painting by Camillo Landriani.

The statues in the wooden choir (1579–85) are the original plaster models created for the spires of the Duomo by 19th-century artists. The Cappella del Rosario, built on the right of the choir (1673) by Gerolamo Quadrio, has marble dressing and is decorated with canvases by Camillo Procaccini depicting The Legend of Mary.

On the left-hand side of the church is the monastery cloister, with remains of noble tombs and ancient tombstones, and a Baroque sacristy, with furniture made by Quadrio in 1692

Part of the Baroque sacristy, Santa Maria del Carmine

⓫ San Simpliciano

Piazza San Simpliciano 7. **Map** 3 B4.
Tel 02-86 22 74. Ⓜ 2 Lanza.
🚎 2, 4, 12, 14. 🚌 43, 57, 61, 94.
Open 9am–noon, 2:15–7pm
Mon–Fri; 9:30am–7pm Sat & Sun.
✝ 7:30am (Sep–Jun), 6pm Mon–Fri;
6pm pre-hols; 8am (Sep–Jun),
8am (except Jul & Aug), 10 & 11:30am,
6pm hols.

The church was founded by Sant'Ambrogio in the 4th century as the Basilica

Virginum and completed in 401. It is preceded by a porch and once had open galleries on either side where penitents and new converts could take part in Mass. The façade, decorated with glazed plates, was added in 1870 by Maciachini, who retained the main portal. The capitals have 12th-century carvings of the processions of the Wise and Foolish Virgins. Fourteenth century frescoes have been discovered in the first chapel on the right, and in the fourth is Enea Salmeggia's Miracle of St Benedict (1619). The apse is frescoed with the Coronation of the Virgin by Bergognone (1508). The Neo-Classical altar covers the wooden choir (1588), and on either side are two organ pedestals frescoed by Aurelio Luini in the 1500s. The transept leads to the Early Christian Sacellum of San Simpliciano (closed), built to house the remains of San Simpliciano and of martyrs.

San Simpliciano, the Three Martyrs and the Carroccio

Lunette over one of the doors of San Simpliciano

St Ambrose asked the young Sisinius, Martirius and Alexander to go to Anaunia (today Val di Non) in northern Italy to spread Christianity. In 397 they were martyred and the bodies were given to Bishop Simpliciano, who buried them in the Basilica Virginum. According to legend, the martyrs were decisive in leading the Milanese to victory in the battle of Legnano against Barbarossa (1176). On that occasion three white doves flew out of the basilica and landed on the Carroccio (cart), the symbol of Milan, waiting to be blessed before the battle. On 29 May the city commemorates this event with a solemn ceremony.

❼ Pinacoteca di Brera

The Brera art gallery holds one of Italy's most important art collections, featuring masterpieces by leading Italian artists from the 13th to the 20th centuries, including Raphael, Mantegna, Piero della Francesca and Caravaggio. The Pinacoteca is housed in the late 16th–early 17th-century palazzo built for the Jesuits in place of the Santa Maria di Brera Humiliati monastery. The Jesuits made this into a cultural centre by establishing a prestigious school, a library and the astronomical observatory – all activities supported by Empress Maria Theresa of Austria, who founded the Accademia di Belle Arti after the Jesuit order was suppressed (1773).

Portrait of Moisè Kisling
Amedeo Modigliani painted this work in 1915, reflecting his interest in African sculpture. (Room 10)

Finding the Body of St Mark
The bold perspective and almost supernatural light in the room where the saint's body is found make this canvas (1562–6) one of Tintoretto's masterpieces. (Room 9)

Mocchirolo Chapel

Key

- ▢ Jesi Collection (20th-century art)
- ▨ 13th–15th-century Italian painting
- ▨ 15th–16th-century Venetian painting
- ▢ 15th–16th-century Lombard painting
- ▨ 15th–16th-century Central Italian painting
- ▦ 17th–18th-century Italian, Flemish and Dutch painting
- ▢ 18th–19th-century Italian painting

Twin staircases
lead to the entrance to the gallery on the first floor.

The Kiss
This canvas by Francesco Hayez (1859) is one of the most reproduced 19th-century Italian paintings – a patriotic and sentimental work epitomizing the optimism that prevailed after Italy's unification. (Room 37)

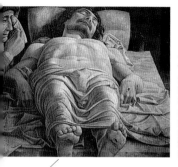

★ Dead Christ
This masterpiece by Mantegna (c.1480) is striking for its intense light and bold fore-shortening. The work was among the artist's possessions at the time of his death. (Room 7)

VISITORS' CHECKLIST

Practical Information
Via Brera 28. **Map** 3 C4.
Tel 02-72 26 32 64.
Open 8:30am–7:15pm Tue–Sun (last adm: 45 mins before closing).
Closed Mon, 1 Jan, 1 May, 25 Dec. 🅿 ♿ 🅰 📷
W brera.beniculturali.it

Transport
Ⓜ 1, 3 Duomo, 2 Lanza.
🚊 1, 4, 12, 14, 27. 🚌 61.

Room 15 has works by painters active in Lombardy from the late 15th to the mid-16th century, including Bergognone, Luini, Bramantino and Vincenzo Foppa.

The courtyard with twin columns is the work of Richini (17th century).

★ Montefeltro Altarpiece
Piero della Francesca painted this great work in 1475 for Federico da Montefeltro, the Duke of Urbino, who is portrayed dressed in a Milanese suit of armour. (Room 24)

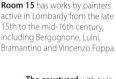

Gallery Guide

The Brera Gallery has 38 rooms, with works arranged in chronological order. The only exception is Room 10, where the Jesi and Vitali collections are on display. It includes 20th-century works which will be exhibited elsewhere in future. The paintings are also grouped together by schools of painting (Venetian, Tuscan, Lombard, etc.). The Sala della Passione on the ground floor is used for temporary exhibitions.

Entrance

★ The Marriage of the Virgin
Raphael signed and dated (1504) his masterful altarpiece on the temple in the background. Some scholars say the young man breaking the staff is a self-portrait of the artist. (Room 24)

Exploring the Pinacoteca di Brera

The original nucleus of the Brera Gallery consisted mainly of plaster casts and drawings used as models for the art students of the Accademia di Belle Arti (founded in 1776). This collection was augmented with works from suppressed churches in Northern Italy and was officially opened in 1809, the paintings being arranged in rows on the wall, from floor to ceiling. The Pinacoteca became independent from the Accademia in 1882, and its fine collection further expanded through 19th- and 20th-century donations. The gallery has always suffered from lack of space, but there are plans to use the adjacent Palazzo Citterio.

The City Rises (c.1910) by Umberto Boccioni

Jesi Collection

The 72 works donated by Emilio and Maria Jesi in 1976 and 1984 are on show in room 10. The collection, mostly by Italian artists, covers the 1910–40 period. Key works include *Portrait of Moisè Kisling (see p116)* by Modigliani, Umberto Boccioni's *Brawl in the Galleria* (1911) and *The City Rises* (a study for the canvas now in the New York MOMA), Carlo Carrà's *The Metaphysical Muse* (1917) and still lifes by Giorgio Morandi, as well as sculpture by Medardo Rosso, Arturo Martini and Marino Marini.

13th–15th-Century Italian Painting

The section given over to 13th–15th-century Italian art (rooms 2–4) includes frescoes from the Oratory at Mocchirolo, painted by an unknown Lombard master in around 1365–70. Among the gold-background works are the *Santa Maria della Celestia Polyptych* by Lorenzo Veneziano (14th century), Ambrogio Lorenzetti's *Madonna and Child* and *Christ the Judge* by Giovanni da Milano. A fine example of the International Gothic style is the *Valle Romita Polyptycb* by Gentile da Fabriano, flanked by Stefano da Verona's *Adoration of the Magi* (1435), in which the viola and carnation at the feet of Jesus symbolize his humility and the Passion.

15th–16th-Century Venetian Painting

Rooms 5 and 6 feature works by 15th–16th-century artists active in the Veneto such as Giovanni d'Alemagna and Antonio Vivarini, who painted the *Praglia Polyptych* (1448). Room 6 has Mantegna's *St Luke Altarpiece*

(1453–4). Giovanni Bellini is represented by two Madonnas with Child and Carpaccio by *Legend of the Virgin*. There are portraits by Lorenzo Lotto in room 7, alongside Mantegna's masterpiece *Dead Christ* and Bellini's *Pietà* (c.1470). *St Mark Preaching in Alexandria* (room 8) was painted for the Scuola Grande in St Mark's in Venice by Giovanni and Gentile Bellini.

The following room has works by Titian and Paolo Veronese, as well as the *Finding of the Body of St Mark*, which Tintoretto painted for Tommaso Rangone, who is portrayed as the kneeling man in the middle of the scene.

15th–16th-Century Lombard Painting

A large collection of 15th–16th-century Lombard paintings is exhibited in rooms 15, 18 and 19. The leading figure, Vincenzo Foppa, is represented by the *Polittico delle Grazie* (c.1483). An unknown master contributed the *Sforzesca Altarpiece* (1494), showing Lodovico il Moro and his family worshipping the Madonna. This room also has works by Bergognone, Gaudenzio Ferrari – an artist with a marked narrative vein, as can be seen in *Martyrdom of St Catherine* – and Bramantino's *Crucifixion*. Works influenced by Leonardo da Vinci include the small paintings

Gentile da Fabriano's Valle Romita Polyptych

Supper at Emmaus, painted by Caravaggio in 1606

for private chapels by De Predis and Luini *(Madonna del Roseto)*, while the Cremona area is represented by names such as Boccaccino, Campi and Piazza.

15th–16th-Century Central Italian Painting

Rooms 20–23 illustrate artistic movements in the regions of Emilia and Marche. The Ferrara school is represented by its leading artists, Cosmè Tura, Francesco del Cossa and Ercole de' Roberti (whose *Madonna and Child among Saints* was painted around 1480). Correggio's *Nativity* is a major Emilian school work, while painting in Le Marche is documented by the works of Carlo Crivelli, including his *Madonna della Candeletta* (1490–91), rich in symbols.

Room 24 houses the two best-known masterpieces in the Brera. Piero della Francesca's *Montefeltro Altarpiece* (c.1475), was commissioned by Federico da Montefeltro. The egg suspended from its shell is a symbol of the Creation and of the Immaculate Conception. Next is Raphael's splendid *The Marriage of the Virgin (see p117)*.

Christ at the Pillar is a rare painting by Bramante, while works by Bronzino and Genga represent Mannerism.

17th–18th-Century Italian, Flemish and Dutch Painting

Room 28 features works by the Bolognese school, founded by the Carracci, including Guido Reni and Guercino. The next room boasts Caravaggio's *Supper at Emmaus* (1606), in which the appearance of Christ occurs in a setting illuminated only by the light emanating from Jesus's face. Lombard artists shown in room 30 are Cerano, Morazzone and Giulio Cesare Procaccini, who painted the *Martyrdom of Saints Rufina and Secunda* together. Baroque painting is represented in rooms 31–33 by Pietro da Cortona and the still lifes of Baschenis. Among the non-Italian artists are Rubens *(Last Supper, 1631–2)*, Van Dyck, Rembrandt *(Portrait of the Artist's Sister, 1632)*, El Greco and Brueghel the Elder *(The Village)*.

Madonna della Candeletta by Crivelli

18th–19th-Century Italian Painting

The following rooms cover various genres in 18th-century Italian art. Large-scale religious paintings are displayed in room 34 with works by the Neapolitan Luca Giordano and Giovan Battista Tiepolo's *Madonna del Carmelo* (1721–7), intended to be viewed from the side. Another Venetian artist, Piazzetta, has his *Rebecca at the Well* displayed in room 35.

Giacomo Ceruti (Il Pitochetto) represents "genre painting", which was popular in the 18th century. This is followed by Venetian *vedutismo* views by Bernardo Bellotto, Guardi and Canaletto. The works of Bellotto and Canaletto are characterized by their bright light and precision of detail (the latter even used a camera obscura to help him render this "photographic" effect).

Portraiture is best exemplified by Fra Galgario *(Portrait of a Gentleman)*. A representative 19th-century painting is Andrea Appiani's Neo-Classical *Olympus*, while the Macchiaioli movement is on display with works by Silvestro Lega and Giovanni Fattori, among others. The Brera also has paintings by the leading exponent of Lombard Romanticism, Francesco Hayez: his famous *The Kiss* and several portraits. The gallery closes with Divisionist Giuseppe Pelizza da Volpedo's *The Flood* (1895–7), a hymn to the struggle of the working class, and an early version of his *Fourth Estate*, now on display at the Museo del Novecento *(see p56)*.

⑫ Sant'Angelo

Piazza Sant'Angelo 2. **Map** 4 D3.
Tel 02-63 24 81. 🚌 43, 94. **Open**
6:30am–8pm daily. 🚶 7, 8, 10am
& 7pm Mon–Sat; 10, 11am, 12:15 &
7pm hols.

Built in 1552 by Domenico
Giunti to replace the older
Franciscan church outside the
Porta Nuova, which had been
demolished to make room
for the Spanish ramparts,
Sant'Angelo is an important
example of 16th-century
Milanese architecture. The
nave is separated from the
presbytery by a triumphal
arch with the *Assumption of
Mary* by Legnanino (17th
century). There are many 16th-
and 17th-century paintings in
the chapels. The first one on the
right has canvases by Antonio
Campi (1584) and a copy of the
*Martyrdom of St Catherine of
Alexandria* by Gaudenzio Ferrari
(the original is in the Brera);
the second has Morazzone's
St Charles in Glory.

⑬ Santa Maria Incoronata

Corso Garibaldi 116. **Map** 3 C2.
Tel 02-65 48 55. Ⓜ 2 Garibaldi.
🚌 43, 70, 94. **Open** 7:15am–1:30pm,
4–7pm Mon–Fri, 8am–12.30pm,
4–7:30pm Sat–Sun. 🚶 7:30 & 9:30am,
6:30pm Mon–Fri, 9:30am, 6:30pm
Sat; 8:30, 10 & 11:30am, 6:30pm
public hols.

This church consists of two
buildings designed by
Guiniforte Solari, which
were merged in 1468.
The left one was built
for Francesco Sforza
in 1451 and the other
was built soon
afterwards for his wife. brick
façade is double, as is the
nave, which has two apses
with 15th and 17th-century
frescoes. In the right-hand
chapels are plaques in
memory of Sforzesco
court personages. The
chapels opposite have
frescoes by Montalto
and Bernardino Zenale (the
fresco in the first chapel is
attributed to Zenale).

The Cimitero Monumentale, with tombs
and shrines produced by famous sculptors

⑭ Cimitero Monumentale

Piazzale Cimitero Monumentale.
Map 3 A1. **Tel** 02-88 46 56 00.
Ⓜ 5 Monumentale. 🚋 2, 4, 12, 14.
🚌 37. **Open** 8am–6pm Tue–Sun
(to 1pm hols; last entry 5:30pm).
Free map of the cemetery available
at the entrance.

Extending over an area of
250,000 sq m (300,000 sq yds),
the Cimitero Monumentale
was begun by Carlo Maciachini
in 1866. The eclectic taste of
the time dictated the use of
various styles for the cemetery,
from mock-Lombard
Romanesque to Neo-Gothic,
with touches of Tuscan thrown
in. The linchpin of the structure
is the Famedio *(Famae Aedes)*,
or House of Fame, a sort of
pantheon of illustrious
Milanese and non-
Milanese buried here.
Author Alessandro
Manzoni, Luca
Beltrami, the
architect who
oversaw
restoration
of the
Castello Sforzesco,
the patriot Carlo
Cattaneo and the
Nobel Prize-winning
poet Salvatore
Quasimodo all have
tombs in this
cemetery. There
are also busts of
Garibaldi, Verdi
and Cavour. The
Romantic painter Hayez lies
in the crypt. A visit to the
Cimitero Monumentale,

Sculpture by Fontana,
Cimitero Monumentale

which is a kind of open-air
museum of art from the late
19th century to the present,
begins at the large square
inside, which contains the
tombs of important Milanese
figures. Around the square are
monumental shrines and the
Civico Mausoleo Palanti, an
enormous mausoleum with
a crypt, used as an air-raid
shelter in 1943. Among its
tombs are those of comic
actor Walter Chiari and
Hermann Einstein, Albert's
father. On the terraces, to
the left are the Elisi (sculpted
by Francesco Penna, 1916)
and Morgagni tombs, and
an epigraph by Benito
Mussolini commemorating
a disastrous aeroplane crash.
In the central avenue are
two tombs designed and
sculpted by Enrico Butti: that
of Isabella Casati, *Young Woman
Enraptured by a Dream,* a typical
Lombard realist work (1890),
and the Besenzanica shrine
with *Work* (1912). On the right,
is the monumental Toscanini
tomb (Bistolfi, 1909–11), built
for the conductor's son.

Among other monumental
tombs for major figures in
Milanese life are those of
Carlo Erba, Bocconi, Campari
and Falck. Many famous
sculptors made pieces for
this place: Leonardo Bistolfi,
Giacomo Manzù, Odoardo
Tabacchi, Adolfo Wildt and
Lucio Fontana. The two
enclosures beside the Famedio
are for Jews and non-Catholics,
with the remains of sculptor
Medardo Rosso, publishers
Arnoldo Mondadori and Ulrico
Hoepli and Jules Richard,
founder of the Richard-Ginori
ceramics industry.

⑮ Hangar Bicocca

Via Chiese 2. **Tel** 02-66 11 15 73.
Ⓜ 1 Sesto Marelli. 🚌 51, 87.
Open 11am–1pm Thu–Sun.
Closed 1 Jan, 1 May, 2 Jun, 25 &
26 Dec. 🚻 🖥 hangarbicocca.org

Housed in a former factory
building (part of an industrial
complex owned by Ansaldo-
Breda-Pirelli), Hangar Bicocca

The Stazione Centrale, with its spectacular iron and glass roof

is the result of a massive reno-vation project to redevelop the area. As a space devoted to the production, exhibition and promotion of contemporary art, it offers some of the best cultural programmes in Milan, including activities for kids.

Just beyond the entrance, visitors are welcomed by Fausto Melotti's *La sequenza* (1981), a site-specific installation made of steel floating in a bed of ornamental grasses and wild flowers designed by the Milan-based architect Marco Bay. Inside there is another site-specific master-piece: Anselm Kiefer's *The Seven Heavenly Palaces*. Created in 2004, it is considered one of the most important works by this German artist.

⓰ Pirelli Building

Piazzale Duca d'Aosta-Via Pirelli. **Map** 4 E1. Ⓜ 2, 3 Centrale. 🚊 2, 9, 33. 🚌 60, 82. **Closed** to the public.

The symbol of postwar reconstruction in Milan, the Pirelli Building, affectionately called "Pirellone" (big Pirelli) by the Milanese, was built in 1955–60. It was designed by a group of leading architects and engineers: Giò Ponti, Antonio Fornaroli, Alberto Rosselli, Giuseppe Valtolina, Egidio Dell'Orto, Pier Luigi Nervi and Arturo Danusso. At 127 m (417 ft) high, it was the largest reinforced concrete skyscraper

in the world until the 1960s. The slender, elegant edifice occupies only 1,000 sq m (1,200 sq yds) and stands on the site where, in 1872, Giovan Battista Pirelli built his first tyre factory. The skyscraper was constructed as the Pirelli company's main offices. Among the many records established by the "Pirellone" was that it was the first building in Milan taller than the Madonnina on the Duomo (108.50 m, 356 ft). As a token of respect, a small statue of the Virgin Mary was placed on the Pirelli roof. Since 1979 the building has been the headquarters of the regional government of Lombardy. Next door is the luxurious Excelsior Hotel Gallia, opened in the 1930s.

The Pirelli Building, symbol of Milan's postwar reconstruction

⓱ Stazione Centrale

Piazzale Duca d'Aosta. **Map** 4 F1. Ⓜ 2, 3 Centrale. 🚊 5, 9. 🚌 42, 60, 81, 87, 90, 91, 92.

Milan's main railway station is one of the largest and perhaps the most monumental in Europe. Ulisse Stacchini's project design was approved and ready in 1912, but construction work proved so slow that the building was not opened until 1931. The new railway station replaced one located in present-day Piazza della Repubblica.

The building is dressed in Aurisina stone, and was clearly inspired by the late Art Nouveau style in vogue in the early 20th century, in marked contrast with the austere 1930s architecture of the surrounding buildings.

The façade is 207 m (679 ft) wide and 36 m (118 ft) tall and is crowned by two winged horses. The large arcades link up with the Galleria dei Transiti, a gallery decorated with four medallions by Giannino Castiglioni representing Labour, Commerce, Science and Agriculture. In the large ticket office hall, flights of steps lead up to the huge departures and arrivals lobby, with tile panels representing the cities of Milan, Rome, Turin and Florence.

The massive building is a landmark in Milan and second only to the cathedral in size. There are numerous shops inside, and some are open 24 hours a day.

Casa Galimberti, decorated with wrought iron and tile panels

⑱ Bastioni di Porta Venezia

Map 4 E3. Ⓜ 1 Porta Venezia, 3 Repubblica. 🚊 5, 9, 33.

What is today a major road was once part of the walls built to defend the city in 1549–61 by the Spanish governor Ferrante Gonzaga. In 1789 the walls became a tree-lined avenue for walking and coach parking. The Porta Venezia ramparts, flanked by the Giardini Pubblici, link Piazza della Repubblica and Piazza Oberdan. The former was laid out in 1931 when the 19th-century railway station was demolished and rebuilt 800 m (2,624 ft) away and greatly enlarged to cope with increasing traffic resulting from the opening of the St Gotthard (1882) and Simplon (1906) passes through the Alps.

Not far from the piazza, in Via Turati, is the Palazzo della Permanente, designed by Luca Beltrami in 1885 as the home of the Permanent Fine Arts Exhibition and now used for temporary exhibitions.

Piazza Oberdan is dominated by Porta Venezia, the city gate rebuilt in 1828 on the site of the Spanish gate of the

Plaque commemorating the *lazzaretto*

same name and used as a customs toll station. The two buildings are decorated with statues and reliefs concerning the history of Milan. Porta Venezia separates Corso Venezia and Corso Buenos Aires, a major commercial thoroughfare.

In 1488–1513, Lazzaro Palazzi chose a site beyond the gate to build the *lazzaretto*, a hospital for plague victims commissioned by Lodovico il Moro. The few remains from the 1880 demolition can be seen in Via San Gregorio. A slight detour from Piazza Oberdan towards Viale Piave will take you past some interesting Art Nouveau style buildings: Casa Galimberti, designed by Giovan Battista Bossi in 1903–4, decorated with wrought iron and panels of ceramic tiles, and the Hotel Diana Majestic.

⑲ Planetarium

Corso Venezia 57. **Map** 4 E4. **Tel** 02–88 46 33 40. Ⓜ 1 Porta Venezia, Palestro. 🚊 9. **Open** Lectures 9pm Tue & Thu; 3 & 4:30pm Sat & Sun. 🅿 📷 ♿ 🆆 **comunemilano.it/planetario**

Donated to the city by the publisher Ulrico Hoepli, the Planetarium was built in 1930 in Classical style by Piero Portaluppi. The projection hall features a large hemispherical dome (20 m (65 ft) in diameter), with the skyline outlined just as it was when the Planetarium first opened, and 300 swivelling seats to gaze at the movements of the stars in absolute comfort. The multimedia projection system reproduces the stars as seen from any point on Earth, whether in the past, present or future.

In addition to the shows, the Planetarium offers guided tours aimed at different levels of knowledge, including tours for students of the subject, and a lively programme of scientific and popular-level lectures on astronomy. There are also special events for students on Sundays.

⑳ Museo di Storia Naturale

Corso Venezia 55. **Map** 4 E4. **Tel** 02–88 46 33 37. Ⓜ 1 Porta Venezia, Palestro. 🚊 9. **Open** 9am–5:30pm (last adm: 5pm) Tue–Sun. **Closed** Mon, 1 Jan, Easter, 1 May, 15 Aug, 25 Dec. 📷 ♿ Lecture hall, library.

The museum of Natural History was founded in 1838 with the donation of the Giuseppe de Cristoforis and Giorgio Jan collections. The building was constructed in Neo-Romanesque

Reconstruction of a dinosaur skeleton, Museo di Storia Naturale

style and with terracotta decoration in 1893 by Giovanni Ceruti. The museum has a specialist library holding more than 30,000 volumes, including sections on mineralogy and zoology. On the ground floor are the mineralogy and entomology collections, and part of the Museo Settala, which was created by a canon named Manfredo. It features a series of scientific instruments and natural history specimens of varied provenance. In the palaeontology halls there are reconstructions of dinosaurs such as the Triceratops and a large Allosaurus skeleton. The ground floor also has displays of molluscs and insects. The upper floor is reserved for reptiles, cetaceans and mammals. There are also several reconstructions of animal habitats and an area dedicated specifically to Italian fauna and protected nature reserves in Italy.

The Giardini Pubblici, a rare area of greenery in Milan

㉑ Giardini Pubblici

Corso Venezia, Via Palestro, Via Manin, Bastioni di Porta Venezia. **Map** 4 E4. Ⓜ 1 Porta Venezia, Palestro, 3 Repubblica, Turati. 🚋 1, 9, 33. 🚌 94. **Open** 6:30am–sunset daily.

The public gardens extend for about 160,000 sq m (192,000 sq yds) and form the largest city park in Milan. They were designed by Piermarini in 1786 and enlarged in 1857 by Giuseppe Balzaretto, who annexed Palazzo Dugnani and its garden. Further changes were made by Emilio Alemagna after the international exhibitions held in 1871–81.

The gardens are home to a wide range of tree species, including fir, beech, linden, elm and an ancient plane tree. In May/June, the gardens play host to Orticola, an annual plant and flower market (*see p39*).

The park is home to the Padiglione del Caffè (1863), now a nursery school, the Museo di Storia Naturale and the Planetarium. Also immersed in the gardens is the popular Bar Bianco. This Milan institution has plenty of outside seating and is open daily from 8am to 7pm.

㉒ Villa Belgiojoso – Galleria d'Arte Moderna

Via Palestro 16. **Map** 4 E4. **Tel** 02-88 44 59 57. Ⓜ 1 Palestro. 🚋 1. 🚌 61, 94. **Open** 9am–5:30pm Tue–Sun (last adm: 5pm). **Closed** 1 Jan, Easter, 15 Aug, 25 Dec. ♿ 📷 Giardini di Villa Belgiojoso Bonaparte: **Open** only to adults accompanying children. 9am–noon, 2–7pm daily (Mar, Oct: to 6pm, Nov–Feb: to 4pm). 🌐 gam-milano.com

Milan's modern art gallery is housed in a splendid Neo-Classical villa built by the Austrian architect Leopold Pollack in 1790 for Count Lodovico Barbiano di Belgioioso. It was lived in by Napoleon in 1802 and later by Marshal Radetzky. Furnishings and frescoes decorate the main floor; the top attraction here is the dining room, with a *Parnassus* by Appiani. The gallery is devoted to 19th-century art movements in Italy, from the Romanticism of Francesco Hayez and Il Piccio to Scapigliatura, and from Divisionism to Macchiaioli, with artists like Fattori and Lega.

The Padiglione di Arte Contemporanea (PAC) is located next to Villa Belgiojoso and is its contemporary art extension.

It is one of the first examples of architecture in Italy designed specifically for contemporary art, similar to the European Kunsthalle, which opened in 1954. Designed by the architect Ignazio Gardella, it is built around a central volume on three levels.

The ground-floor level boasts large windows that face the beautiful garden of Villa Reale. Temporary exhibitions are held throughout the year.

Antonio Canova's bronze of Napoleon

The Neo-Classical Villa Belgiojoso, home to the Galleria d'Arte Moderna

㉓ Corso Venezia

Formerly called Corso di Porta Orientale, this famous and popular street was named after the gate in the medieval walls corresponding to present-day Via Senato. The same name was given to the quarter, whose emblem is the lion on the column in front of the church of San Babila. Corso Venezia was lined with relatively few buildings and bordered by kitchen gardens and orchards until the mid-18th century, when the reforms carried out by Maria Theresa of Austria led to the construction of the numerous patrician palazzi that make this one of Milan's most elegant streets.

Locator Map
See Street Finder map 4

Three inner courtyards lead to the garden.

On the balustrade are statues of the *Dei Consenti* (the 12 chief Roman gods) by Pompeo Marchesi and Grazioso Rusca.

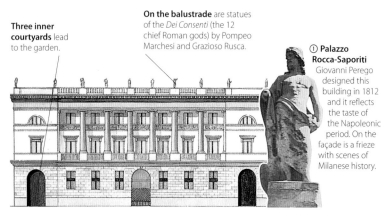

① **Palazzo Rocca-Saporiti**
Giovanni Perego designed this building in 1812 and it reflects the taste of the Napoleonic period. On the façade is a frieze with scenes of Milanese history.

② **Palazzo Castiglioni**
This palazzo was built by Giuseppe Sommaruga in 1904. There were once two female nudes on the façade (later removed), hence its name *Ca' di Ciapp* (House of Buttocks).

On the first floor is a lovely three-flight staircase and the Sala dei Pavoni.

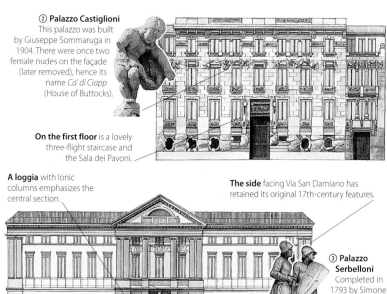

A loggia with Ionic columns emphasizes the central section.

The side facing Via San Damiano has retained its original 17th-century features.

③ **Palazzo Serbelloni**
Completed in 1793 by Simone Cantoni, this palazzo played host to Napoleon and Vittorio Emanuele.

④ ★ **Casa Fontana-Silvestri**
This rare example of a Renaissance residence in Milan was built in the late 15th century by Angelo Fontana. The windows on the façade are framed in brick and the portal by candelabrum columns.

VISITORS' CHECKLIST

Practical Information
Map 4 E4. Palazzi not open to public. San Babila: Piazza San Babila. **Tel** 02-76 00 28 77.
Open 7:30am–noon, 3:30–7pm daily. 🕐 8, 8:30 & 10:30am, 6:30pm Mon–Fri; 8 & 10:30am, 6:30pm Sat; 8, 9:30 & 11am, 12:30 & 6:30pm Sun, hols.

Transport
Ⓜ 1 Porta Venezia–Palestro–San Babila. 🚋 9. 🚌 54, 61, 94.

Bramante is thought by a number of scholars to have worked on the decoration of the façade.

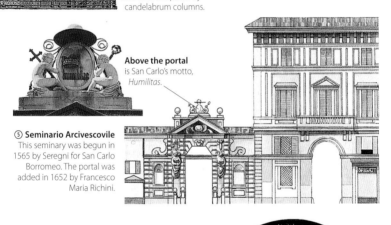

Above the portal
is San Carlo's motto, *Humilitas*.

⑤ **Seminario Arcivescovile**
This seminary was begun in 1565 by Seregni for San Carlo Borromeo. The portal was added in 1652 by Francesco Maria Richini.

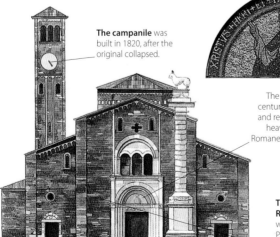

The campanile was built in 1820, after the original collapsed.

⑥ ★ **San Babila**
The church was built in the 11th century over a 4th-century basilica and rebuilt in the 1500s. The rather heavy-handed restoration of the Romanesque original began in 1853.

The present-day Neo-Romanesque façade
was designed in 1906 by Paolo Cesa Bianchi, who also built the high altar.

TWO GUIDED WALKS IN MILAN

Most visitors travel around by Metro and come away with the impression that Milan offers little more than the Gothic-spired Duomo, the famed *Last Supper* and some chillingly expensive fashion boutiques. But by strolling around at a slower pace, you can find a Milan of great art, deep history and glorious monuments. The first walk investigates the hidden heart of Milan's historic centre, from church gems to fantastical façades tucked just off busy modern thoroughfares, and from designer boutiques to the elegant townhouses of

Milan's 19th-century elite. The second walk examines the ages of Milan, from its Roman roots to Palaeochristian basilicas rich in mosaics and frescoes, and from the medieval Castello Sforzesco to Renaissance master-pieces by the likes of Bellini, Mantegna and Leonardo da Vinci. In fact, Leonardo pops up frequently on this walk in all his guises, from artist to inventor to engineer. The walk ends at the Navigli, a thriving restaurant and nightlife district based around the remnants of a canal system that the multi-talented Leonardo helped design.

CHOOSING A WALK

The Two Walks
This map shows the location of the two guided walks in relation to the main sightseeing areas of Milan *(pp16–17)*.

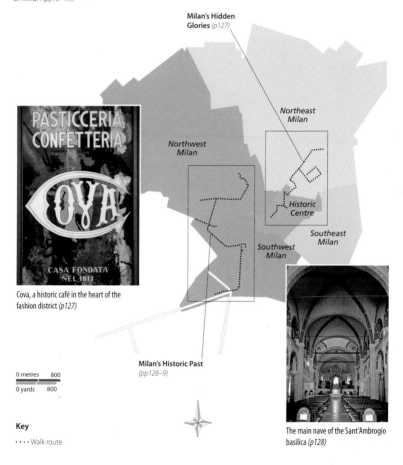

Milan's Hidden Glories *(p127)*

Northeast Milan

Northwest Milan

Historic Centre

Southeast Milan

Southwest Milan

Cova, a historic café in the heart of the fashion district *(p127)*

Milan's Historic Past *(pp128–9)*

| 0 metres | 800 |
| 0 yards | 800 |

Key

•••• Walk route

The main nave of the Sant'Ambrogio basilica *(p128)*

A 90-Minute Walk Around Milan's Hidden Glories

Milan's beauty is not immediately obvious. With a few exceptions, such as the Duomo and the Galleria, the city's glories are hidden. This walk takes in stunning Baroque façades lost amid bland buildings, and tours the fashion boutiques in the "Golden Rectangle".

Around the Duomo

Begin at the jewel-box church of Santa Maria presso San Satiro ① *(see p57)*. Encased by modern buildings it can be hard to find (it's down a short alley off Via Torino). A right down Via Speronari leads to its 10th-century bell tower. Leave the church, turn left up Via Mazzini into Piazza del Duomo ② *(see pp46–7)* and ascend to the cathedral's roof ③ *(see pp48–51)* for panoramic views. Descend and stop for a drink at the renowned Zucca in Galleria ④ *(see p185)*, which lies near the entrance to the Galleria Vittorio Emanuele II ⑤ *(see p52)*, a 19th-century shopping arcade. Stroll through its glass-roofed atrium, ensuring good luck by stomping on the testicles of the mosaic bull near the centre. Emerge at Piazza della Scala ⑥, for the splendid Teatro alla Scala opera house ⑦ *(see pp54–5)* and pay your respects to Verdi in the attached Museo Teatrale.

Cross the square and walk behind Palazzo Marino ⑧ *(see p52)* to the Counter-Reformation church of San Fedele ⑨ *(see p52)*. Head northeast along its left flank past the surreal Casa degli Omenoni ⑩ *(see p53)*. Turn left on Via Morone

at the 18th-century Palazzo Belgioioso ⑪ and turn right onto Via Manzoni ⑫ *(see p110)*, lined with grand palazzi.

The Shopping District

Admire the magnificent Grand Hotel et de Milan ⑬, where Giuseppe Verdi died in 1901, then turn right onto Via Montenapoleone, the

Key

· · · Walk route

⑦ The Theatre Museum, part of the La Scala opera house

heart of the fashion district. Versace, Gucci and Prada all have boutiques here. Continue along the road until you reach Cova ⑭ *(see p185)*, an elegant café famous for its *panettone*.

Turn left and left again onto Via della Spiga, home to chic Dolce & Gabbana ⑮. Turn left onto Via Gesù and half way down is Museo Bagatti Valsecchi ⑯ *(see p111)*, a refined town-house filled with 15th- to 17th-century furnishings. At the end of the road turn right and right

again onto Via Manzoni. Walk through Archi di Porta Nuova ⑰ *(see p111)*, a medieval gate with Roman funerary reliefs, and head to Giardini Pubblici ⑱ *(see p122)*, a welcome respite from the urban streetscape.

⑭ Cova, a Milanese must for an elegant coffee break since 1817

Tips for Walkers

Starting point: Santa Maria presso San Satiro, off Via Torino.
Length: 2.8 km (1.7 miles).
Getting there: Duomo station.
Best time for walk: Morning.
Stopping-off points: Historic cafés such as Zucca and Cova.

For keys to symbols *see back flap*

A Two-Hour Walk Around Milan's Historic Past

Milan is a city that tends to keep its history largely buried under a modern, business-orientated veneer. The following walk seeks out the remnants of Roman, medieval and Renaissance Milan while paying homage to the city's most famous adopted son, Leonardo da Vinci. The Renaissance master has left a distinctive stamp on the city. Examples of his genius are scattered all around town, from *The Last Supper* fresco to models of his inventions in the Museo della Scienza e della Tecnica, not to mention the surviving canals that were once part of a vast and intricate waterway system Leonardo helped plan.

④ Santa Maria delle Grazie, home to Leonardo's famous *Last Supper*

From the Castello Sforzesco to Leonardo's *Last Supper*

Begin at Milan's splendid 15th-century castle ① *(see pp66–9)*, which houses archaeological artifacts, paintings and sculptures. From the front gate, head towards Largo Cairoli and then turn right into Via San Giovanni sul Muro. At the junction with Via Meravigli turn right into Corso Magenta. Follow it west, and across from the Rococo Palazzo Litta ② *(see p76)*, you will see

⑦ The cloistered entrance to the basilica of Sant'Ambrogio

Tips for Walkers

Starting point: Castello Sforzesco.
Length: 4.9 km (3 miles).
Getting there: Cairoli metro station.
Best time for walk: Morning.
Stopping-off points: Not far from the Castello Sforzesco is the genteel Marchesi pastry shop *(see p184)*, or you can stop at the Art Nouveau Bar Magenta in Via Carducci *(see p184)*. The walk ends in Milan's best district for wine bars and eateries.

the Museo Archeologico ③ *(see p76)* – its cloisters preserve a bit of the city's Roman-era walls. Keep moving west on Corso Magenta to the church of Santa Maria delle Grazie ④ *(see p73)*, where you will find Leonardo's *Last Supper (see pp74–5)*. (Tickets to see this fresco should be booked at least six weeks in advance.)

Roman and Medieval Milan

Trace your steps back along Corso Magenta and turn right at Via Carducci. At the bottom of this street is the Pusterla di Sant'Ambrogio ⑤ *(see p88)*, a remnant of the medieval city gates. Turn right into Via San Vittore for the Museo della Scienza e della Tecnologia Leonardo da Vinci ⑥ *(see p90)*, which contains models of Leonardo's inventions built to the master's sketches.

Double back along Via San Vittore to visit Sant'Ambrogio ⑦ *(see pp86–9)*, a 4th-century basilica with Palaeochristian mosaics, medieval carvings, and Renaissance frescoes. Head down Via de Amicis, angling left at Piazza Resistenza Partigiana to continue along Via GG Mora ⑧. This street curves slightly since it follows the track of the interred Olona River. In ancient times this stream joined with the Nirone, Seveso and Vetra rivers at Corso di Porta Ticinese. The Vetra used to run

Leonardo-designed wooden model

south through what is now Piazza della Vetra and the Parco delle Basiliche ⑨. Head up Via Pio IV and turn left on Corso di Porta Ticinese for the church of San Lorenzo alle Colonne ⑩ *(see pp82–3)*. This magnificent 4th-century church is preceded by a set of freestanding Roman columns ⑪, probably the portico to a 2nd-century pagan temple, dismantled and moved here when the church was built.

Continue south along Corso di Porta Ticinese and go through the medieval Porta Ticinese ⑫ *(see p84)*, built as part of the city's 12th-century walls and modified in the 1860s. Keep following the road until you reach Sant'Eustorgio ⑬ *(see p92)*, a 4th-century

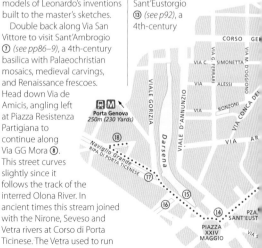

CORSO GE
VIA C. SIMONETTA
VIA M. D'OGGIONO
VIA G. FERRARI
VIALE GORIZIA
VIA ALESSI
VIALE D'ANNUNZIO
VIA RONZONI
VIA CONCA DEL
VIA AR
Porta Genova
250m (230 Yards)
Navilio Grande
RIPA DI PORTA TICINESE
Darsena
⑱
⑰
⑯
⑮
⑭
PZA.
SANT'EUST
PIAZZA
XXIV
MAGGIO
VIA S

church hiding behind an insipid 19th-century façade. Beyond the main church and behind the altar lies the Cappella Portinari, a masterpiece of early Renaissance architecture gorgeously frescoed with the story of St Peter Martyr by Vincenzo Foppa. The church houses a vast marble arch carved in the 1330s.

Along the Navigli

One more road south, past the confusingly named Porta Ticinese ⑭ (unlike its medieval namesake up the street, this

⑬ The façade of Sant'Eustorgio hides a 4th-century church

Neo-Classical pile dates from 1801–14), and you are in the Piazza XXIV Maggio. This marks the intersection of the last

basin at the confluence of the underground Olona River and two canals.

The canal closest to the square is the Naviglio Pavese ⑯, running 33 km (20.5 miles) south to the Ticino River, near Pavia. Once the busiest canal in the entire system, since 1978 it has served as a very long irrigation ditch.

To the southwest of the Darsena is the Naviglio Grande ⑰ *(see p91)*, a 50-km (31-mile) waterway connecting Milan to the Ticino since 1177. This now merely irrigates fields south of the city. Walk along its far

Key

••• Walk route

significant remnant of Milan's once-vast system of *navigli* (canals). The system was begun in the 12th century and expanded under Lodovico il Moro, who turned to Leonardo for help with the plans. At its late 19th-century peak, the system included 150 km (93 miles) of canals along which 8,300 boats hauled 350,000 tons of merchandise a year, making Milan the 13th-busiest port in Italy – impressive for a land-locked city. The canals' import-ance faded with the rise of the railways, and from the 1930s they were slowly filled in. West of Piazza XXIV Maggio stretches the main "port", the 1603 Darsena ⑮, an artificial

embankment (Alzaia Naviglio Grande) to the blind alley of Vicolo dei Lavandai ⑱, down which is a pretty miniature canal of stone washbasins covered by a tiled roof.

The Navigli has blossomed into Milan's trendiest bar and restaurant zone, packed with wine bars, trattorias, pizzerias and jazz clubs and is the pefect place for a post-walk drink or lunch. Porta Genova metro station is a short stroll from here.

⑱ The pretty Vicolo dei Lavandai

Harbour at Menaggio, Lake Como ▶

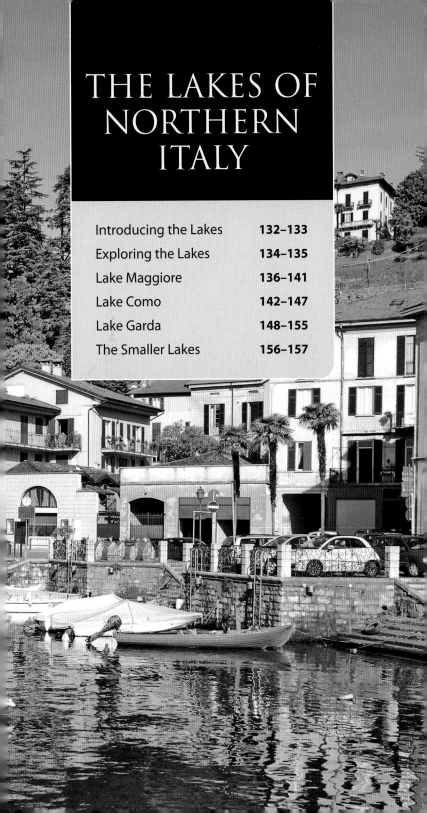

THE LAKES OF NORTHERN ITALY

THE LAKES OF NORTHERN ITALY

Appreciated by the ancient Romans for their beautiful location and mild climate, the lakes of Northern Italy – most of which are in Lombardy – are deservedly renowned for the fascinating and unique combination of magnificent scenery and historic and artistic heritage that characterizes the lakeside towns.

Besides Lake Maggiore, Lake Como and Lake Garda, there are smaller and less well-known bodies of water such as the lakes of Orta, Varese, Iseo and Idro. All these lovely lakes are the result of glaciation in the Pleistocene era, which enlarged clefts already in the terrain. The lake shores were inhabited during the prehistoric period – traces of ancient civilizations have been found almost everywhere – and for the most part were colonized by the Romans, as can be seen in the grid street plans of many towns and in the villas at Lake Garda. Churches, sanctuaries and castles were built here in the Middle Ages. In the winter the shores of the lakes can be battered by winds from Central Europe, but the climate remains quite mild thanks to the water. Typical Mediterranean vegetation can be seen everywhere: vineyards, olive trees, oleanders and palm trees. The many splendid villa gardens along the lakes' shores enhance the environment, and nature reserves have been established to protect some stretches. In the 18th century a visit to the lake region was one of the accepted stages on the Grand Tour, the trip to Europe considered essential for the education of young people of good birth. These shores were also favourites with writers, musicians and artists such as Goethe, Hesse, Klee, Toscanini, Stendhal, Byron, Hemingway and Nietzsche. The numerous vantage points, connected to the shore by funiculars, narrow-gauge trains and cable cars, offer truly spectacular views over the landscape.

The town of Menaggio, on Lake Como

◀ The Castello Scaligero on Lake Garda

Exploring the Lakes

The larger lakes offer the best facilities for visitors, with hotels, restaurants and cafés lining the lake front. The lake shores are dotted with pretty villages, castles (Sirmione sul Garda), villas and gardens such as Villa Taranto or the Vittoriale, the residence of the poet D'Annunzio at Lake Garda, as well as a number of small local museums. In summer, you may be able to participate in cultural events such as the famous Settimane Musicali di Stresa music festival at Lake Maggiore. Although the smaller lakes offer fewer facilities, they are very peaceful, unspoilt places.

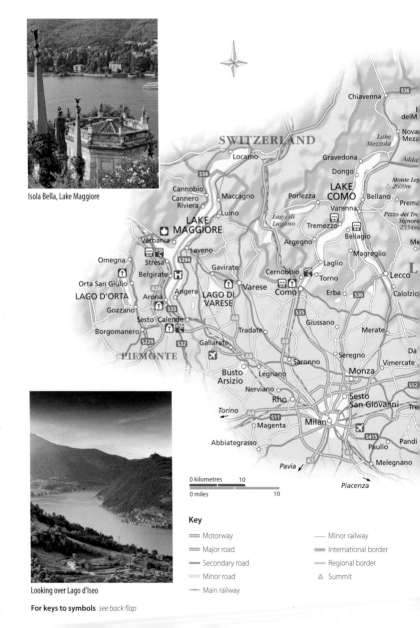

Isola Bella, Lake Maggiore

Looking over Lago d'Iseo

Key

═══ Motorway

═══ Major road

─── Secondary road

─── Minor road

▬▬ Main railway

─── Minor railway

▬▬▬ International border

▬▬▬ Regional border

△ Summit

0 kilometres 10

0 miles 10

For keys to symbols *see back flap*

The pretty, colourful harbour of the town of
Bellagio, on Lake Como

Locator Map

Getting There

The lakes of Northern Italy can be reached via Malpensa and Linate airports in Milan, Orio al Serio airport in Bergamo and Catullo airport in Verona. There are also good connections by motorway from Milan: the A8 *autostrada* goes to lakes Maggiore and Varese, the A9 to Lake Como, and the A4 to Iseo and Garda. Traffic on the major and minor roads is often heavy, so make allowances when planning. Boat services on the three major lakes are quite efficient; they go to the islands and towns around the lakeside and are an enjoyable way of getting about.

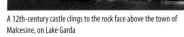

A 12th-century castle clings to the rock face above the town of
Malcesine, on Lake Garda

The Lakes

Lake Maggiore

With borders in Piedmont, Lombardy and the Ticino canton in Switzerland, Lake Maggiore, or Verbano, is the second largest lake in Italy (212 sq km, 82 sq miles) and has a maximum depth of 372 m (1,220 ft). For the most part it is fed and drained by the Ticino river, and is also fed by the Toce. The towns around the shore were embellished with churches and paintings from 1449 onwards, thanks to the wealthy Borromeo family, and with villas and gardens in the 18th–19th centuries. The opening of the Simplon pass and the introduction of ferry services (1826) helped trade to develop in the area.

Magaduno
Vira
Locarno
San Nazzaro
Ascona
Gerra-Gambarogno
Sant'Abbondio
Porto Ronco
Isola di Brissago
Brissago
Maccagno
Luin
Cannobio **8**
Gannero Riviera
Pieggio
Veltrav
Ghiffa
Intra
Verbania **7**
Isola Madre

5 ★ Isole Borromee
Of the three islands, the best known is Isola Bella, named after Isabella d'Adda, wife of Charles III Borromeo.

The two castles of Malpaga, built in the 13th–14th century on two islets at the foot of Mount Carza, belonged to the Mazzardites, the pirates who raided the lake.

4 Stresa
This old fishermen's village began to become a tourist attraction thanks to the descriptions of famous writers such as Stendhal, Byron and Dickens.

★ Villa Taranto
One of Italy's best-known botanic gardens was founded here in 1931 by an Englishman called McEacharn in an area of about 16 ha (40 acres). Many examples of species of plants from all over the world, including *Victoria amazonica*, are grown here (*see p140*).

⓫ ★ Santa Caterina del Sasso Ballaro
Perched on a rocky spur near Laveno, this monastery is one of the most enchanting sights on Lake Maggiore. It was built by a local merchant in the 12th century to fulfil a vow made when he was saved from a storm.

⓬ ★ Rocca di Angera
The imposing medieval fortress of the Borromeo family has 14th- and 15th-century frescoes. It now houses the Doll Museum.

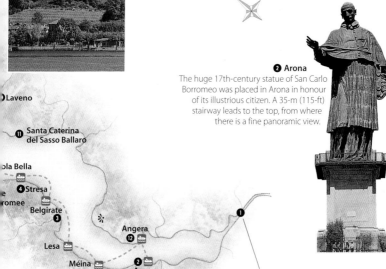

❷ Arona
The huge 17th-century statue of San Carlo Borromeo was placed in Arona in honour of its illustrious citizen. A 35-m (115-ft) stairway leads to the top, from where there is a fine panoramic view.

Sesto Calende The town museum in Piazza Mazzini contains objects found in nearby Bronze Age sites.

VISITORS' CHECKLIST

Practical Information
ℹ Local tourist bureau.
ⓦ navlaghi.it

Transport
🚆 FS Stazione Centrale (89 20 21); Ferrovie Nord Milano Cadorna Station (800 500 005).
🚌 SAFduemila (0323-55 21 72); Autolinee Varesine (0332-73 11 10).
⛴ Navigazione Lago Maggiore (800-55 18 01).

Sights at a Glance

❶ Sesto Calende
❷ Arona
❸ Lesa and Belgirate
❹ Stresa
❺ Isole Borromee
❻ Baveno
❼ Verbania
❽ Cannobio
❾ Luino
❿ Laveno
⓫ Santa Caterina del Sasso Ballaro
⓬ Rocca di Angera

Key

-- Ferry routes

0 kilometres   2
0 miles   2

For keys to symbols *see back flap*

Boats anchored in a harbour in Sesto Calende

❶ Sesto Calende

Varese. 10,974. IAT (mid-Mar–Oct only), Viale Italia 3 (0331-92 33 29). **prosestocalende.it**

The town at the southern tip of Lake Maggiore marks the end of two motorways leading to the Verbano region. The road to Arona goes to **San Donato**, known as "La Badia" or abbey, a 9th-century basilica rebuilt in the 11th–12th century. The capitals have sculpted figures of animals and humans. There are frescoes from the 15th and 16th centuries in the nave and from the 18th century in the crypt. South of Sesto, near Golasecca, are Iron Age tombs (9th–5th century BC), part of the civilization named after the place. State road 33 to Arona will take you to the **Lagoni di Mercurago Regional Park**, with varied bird species and the remains of ancient villages.

Abbazia San Donato
Via San Donato 6. **Tel** 0331-92 42 71. **Open** 8am–7pm daily.

Lagoni di Mercurago Regional Park
Via Gattico 6, Mercurago. **Tel** 0322-24 02 39. **parchilagomaggiore.it**

❷ Arona

Novara. 15,000. Largo Duca d'Aosta (0322-24 36 01). antiques, 1st Sun of month (Feb–Nov).

Arona once occupied an important trading position between Milan and the lake and mountain regions of Northern Italy. Because of its strategic location, a Rocca or fortress (the twin of the one at Angera; *see p141*), was built here; it was enlarged by the Borromeo and dismantled by Napoleon. Corso Marconi has a view of the Rocca at Angera, and leads to Piazza del Popolo. Here are the 15th-century Casa del Podestà, with an arched portico, and the 16th-century Madonna di Piazza church. Santi Martiri has 15th-century paintings by Bergognone, and Santa Maria Nascente has an altarpiece by Gaudenzio Ferrari (1511).

Just north of the centre is a massive **statue of San Carlo**. It was designed by Cerano in 1614 and finished in 1697. In the church of San Carlo there is a reconstruction of the room where San Carlo was born.

Villa Ponti is a mid-18th-century villa with Baroque and Art Deco decoration. It stands in a garden with a nymphaeum and a fountain.

Statue of San Carlo
Piazza San Carlo.
Tel 0322-24 96 69.
Open Mar: 9am–12:30pm, 2–4:30pm Sat & Sun; Apr–Sep: 9am–12:30pm, 2–6:30pm daily; Oct: 9am–12:30pm, 2–6:30pm Sat & Sun; Nov & Dec: 9am–12:30pm, 2–4:30pm Sat & Sun except 1 Nov, 8, 25 & 26 Dec. Children under eight are not allowed inside the statue. **Closed** Jan, Feb.

Villa Ponti
Via San Carlo 63.
Tel 0322-446 29.
Closed to the public.

❸ Lesa and Belgirate

Lesa (Novara). 2,400. Belgirate (Verbania). 600. IAT, Via Portici, Lesa (0322-77 20 78).

Lesa lies on a particularly charming stretch of the lake between Arona and Stresa, and has been popular as a resort for noble Lombard families since the 18th century. The **Museo Manzoniano di Villa Stampa** has mementos of author Alessandro Manzoni, who was a guest here. The hamlet of Villa boasts the Romanesque church of San Sebastiano.

Once past Lesa, continue to Belgirate and its charming historic centre, whose houses have porticoes and porches. This village also commands a panoramic view of the lake. It was a haunt of philosopher Antonio Rosmini and poet Guido Gozzano.

On the hills 4 km (2 miles) from Belgirate is the13th-century **Castello Visconteo**, decorated with frescoes of the period. Nearby is the Romanesque church of San Michele, with a leaning bell tower.

Museo Manzoniano di Villa Stampa
Via alla Fontana 18, Lesa. **Tel** 0322-764 21. **Open** Aug only: 10am–noon Thu, 5–9pm Sat & Sun (by appt only).

Castello Visconteo
Via Visconti 1, Massino Visconti. **Tel** 329-475 37 83 **Open** by arrangement only.

The square in Arona with the huge statue of San Carlo Borromeo

❹ Stresa

Verbania. 🚠 5,200. ℹ️ IAT, Piazza
Marconi 16 (0323-301 50 or 0323-31
308). 🌐 **stresaturismo.it**

The origins of medieval Strixia,
dating from before 1000, are
partially hidden by the palazzi
and villas built for the aristocracy in the late 19th–early
20th century, partly because
of the opening of an electric
rack-railway (the first in Italy),
which goes to the top of
Mount Mottarone. The town is
now a centre for conferences
and tour groups, attracted
by the easy access to the
Borromean islands. On the
lakefront are 19th-century
villas, Sant'Ambrogio (18th
century) and the **Villa Ducale**
(1770), with mementos of
19th-century philosopher
Antonio Rosmini, who died
here (the villa is now the
Rosmini Study Centre). Mount
Mottarone (1,491 m, 4,890 ft),
a ski resort, has a view from
the Alps to the plain.

🏛️ **Villa Ducale Centro di
Studi Rosminiani**
Corso Umberto I 15. **Tel** 0323-
300 91. **Open** 9–11:45am,
3–5:45pm Mon–Fri.

🌳 **Parco di Villa
Pallavicino**
State road 33.
Tel 0323-324 07.
Open mid-Mar–Oct:
9am–5pm Mon–Fri. 🚻
♿ 🚼 🅿️ 🌐 **parcozoo
pallavicino.it**

This villa near Stresa is famous
for its gardens. The luxuriant
English garden has centuries-old
plants as well as exotic creatures
such as llamas and pelicans.

Borromeo Palace garden on Isola Bella, overlooking Lake Maggiore

❺ Isole Borromee

Verbania. 🚢 from Arona, Laveno,
Stresa, Baveno, Pallanza. To Isola
Madre and Isola Bella: tel. 0322-23
32 00 or 800 55 18 01. **Open** late
Mar–mid-Oct: 9am–5:30pm daily.
Closed Nov–Mar. 🎫 🅿️ by appt. ♿
🌐 **borromeoturismo.it**

These three islands, which can
be reached easily from Stresa,
became famous thanks to the
Borromeo family, who built
elegant palazzi and magnificent
gardens there. The loveliest
is **Isola Bella**, an old fishing
village transformed
from 1632 to
1671 by the
Borromeo
family into a
lovely complex
consisting of a
Baroque palazzo and
a terraced Italian-
style garden with rare plants.
Inside are a music room (where
Mussolini met British and
French officials in 1935), the Sala
di Napoleone (where Napoleon

A fountain
at Villa Pallavicino

stayed in 1797), a ballroom,
throne room and bedroom with
17th-century decoration and
furnishings and paintings by
Carracci, Cerano and Tiepolo.
The six grottoes are decorated
with shells and pebbles.

Isola Madre, the largest
island, boasts an 18th-century
villa with a garden where white
peacocks roam freely; it has
rare plants as well as azaleas,
rhododendrons and camellias.
The villa has period furnishings
and a collection of 18th- and
19th-century puppet theatres.

Tiny **Isola dei Pescatori**, once
the leading fishing village, has
retained its quaint atmosphere
and architecture.

❻ Baveno

Verbania. 🚠 5,000. ℹ️ IAT, Piazza
della Chiesa 8 (0323-92 46 32).

Made famous by its pink granite
quarries, which among other
things supplied the stone for
the Galleria Vittorio Emanuele II
in Milan (see p52), Baveno
became a fashionable resort
in the mid-19th century, entertaining guests such as Queen
Victoria, who stayed in the
Villa Clara (now Villa Branca) in
1879. A major attraction is Santi
Gervasio e Protasio, with its 12th-
century facade and 15th-century
octagonal baptistery with
Renaissance frescoes. Going
towards Verbania, take the
turn-off for San Giovanni at
Montorfano, one of the loveliest
churches in the area.

The garden at Villa Pallavicino, the home of many species of animals

❼ Verbania

🏠 31,000. **ℹ** IAT, Corso Zanitello 6–8 (0323-55 66 69); Pro Loco, Viale delle Magnolie 1 (0323-55 76 76). 🏛 antiques, Jul & Aug: 8pm–midnight Fri.

Pallanza and Intra were merged in 1939 to create the town of Verbania (capital of the Verbano-Cusio-Ossola province established in 1992). The former, facing the Borromeo gulf, is the seat of the municipal government and has retained its medieval aspect and atmosphere. The latter dominates the promontory of Castagnola and has a Baroque and Neo-Classical flavour. Intra, the main port of call on the lake and one of its major industrial centres, was the regional leader in textile manufacturing in the 18th century. Pallanza was the only town in Lake Maggiore not under Borromeo dominion, and it has some of the most important monuments. These include Romanesque Santo Stefano, the parish church of San Leonardo and 18th-century Palazzo Viani Dugnani, home to the **Museo del Paesaggio**, which has an exhibit of 16th–20th-century landscape paintings, sculpture by Arturo Martini and Giulio Branca and a plaster-cast gallery. Isolino di San Giovanni was a favourite refuge of Arturo Toscanini. In the environs is 16th-century Madonna di Campagna, with

Effigy of McEacharn, who created the Villa Taranto gardens

a small Romanesque campanile and frescoes by Gerolamo Lanino and Camillo Procaccini (16th–17th centuries).

🏛 Museo del Paesaggio

Via Ruga 44. **Tel** 0323-55 66 21. **Open** Apr–Oct: 10am–noon, 3:30–6:30pm Tue–Sun.

Environs
🌳 Giardini di Villa Taranto

Via Vittorio Veneto, Pallanza. **Tel** 0323-55 66 67. **Open** mid-Mar–Oct: 8:30am–6:30pm (to 5pm Oct). 🅿 🚤 ♿ 🏪

In 1931 a Scottish captain named Neil McEacharn created one of the outstanding botanical gardens in Europe on the Castagnola promontory, using the lake water for irrigation. He is buried in the small park church. McEacharn exploited the valley terrain, creating terraced gardens, a winter garden and a marsh garden among small falls and water lily ponds. He donated the Villa Taranto garden to the Italian state and it was opened to the public in 1952. It has a range of exotic plants, including *Victoria amazonica* in the glasshouses. Azaleas, dahlias and rhododendrons (over 300 varieties) look wonderful in full flower.

❽ Cannobio

Verbania. 🏠 5,300. **ℹ** IAT, Via Antonio Giovanola 25 (0323-712 12). 🌐 procannobio.it

This pleasant tourist resort is the last Italian town on the Piedmontese side of the lake. It still retains its old medieval character, exemplified in the Palazzo della Ragione or Palazzo Parrasio, the town hall with a 12th-century Commune Tower. The Santuario della Pietà, which was rebuilt by San Carlo Borromeo in 1583, contains a fine altarpiece by Gaudenzio Ferrari. In nearby Val Cannobina, the Orrido di Sant'Anna is worth

Cannobio, on the Piedmontese side of the lake

a visit. This deep gorge was carved out of the rock by the Cannobino river.

❾ Luino

Varese. 🏠 14,400. **ℹ** IAT, Via Chiara 1 (0332-53 00 19).

Luino, which occupies a cove on the eastern side of the lake, is a town dating from ancient Roman times. Its name may have derived from the Luina torrent or perhaps from the local term *luina* (landslide). In the Middle Ages it was contested by the leading Como and Milanese families and became famous when Garibaldi landed here in 1848 with a group of volunteers and routed an entire Austrian detachment.

The large railway station (1882) shows how important the town was when it linked Italy with Central Europe, a position that declined when railway traffic shifted to Chiasso. Luino's market was founded by an edict of Charles V in 1541 and is still a tourist attraction. San Pietro in Campagna has frescoes by Bernardino Luini and a lovely Romanesque bell tower; the oratory of the Chiesa del Carmine dates back to 1477. A must is a visit to the town's symbol, the 17th-century oratory of San Giuseppe.

The harbour in Laveno, once an Austrian naval base

⓾ Laveno

Varese. 🗺 8,800. 🛈 IAT, Piazza Italia 2 (0332-66 87 85).

The name of this town goes back to Titus Labienus, the Roman general who was Caesar's legate in Cisalpine Gaul. Laveno was important strategically because of its port, the only natural harbour on Lake Maggiore. During their period of rule, the Austrians moored the gunboats controlling the lake here. Today the town is the main ferry point for the Piedmontese shores. The Ferrovie Nord railway linked Laveno to Varese and Milan, fostering commercial development, especially in the field of ceramics with the founding of well-known Società Ceramica Italiana Richard-Ginori, in 1856. In the town centre, the garden in the Villa Frua (18th century) is worth visiting. A cable car goes up to Sasso del Ferro, at 1,062 m (3,483 ft), behind Laveno with fine views of the lake, Monte Mottarone and Monte Rosa.

⓫ Santa Caterina del Sasso Ballaro

Via Santa Caterina 13, Leggiuno. **Tel** 0332-64 71 72. **Open** timings vary, call ahead or check website for details. 🕐 4:30pm hols. 📷
🌐 santacaterinadelsasso.com

To get to this small monastery perched on a steep rock 18 m (59 ft) above the lake, you can either climb the 240 steps near Leggiuno or take the boat and enjoy the lovely views. The place was founded in the mid-12th century by a local merchant. The Dominicans arrived in 1230 and after numerous changes in fortune have since returned. Over the centuries the original building was enlarged and rebuilt, as can be seen by the different architectural styles. The chapter at the entrance has important 14th–15th-century frescoes, including a *Crucifixion with Armigers*. In the second portico the 17th-century fresco, only partly preserved, represents a *Dance of Death*. The frescoes inside the church were executed in the 16th century, and the *Madonna and Child with Saints* on the high altar dates from 1612. By the entrance porticoes there is a large wine press made in 1759.

14th–15th-century frescoes, Rocca di Angera

⓬ Rocca di Angera

Fortress and museum: Via Rocca, Angera. **Tel** 0331-93 13 00. **Open** Apr–Oct: 9am–5:30pm daily. 🚫 ♿ 📷 🚭

A majestic fortress, probably built over the ruins of an ancient Roman fortification, the Rocca once belonged to the archbishops of Milan. In the 13th century it was taken over by the Visconti family and in 1449 was granted as a fief to the Borromeo family, who still own it. The Visconti building has single and double lancet windows and partly lies against the earlier castle tower. The frescoes in the halls are well worth a look, especially those in the Salone Gotico, with a cycle of the *Battles of Ottone Visconti against the Torriani* (14th century). The vaults in this hall are decorated with the Visconti coat of arms, while those in the other rooms have geometric patterns and signs of the Zodiac. The Borromeo wing has frescoes removed from Palazzo Borromeo in Milan in 1946, with *Aesop's Fables* by the school of Michelino da Besozzo (15th century). The Rocca is used for art shows and is also home to the **Museo della Bambola** (Doll Museum) in the Visconti wing, one of the best of its kind in Europe, created with the collection of Princess Bona Borromeo. Besides dolls and doll's houses, it contains books, games and children's clothing.

Santa Caterina del Sasso Ballaro, built on a cliff overlooking the lake

…omo

… is also known as Lario, is the third largest
in Italy and the deepest (410 m, 1,345 ft). It is shaped like
a sprawling upside-down Y, with the arms of Como, Lecco
and Colico. The Como shore is the most developed, with
numerous restaurants and hotels, as well as a scenic road
that follows the ancient Strada Regina, lined with elegant
villas and aristocratic gardens. The Lecco area has more
stark scenery and small coves. You may spot the typical
"Lucia" boats, named after the heroine in Manzoni's *The
Betrothed*, which was partly set here.

⓬ ★ Bellagio
Its position at the junction of the
arms of the lake and the spectacular
view from the Spartivento point
make this one of the most popular
spots on Lake Como.

The bell tower on
Santa Maria Maddalena
at Ossuccio is one of
the symbols of the lake.

❶ ★ Como
Construction of Como's Duomo began
in 1396 and ended in 1740 with the
huge dome. Next to it is the elegant
13th-century Broletto, the old town hall.

Menaggio

Sala
Comacina   Lenno   Cadena
                      Tremezzo
Isola   ❹   ❺
Comacina ❸

Argegno

Lake Como

Lezzeno

0 kilometres   5

0 miles   5

Nesso

Careno

Torrigia

Ùrio

Moltrasio

Pognana
Lario
❸
Torno

Cernobbio ❷

Belvio

Travernola

Como ❶   Brunate

Key

– – Ferry routes

❷ Cernobbio
The 16th-century Villa d'Este
in Cernobbio, now a famous
hotel, is surrounded by
beautiful landscaped
gardens with many fountains.

❼ Gravedona

Santa Maria del Tiglio in Gravedona is the most famous Lombard Romanesque construction in the Alto Lario region. Its main features are the layers of black and white stone and the unusual octagonal bell tower set into the façade.

VISITORS' CHECKLIST

Practical Information
ℹ️ Local information bureaux.
🌐 navlaghi.it

Transport
🚆 FS: Milan–Chiasso line (89 20 21); Ferrovie Nord Milano: (031-30 48 00 or 800 500 005). 🚌 ASF Autolinee, Piazza Matteotti, Como (031-24 72 47). ⛴ Navigazione Lago di Como (800-55 18 01 (freefone) or 031-57 92 11).

Lake Mezzola, separated from the Lario region by silt from the Adda river, is a nature reserve inhabited by grey herons.

The **"crotti"** are typical mountain caves in the upper Lario region, used as wine cellars since the 19th century.

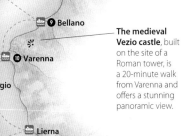

The medieval **Vezio castle**, built on the site of a Roman tower, is a 20-minute walk from Varenna and offers a stunning panoramic view.

❿ Varenna

Some of the paths in this village, one of the best preserved on the lake, consist of steps and raised boardwalks perched over the water.

❺ ★ Tremezzo

The Villa Carlotta in Tremezzo was a wedding gift for Carlotta of Prussia (1843). Inside there is a copy of Canova's *Cupid and Psyche*.

Sights at a Glance

❶ Como
❷ Cernobbio
❸ Isola Comacina
❹ Lenno
❺ Tremezzo
❻ Menaggio
❼ Gravedona
❽ Abbazia di Piona
❾ Bellano
❿ Varenna
⓫ Lecco
⓬ Bellagio
⓭ Torno

For keys to symbols *see back flap*

❶ Como

🏔 85,200. 𝑖 IAT, Piazza Cavour 17 (031-26 97 12). 🅦 lakecomo.org

Comum was founded by the Romans in 196 BC and in the 12th century fought against Milan as an ally of Barbarossa, who built the medieval walls. In 1335 Como came under Visconti rule and in 1451 under Sforza rule. The town shared Milan's fate under Spanish and Austrian domination, becoming part of the Kingdom of Italy in 1859.

Como's many Romanesque churches include the 12th-century San Fedele and the jewel of the Comacine masters, 11th-century Lombard–Romanesque Sant'Abbondio.

The **Duomo**, begun in 1396, is dominated by Filippo Juvarra's Baroque dome. The sculpture on the Gothic façade and the Porta della Rana door were executed by Tommaso and Jacopo Rodari (c.1500). The nave and side altars are decorated with 16th-century tapestries and canvases by Ferrari and Luini. Next to the Duomo is the Romanesque-Gothic Broletto (1215).

The **Tempio Voltiano** (1927) contains relics of the physicist Alessandro Volta from Como, who gave his name to "voltage". The Casa del Fascio (1936) exemplifies Italian Rationalist architecture. **Villa Olmo**,

Piazza del Duomo in Como, the birthplace of Pliny the Elder

designed by Simone Cantoni in 1797, has frescoed rooms and a park. A funicular goes up to **Brunate**, with spectacular views of Como and popular hiking trails.

🏛 **Duomo**
Piazza Duomo. **Tel** 031-26 52 44.
Open 7:30am–7:30pm daily.

🏛 **Tempio Voltiano**
Viale Marconi. **Tel** 031-57 47 05.
Open 10am–6pm Tue–Sun. 🅿

🏛 **Villa Olmo**
Via Cantoni 1. **Tel** 031-57 19 79.
Open 10am–8pm Tue–Fri, 10am–10pm Sat & Sun (times may vary in the summer months). **Closed** hols. 🅿

❷ Cernobbio

Como. 🏔 7,000. 𝑖 Via Regina 33b (031-51 01 98) (open Apr–Sep); Piazza Cavour 17, Como (031-26 97 12).

Cernobbio marks the beginning of a series of splendid villas that have made the western side of the lake famous. **Villa d'Este**, built by Pellegrino Tibaldi in 1570 for the Gallio family, became a luxury hotel in 1873, frequented by princes and actors. The rooms have period furnishings and are used for conferences. The villa stands in an Italianate garden with a nympheum. The 18th-century

The Villa d'Este in Cernobbio, once host to the Duke of Windsor and Mrs Simpson

Villa Erba (now a conference centre) is known for its interior (visits by request): the Salone da Ballo, chapel and Sala delle Nozze, decorated by architect Giocondo Albertolli, are lovely.

🏨 **Hotel Villa d'Este**
Via Regina 40. **Tel** 031-34 81.
Closed Nov–Mar.

🏨 **Villa Erba**
Largo Visconti 4. **Tel** 031-34 91. **Closed** to the public. The Luchino Visconti rooms can be booked for group visits.

❸ Isola Comacina

Como. 𝑖 IAT, Piazza Cavour 17, Como (031-26 97 12). 🚌 (as far as Sala Comacina, then by boat).

The only island on Lake Como has been inhabited since Roman times. It was fortified by the Byzantines and enjoyed a

From Mulberry to Silk

Como produces about 80 per cent of Europe's silk. Silk worms were imported in the 14th century and production thrived in the 17th century with the large-scale cultivation of mulberries, the worms' food. Silk thread was woven and sent on the "silk route" in Austria and Bavaria. Competition from Chinese silk now forces Como to concentrate on quality silk, as shown in the Museo della Seta (Silk Museum) in Como.

Cocoons

period of splendour in the Middle Ages. The people of Como conquered the fortress in 1169 and destroyed the seven churches on the island. The ruins, along with those of a mosaic-decorated baptistery, were found after World War II and are now being studied.

Sala Comacina, where boats depart for the island, has an 18th-century church with a fresco by Carlo Carloni, and the villa of Cesare Beccaria, where Manzoni was a guest.

❹ Lenno

Como. 1,800. IAT, Piazza Cavour 17, Como (031-26 97 12).

This town is famous for the **Villa del Balbianello**, built by Cardinal Durini in the 17th century onto a 16th-century building attributed to Pellegrini. The magnificent garden has a loggia with a view of Isola Comacina on one side and the Tremezzina bay on the other. Access to the villa is by boat from Sala Comacina.

Also worth a visit are the octagonal baptistery and church of Santo Stefano, built in the 11th century over a Roman building and decorated with frescoes by Luini. Above the town is the Cistercian abbey of Acquafredda, rebuilt in the 17th century, with frescoes by Fiammenghino. At nearby Giulino di Mezzegra, the Fascist dictator Benito Mussolini and his mistress Claretta Petacci were executed on 28 April 1945.

Villa Carlotta, built in the 18th century by Marchese Giorgio Clerici

🏛 Villa del Balbianello
Via Comoedia 5, Lenno. **Tel** 0344-561 10 (FAI). Garden: **Open** mid-Mar–mid-Nov: 10am–6pm Tue, Thu–Sun. Villa: **Open** by appt only.

❺ Tremezzo

Como. 1,300. IAT, Via Regina 3 (0344-404 93) (open Apr–Sep); Piazza Cavour 17, Como (031-26 97 12).

This lakeside town is a major tourist resort and home to the 18th-century **Villa Carlotta**. The residence, surrounded by a terraced garden with landscaped staircases, was converted in the 1800s into a Neo-Classical villa. It houses paintings by Hayez, furniture by Maggiolini and sculpture pieces by Canova, including a copy of *Cupid and Psyche* and *Terpsichore*. Among the rooms decorated with stuccowork is one with Appiani's frescoes

taken from the Palazzo Reale in Milan. The villa is famous for its garden, with over 150 species of rhododendrons and azaleas.

🏛 Villa Carlotta
Via Regina 2b. **Tel** 0344-404 05. **Open** timings vary, call ahead or check website for details. 📷 🌐 villacarlotta.it

❻ Menaggio

Como. 3,200. IAT, Piazza Garibaldi 8 (0344-329 24). 🌐 menaggio.com

The name Menaggio supposedly derives from two Indo-European words: *men* (mountain) and *uigg* (water), referring to the mouth of the Sanagra river on which the town lies. Menaggio is the leading commercial centre in the upper Lario region and a popular tourist resort. It is dominated by the ruins of a castle and has preserved some of its medieval layout. Of note are the parish church of Santo Stefano, the Baroque architecture of which conceals its Romanesque origin and 17th-century San Carlo, with a fine painting by Giuseppe Vermiglio (1625). The lakeside promenade, with arcaded houses and villas, is a must-see. Past Menaggio, at Loveno, is the Neo-Classical Milyus-Vigoni villa with family portraits by Francesco Hayez. Around it is a lovely park, designed by Balzaretto in 1840.

Menaggio, a lakeside town especially popular with British visitors

Palazzo Gallio, designed by architect Pellegrino Tibaldi in 1583

❼ Gravedona

Como. 2,800. Piazza Trieste (0344-850 05); IAT, Piazza Cavour 17, Como (031-26 97 12).

A fortified town of some importance in Roman times, Gravedona was destroyed by the people of Como in the 13th century because it was allied with Milan. It later became capital of the small Tre Pievi republic. The town then declined and was ceded to Cardinal Tolomeo Gallio, who in 1583 asked Tibaldi to build Palazzo Gallio. Gravedona is known for the church of **Santa Maria del Tiglio** (12th century). The aisled nave with tall galleries houses a 12th-century wooden crucifix, a floor mosaic dating from the 6th century and various 12th–14th-century frescoes. Santi Gusmeo e Matteo was frescoed by Fiammenghino, while Santa Maria delle Grazie (1467) contains 16th-century frescoes. Nearby Dongo is an ancient village known for the Falck steelworks, responsible for building the metal parts of the *Italia* and *Norge* airships. Above Gravedona, at Peglio, is the Sant'Eusebio complex, with fine 17th-century frescoes in the church. The Spanish fort in the outskirts was built in 1604 to guard the Adda river plain.

⬆ Santa Maria del Tiglio
Piazza XI Febbraio. **Tel** 0344-852 61. **Open** 8:30am–5pm winter (till 7pm summer).

❽ Abbazia di Piona

Via Santa Maria di Piona 1, Colico. **Tel** 0341-94 03 31. **Open** 8:30am–noon, 2–6pm daily.

A promontory on the north-eastern shore of the lake conceals this extraordinary abbey built by Cluniac monks in the 11th century. The exterior of Romanesque San Nicolao is adorned with small arches and pilasters. The bell tower dates from 1700 and the cloister (1252–7) has sculpted capitals with fantastic figures. There are 13th-century frescoes here as well as in the apse.

❾ Bellano

Lecco. 3,400. IAT, Via Nazario Sauro 6, Lecco (0341-29 57 20).

In the middle ages Bellano was the summer residence of Milanese bishops and it has preserved its medieval character. Among houses with wrought-iron coats of arms is the church of Santi Nazaro, Celso e Giorgio, the work of Campionese masters (14th century). Santa Marta houses a *Pietà* executed in 1518. However, the main appeal of Bellano is the **Orrido**, a deep gorge created by the Pioverna torrent.

Orrido
Tel 0341-82 11 24. **Open** Apr–Jun & Sep: 10am–1pm, 2:30–7pm daily; Jul–Aug: 10am–7pm daily; Oct–Nov & Mar: 10am–12:30pm, 2:30–5pm Sat & Sun; Dec–Feb: 2–5pm Sat & Sun.

❿ Varenna

Lecco. 800. Pro Loco (Aug only), Via IV Novembre 3 (0341-83 03 67).

This splendid village of Roman origin, with a perfectly intact medieval layout, was a haven for the inhabitants of Isola Comacina when the citizens of Como burned the island (1169). The 14th-century church of San Giorgio has an altarpiece by Pietro Brentani (1467), while Santa Marta houses the parish art gallery. Varenna is famous for **Villa Cipressi**, with its terraced garden, and **Villa Monastero**, built over a Cistercian monastery. All around the town were quarries for the black Varenna marble used in the Milan Duomo *(see pp48–51)*. Since 1921 Mandello del Lario has housed the **Moto Guzzi factory**, with a Motorcycle Museum.

Villa Cipressi
Via IV Novembre 18. **Tel** 0341-83 01 13. **Open** (garden) Mar–Oct: 9am–6pm daily. **Closed** Nov–Feb.

Villa Monastero
Via Polvani 2. **Tel** 0341-29 54 50. **Open** Villa: Mar–July & Sep: 9:30am–7pm Fri–Sun & hols; Aug: 9:30am–7pm daily. Garden: May–Oct: 9:30am–7pm daily (check website as times may vary). **Closed** Nov–Feb. villamonastero.eu

The exterior of Villa Cipressi, overlooking Lake Como

🏛 **Museo Moto Guzzi
della Motocicletta**
Via Parodi 57, Mandello del Lario.
Tel 0341-70 92 37. **Open** 3–4pm Mon–
Fri. **Closed** hols. 🅦 **motoguzzi.it**

⓫ Lecco

🏠 46,000. 🛈 IAT, Via Nazario Sauro 6
(0341-29 57 20). 🅦 **aptlecco.com**

Lecco lies on the southern tip
of the arm of the lake of the
same name. It was inhabited in
prehistoric times and fortified
in the 6th century AD. In the
1300s it was taken over by
Azzone Visconti, who built
the Ponte Vecchio.

Manzoni set his novel
I Promessi Sposi (The Betrothed)
here. Mementos of his life
can be found in his childhood
home, the **Casa Natale di
Manzoni** at Caleotto, which also
houses the Galleria Comunale
d'Arte. In the centre are the
Teatro della Società (1844) and
San Nicolò, whose baptistery
chapel has 14th–15th-century
frescoes. The **Museo di Storia
Naturale** in the 18th-century
Palazzo Belgioioso is also of
interest. Sites described by
Manzoni in his novel have been
identified, including the castle
of the Unnamed at Vercurago,
and Lucia's home at Olate.
Near Civate is Romanesque
San Pietro al Monte (12th
century), with frescoes and
reliefs depicting the Passion.
A turn-off on the road to
Bellagio leads to the Madonna
del Ghisallo sanctuary.

The Italian writer Manzoni, author of
The Betrothed

A drawing room in Villa Serbelloni overlooking the lake

🏛 **Casa Natale di Manzoni**
Via Guanella 1. **Tel** 0341-48 12 47. **Open**
9:30am–5:30pm Tue–Sun. 🐾 ♿

🏛 **Palazzo Belgioioso and
Museo di Storia Naturale**
Corso Matteotti 32. **Tel** 0341-48
12 48. **Open** 9:30am–2pm Tue–
Sun. **Closed** 1 Jan, Easter, 15
Aug, 1 May, 25 & 26 Dec. ♿

⛪ **San Pietro al Monte:**
Civate. **Tel** 0341-55 07 11.
Open call ahead for
opening times.
🅦 **amicidisanpietro.it**

⓬ Bellagio

Como. 🏠 3,050.
🛈 Piazza Mazzini (031-
95 02 04). 🅦 **bellago
lakecomo.com**

Known since antiquity for its fine
climate and scenery, Bellagio
still has its medieval layout, with
stepped alleyways. It became
the site of splendid noble villas
in the 1700s and then became a
famous resort town in the 19th
century. Among the attractive
residences, the loveliest are **Villa
Serbelloni** and **Villa Melzi d'Eril**.
In 1870 the former became a
hotel that numbered Winston
Churchill and J F Kennedy
among its guests. The Neo-
Classical Villa Melzi was built in
1810 by Giocondo Albertolli. The
interior is not open to the public,
but the Museo Archeologico, the
chapel and the gardens are. Near
the town are the 18th-century

Trivulzio and Trotti villas. Do not
miss the 12th-century San Giacomo, with its pulpit decorated
with symbols of
the Evangelists.

🏛 **Villa Serbelloni**
Piazza della Chiesa. **Tel** 031-
95 15 55. **Open** for guided
visits only, mid-Mar–mid-
Nov: 11am and 3:30pm
Tue–Sun. 🐾 🔲 for
groups of up to 30 people
(book ahead).

🏛 **Villa Melzi d'Eril**
Lungolario
Marconi.
Tel 339 45 73 838.
Open 9:30am–
6:30pm end Mar–Oct. 🐾

One of the statues at
Villa Melzi d'Eril

⓭ Torno

Como. 🏠 1,200. 🛈 IAT, Piazza
Cavour 17, Como (031-26 97 12).

The village of Torno boasts
the churches of Santa Tecla,
which has a beautiful marble
portal dating from 1480, and
the 14th-century San Giovanni,
with its remarkable Renaissance
door. However, Torno is best
known for the Villa Pliniana,
built in 1573 (and attributed to
Tibaldi) for Count Anguissola,
the governor of Como.
The villa is surrounded by a
park and stands right by the
lake. The writers Foscolo,
Stendhal and Byron, and
composer Rossini have all
been guests here.

Lake Garda

Italy's largest lake was created by glaciation. The scenery is varied, with steep, rugged cliffs at the northern end and softer hills southwards, where the basin widens and Mediterranean flora prevails. Over the centuries the praises of Lake Garda have been sung by such greats as Catullus, Dante and Goethe, and today it caters for luxury holidays and tour groups alike. Garda is an ideal spot for windsurfing and sailing, and it hosts famous regattas such as the Centomiglia.

❷ ★ Desenzano del Garda
This is one of the liveliest and most popular towns on Lake Garda. The Roman villa, built in the 4th century and discovered in 1921, has some beautiful mosaics *(see above)*.

❺ ★ Gardone Riviera
In this pleasant tourist resort is the Vittoriale degli Italiani, where the writer Gabriele D'Annunzio lived from 1921 to 1938. It embodies the decadence of which this poet and novelist was a great exponent.

Villa Bettoni in Bogliaco (1756) has elegant frescoed rooms with masterpieces by Reni and Canaletto, as well as a garden with a nymphaeum.

Toscolano Maderno

Gardone Riviera

Salò ❹

Fasano

The Valtènesi and San Felica del Benaco ❸

Isola di Garda

Manerba

Moniga del Garda

Desenzano ❷

❶ Sirmione

San Pietro in Mavino

❶ ★ Sirmione
This Roman villa, which extends over a large area and was once thought to be the residence of the Latin poet Catullus, is one of the most impressive examples of an ancient Roman dwelling in Northern Italy.

Key

– – Ferry routes

0 kilometres 5

0 miles 5

❼ Limone sul Garda
The abundance of citrus trees grown here is supposedly the reason why the locals have the longest life expectancy in Italy.

VISITORS' CHECKLIST

Practical Information
ℹ️ Local information bureau. Navigazione Lago di Garda (freefone 800-55 18 01).
🌐 navlaghi.it

Transport
🚊 FS Milan–Venice line (89-2021). 🚌 Azienda Provinciale Trasporti di Verona (045-805 78 11) or Società Italiana Autoservizi (840-62 00 01). 🚢

❽ Riva del Garda

Torbole

Limone sul Garda ❼

Campione del Garda

❾ Malcesine

ano

Isola di Trimelone

Porta di Brenzone

Castelletto de Brenzone

Pai

❿ Torri del Benaco

⓫ Garda

Bardolino ⓬

Lazise

ardaland ⓮

⓭ Peschiera del Garda

At Torbole, now a surfers' paradise, Venetian ships – which defeated the Visconti in 1440 – were reassembled after being transported along the Val d'Adige.

Punta San Vigilio was named after the bishop from Trent who brought Christianity to the area in the 4th century.

The Camaldolite Hermitage (16th century), which allowed women visitors only since 1993, has a splendid panoramic view.

Sights at a Glance

❶ Sirmione
❷ Desenzano del Garda
❸ The Valtènesi and San Felice del Benaco
❹ Salò
❺ Gardone Riviera
❻ Toscolano Maderno
❼ Limone sul Garda
❽ Riva del Garda
❾ Malcesine
❿ Torri del Benaco
⓫ Garda
⓬ Bardolino and Lazise
⓭ Peschiera del Garda
⓮ Gardaland

❿ Torri del Benaco
The economy of this small town, which thanks to its strategic position controls access to the upper lake region, is based on tourism and fishing. The townspeople have enjoyed special fishing privileges since the 1400s.

For keys to symbols see back flap

❶ Sirmione

Brescia. 🔼 8,200. 🛈 Viale
Marconi 8 (030-91 61 14).
W comune.sirmione.bs.it

Roman Sirmio lay in the
hinterland and only the villa
quarter faced the lake. In the
13th century the Scaligeri lords
of Verona turned it into a fortress
to defend Lake Garda. In 1405
Sirmione was taken over by
Venice, which then ruled until the
18th century. The main focus of
the town is the **Rocca Scaligera**,
a castle built by Mastino I della
Scala (13th century), the inner
basin of which served as shelter
for the Veronese boats. Roman
and medieval plaques are in
the entrance arcade.

Fifteenth-century Santa Maria
Maggiore, built over a pagan
temple, has a Roman column
in its porch, while the campanile
was a Scaligera tower. The
interior has 15th- and 16th-
century frescoes and a
15th-century Madonna.

The **spas** use the water from
the Boiola spring, known since
1546. San Pietro in Mavino,
re-built in 1320, boasts fine
13th– 16th-century frescoes.
Sirmione is also famous for the
so-called **Grotte di Catullo**, a
huge Roman residence built in
the 1st centuries BC–AD. The
most evocative rooms are the
Grotta del Cavallo, the
Cryptoporticus and the pool.
The Sala della Trifora del Paradiso
and Sala dei Giganti overlook the
lake. The Antiquarium has finds
from the villa, including a mosaic
of a seascape and a portrait of
Catullus (1st century BC).

🏰 Rocca Scaligera
Piazza Castello. **Tel** 030-91 64 68.
Open 8:30am–7:30pm Tue–Sat,
8:30am–2pm Sun. **Closed** hols. 🖾

Terme Catullo (Spa)
Piazza Castello. **Tel** 030-990 49 23 (for
bookings). W **termedisirmione.com**

🌀 Grotte di Catullo
Via Catullo. **Tel** 030-91 61 57.
Open Apr–Sep: 9am–6pm Tue–Sun;
Oct–Mar: 9am–4pm Tue–Sun.
Closed Mon (Tue if Mon is hol). 🖾

Christ Enthroned with Angels and Saints,
San Pietro in Mavino

❷ Desenzano del Garda

Brescia. 🔼 27,000. 🛈 Via Porto
Vecchio 34 (030-374 87 26).
🔲 (antiques, 1st Sun of month
(except for Jan & Aug).

Probably founded by the
Romans on a site inhabited since
prehistoric times, Desenzano was
taken over by Venice in the 15th
century, when it became the
leading lakeside town. Since the
19th century it has been a tourist
resort. The heart of the town

centre is Piazza Malvezzi, home
to an antiques market known
for its silverware and prints.
The 16th-century town hall and
Provveditore Veneto buildings
are also here. In the **Duomo**
(16th century) is a fine *Last Supper*
by Tiepolo. The **Museo Civico
Archeologico**, in the cloister
of Santa Maria de Senioribus,
contains displays of Bronze-Age
finds and the oldest known
wooden plough (2000 BC).

The **Villa Romana** was built
in the 4th century AD and
rediscovered in 1921. It had
been covered by a landslide,
which preserved some lovely
mosaics with geometric motifs
such as the *Good Shepherd* and
Psyche and Cupids. Finds from
the villa are in the Antiquarium.

🏛 Duomo
Piazza Duomo. **Tel** 030-914 18 49.
Open 9:30am–noon, 3:30–6pm daily
(to 6:30pm May–Sep).

🏛 Museo Civico Archeologico
Via T. Dal Molin 7. **Tel** 030-914 45 29
or 030-999 42 75. **Open** 9am–1pm
Tue–Wed, 3–7pm Thu–Fri, 2:30–7pm
Sat, Sun & hols.

🏛 Villa Romana
Via Crocifisso 2. **Tel** 030-914 35 47.
Open Mar–14 Oct: 8:30am–7pm
Tue–Sun; 15 Nov–Feb: 8:30am–5pm
Tue–Sun. **Closed** Mon (Tue if Mon
is hol). 🖾

❸ The Valtènesi and San Felice del Benaco

Brescia. 🔼 3,400. 🛈 Via Portovecchio
34, Desenzano del Garda (030-374 87 26).

The area between Desenzano
and Salò, called Valtènesi, is
rich in medieval churches and
castles. At Padenghe, the Rocca
(9th–10th century) is reached
by a drawbridge. Nearby is
12th-century Sant'Emiliano.
The houses in Moniga del Garda
are protected by a 10th-century
wall with turrets. Here stands
Santa Maria della Neve, built in
the 14th century. The Rocca di
Manerba del Garda (8th century)
lies on a headland over the lake
where a castle once stood. The
ruins have become part of a
regional park. At Solarolo, the

The Rocca Scaligera at Sirmione, with its tower and battlements

Cappella del Santissimo Sacramento, Salò Duomo (18th century)

15th-century Santissima Trinità has a fresco cycle with the *Last Judgment*, while prehistoric finds from this area can be seen at the **Parco Archeologico Naturalistico della Rocca**. The bay between the Punta Belvedere and Punta San Fermo headlands is dominated by San Felice del Benaco. To the south is the Madonna del Carmine sanctuary (1452) containing outstanding 15th- and 16th-century frescoes. In the town centre the parish church has a *Madonna and Saints* by Romanino. Opposite Punta San Fermo is Isola di Garda. It is said that the Franciscans in the 13th-century monastery introduced citrus fruit cultivation to Lake Garda.

🔼 Parco Archeologico Naturalistico della Rocca

Via Rocca 20, Manerba del Garda. **Tel** 339 613 72 47. **Open** Apr–Sep: 10am–8pm daily; Oct–Mar: 10am–6pm Thu–Sun.

❹ Salò

Brescia. 🔼 10,700. ℹ️ Piazza San Antonio 4 (0365-214 23).

A former Roman town, in 1337 Salò became the seat of the Consiglio della Magnifica Patria, the governing body of 42 towns which met in the palazzo built by Sansovino in 1524 (now the Museo Archeologico). The late Gothic cathedral has a *Madonna and Saints* by Romanino (1529) and an altarpiece from 1476. The Centro Culturale Santa Giustina, formerly a church, now houses **MuSa (Museo di Salò)**, whose collections include the Museo del Nastro Azzurro, a military museum. Palazzo Terzi-Martinengo at Barbarano was the seat of Mussolini's Salò puppet government.

🏛️ MuSa (Museo di Salò)

Via Brunati 9. **Tel** 0365-20 553. **Open** May–early Nov: times vary. Call or see website for details. 🏞️
Ⓦ museodisalo.it

Vines, Churches and Castles

The Valtènesi area is known for its vineyards, where the rosé wine Chiaretto della Riviera del Garda is produced. A visit to the wineries

The medieval church of San Pietro in Lucone

here offers a chance to visit the inland region of this side of Lake Garda and also see the medieval fortresses of Soiano del Lago, Puegnago sul Garda and Polpenazze del Garda. In the cemetery of Polpenazze del Garda is the Romanesque church of San Pietro in Lucone, with its 15th-century frescoes depicting the lives of St Peter and the Apostles.

❺ Gardone Riviera

Brescia. 🔼 2,700. ℹ️ Corso Repubblica 8 (0365-203 47).

Boasting the highest winter temperatures in Northern Italy, Gardone Riviera became a fashionable tourist resort in the late 19th century because of its mild dry climate, which is beneficial for those suffering from lung ailments. Two celebrated villas in the area are Villa Alba and Villa Fiordaliso.

Gardone is also famous for the **Vittoriale degli Italiani**, Gabriele D'Annunzio's residence, where the poet collected over 10,000 objects including works of art, books and mementos, which he later donated to the state. In the garden are the Prioria, his residence, the Schifamondo with mementos, the Auditorium and the Mausoleum. On display are objects related to his exploits during and after World War I, such as his motor boat and aeroplane.

Another attraction is the **Giardino Botanico Hruska**, a fine botanical garden with over 2,000 Alpine, Mediterranean and subtropical species of plants.

D'Annunzio, who lived out his days at the Vittoriale degli Italiani

🏛️ Vittoriale degli Italiani
Gardone. **Tel** 0365-29 65 11. **Open** Apr–Sep: 8:30am–8pm daily; Oct–Mar: 9am–5pm daily. 🏞️ House: **Open** Apr–Sep: 9:30am–7pm Tue–Sun; Oct–Mar: 9am–1pm, 2–5pm Tue–Sun (last adm: 1 hour before closing). 🏞️ 🎫 🏠 Ⓦ vittoriale.it

🔼 Giardino Botanico Hruska
Via Roma 2. **Tel** 0365-203 47 (IAT Gardone). **Open** 15 Mar–15 Oct: 9am–7pm daily. 🏞️

Canvas by Celesti in the Santi Pietro e Paolo parish church, Toscolano

❻ Toscolano Maderno

Brescia. 🗻 8,100. 🛈 Via Sacerdoti, Maderno (0365-54 60 83).

This town is made up of the two villages of Toscolano and Maderno. Sights of interest at Maderno are the Romanesque church of Sant'Andrea, with a panel by Paolo Veneziano, and the parish church of Sant'Ercolano, with paintings by Veronese and Andrea Celesti. Here the Gonzaga family built the Palazzina del Serraglio (17th century) for Vincenzo I's amorous assignations. Toscolano, ancient Benacum, was the largest town on Lake Garda in Roman times. At Santa Maria del Benaco, with 16th-century frescoes, archaeologists found Roman and Etruscan objects and the ruins of a mosaic-decorated villa (1st century AD). The parish church of Santi Pietro e Paolo has 22 canvases by Andrea Celesti. Gargnano boasts San Giacomo di Calino (11th–12th century) and San Francesco (1289), whose cloister has Venetian arches. Another sight is Villa Feltrinelli, Mussolini's residence during the Republic of Salò.

❼ Limone sul Garda

Brescia. 🗻 1,100. 🛈 Lungolago 15 (0365-954 265).

Known for its mild climate, Limone may have been named after the lemon tree terraces (no longer used) typical of this area. Or the name may derive from *Limen* (border), since the Austrian frontier was here until 1918. In the town centre are the 15th-century church of San Rocco and a parish church (1685), with canvases by Celesti. Near Tignale is the **Montecastello Sanctuary** (13th–14th century) with a *Coronation of the Virgin* (14th century) and medallions by the school of Palma il Giovane. Towards Tremosine is the Brasa river gorge, in a panoramic setting.

🏠 **Montecastello Sanctuary**
Via Triboldi, Tignale. **Open** mid-Apr–Oct: 9am–6pm daily (May–Sep: 9am–5pm Sun). **Tel** 0365-730 19.

❽ Riva del Garda

Trento. 🗻 16,000. 🛈 Largo Medaglie d'Oro (0464-55 44 44).
🌐 gardatrentino.it

Situated at a strategic point on the northern tip of the lake, in the Trentino region, Riva was under Austrian rule until 1918. The Rocca and Torre Apponale (13th century) were built to defend the town; an angel, the town symbol, tops the tower. In the square opposite are Palazzo Pretorio (1370) and Palazzo del Provveditore (1482). The 12th-century Rocca is the home of the **Museo Alto Garda (MAG)**, with 14th–20th-century paintings. Santa Maria Assunta has two canvases by Piazzetta, while the octagonal, richly frescoed Inviolata (1603) has works by Palma il Giovane. The impressive waterfalls of the Varone river, above Riva, are 80 m (262 ft) high.

Nearby Torbole was described by Goethe in *Italian Journey* and is a popular spot for sailing.

🏛 **Museo Alto Garda (MAG)**
Piazza Cesare Battisti 3. **Tel** 0464-57 38 69. **Open** end Mar–Oct, 27–30 Dec, 2–6 Jan: 10am–6pm Tue–Sun (Jun–Sep: 10am–6pm daily). **Closed** Nov–Feb. 🏞

❾ Malcesine

Verona. 🗻 3,700. 🛈 Seasonal office: Via Gardesana 238 (045-740 00 44).

Deposition (15th century), Malcesine parish church

One of the most fascinating towns along the lake shore, Malcesine stands on a stretch of impervious rock, hence the name *mala silex*, inaccessible rock. The 12th-century **Castello** was rebuilt by the Scaligeri of Verona in 1277. It houses the Museo di Storia Naturale del Garda e del Monte Baldo, the lake's natural history museum, which among other things shows how the Venetians transported ships to Torbole (1438–40). The parish church contains a 16th-century Deposition. Towering above Malcesine is Monte Baldo (2,218 m, 7,275 ft), accessible by cable car, with nature trails and stunning views.

The Legend of Maria (c.1614–20) by Martino Teofilo Polacco, in the Inviolata at Riva del Garda

The harbour at Torri del Benaco

⊞ Castello Scaligero
Via Castello. **Tel** 045-657 03 33.
Open Apr–Oct: 9:30am–7:30pm
daily; Nov–Mar: 11am–6pm Sat, Sun
& hols.

⑩ Torri del Benaco

Verona. 2,500. Via Fratelli
Lavanda (045-722 51 20).

Roman Castrum Turrium was
a major stop between Riva
and Garda and has preserved
the typical grid plan. Due to
its strategic position, Torri was
fortified and a castle was built;
it is now a **museum**, with old
farm tools and prehistoric finds.
Santissima Trinità has some
15th-century frescoes.

⊞ Museo del Castello
Via Fratelli Lavanda. **Tel** 045-629 61 11.
Open mid-Jun–mid-Sep: 9:30am–
1pm, 4:30–7:30pm daily; mid-Sep–Oct
& Apr–mid-Jun: 9:30am–12:30pm,
2:30–6pm daily.

⑪ Garda

Verona. 4,000. Piazzetta
Donatori di Sangue (045-627 03 84).

Built around a small bay, Garda
was one of the major towns
along the lake, controlling the
southern basin. Its name,
then given to the lake as well,
comes from the German *Warten*
(fortress), referring to the wall
around the historic centre
with its small port, accessible
through the Torre dell'Orologio
tower and gate. Among the
historic buildings are the
15th-century Palazzo del
Capitano, the losa, the dock

of Palazzo Carlotti designed by
Sanmicheli, and **Santa Maria
Maggiore** (18th century) with
a painting by Palma il Giovane
and a 15th-century cloister. At
the new port is Villa Albertini,
with an English-style park,
while at Punta San Vigilio is Villa
Guarienti (1542), designed by
Sanmicheli, where the WWF
offers a tour of the Bronze Age
rock engravings.

⊞ Santa Maria Maggiore
Piazzale Roma. **Tel** 045-725 68 25.

⑫ Bardolino and Lazise

Verona. 6,800. Bardolino
Piazzale Aldo Moro (045-721 00 78).
antiques, 3rd Sun of month.

The Cornicello and Mirabello
headlands enclosing Bardolino
made it a natural harbour.
Originally it was a prehistoric
settlement and then became
a Roman camp. The
historic centre has
two early medieval
churches, San Zeno
and San Severo.
The first still has
its 9th-century
Carolingian cruciform
structure. Roman-
esque San Severo
was founded in
the 9th century but
rebuilt in the 12th.
It has 12th–13th-
century frescoes with
battle scenes and
biblical episodes,
and a 10th-century
crypt. Among the
civic buildings is the

Loggia Rambaldi, in the Rambaldi
family palazzo. Bardolino is also
famous for its wine.
Lazise also boasted a prehistoric civilization. A castle
was built in the 11th century
and the lords of Verona erected
the walls in the 1300s. The
16th-century Venetian Customs
House is all that remains of
the old harbour. Next to it is
San Nicolò (12th century), with
Giotto school frescoes.

⊞ Terme di Villa dei Cedri
Piazza di Sopra 4, Località Colà
di Lazise. **Tel** 045-759 09 88.
Open 9am–9pm Mon–Thu, 9–2am
Sat, 9am–11pm Fri & Sun.

⑬ Peschiera del Garda

Verona. 10,000. Piazzale
Betteloni 15 (045-755 16 73).
tourism.verona.it

Peschiera has retained its
military image more than any
other town on Lake Garda.
The old town lies on an island
surrounded by a star-shaped
wall – "a fortress beautiful
and strong", says Dante. The
walls were reinforced by
the Scaligeri of Verona, rebuilt
for the new Venetian rulers
by Sanmicheli in 1556, and
completed with two forts by the
Austrians two centuries later.
Besides the frescoed 18th-
century San Martino, there is
the 16th-century Madonna
del Frassino sanctuary.

Lake Garda as seen from a harbour in Peschiera

⓮ Gardaland

This theme park was opened in 1975 and is one of the largest in Italy (500,000 sq m, 600,000 sq yds). The 32 attractions range from the rollercoaster to reconstructions of the pyramids and a jungle, the Gardaland Theatre and the Fantasy Kingdom, all ideal for families with children. The fun park facilities are good, including a wide range of refreshments, theme shops and souvenir photos. At busy times queues are kept informed about the length of the wait.

Locator Map

▨ Gardaland

Space Vertigo
There's a bacteriological alarm in the space station – everyone must escape! The only hope is to jump into space at top speed from a 40-m (131-ft) high tower. Thrills galore for everyone.

Ramses the Awakening
Lovers of ancient Egypt can enter the temple of Abu Simbel and explore the dark corridors while shooting laser guns.

KEY

① **The floating tree trunks** of the Colorado Boat confront the canyon rapids.

② **Magic Mountain**, a super-fast rollercoaster, is one of the most famous rides of all, with two hairpin bends and two death-defying spins. Only for the most intrepid of visitors.

③ **Monorail station**

④ **Top Spin**

⑤ **Ice Age 4D**

⑥ **Raptor** is a winged rollercoaster that takes you on a flight of near-misses at breathtaking speed.

⑦ **Mammoth**

⑧ **Escape from Atlantis**

Gardaland Theatre
The park's actors take to the stage every day to provide entertainment for both adults and children.

Jungle Rapids
Climb aboard a rubber dinghy and travel over the rapids of a canyon, past a volcano, into the heart of mysterious and magical Southeast Asia with its temples.

VISITORS' CHECKLIST

Practical Information
Peschiera del Garda. **Tel** 045-644 97 77. **Open** Apr–mid-Jun & second week Sep–end Sep: 10am–6pm daily; mid-Jun–first week Sep: 10am–11pm daily; Oct: weekends only & 31 Oct; Dec–first week Jan: 10am–6pm weekends and Christmas hols. **Closed** Nov, mid-Jan–end Mar. 🅿️ (free for ♿ and children under 1 m (3 ft) tall). ✂️
Ⓦ **gardaland.it**

0 metres   100
0 yards   100

★ Blue Tornado
Even more exciting than the rollercoaster, this attraction offers visitors the opportunity to experience first-hand the thrills of piloting an American fighter plane.

Prezzemolo
Gardaland's mascot, Prezzemolo (Parsley) the dragon, is always at the park entrance to welcome all visitors.

★ Fantasy Kingdom
Younger children will love this! The talking trees, singing animals and puppet show will keep them entertained for hours.

The island of Orta San Giulio on Lago d'Orta

Lago d'Orta

i APTL, Via Panoramica, Orta–San Giulio (0322-90 51 63). FS Novara-Domodossola line (848-88 80 88). Nav. Lago d'Orta (345-517 00 05).

Lake Orta, or Cusio, is the westernmost lake in the lower Alps region, characterized by soft hills and scenery. Villages are dotted around the lake, along the shore or perched among green terracing. The Mottarone, a ski resort, and the other mountains surrounding the lake offer attractive hiking trails.

As far back as the 1700s, Orta was a tourist attraction and many villas were built in large parks. The chief town is Orta San Giulio, on a promontory in the middle of the lake. The village alleyways wind around Piazza Motta, on which lies the Palazzetto della Comunità (1582) and where the stepped Motta ascent begins. Opposite the square is the island of San Giulio, converted to Christianity by the Greek deacon Julius, who built the 4th-century **basilica**. The church was restored in the 11th–12th centuries and has a 12th-century Romanesque marble pulpit and 15th-century frescoes. Next door is the Palazzo del Vescovo (16th–18th century). The UNESCO World Heritage site of **Sacro Monte** is a sanctuary built in 1591 on the rise above Orta.

Dedicated to St Francis, it consists of 20 chapels with 17th–18th-century terracotta statues and frescoes. Opposite, perched over a steep quarry, is the Madonna del Sasso sanctuary (1748).

On the northern tip of the lake is Omegna, whose medieval quarter boasts the late Romanesque collegiate church of Sant'Ambrogio.

At Quarna there is the **Museo Etnografico e dello Strumento Musicale a Fiato**, with displays of wind instruments, made in this village for centuries. Other interesting villages are Vacciago di Ameno, with the Calderara Collection of contemporary art, featuring 327 international avant-garde works of the 1950s and 1960s; Gozzano, with the church of San Giuliano (18th century),

Figure on the pulpit, San Giulio

Palazzo Vescovile and the seminary; and, lastly, Torre di Buccione. San Maurizio d'Opaglio has a curious attraction: a museum devoted to the production of taps.

🏛 **Basilica di San Giulio**
Isola di San Giulio. APTL, ring road, Orta San Giulio (0322-90 56 14). **Open** Easter–Sep: 9:30am–6pm daily; Oct–Easter: 11am–6pm Mon.

🏛 **Sacro Monte**
Via Sacro Monte. **Tel** 0322-91 19 60. Chapels: **Open** summer: 8:30am–6:30pm daily; winter: 9am–4:30pm daily (5pm hols). **Closed** 1 & 6 Jan, 25, 26 & 31 Dec.

🏛 **Museo Etnografico e dello Strumento Musicale a Fiato**
Via Roma, Quarna Sotto. **Tel** 0323-82 63 68. **Open** Jul–Aug: 2:30–6:30pm Tue–Fri, 10:30am–12:30pm, 2:30–6:30pm Sat & Sun.

Lago di Varese

i IAT, Via Romagnosi 9, Varese (0332-28 19 13). Ferrovie Nord Milano, Milan–Laveno line to Gavirate (02-72 49 49 49). Autolinee Varesine (0332-73 11 10).

This lake basin was created by glacial movement during the Quaternary era. It offers pleasant scenery, with rolling hills and the Campo dei Fiori massif. In prehistoric times it was inhabited by a prehistoric civilization, the important remains of which were found on the island of Isolino Virginia (which can be reached from Biandronno), where they are on display at the **Museo Preistorico**, a UNESCO heritage site.

Part of the lake shore is now protected as the Brabbia marsh nature reserve. Not far away, at Cazzago Brabbia, are ice-houses used to conserve fish in the 18th century. On the northern tip of the lake, at Voltorre di Gavirate,

Fishing boats along the shores of the Lago di Varese

the **Chiostro di Voltorre** is worth a visit. It was part of a 12th-century Cluniac monastery and is now used for exhibitions. On the slopes of Campo dei Fiori you can see the lake of the UNESCO site **Sacro Monte** di Varese, a sanctuary made up of 14 17th-century chapels with frescoes and life-size statues.

🏛 Museo Preistorico
Isolino Virginia. **Tel** 0332-25 54 85 (Musei Civici di Varese). **Open** Apr–Sep: 2–6pm Sat & Sun (Oct: 2–6pm Sun). 🎫 🖼 (book in advance).

⬆ Chiostro di Voltorre
Voltorre di Gavirate. **Tel** 0332-73 14 02. **Open** 10am–12:30pm, 2–5pm Tue–Sun (Apr–Sep: until 6pm).
🌐 museoartemoderna.it

⬆ Sacro Monte
Varese. **Tel** 0332-22 92 23. **Open** 8am–noon, 2–6pm daily.

Lago d'Iseo
ℹ IAT, Lungolago Marconi 26, Iseo (030-98 02 09). 🚆 FS to Brescia, then Ferrovie Nord Milano (02-20 222). 🚌 SAB (west side, 035-28 90 11); SIA (east side, 030-377 42 37). 🚢 Navigazione Lago d'Iseo (035-97 14 83). 🌐 lagodiseo.org

Lake Iseo, also known as Sebino, extends between the provinces of Bergamo and Brescia. It is the seventh-largest lake in Italy and the fourth in Lombardy, created by a glacier descending from the Val Camonica. The chief towns here are Iseo, Sarnico, Lovere and Pisogne. The historic centre of Iseo has kept its medieval character, with the church of Sant'Andrea (1150), the Neo-Classical interior of which contains a painting by Hayez. Next to this is the tomb of the feudal landowner Giacomo Oldofredi and, on a hill at the entrance to the town, the Castello degli Oldofredi (both built in the 14th century), which in 1585 became a Capuchin monastery. At Provaglio d'Iseo there is the San Pietro in Lamosa Cluniac monastery, founded in 1030. Its 11th–12th-century Romanesque church has frescoes by the school of Romanino. Sarnico, at the southern end of the lake, was an important commercial and industrial town. Among the Art Nouveau houses built here by Giuseppe Sommaruga is Villa Faccanoni (1912), one of the best examples of this style.

The road that follows the western side of the lake rounds the Corno headland, which has fine views of Monte Isola, the largest lake island in Europe, with its typical villages, dominated by the Madonna della Ceriola sanctuary and the 15th-century Rocca Oldofredi. At the northern end of the lake is Lovere, which has medieval tower-houses.

On the lakeside is the **Galleria dell'Accademia Tadini**, featuring fine works of art ranging from the 14th to the 20th century, including Jacopo Bellini, Strozzi, Tiepolo, Hayez and Canova. The church of Santa Maria in Valvendra (1483) has paintings

The Piramidi di Zone pinnacles, some reaching 30 m (98 ft)

by Floriano Ferramola and Moretto and a 16th-century wooden altarpiece on the high altar. At Pisogne is Santa Maria della Neve (15th century), with scenes of the Passion frescoed by Romanino (1534). From here you can go to the Val Camonica rock engravings park. The lake is also famous for its lovely scenery, including the Piramidi di Zone, pinnacles protected from erosion by the rock massif above them, and the Torbiere d'Iseo, a marshy area with peat bogs.

🏛 Galleria dell'Accademia Tadini
Via Tadini 40, Lovere. **Tel** 035-96 27 80. **Open** May–Sep: 3–7pm Tue–Sat, 10am–noon, 3–7pm Sun & hols; Apr & Oct: 3–7pm Sat, 10am–noon, 3–7pm Sun & hols. **Closed** Nov–Mar. 🎫 ♿

Lago d'Idro
ℹ Pro Loco, Via Trento 16, Idro (0365-832 24). 🚌 SIA (030-377 42 37). 🌐 lagodidro.it

The highest large lake in Lombardy (368 m, 1,207 ft above sea level) was turned into an artificial basin in 1932 to provide irrigation and hydroelectricity. It is dominated by the Rocca di Anfo, a fortress with a splendid panoramic view that was built over older fortifications by the Venetians in 1450, and then rebuilt many times. From here you can reach Bagolino, with its charming stone houses and San Rocco (1478), which contains a fresco cycle by Giovan Pietro da Cemmo.

Rocca Oldofredi, Monte Isola, the Martinengo residence since the 1500s

TRAVELLERS' NEEDS

WHERE TO STAY

Milan tends to cater mostly to businessmen and women; and the majority of hotels are, therefore, modern and geared to their needs, offering in-room work facilities. However, it is also possible to find atmospheric old hotels and charming guesthouses in the historic heart of the city. Accommodation generally comes in the medium to high price range with either private parking or garage facilities nearby. Hotels, especially those with four stars and above, often have prestigious restaurants that are among the finest in the city. It is best to book accommodation in advance, especially during the international fashion

shows (held in February and March as well as September and October) and the top trade fairs. However, independent travellers should be able to secure good accommodation on arrival, even if they have not booked ahead. At the lakes, the choice ranges from guesthouses to fascinating historic hotels, which have drawn visitors and celebrities from all over the world since the 19th century. The most luxurious of these are in charming 17th- and 18th-century villas, with flower-filled terraces, health clubs and heated pools. For more information regarding accommodation in Milan and at the lakes, see pages 162–5.

Choosing a Hotel

The Italian for hotel is *albergo*. A *pensione* or *locanda* theoretically indicates a more modest guesthouse, but in practice the distinctions are quite blurred.

Most of the hotels in Milan are concentrated in the Buenos Aires–Stazione Centrale area, near the Fieramilanocity and in the Città Studi district. The first group is situated for the most part in Piazza della Repubblica and near the main railway station, which is practical for visitors who arrive on a short stay. Some of the more interesting hotels are the luxurious **Seven Stars Galleria** *(see p162)*, in the Galleria

A luxuriously furnished room in Grand Hotel Tremezzo *(see p164)*, Tremezzo

The opulent lobby of Palazzo Parigi Hotel & Grand Spa Milano *(see p162)*

Vittorio Emanuele II, and the **Hotel Principe di Savoia** *(see p163)*, decorated in the 1930s style. Around the Fiera, hotels cater for professional and business visitors, while at Città Studi travellers can find clean, inexpensive two-star hotels. In the historic centre, a few charming hotels still remain. The **Gran Duca di York** *(see p162)* has an intimate, boutique atmosphere. The **Palazzo Parigi Hotel & Grand Spa Milano** *(see p162)* is quite an elegant hotel as well.

At the lakes, hotels are more geared to holidaymakers as well as families. Some of Italy's most famous luxury hotels are situated around lake shores. Lake Como boasts luxury hotels such as the **Grand**

Hotel Villa Serbelloni *(see p164)* at Bellagio and **Grand Hotel Tremezzo** *(see p164)* at Tremezzo, while at Lago d'Iseo there is **L'Albereta** *(see p165)* in Erbusco and at Lago d'Orta the grand **Villa Crespi** *(see p165)*, located in Orta San Giulio.

Booking

Accommodation in Milan and the Lakes can often be booked online, or by calling the hotel, with a confirmation generally sent by email. Almost all of the Milanese hotels have email facilities and some, usually the upmarket ones, have websites where visitors can book directly online. The hotel will probably ask for a credit card number in advance.

◄ Lakeside seating at the tavern-style Locanda San Vigilio, Lake Garda

The Grand Hotel Villa Serbelloni *(see p164)* at Lake Como

Grading

Along with the rest of Italy, hotels in Milan and at the lakes are classified by a star system, from one (the lowest) to five stars. One-star hotels are basic, while those with two-stars usually offer bed and breakfast, but may not have private bathrooms. Three-star hotels offer en-suite bathrooms. Four-star and five-star hotels generally have added services such as restaurants and wellbeing facilities.

At the lakes, accommodation ranges from luxury hotels to family-run guesthouses. There are also youth hostels and campsites with tents as well as camper vans (RVs). Some also have self-catering apartments.

Prices

Accommodation in Milan is generally expensive and as the city is primarily a business destination there is little seasonal variation in pricing. Tariffs increase dramatically when the fashion shows are held and when there are major trade shows at the Fiera, which is quite often. For a hotel bargain, visit Milan in August when most locals leave the city to go on holiday.

At the lakes, prices vary according to the season. In spring and summer, the peak tourist seasons, prices are higher. Note that August is the busiest time. Many hotels expect you to take full board, especially in the summer months. Some hotels close for winter. By law, prices have to be displayed in every hotel bedroom. Beware of extras, such as expensive mini-bar drinks and in-room phone charges. Milanese law also states that hotels must issue a receipt on payment, and the receipt should be kept until you leave Italy.

Children

In general, children are welcomed everywhere in Italy. Hotels around the lakes tend to be better equipped for children than the business hotels of Milan. Babysitting services are also offered by some large hotels at the lakes.

Pets

For those travelling with a pet, some hotels actively welcome animals and provide special facilities for them, especially at the lakes. In Milan it is more difficult to find hotels and guesthouses that accept pets. It is always a good idea to check these details when booking.

Recommended Hotels

The accommodation listed in this guide has been carefully selected to reflect the range available in and around Milan and the lakes. **Luxury** hotels number among the most upmarket options in town with high standards of rooms and service. Properties in the **Apartment** category are for those who enjoy the flexibility of a self-catered stay. Milan and the lakes have many inexpensive options for basic, but neat and clean places to stay; these have been grouped under **Value for Money**. **Modern** defines a level of comfort provided by standard contemporary conveniences. **Boutique** refers to the most fashionable of stylish hotels. A variety of locations and price tags is covered. DK Choice highlights those places deserving of special mention for some exceptional feature such as a scenic location, impeccable service, other unique aspects or innovative touches.

Neutral colours and sleek elegance at the Armani Hotel Milano *(see p162)*, Milan

Where to Stay

Milan

Historic Centre

Gran Duca di York €€
Boutique **Map** 7 B1
Via Moneta 1, 20123
Tel 02 87 48 63
W ducadiyork.com
An elegant hotel, with frescoes
and art on the walls, housed in
an 18th-century palazzo.

Hotel Ambasciatori €€
Modern **Map** 8 D1
Galleria del Corso 3, 20122
Tel 02 76 02 02 41
W ambasciatorihotel.it
Centrally located with a fresh,
contemporary decor and stylish
rooms, restaurants and bars.

Hotel Dei Cavalieri €€
Value for Money **Map** 7 C2
Piazza Giuseppe Missori 1, 20123
Tel 02 88 571
W hoteldeicavalieri.com
Located just minutes from Milan's
Duomo, museums and shops,
this hotel offers lovely rooms
and a top-floor restaurant.

Hotel Milano Scala €€
Value for Money **Map** 3 C4
Via dell'Orso 7, 20121
Tel 02 87 09 61
W hotelmilanoscala.it
The opera-themed rooms build
on the hotel's proximity to the
Teatro alla Scala. The superb on-
site restaurant serves organic food.

Armani Hotel Milano €€€
Luxury **Map** 4 D5
Via Manzoni 31, 20121
Tel 02 88 83 88 88
W armanihotels.com
With sumptuous guestrooms,
gourmet cuisine and an out-
standing spa, this a seriously
stylish place.

Boscolo Milano
Autograph Collection €€€
Luxury **Map** 4 D5
Corso Matteotti 4–6, 20121
Tel 02 77 67 96 11
W milano-boscolo.com
Five-star hotel that features
luxurious yet quirky sculptural
decor. Facilities include a spa.

The Gray €€€
Boutique **Map** 7 C1
Via San Raffaele 6, 20121
Tel 02 72 08 95 1
W hotelthegray.com
Housed in a famous Art Nouveau
building, this hotel has beautiful
rooms, two restaurants and a
fitness suite.

DK Choice

Palazzo Parigi Hotel &
Grand Spa Milano €€€
Luxury **Map** 3 C4
Corso di Porta Nuova 1, 20121
Tel 02 62 56 25
W palazzo-parigi-spa-rn.com
This absolutely beautiful five-
star hotel is richly decorated
and has amenities that include
gardens, tennis courts and a
gourmet restaurant. The roof-
top terrace affords great views.

DK Choice

Seven Stars Galleria €€€
Luxury **Map** 7 C1
Via Silvio Pellico 8, 20121
Tel 02 89 05 82 97
W sevenstarsgalleria.com
Seven-star hotel housed in
the national monument of
Galleria Vittorio Emanuele II.
Suites furnished with antiques
overlook the galleria. Extras
include private butlers, limousine
transfers and fine dining options.

Price Guide

Prices are based on one night's stay in
high season for a standard double room,
inclusive of service charges and taxes.

€	under €150
€€	€150 to €280
€€€	over €280

Straf €€€
Boutique **Map** 7 C1
Via San Raffaele 3, 20121
Tel 02 80 50 81
W straf.it
Hidden behind an 1883 Neo-
Classical façade, is this ultra-
modern hotel. Only a few
minutes from the Duomo.

Northwest Milan

Barcelò Milan €
Boutique
Via Stephenson 55, 20157
Tel 02 33 28 61 11
W barcelo.com
A well-recognized architectural
landmark of the city with rooms,
spa and restaurant that are
equally impressive.

Ariosto Hotel €€
Value for Money **Map** 2 E5
Via Ariosto 22, 20145
Tel 02 481 78 44
W hotelariosto.com
Set in an Art Nouveau building
with period features, this is a
charming hotel with rooms
around a courtyard garden.

Enterprise Hotel €€
Value for Money **Map** 2 D1
Corso Sempione 91, 20149
Tel 02 31 81 81
W enterprisehotel.com
Chic hotel in a former radio
factory. Relax in Le Terme di Kyoto,
the hotel's seventh-floor spa, or
dine at its superb restaurant.

Milan Royal Suites €€
Apartment **Map** 2 F5
*Different locations around the Santa
Maria delle Grazia church district*
Tel 02 39 66 94 31
W milanroyalsuites.com
Luxurious, well-equipped
apartments located around the
Santa Maria delle Grazie, home
to Da Vinci's *The Last Supper*.

Southwest Milan

Hotel dei Fiori €
Value for Money **Map** 6 F5
Via Renzo e Lucia 14, 20142
Tel 02 843 64 41
W hoteldeifiori.com
A pleasing three-star hotel with
comfortable soundproofed

A lavishly appointed room in the upmarket Palazzo Parigi Hotel

Stylish room featuring sports themed decor in The Yard Milano

rooms – a peaceful haven despite the busy road. Located close to Navigli's nightlife.

Atahotel Quark
Due Residence €€
Apartment
Via Lampedusa 11/3, Ripamonti Corvetto, 20141
Tel *02 89 52 61*
W atahotels.it
In a lovely leafy area, these apartments are large, bright and fully equipped with kitchen facilities.

Nhow Milano €€
Boutique **Map** 6 D4
Via Tortona 35, 20144
Tel *02 489 88 61*
W nhow-milan.com
From the foyer seating to loft-style rooms, eclectic colours lift Nhow above the ordinary. There is a gym, terrace bar and restaurant on site.

DK Choice

The Yard Milano €€
Boutique **Map** 7 B3
Piazza XXIV Maggio 8, 20123
Tel *02 89 41 59 01*
W theyardmilano.com
Ultra-chic suites and apartments with a sports theme. Cricket bats or model sailing yachts, anything sporty could feature in the decor. Public areas afford an equally edgy look. Located in one of Milan's liveliest nightlife districts.

Carrobbio €€€
Luxury **Map** 7 B2
Via Medici 3, 20123
Tel *02 89 01 07 40*
W hotelcarrobbiomilano.com
Chic rooms and suites with private gardens. The 1930s architecture and period furniture contribute to a distinguished stately ambience.

Hotel Pierre Milano €€€
Luxury **Map** 7 A2
Via De Amicis 32, 20123
Tel *02 72 00 05 81*
W hotelpierremilano.it
Nice blend of historical references and contemporary style. Excellent service and amenities, a piano bar and an à la carte restaurant.

Magna Pars Suites Milano SLH €€€
Value for Money **Map** 6 E4
Via Forcella 6, 20144
Tel *02 833 83 71*
W magnapars-suitesmilano.it
Housed in a contemporary complex, these suites are five-star luxury. The leather sofas and a private library are a nice touch.

Southeast Milan

Hotel 22 Marzo €
Value for Money **Map** 8 F1
Piazza Santa Maria del Suffragio 3, 20129
Tel *02 70 10 70 64*
W hotel22marzo.com
Family-run establishment that offers comfortable rooms at a convenient location.

Town House 31 €€
Boutique **Map** 4 F5
Via Goldoni 31, 20129
Tel *02 701 56*
W townhousehotel.com
Welcoming hotel, with rooms and public spaces sensitively designed to soothe and relax. Serves cocktails in its garden in summer.

Vittoria €€
Modern **Map** 8 F1
Via Pietro Calvi 32, 20129
Tel *02 545 65 20*
W hotelvittoriamilano.it
Bright and colourful with a touch of the classic. Breakfast in the garden in summer. Not far from the Duomo.

Northeast Milan

Hotel Michelangelo €
Modern **Map** 4 F1
Piazza Luigi di Savoia 6, 20124
Tel *02 675 51*
W michelangelohotelmilan.com
Contemporary hotel with emphasis on colour and smart lighting. Convenient location.

Hotel Cavour €€
Boutique **Map** 3 C4
Via Fatebenefratelli 21, 20121
Tel *02 62 00 01*
W hotelcavour.it
Elegant decor and an impeccable foyer. Close to the Teatro alla Scala and the Brera arts quarter.

Hotel Fenice €€
Modern **Map** 4 F3
Corso Buenos Aires 2, Piazza Venezia, 20124
Tel *02 29 52 55 41*
W hotelfenice.it
Cheerful, modern hotel. Very well located for shopping as well as a taste of local life.

Hotel Manin €€
Boutique **Map** 4 D4
Via Daniele Manin 7, 20121
Tel *02 659 65 11*
W hotelmanin.it
Family run since 1904, this 4-star hotel is well located, has great ambience and every modern facility.

Residenza delle Citta €€
Apartment **Map** 4 F1
Via Mauro Macchi 79, 20124
Tel *02 66 70 01*
W residenzadellecitta.it
A complex of 31 apartments with a fitness centre and a terrace. Close to Milan's fashion district.

Bulgari €€€
Luxury **Map** 3 C4
Via Privata Fratelli Gabba 7b, 20122
Tel *02 805 80 51*
W bulgarihotels.com
From luxurious rooms to a world-class spa, it is all pure luxury at this hotel housed in a palazzo.

Grand Hotel et de Milan €€€
Luxury **Map** 4 D4
Via Manzoni 29, 20121
Tel *02 72 31 41*
W grandhoteletdemilan.it
Lots of old world charm at this landmark hotel with the likes of Verdi in the guest book.

Hotel Principe Di Savoia €€€
Luxury **Map** 4 D2
Piazza della Repubblica 17, 20124
Tel *02 623 01*
W dorchestercollection.com
One of the city's top hotels with a fitness suite, spa club and a gourmet restaurant. Classy rooms.

For more information on types of hotels *see page 161*

Lake Maggiore

DK Choice

**BAVENO: Grand Hotel
Splendid** €€€
Luxury
Strada del Sempione, 28831
Tel *0323 92 45 83*
w zaccherahotels.com
Fabulous amenities at this hotel
on Lake Maggiore include a
health club and a private beach.
The restaurant boasts stunning
views of the lake, as do the
spacious rooms with balconies.

BELGIRATE: Villa Carlotta €€
Value for money
Via Mazzini 121-125, 28832
Tel *0322 764 61*
w villacarlottalagomaggiore.it
Classic decor lends an old-
fashioned charm to this villa
located beside the lake.

CANNERO: Hotel Cannero €
Value for money
Piazza Umberto I 2, 28821
Tel *0323 78 80 46*
w hotelcannero.com
This stylish hotel with a pool,
tennis court and a restaurant sits
on the lake's Piedmontese shore.

CANNOBIO: Hotel Cannobio €€
Boutique
Piazza Vittorio Emanuele III 6, 28822
Tel *0323 73 96 39*
w hotelcannobio.com
Centrally located on the lakeside
promenade; romantic ambience.

STRESA: Hotel Regina Palace €€
Value for money
Corso Umberto 1 29, 28838
Tel *0323 93 69 36*
w reginapalace.it
Elegant, modern hotel housed
in an Art Nouveau building.
Amenities include spa and pool.

**STRESA: Hotel Villa e
Palazzo Aminta** €€€
Boutique
Via Sempione Nord 123, 28838
Tel *0323 93 38 18*
w villa-aminta.it
Delightful villa complete with
chandeliers, *trompe-l'oeil* paintings,
Murano glass lamps and lavish
furnishings. Private beach and pier.

VERBANIA: Hotel Ancora €€
Boutique
Corso Mameli 65
Tel *0323-53 951*
w hotelancora.it
Enjoy minimalist design in a
central location facing the old
harbour. Open mid-Mar–mid-Nov.

Picturesque view of the lake from the balcony of a room in Grand Hotel Tremezzo

**VERBANIA:
Hotel Residence Zust** €€
Value for money
Via Ticino 39, 28921
Tel *0323 40 25 04*
w hotelzust.com
Set in lovely gardens, with a pool
and a children's playground. Fine
views of the lake.

Lake Como

BELLAGIO: Hotel Belvedere €€
Value for money
Via Valassina 31, 22021
Tel *031 95 04 10*
w belvederebellagio.com
Grand old house that has been
in the same family since 1880.
Elegant guestrooms and a
relaxing lakeside location.

**BELLAGIO: Grand Hotel Villa
Serbelloni** €€€
Luxury
Via Roma 1, 22021
Tel *031 95 02 16*
w villaserbelloni.com
A dramatic headland location
and opulent decor distinguish
this converted aristocratic
home. Superb spa.

COMO: Avenue Hotel €€
Boutique
Piazzolo Terragni 6, 22100
Tel *031 27 21 86*
w avenuehotel.it
Creative decor, furniture and art
on the walls. Lots of designer
shopping nearby.

COMO: Palace Hotel €€
Value for money
Lungo Lario Trieste 16, 22100
Tel *031 233 91*
w palacehotel.it
Located close to Como Cathedral,
this attractive hotel has modern
rooms, an elegant restaurant
and gardens beside a lake.

DOMASO: Villa Vinicia €€
Apartment
Via Regina 135, 22013
Tel *339 621 82 47*
w villavinicia.it
Seven chic apartments in a
17th-century villa with period
furniture. Garden and pool.

LECCO: Albergo Nicolin €
Value for money
Via Ponchielli 54, 23900
Tel *0341 42 21 22*
w ristorantenicolin.it
Homely, welcoming hotel that
offers nine modern rooms, a
good restaurant and gardens.

TREMEZZO: Hotel Villa Marie €€
Value for money
Via Regina 30, 22019
Tel *0344 404 27*
w hotelvillamarie.com
Lovely rooms in a beautiful
harbourside setting. Panoramic
views, pool and gardens.

DK Choice

**TREMEZZO: Grand Hotel
Tremezzo** €€€
Luxury
Via Regina 8, 22019
Tel *0344 424 91*
w grandhoteltremezzo.com
This 1910 Art Nouveau-style
palazzo is one of the oldest
hotels on Lake Como. The rooms
are romantic, the gourmet restaurant refined, and the tranquil
spa has an infinity pool. Amid
lush gardens on the lake's shore.

VARENNA: Hotel du Lac €€
Value for money
Via del Prestino 11, 23829
Tel *0341 83 02 38*
w albergodulac.com
Built in 1823 right on the
water's edge; great views
from many of the rooms as
well as the terrace restaurant.

VARENNA: Hotel Royal Victoria €€€
Luxury
Piazza S Girogio 2, 23829
Tel *0341 81 51 11*
[w] royalvictoria.com
Named after one-time guest Queen Victoria, this hotel, in a lakeside setting, is supremely elegant.

Lake Garda

DESENZANO DEL GARDA: The Tower of the Old King €
Value for money
Via Castello 66, 25015
Tel *338 706 3578*
[w] thetoweroftheoldking.it
Close to the shore, next to the castle. Plenty of antiques and soothing decor in gentle pastels.

DESENZANO DEL GARDA: Hotel Bonotto €€
Value for money
Viale Antonio Gramsci 40, 25015
Tel *030 91 21 021*
[w] hotelbonottodesenzano.it
Lovely hotel with contemporary rooms, a breakfast hall and a terrace with panoramic views.

DESENZANO DEL GARDA: Hotel Villa Rosa Desenzano €€
Modern
Lungolago c. Battisti 89, 25015
Tel *030 914 19 74*
[w] villarosahotel.eu
Neo-Classical villa overlooking the lake, converted to offer plush rooms and a romantic restaurant.

GARDONE RIVIERA: Grand Hotel Fasano €€€
Luxury
Corso Zanardelli 190, 25083
Tel *0365 29 02 20*
[w] ghf.it
Former hunting lodge set in a parkland, with classic Italian-style decor. Fine-dining restaurant and a glamourous spa as well.

Rustic but stylish interiors of Agriturismo Villa Bissiniga, Salò

The stunning stately Villa Crespi, Orta San Giulio

GARGNANO: Lefay Resort & Spa Lago Di Garda €€€
Luxury
Via Angelo Feltrinelli 118, 25084
Tel *0365 24 18 00*
[w] lefayresorts.com
Spa resort in a tranquil, natural park setting with lake views. Eco-friendly rooms and public areas.

LIMONE SUL GARDA: Park Hotel Imperial €€€
Luxury
Via Tamas 10b, 25010
Tel *0365 95 45 91*
[w] parkhotelimperial.it
Immaculate gardens around a lagoon-style pool. Elegant rooms with balconies. Wellness centre.

RIVA DEL GARDA: Hotel Lido Palace €€€
Luxury
Viale Giosuè Carducci 10, 38066
Tel *0464 02 18 99*
[w] lido-palace.it
Chic rooms and a Michelin-starred restaurant in a *belle époque* building. State-of-the-art spa complex.

DK Choice

SALÒ: Agriturismo Villa Bissiniga €
Value for money
Via Brissi, off Via Renzano, Salò
Tel *0365 198 04 04*
[w] villabissiniga.com
Belle époque villa surrounded by vineyards. Rustic, but well-equipped rooms, some with harbour views. Botanical routes wind through a verdant garden.

SALÒ: Villa Arcadio Hotel €€
Value for money
Via Palazzina 2, 25087
Tel *0365 422 81*
[w] hotelvillaarcadio.it
Beautifully peaceful, this former monastery offers modern rooms with rustic features.

Lago d'Iseo

DK Choice

ERBUSCO: L'Albereta €€€
Luxury
Via Vittorio Emanuele 23, 25030
Tel *030 776 05 50*
[w] albereta.it
Surrounded by gardens and vineyards, this quiet, award-winning hotel in a Neo-Renaissance country mansion is an experience, not just a place to stay. Gourmet restaurant on site.

ISEO: Araba Fenice Hotel €€
Boutique
Via Fenice 4, 25049
Tel *030 982 20 04*
[w] arabafenicehotel.it
An elegant, historic hotel on the water's edge. Boasts lovely rooms and a fine-dining restaurant.

PISOGNE: La Pieve di Pisogne €€
Modern
Via Don G. Recaldini 1, 25055
Tel *0364 862 14*
[w] lapievedipisogne.it
Contemporary hotel with a red façade and pretty gardens. Superb restaurant and wellness centre.

Lago d'Orta

ORTA SAN GIULIO: Hotel San Rocco €€
Value for money
Via Gippini 11, 28016
Tel *0322 91 19 77*
[w] hotelsanrocco.it
A charming hotel in a converted 17th-century convent. Enjoy a spa, lake boat tours and fine dining.

DK Choice

ORTA SAN GIULIO: Villa Crespi €€€
Luxury
Via Fava 18, 28016
Tel *0322 91 19 02*
[w] villacrespi.it
Built in 1879 in Middle-Eastern architectural style – it even has a minaret! – this exotic hotel boasts a spectacular setting and a Michelin-starred restaurant.

PETTENASCO: Giardinetto €€
Boutique
Via Provinciale 1
Tel *0323 891 18*
[w] giardinettohotel.com
This former trattoria with a waterfront setting offers lovely rooms and a well-stocked cellar.

For more information on types of hotels *see page 161*

WHERE TO EAT AND DRINK

Milan is a cosmopolitan city and offers a wide range of restaurants in all price categories. As well as Milanese and Tuscan cooking – the latter has become a real speciality of the city – ethnic cuisine has recently come to the fore, reflecting the city's multicultural character. There are restaurants offering skillfully prepared fish and seafood, along with meat, as well as osterias and pizzerias for informal dining.

Sunday brunch has become part of the Milanese lifestyle. Restaurants are at their most crowded at weekends, and it is often best to book in advance. At the Lakes, there are restaurants with terraces overlooking the water, and cafés with tables outside. Menus are dominated by fish dishes and local specialities. This introduction gives a number of tips to help you experience the pleasures of eating out in Milan.

Choosing a Restaurant

In Milan, the Brera and Navigli districts are filled with both trendy restaurants and inexpensive eateries. The theatre crowd mostly congregates at **Caffe Verdi di Rosso Maria** (see p173), while vegetarians head for **Joia** (see p175), which also serves a few fish dishes. Those on a budget will find many options around the Navigli, such as the Neapolitan-inspired **Pizzeria Tradizionale con Cucina di Pesce** (see p171) and **Premiata Pizzeria** (see p171). Near Porta Genova is **Osteria dei Binari** (see p172 serving Lombard and Piedmontese dishes. The **Raw Fish Café Centro Ittico** (see p175) and **Malavoglia** (see p173) near the fish market, have excellent fresh fish.

Classic restaurants in the city centre include **Boeucc** (see p170 and the historic

The Premiata Pizzeria sign, Milan (see p171)

Savini (see p170), both of which specialize in traditional Milanese cuisine.

Some of Italy's best places to eat are set in beautiful locations near the Lakes. At Lake Maggiore, **Il Sole di Ranco** (see p176) is one of Italy's finest, while at Lake Como good places to eat include **Barchetta** (see p177) at Bellagio and **Raimondi** (see p178), a well-known gourmet restaurant. At Erbusco (Lago d'Iseo) is **Gualtiero Marchesi** (see p180), the restaurant of Italy's celebrated chef. Lake Garda also boasts excellent eateries, such as **Villa Fiordaliso** (see p179), at Gardone, while at Lago d'Iseo, **La Foresta** (see p181) is famous for its fish, all landed by the owner.

To prevent disappointment, book a table ahead if there is a restaurant you are particularly keen on trying.

The well-equipped bar at 10 Corso Como (see p173), Milan

Eating Hours

Lunch is generally served at Milanese restaurants between 12:30 and 2:30pm. Dinner is usually at about 7:30pm and goes on until late. Sunday brunch is served from 11am onwards. Note that some restaurants close during the month of August.

Etiquette

The Milanese are very dress-conscious and usually dress up for dinner. Restaurants and bars must provide separate no-smoking areas or face a fine. Smokers who light up in no-smoking areas are also liable to a fine. At cafés and restaurants that do not have sealed-off areas, smoking is limited to outside tables only.

Types of Restaurants

Milan offers an unusually wide range of cuisines for an Italian city. Besides traditional Milanese

Outside tables in a pretty terrace setting at La Foresta (see p181), Lago d'Iseo

cooking, Italian regional cuisines, from Tuscan to Piedmontese, Neapolitan and Sicilian, are becoming increasingly popular. Visitors can also find Asian, North African and Mexican food of all kinds.

There are several different types of restaurants. Traditionally, a *ristorante* is smarter and more expensive than an *osteria* or a trattoria, but the divisions are becoming increasingly blurred. A pizzeria is usually an inexpensive place to eat and many serve pasta, meat and fish dishes as well as pizza. Those with *forno a legna* (wood-fired ovens) are the most highly rated. An *enoteca* or *vineria* is a place to taste wine and sample snacks.

At the Lakes, menus almost always feature local fish such as carp, tench and shad. Additionally, visitors will find regional specials – in particular Piedmontese, Valtellinese and Veneto dishes.

Table setting at Cracco *(see p170)*

Reading the Menu

A classic Italian dinner begins with an *antipasto* or starter. The first course *(il primo)* is likely to be pasta or risotto but may be a hearty soup. The main course *(il secondo)* consists of meat or fish served with a side dish of vegetables *(contorno)*. Dessert *(il dessert)* follows and may consist of fruit, ice cream or pastries. Coffee *(il caffè)* comes next, and, perhaps, a digestif.

A typical Milanese dinner might consist of *nervetti*, or *nervitt* (calf cartilage with oil, vinegar and onions), followed by *risotto alla milanese*, and then a veal cutlet *(cotoletta)*. Other traditional dishes are *ossobuco* (a cut of veal including the bone and its marrow) and *cassoeûla* (a dish of pork and cabbage served with polenta).

Vegetarians will find that many pasta dishes are meat- and fish-free, and that restaurants are increasingly offering pure vegetarian cuisine. Cheeses are also a good option.

Paying

Menus are usually posted outside restaurants, with prices. An unavoidable extra is the cover charge *(coperto)*, which is charged per person. In general Milanese restaurants accept major credit cards, except for some of the smaller, family-run trattorias, where you will need cash. Even restaurants in the smaller villages around the lakes now increasingly accept credit cards.

Wheelchair Access

Not all Milanese restaurants have facilities for the disabled, although more and more establishments are installing slopes and bathrooms for wheelchair users. It is best to telephone the restaurant beforehand, explain the disability and ask for advice.

Children's Facilities

Less expensive places such as trattorias and pizzerias are ideal for children, who may be less welcome in Milan's sophisticated restaurants. Restaurant owners at the Lakes are more accustomed to families with children, and can often provide smaller portions if required.

Recommended Restaurants

The restaurants in this section have been chosen to reflect their quality, amenities and variety of cuisine. Milan and the Lakes have a large number of traditional restaurants as well as eateries serving international cuisine. The restaurant selection includes suggestions for Chinese, Japanese, Indian and Greek cuisine as well as those offering fish and seafood fare or good vegetarian menus. The DK Choice restaurants have been highlighted for a special feature – exquisite food, outstanding setting, an inviting atmosphere or high standards of service.

The elegant dining area at Al Sorriso *(see p181)*, Lago d'Orta

The Flavours of Milan and the Lakes

As a powerhouse of industry, finance and fashion, Milan, more than any other Italian city, has embraced international cuisine. The Milanese are quick to adopt new culinary trends and food fads come and go. But there has also been a long-standing interest in rediscovering the historic cuisine of the region. Like the prosperous city itself, this traditional food is rich. Milanese risottos are laced with butter and Parmesan, and even the local asparagus is likely to arrive at the table topped with an egg and grated cheese. Increasingly chefs are now scaling down the fats and substituting olive oil to suit today's health-conscious palates.

Asparagus

Selection of salami at a delicatessen, Cremona

Milan

The city is surrounded by vast agricultural plains that provide an abundance of fresh produce, including meat, cereals, cheese and vegetables. The Milanese are great meat-eaters – pork, veal and game are all very popular. The region's typical hearty casseroles were once the staples of the local peasant diet, combining whatever meat, grains and vegetables happened to be available. Filling *minestre* soups with added rice or pasta stem from the same tradition. A more elaborate cuisine also developed at the courts of the ruling Visconti and Sforza families. Recipes created there are still being prepared by Milanese chefs today. Spanish rule in the 16th century led to rice being grown with other crops along the Po valley. This was used to make risotto – a direct descendant of paella. Saffron, cultivated locally, was added to flavour Milanese risottos, giving them their characteristic yellow hue. Again, the grain was cooked with anything that was in season to make a filling

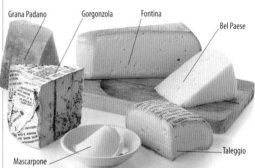
Grana Padano   Gorgonzola   Fontina   Bel Paese   Taleggio   Mascarpone
Mouthwatering range of northwest Italy's excellent cheeses

Local Dishes and Specialities

Rich dishes with meat and offal are traditional Milanese fare. Meals often start with slices of cured meats or the fine-grained *salame di Milano*. Popular main courses include *cassoeûla*, a rich stew of pork, cabbage and sausage, served with polenta; *busecca alla Milanese*, tripe with onion, carrot, sage and celery; and *fritto misto alla Milanese*, fried mixed offal coated in breadcrumbs. Seasonal specialities are *fagiano alla Milanese*, braised spiced pheasant, and *rise spargitt*, rice and asparagus. From the lakes come *alborelle fritte*, tiny fish, floured and deep-fried, and *missoltini*, shad, air-dried then salted and flavoured with bay leaves. A selection of regional cheeses is usually served at the end of a meal.

Panettone

Risotto alla Milanese Rice is cooked slowly with onion, stock, wine, butter, grated Parmesan and golden saffron.

Fresh vegetables for sale at a Milanese greengrocer

meal – vegetables, freshwater fish, meat and game. Milanese risottos still tend to have a seasonal twist. In the autumn, locally grown pumpkin is often added and, in summer, wild strawberries.

During the 18th century, maize (corn) was introduced into the region and polenta – made from maize flour and water – soon became an important staple food. Today, even though pasta is hugely popular, it is just as likely that polenta and rice will be found on the table in Milan.

Rule by Austria in the late 18th century has also left its mark on the Milanese diet. The popular bread-crumbed veal *costoletta Milanese* is a version of *Wiener Schnitzel*, and *panettone* is based on the rich yeast cakes of Central Europe.

The Lakes

Although fishing on the region's deep glacial lakes is no longer a major industry, it still plays a central role in shaping the local diet. Pike, perch, trout, tench, bleak, shad, sardines and eel are plentiful, while carp is more elusive and prized.

Shad, part of a catch of fish from the clear waters of Lake Como

The catch served at lakeside restaurants is often simply fried, grilled or poached, although it is also popular marinated and is used in risottos, soups, pâtés and as a ravioli filling.

The land around Lake Garda is particularly suited for growing vines and olive trees. Light and delicate, Garda extra-virgin olive oil is perfect in salad dressings and can be bought direct from oil mills. Other regional products include capers and a delicious honey sold by local beekeepers.

WHAT TO DRINK

Franciacorta wines The reds and whites from the Lago d'Iseo area are held in high esteem by the Milanese, especially the *spumante*.

Oltrepo Pavese wines More than 20 different varieties, both still and sparkling, are produced in ancient vineyards to the south-west of Milan.

Valtellina wines From the Swiss border, north of Lake Como, these include reds and the unusual raisin-like *sforzato* made from semi-dried grapes.

Garda wines Made from a wide variety of grapes, the reds, whites and rosés from the area around Lake Garda include a light red Bardolino, Garda Classico Groppello and Garda Classico Chiaretto. The white Lugana goes particularly well with lake-fish dishes.

Minestrone The Milanese add beef marrow and rice to their version of this hearty bean and vegetable soup.

Ossobuco Veal shanks are braised very slowly in white wine. The bone marrow is considered a delicacy.

Trota Ripiena Lake trout are stuffed with mushrooms, onion and parsley, then poached in red wine.

Where to Eat and Drink

Milan

Historic Centre

La Rinascente Food Market   €
Café & Patisserie   **Map** 7 C1
Via San Raffaele 2, 20121
Tel *02 885 24 71*
Excellent for a cappuccino while
shopping, lunch or a full dinner.
Located at the top of a depart-
ment store with city views.

Camparino in Galleria   €€
Café & Patisserie   **Map** 7 C1
Galleria Vittorio Emanuele II, 20121
Tel *02 86 45 44 35*
A favourite of composer
Guiseppe Verdi, this historic
café attracts the trendy set.
Enjoy gourmet coffee and
lunch in a spectacular setting.

Al Cantinone   €€€
Italian   **Map** 8 D1
Via Agnello 19, 20121
Tel *02 86 30 15*
Housed in a 17th-century
mansion near the Duomo,
this is a popular eatery that
serves outstanding classic
Tuscan cuisine. Specials include
ossobuco (veal shank).

Boeucc   €€€
Italian   **Map** 4 D5
Piazza Belgioioso 2, 20121
Tel *02 76 02 02 24*   **Closed** *Sat &
Sun lunch*
Costoletta di vitello alla Milanese
(veal Milanese-style) is the
speciality at this historic eatery
in an old palazzo dating
from 1696.

DK Choice

Cracco   €€€
Gourmet   **Map** 7 C1
Via Victor Hugo 4, 20121
Tel *02 87 67 74* **Closed** *Mon & Sat
lunch; Sun*
Michelin-starred chef Carlo
Cracco's restaurant features
tasteful decor and an exquisite
gourmet menu that has made
it one of Milan's favourite spots.
The extensive wine list boasts
2,000 labels. The delicious slow-
roasted pork cheek with scampi
is highly recommended.

La Cupola   €€€
Gourmet   **Map** 7 C1
*Park Hyatt Hotel, Vias Tommaso
Grossi 1, 20121*
Tel *02 88 21 12 34*
Open from breakfast to late
supper, this stylish lounge serves

Italian gourmet classics. Try the
tapas – a speciality – before visiting the nearby Teatro alla Scala.

Le Noir   €€€
Italian   **Map** 7 C1
The Gray, Via San Raffaele 6, 20121
Tel *02 720 89 51*
Cutting-edge design features
set off by subtle changes of
coloured lighting and a selection
of *amuse bouche* is the prime
attraction here.

Savini   €€€
Italian   **Map** 7 C1
Galleria Vittorio Emanuele II, 20121
Tel *02 72 00 34 33*   **Closed** *Sat
lunch; Sun*
In service since 1867, Savini is
known for its *belle époque* decor
and great cuisine. Signature
dishes include black squid risotto
and pigeon breast on crepinette.

VUN   €€€
Gourmet   **Map** 7 C1
*Park Hyatt Milano, Via Tommaso
Grossi 1, 20121*
Tel *02 88 21 12 34*   **Closed** *lunch; Sun
& Mon*
Limoges china and sparkling
glassware set the scene for fine
dining with Mediterranean and
Italian dishes on the menu. Superb
desserts and fabulous wines.

Northwest Milan

DK Choice

Shockolat   €
Café & Patisserie   **Map** 2 F5
Via Boccaccio 9, 20123
Tel *02 481 005 97*   **Closed** *Sun*
Chocolate creations to buy
or enjoy with coffee is the
temptation at this central
café and patisserie. The chocolate fruit tarts and cheesecakes
are legendary. It also has
a wide range of flavoured
chocolate ice cream, including
hazelnut, ginger and amaretto.
Stylish decor and window
seats from which to watch
the world go by.

La Felicità   €€
Chinese   **Map** 3 B5
Via Rovello 3,
Tel *02 86 52 35*
Run by a family from Shanghai,
this simple yet inviting Chinese
spot serves authentic Jiangsu
and Zhejiang cuisine. The
Xiaolongbao dumplings are
well known.

Price Guide
Prices are for a three course meal
for one, including half a bottle of
house wine, and all extra charges.

€	under €30
€€	€30 to €50
€€€	over €50

Tagiura   €€
Italian   **Map** 5 C2
Via Tagiura 5, 20146
Tel *02 48 95 06 13*   **Closed** *Sun*
Serves everything from breakfast
and morning coffees to traditional
Piacenza lunch and dinner classics
that focus on pasta. Try the
delicious pumpkin ravioli.

Tara   €€
Indian   **Map** 2 F3
Via Domenico Cirillo 16, 20154
Tel *02 345 16 35*   **Closed** *Mon lunch*
One of the best Indian restau-
rants in Milan. Atmospheric,
with an Indian decor. *Samosas*
and *Jalfrezi* curry feature on the
menu, plus the eatery's legendary dish, tandoori shellfish.

Taverna della Trisa   €€
Italian   **Map** 2 E2
Via Francesco Ferrucci 1, 20154
Tel *02 34 13 04*   **Closed** *Sun eve
& Mon*
Dine inside or on the summer
garden terrace. The Trentino menu
features their signature dish,
smoked fish trio (salmon, whitefish
and trout) cooked on lava rock.

Trussardi Café   €€
Café & Patisserie   **Map** 3 C5
Piazza della Scala 5, 20121
Tel *02 80 68 82 95*   **Closed** *Sun*
Refined yet informal, with an
open kitchen, this café focuses
its dishes around healthy
ingredients. Menu options
include pasta and ciabattas.

The elegantly decorated dining area
of Cracco

Exterior of the Trussardi alla Scala, an upmarket restaurant famous for gourmet Italian cuisine

B-Floor €€€
Italian **Map** 2 D1
Via General Govone 42,
20155
Tel *02 36 51 73 29* **Closed** *Sat lunch*
Cosy restaurant serving pizza
with mozzarella from
Battipaglia. Starters include
the Italian salami tasting plate
and *gnocco fritto*, with well-
cooked meat dishes and grilled
fish recipes for mains. The
sornetto is a must-try.

Primo Novecento €€€
Italian **Map** 2 D1
Via Ruggero di Lauria 17, 20100
Tel *02 33 61 16 43* **Closed** *Sat lunch*
Subtle lightning, elegant decor
and old sepia photo-graphs of
Milan on the walls; serves Italian
specialities such as seafood
cooked in delicate sauces.

Quattro Mori €€€
Italian **Map** 3 B5
Largo Maria Callas 1, 20121
Tel *02 87 84 83*
Famous for its home-made
pasta, which is used imagi-
natively in the dishes. Fish is
the main draw, but there are
many meat and vegetable
mains too. Great desserts.

Tondo €€€
Italian **Map** 2 D1
Via Stephenson 55, 20157
Tel *02 87 38 75 17*
Tondo offers a large range of
dishes made using fresh, high-
quality ingredients. The menu
features steaks of the best beef,
Italian fish and meat dishes,
home-made pasta and pizza.
Enjoy meals with selected
wines and an assortments of
fresh juices.

DK Choice

Trussardi alla Scala €€€
Gourmet **Map** 3 C5
Piazza della Scala 5, 20121
Tel *02 80 68 82 01* **Closed** *Sat lunch; Sun*
Seriously stylish decor with
crisp linen and subtle lighting,
first-floor à la carte restaurant
has a wall of windows through
which to observe the city.
Oysters with a rose sorbet and
duck in a *bigarade* sauce and
pasta are a must-try. Popular
with the city's tendy crowd.

Southwest Milan

L'Oca Giuliva €
Italian **Map** 7 C4
Viale Bligny 29, 20136
Tel *02 58 31 28 71* **Closed** *Mon lunch*
Homely yet chic decor sets the
scene for imaginative Puglian
dishes. Try the goose ravioli or
capriccio puglia (beef roulade).
Extensive salad and pizza menu.

Pizzeria Tradizionale con
Cucina di Pesce
Italian **Map** 6 D4
Ripa di Porta Ticinese 7, 20144
Tel *02 839 51 33* **Closed** *Wed lunch*
This pizzeria overlooks the canal
and in summer diners can sit
outside. In typical Neapolitan
style the pizzas are cooked in a
wood-fired oven and served
with buffalo mozzarella.

Premiata Pizzeria €
Italian **Map** 7 A4
Via Alzaia Naviglio Grande 2,
20144
Tel *02 89 40 06 48*
Tasteful decor, a lovely courtyard
garden and a menu of excellent

stone oven-cooked pizza, is
the winning combination at
this pizzeria near the canals.

Dal Bolognese €€
Bolognese **Map** 8 E1
Via Cornaggia, corner of Via
Amedei, 20123
Tel *02 62 69 48 45* **Closed** *Sat lunch; Sun*
This restaurant offers traditional
Bolognese dishes such as pump-
kin *tortelli*, lasagna and *tagliatelle*.
Vegetarian options include green
lasagna Bolognese style. Good
selection of wines.

Osteria Grand Hotel €€
Modern Italian **Map** 7 A4
Via Ascanio Sforza 75, 20136
Tel *02 89 51 15 86* **Closed** *Mon–Fri lunch*
Locally sourced ingredients are
plated as imaginative dishes,
accompanied by home-made
mustards, pasta, pâté and desserts.
Good wine cellar of 700-plus labels.

Osteria di Via Pre €€
Italian **Map** 6 F4
Via Casale 4, 20144
Tel *366 159 74 78* **Closed** *Mon lunch; Tue*
Housed in a welcoming old inn,
this eatery specializes in Ligurian
seafood and pasta. The specials
include *pansotti* (pasta filled with
ricotta, lemon and herbs).

Pace €€
Italian **Map** 5 C1
Via G Washington 74, 20146
Tel *02 46 85 67* **Closed** *Wed & Sat lunch*
A wooden-beamed trattoria with
a tasteful decor, this is a local
favourite. The Tuscan menu features *bollito* (stewed meat) with
mostarda, an Italian condiment.

For more information on types of restaurants *see page 167*

Modern art adorning the white walls of the chic Aimo e Nadia

Trattoria Aurora €€
Italian Map 5 B4
Via Savona 23, 20144
Tel *02 89 40 49 78* **Closed** *Mon*
Delightful trattoria in the heart of Milan serving Piedmontese cuisine that features home-made pasta and sauces. Excellent wine selection and superb ice creams.

Aimo e Nadia €€€
Gourmet Map 5 A5
Via Privata Raimondo Montecuccoli 6, 20147
Tel *02 41 68 86* **Closed** *Sat lunch & Sun*
This contemporary haunt of artisans offers a menu of imaginative Italian classics. The truffle risotto and seasonal game are particularly delicious.

Al Pont de Ferr €€€
Modern Italian Map 6 D4
Ripa di Porta Ticinese 55, 20143
Tel *02 89 40 62 77*
Savour traditional Milanese fare with a modern, gourmet-style twist at this *osteria*. Tasting and à la carte menus, good cheese, dessert and wine selection.

Al Porto €€€
Fish & Seafood Map 6 F3
Piazzale Generale Cantore
Tel *02 89 40 74 25* **Closed** *Sun & Mon lunch*
One of Milan's finest seafood restaurants, with specials that include sea bass with olives and seafood risotto. Good Friulian wines and antipasta menu.

Alla Collina Pistoiese €€€
Italian Map 7 C2
Via Amedei 1, 20123
Tel *02 86 45 10 85* **Closed** *Fri & Sat lunch*
Founded in 1938, this *osteria*-style eatery specializes in Tuscan

dishes. Florentine steak with zucchini and mozzarella is a favourite with diners.

Chic'n'Quick €€€
Gourmet Map 7 A4
Via Ascanio Sforza 77, 20141
Tel *02 89 50 32 22* **Closed** *Sun & Mon lunch*
A relaxed yet ultra-modern trattoria, Chic'n'Quick is popular with foodies who appreciated Milanese gourmet cuisine. It offers themed menus, superb wines and artistic desserts.

Osteria dei Binari €€€
Italian Map 6 E3
Via Tortona 1, 20144
Tel *02 89 40 94 28*
Lombardian dishes are served at this *osteria* housed in a *casa di ringhiera* (an authentic Milanese house with a common passage balcony). The *risotto alla Milanese* (rice with saffron) is a speciality.

Osteria Porta Cicca €€€
Modern Italian Map 6 D4
Ripa di Porta Ticinese 51, 20143
Tel *02 837 27 63* **Closed** *Mon; Tue–Sat lunch*
In an old tavern beside the Naviglio Grande canal; Italian fish, meat and pasta dishes are given a modern twist in combinations such as Tuscan ham with figs.

L'Ulmet €€€
Italian Map 7 B2
Via Disciplini, corner Via Olmetto, 20123
Tel *02 86 45 27 18* **Closed** *Sun and Mon lunch*
Delicious *ossobuco* (veal shank) and steak cooked in rich, red wine are among the choice of dishes at this elegant, wooden-beamed restaurant. Superb wine list.

Southeast Milan

Dongio €
Italian Map 8 F4
Via Corio 3, 20135
Tel *02 551 13 72* **Closed** *Sat lunch; Sun*
A rustic ambience as well as a menu of Calabrian and Piacenza cuisine combine to make this trattoria a local favourite. Try the ravioli made with *caciocavallo* cheese.

Da Giacomo €€
Italian Map 4 F5
Via Pasquale Sottocorno 6, 20129
Tel *02 76 02 33 13*
Has thrilled Milan's trendy set for several decades with dishes of white truffles, spider crab and sea bass, cooked Tuscan-style. Upmarket and intimate.

Mauro €€
Modern Italian Map 8 E1
Via Colonnetta 5, 20122
Tel *02 546 17 27* **Closed** *Sat lunch; Mon*
Italian recipes handed down through generations served with a modern twist. Must-try dishes include smoked salmon with *scamorza* cheese and *pappardelle* with scampi.

That's Vapore €€
Italian Map 8 D1
Corso di Porta Vittoria 5, 20122
Popular with locals, this lively trattoria offers an eclectic menu of Italian dishes with a healthy twist. Specials include taster menus, dozens of cheeses, vegetarian dishes and a juice bar.

Trattoria del Pescatore €€
Fish & Seafood Map 8 E4
Via Atto Vannucci 5, 20135
Tel *02 58 32 04 52* **Closed** *Sun*
A local favourite for its excellent fish- and seafood-based fare. Try the mixed fish antipasta platter followed by Catalan lobster. Good wine list. Book ahead.

I Chiostri Di San Barnaba €€€
Italian Map 8 E4
Via San Barnaba 48, 20122
Tel *02 54 66 494*
Housed in a 15th-century former convent complete with cloisters, this stylish place serves authentic Milanese antipasti dishes and mains, and regional wines. Dine alfresco on its outdoor terrace.

Globe Restaurant Lounge Bar €€€
Gourmet Map 8 F1
Piazza 5 Giornate, 20129
Tel *02 55 18 19 69*
Gourmet-style brunch and dinner is the deal at this 8th-floor eatery.

Antipasta dishes include spaghetti with tasty sauces, followed by creative mains. Enjoy great views of the city while dining.

Raw Fish Café Centro Ittico €€€
Fish & Seafood **Map** 4 F1
Corso di Porta Romana 132, 20125
Tel *02 26 14 37 74* **Closed** *Sun*
Contemporary eatery that makes the most of its location, right next to the fish market, serves scallops, squid, octopus, mussels and lobster in imaginative ways.

La Rena Ristorante €€€
Fish **Map** 8 E4
Via Festa del Perdono 1, 20122
Tel *02 76 28 12 74*
This elegant restaurant offers à la carte lunch and dinner menus. Dishes prepared with flair include platters of oysters, prawns, crayfish and truffles.

Northeast Milan

10 Corso Como €
Modern Italian **Map** 3 C2
Corso Como 10, 20154
Tel *02 29 01 35 81*
Housed within designer Carla Sozzani's Milan centre; serves healthy dishes in a bistro-style setting. Innovative selection of salads. Welcoming courtyard.

Be Bop Pizzeria €
Italian **Map** 4 F4
Via Col di Lana 4, 20136
Tel *02 839 69 72*
This popular restaurant serves around 70 different pizzas, some vegan, vegetarian, gluten-free or wheat-free. It has a superb pasta, salad, meat and fish selection.

DK Choice

Da Rino Vecchia Napoli €
Italian **Map** 4 F1
Via Chavez 4, 20131
Tel *02 261 90 56*
Tuck into crispy pizzas with a choice of around 50 toppings at this bustling pizzeria. Try meat-balls with spinach topping, or aubergine with Parmesan, or even a sweet pizza laden with sugared orange slices, juicy pineapple chunks, bananas and strawberries. Their heart-shaped pizzas have even won awards.

Geppo €
Italian **Map** 4 F3
Via Gian Battista Morgagni 37, 20129
Tel *02 29 51 48 62* **Closed** *Sun*
Informal, bistro-style restaurant that serves wafer-thin pizzas with a host of toppings, ranging from ham and cheese to aubergine.

Pizzeria Piccola Ischia €
Italian **Map** 4 F3
Via Gian Battista Morgagni 7, 20124
Tel *02 204 76 13* **Closed** *Wed, Sat & Sun lunch*
Bright and fun pizzeria offering an array of large pizzas, including the classic Neapolitan. Pasta, salads and bread available.

Princi €
Café & Patisserie **Map** 3 C2
Largo La Foppa, 20154
Tel *02 659 90 13*
One of a chain of upscale bakeries where diners can see the bakers at work. Great for light lunches, such as flans and slices of pizza, pastries and coffees.

Serendib €
Sri Lankan **Map** 3 B2
Via Pontida 2, 20121
Tel *02 659 21 39* **Closed** *lunch*
One of the finest Sri Lankan restaurants in the city with a menu of classic Asian dishes. *Biscotti di cocco* is a speciality.

Alla Cucina delle Langhe €€
Italian **Map** 3 C2
Corso Como 6, 20154
Tel *02 655 42 79*
Enjoy Piedmontese cuisine at this stylish eatery comprising two floors. Try the Barolo risotto infused with rich red Barolo wine and topped with Parmesan flakes.

Caffe Verdi di Rosso Maria €€
Café & Patisserie **Map** 3 C5
Via Guiseppe Verdi 6, 20121
Tel *02 86 38 80*
With busts of composers and photographs of opera stars, this café is rich in atmosphere. Just a few steps from the Teatro alla Scala, it offers a range of snacks, light meals and drinks.

Da Ilia €€
Italian
Via Lecco 1, 20124
Tel *02 29 52 18 95* **Closed** *Fri lunch*
An extensive menu of antipasti dishes and home-made desserts top and tail a selection of Italian pasta, meat and fish dishes. The Milanese crusted veal is a special.

Giglio Rosso €€
Italian **Map** 4 F1
Piazza Luigi di Savoia 2, 20124
Tel *02 669 41 74* **Closed** *Sat & Sun lunch*
An elegant contemporary place that is a celebration of Milanese and Tuscan cuisine. Its *risotto alla Milanese* is a local favourite.

Hong Kong €€
Chinese
Via Schiaparelli 5, 20125
Tel *02 670 19 92* **Closed** *Mon lunch*
Richly decorated with silks and elegant antique-style furniture, this restaurant serves Sichuan and Cantonese cuisine. À la carte and fixed price menus. Good wines.

Lon Fon €€
Chinese **Map** 4 E3
Via Lazzaretto 10, 20124
Tel *02 29 40 51 53*
Superb Chinese eatery serving traditional dishes made with the best ingredients. Dumplings with meat, vegetables and prawns, chicken with macadamia nuts as well as Cantonese rice are on offer.

Malavoglia €€
Fish & Seafood **Map** 4 E3
Via Lecco 4, 20124
Tel *02 29 53 13 87* **Closed** *Mon lunch; Sun*
Sicilian-inspired fare includes sweet and sour sardines or shrimp soup, followed by swordfish rolls stuffed with pine nuts and raisins. Good pasta and wines as well.

Neatly arranged tables in the stylish courtyard at 10 Corso Como

For more information on types of restaurants *see page 167*

Massawa €€
African **Map** 4 F4
Via Sirtori 6, 20129
Tel *02 29 40 69 10* **Closed** *Sat & Sun lunch*
One of the few places in Milan offering authentic African cuisine. Eritrean dishes include *tsebhi* with *injera* (a spicy stew with flatbread). Fixed menu or à la carte. Italian dishes available too.

Mykonos €€
Greek **Map** 4 F1
Via Tofane 5, 20217
Tel *02 261 02 09* **Closed** *Tue lunch; Sat & Sun*
Try this Greek taverna's selection of dips such as the Greek *tzatziki*, mains of *souvlaki* (Greek fast food of meat or vegetables grilled on skewers) and home-made desserts.

Obikà €€
Italian **Map** 3 B4
Via Mercato corner Via dei Fiori Chiari, 20121
Tel *02 86 45 05 68*
Obikà serves different kinds of buffalo mozzarella and dishes such as rolls of mozzarella filled with speck and courgettes or salmon and roquette and pizza. Try the tiramisù for dessert. Good selection of wines and beers.

Osteria La Piola €€
Milanese
Viale Abruzzi 23, 20131
Tel *02 29 53 12 71* **Closed** *Sun*
This eatery offers a variety of traditional Milanese and regional dishes. Don't miss the risotto with *ossobuco* and the *cotoletta alla milanese* (Milanese cutlets). Good selection of desserts and wines.

Osteria del Treno €€
Modern Italian **Map** 4 E2
Via San Gregorio 46, 20124
Tel *02 670 04 79* **Closed** *Sat & Sun lunch*
The chef at this attractive *osteria* takes his inspiration from the Slow Food philosophy, creating

tasty dishes such as gnocchi with cocoa and gorgonzola.

Piccola Cucina €€
Italian **Map** 4 F4
Viale Piave 17, 20129
Tel *02 76 01 28 60* **Closed** *Lunch; Sun*
A local favourite, this restaurant is a tastefully decorated place. Specials change daily, but typically have dishes such as gnocchi with a gorgonzola and thyme sauce.

Piero e Pia €€
Italian **Map** 4 F4
Piazza Aspari 2, 20219
Tel *02 71 85 41* **Closed** *Sun*
Warm and welcoming family-run restaurant famous for its excellent cuisine from the Piacenza region. The risotto with pumpkin and black truffles is delicious. Also serves superb desserts such as eggnog and caramel parfait.

Rigolo €€
Italian **Map** 3 C3
Largo Treves, Via Solferino, 20121
Tel *02 86 46 32 20* **Closed** *Mon*
Ossobuco alla Milanese (veal) and steak tartare with crostini delight the trendy diners who frequent the Brera district where this historic inn is located.

Tomoyoshi Endo €€
Japanese **Map** 4 E2
Via Fabio Filzi 8, 20124
Tel *02 66 98 61 17* **Closed** *Sun*
One of three restaurants in Milan run by the husband-and-wife team of Kato and Masako Shozo. The creative 120-dish menu leads with excellent sushi. Fine wine list.

Trattoria Al Matarel €€
Italian **Map** 3 B3
Corso Garibaldi 75, 20121
Tel *02 65 42 04* **Closed** *Tue; Wed lunch*
With the look of a traditional village trattoria, Al Matarel is a always packed. Their signature dish is *cassoeula* (pork stew). The menu also features lots of pasta and risottos dishes.

I Valtellina €€
Italian
Via Taverna 34, 20134
Tel *02 756 11 39* **Closed** *Fri; Sat lunch*
The country-house decor, and an extensive menu of dishes prepared with quality ingredients, never fail to wow diners. Dine inside or alfresco on the terrace.

Akropolis €€€
Greek
Via Accademia 56, 20131
Tel *02 26 15 430* **Closed** *Sat & Sun lunch*
Delicious Greek fare served in an elegant atmosphere. The menu features *feta saganaki* (fried feta with honey and sesame seeds), meat and fish dishes as well as *tzatziki* with different ingredients. Sit outside in the covered and heated area in winter.

Il Baretto al Baglioni €€€
Italian **Map** 4 E5
Via Senato 7, 20121
Tel *02 78 12 55*
Complete with wood panels and hunting scenes, this refined restaurant is styled along the lines of an English lounge bar. Gastronomic-style dishes are served with excellent wines.

Bulgari €€€
Gourmet **Map** 3 C4
Via Privata Fratelli Gabba 7b, 20122
Tel *02 805 80 52 33*
This luxurious hotel restaurant on the edge of the Botanical Gardens excels in gastronomic cuisine. Dine on crusted veal or sea urchins, saffron risotto and hand-rolled profiteroles with fruit.

DK Choice

Il Coriandolo €€€
Italian **Map** 3 C5
Via dell'Orso 1, 20121
Tel *02 869 32 73*
The emphasis is on fresh, quality food and wine at Il Coriandolo. Fresh fish appears on the menu as an excellent appetizer for two to share and as mains such as a crusted Orbetello sea bass with tomato au gratin. Meat mains are creative: veal with lime cream, or beef with Treviso chicory and Parmesan to name a few.

Da Giannino €€€
Italian **Map** 8 F1
Via Vittor Pisani 6, 20135
Tel *02 66 98 69 98* **Closed** *Sat & Sun lunch*
A lavish *belle époque* dining hall provides the setting for a fine menu of Tuscan-Milanese

Classy Old English decor at Il Baretto al Baglioni

Key to Price Guide *see page 170*

A selection of wines at Joia, an upmarket vegetarian restaurant

dishes. The veal cutlet is served pink and the white truffles and tiramisu are a big draw.

I Sapori del Mare　€€€
Fish & Seafood　**Map** 4 F5
Via Carlo Goldoni 58, 20129
Tel *02 71 36 69*　**Closed** *Mon & Sun lunch*
Murals of sea scenes and an aquarium provide the backdrop to those dining at this fish and seafood restaurant. Try one of the three favourites: clam chowder, Catalan prawn risotto or Sardinian monkfish.

Il Teatro　€€€
Gourmet　**Map** 4 D5
Four Seasons Hotel, Via Gesu 6-8, 20121
Tel *02 770 88*
Elegant restaurant, complete with crisp linens and sparkling glassware, that excels in Milanese gastro dishes. Veal with black truffles is a special. Sunday brunch is also served.

Joia　€€€
Vegetarian　**Map** 4 E3
Via Panfilo Castaldi 18, 20124
Tel *02 29 52 21 24*　**Closed** *Sat lunch; Sun*
Discover this unexpected treasure – a gourmet restaurant offering mostly vegetarian dishes, including its signature (and obviously meat-free) *foie gras*. Artful plating and a very popular tasting menu.

Nobu Armani　€€€
Japanese　**Map** 4 E2
Via Gastone Pisoni 1, 20121
Tel *02 62 31 26 45*　**Closed** *Sun lunch*
Fine Japanese gourmet cuisine prepared by master chef Nobu Matsuhisa. The menu includes

scallops with wasabi and black cod with miso. Located inside the Armani store.

Lake Maggiore

ARONA: Del Barcaiolo　€€
Italian
Piazza del Popolo 23, 28041
Tel *0322 24 33 88*　**Closed** *Wed lunch*
Housed in a centuries-old palazzo complete with wooden beams, this place focuses on Piedmontese cuisine. The chargrilled fish and meat is complemented by the home-made pasta.

ARONA: Taverna del Pittore　€€
Gourmet
Piazza del Popolo 39, 28041
Tel *0322 24 33 66*　**Closed** *Mon*
Winning combination of simple Tuscan dishes and elaborate gourmet-style cuisine, especially fish, at this lakeside eatery. Located in Arona's main square.

ARONA: La Vecchia Arona　€€
Italian
Lungolago Marconi 17, 28041
Tel *0322 24 24 69*　**Closed** *Fri*
Intimate restaurant right on the lakeside serving home-made pâtés and pasta, followed by Piedmontese meat and fish dishes. Tempting desserts.

CANNOBIO: Del Lago　€€
Italian
Via Nationale 2, 28822
Tel *0323 705 95*　**Closed** *Tue & Wed lunch*
Water almost laps the terrace of this lakeside restaurant at the Del Lago hotel. The cuisine remains faithful to Lombardy and Piedmont

with staples such as *ossobuco* and *Vitello tonnato* (veal with tuna cream sauce) on the menu.

CANNOBIO: Osteria Vino Divino　€€
Modern Italian
Strada della Valle Cannobina 1, 28822
Tel *0323 719 19*　**Closed** *lunch*
A bright *osteria* created in an old stable block, excels in classic dishes with a modern twist. Try deer teamed with a berry omelette or veal with pistachio cream. Good cheeses and wines.

CANNOBIO: Porto Vecchio　€€€
Gourmet
Hotel Cannobio, Piazza Vittorio Emanuele III 6, 28822
Tel *0323 73 96 39*　**Closed** *Tue*
The rattan chairs and lamps give this little restaurant a chic feel. The terrace overlooks the lake. À la carte menu with excellent fish and seafood dishes.

LAVENO: Il Porticciolo　€€€
Modern Italian
Via Fortino 40, 21014
Tel *0332 66 72 57*
Savour *foie gras* with cream kumquats, cannelloni with cod, ravioli stuffed with trout or veal with lemongrass among other innovative dishes at this seriously stylish restaurant.

LUINO: Gelateria Cagliani　€
Café & Patisserie
Via Dante 65, 21016
Tel *0332 53 30 06*
Bright and welcoming ice cream parlour in the heart of Luino, popular with locals and visitors. Tempts with superb creamy ice cream, in dozens of flavours.

For more information on types of restaurants *see page 167*

Shaded outdoor seating in the well-manicured garden fronting La Rampolina, Stresa

LUINO: Osteria degli Antichi Sapori €€
Italian
Via Voldomino 3, 21016
Tel *0332 51 02 77*
A welcoming family-run *osteria* serving a menu of local dishes, including fish platters and their famous risotto with pistachio and brie. The emphasis is on flavour and fresh ingredients.

LUINO: Ristorante Sibilla Pizzeria €€
Italian
Via XXV Aprile 81, 21016
Tel *0332 53 10 01*
The aroma of pizza, fresh from the oven, attracts passers-by to this friendly little pizzeria. The Margherita pizza with a thick, crusty base and lots of buffalo mozzarella is a favourite.

DK Choice

MACCAGNO: Acquadulza €€
Italian
Lungolago Girardi 4, 21010
Tel *0345 83 40 932*
Housed in a gorgeous old building with a vibrant decor, Acquadulza is one of the region's trendiest lounges. Innovative antipasti dishes such as salmon croquettes with salsa preceed mains of *fusilli alla sorrentina* or *frittura di calamari e zucchini* (squid and aubergine). Extensive wine list from all Italian regions.

MACCAGNO: La Gabella €€€
Italian
Via Marconi 19, 21010
Tel *0332 56 15 26*   **Closed** *Tue lunch; Mon*
Located beside the lake with access via a private harbour, La Gabella specializes in fresh fish with home-made sauces, and a range of pizza and pasta dishes.

PALLANZA: Osteria dell'Angolo €
Italian
Piazza Garibaldi 35, 28048
Tel *0323 55 63 62*
This small, traditionally decorated tavern is one of the town's best-kept secrets. The menu focuses on Lombardy and Piedmontese veal and seafood dishes.

PALLANZA: Milano €€
Italian
Corso Zannitello 2, 28922
Tel *0323 55 68 16*   **Closed** *Tue*
In a Neo-Gothic mansion on the banks of the lake, fish and organic garden produce are transformed into dishes of exemplary flavour and served with style. Lovely terrace with views.

DK Choice

RANCO: Il Sole di Ranco €€€
Gourmet
Piazza Venezia 5, 21020
Tel *0331 97 65 07*   **Closed** *Tue (except summer)*
Elegant restaurant, surrounded by parkland with the prettiest of terraces for al fresco dining in summer. Lobster perfumed with orange, followed by blue cheese lasagna or sea bass cooked in clay with iced mustard are just some of the gourmet dishes prepared in chef Carolo Brovelli's kitchen. Good cellar.

SESTO CALENDE: La Biscia €€
Fish & Seafood
Piazza de Cristoforis 1, 21028
Tel *0331 92 44 35*   **Closed** *Sun dinner; Mon*
Fish and seafood dishes dominate the menu of this bright and elegant restaurant beside the lake. Try its renowned – flambéed shrimp on leeks. Good wine and dessert menu.

SESTO CALENDE: Zen €€
Japanese
Via Manzoni 48, 21018
Tel *0331 91 38 35*   **Closed** *Tue lunch*
The fixed-price all-you-can-eat option is excellent value at this popular Japanese restaurant. Sushi, sashimi and tempura, plus a wide choice of fish dishes.

SESTO CALENDE: MoMa l'Ospite e il Gusto €€€
Italian
Piazza Federico Berera 18, 21018
Tel *0331 92 34 73*   **Closed** *Mon lunch; Tue*
The menu typically features venison marinated with fennel or sturgeon carpaccio to start, followed by meat, fish and pasta options at this fashionable eatery. Excellent wine list.

STRESA: Piemontese €€
Modern Italian
Via Mazzini 25, 28838
Tel *0323 302 35*   **Closed** *Mon*
Traditional cuisine is given a modern twist and served on the vine-covered terrace which allows for alfresco dining in summer. The pâté with fondue is a special.

DK Choice

STRESA: La Rampolina €€
Italian
Road to Someraro 13, 28838
Tel *0323 92 34 15*   **Closed** *Mon*
Decorated in bright pink and cream, and overlooking a lake, this eatery is a gem. The kitchen takes the freshest mushrooms and chestnuts from the forest, fish from the lake, and Ossola Valley cheese and creates exceptional Piedmontese dishes. In addition, its pizzeria serves wood-fired oven pizzas.

VERBANIA: Boccon di Vino €€
Italian
Via Troubetzkoy 86, 28900
Tel *0323 64 40 39*   **Closed** *Tue*
The Piedmontese fare served at this lakeside tavern is of gastronomic standard. Fine wines accompany dishes such as prawns with cognac, and beef tartare Fassona.

VERBANIA: Chi Ghinn €€
Italian
Via Maggiore 21, Bèe 28900
Tel *0323 563 26*   **Closed** *Tue*
This absolutely beautiful renovated villa, with cream walls and crisp linens, is a must-visit. It lies in the tiny village of Bèe and serves Italian fish dishes.

Exterior of Barchetta, a classic terrace restaurant in Bellagio

VERBANIA: Little Italy €€
Italian
Via Guglielmazzi 25, 28900
Tel *0323 50 45 46*
This warm, family-run *osteria* specializes in traditional dishes made with recipes handed down through the generations. Try the *Scalopine di vitello* (veal). Regional wines on offer as well.

DK Choice

VERBANIA: Il Portale €€€
Italian
Via del Sassello 3, 28922
Tel *0323 50 54 86* **Closed** *Mon–Fri lunch in winter; Mon lunch in summer*
Artfully presented antipasti dishes such as noodles with rabbit, and mains of whitefish stuffed with shrimps and blue cheese, feature on the menu of the elegantly decorated Il Portale. Good choice of desserts and wines. Tasting and special diet menus are also available.

Lake Como

BELLAGIO: Silvio €
Fish & Seafood
Via Paolo Carcano 12, 22021
Tel *031 95 03 22*
Run by a fisherman whose catch appears in creative dishes such as perch served *a cagnon* (with rice) and Parmesan or fish mousse ravioli. Stylish decor and fine wines.

BELLAGIO: Barchetta €€
Italian
Salita Mella 13, 22021
Tel *031 95 13 89*
Established in 1887, this popular, eatery specializes in fish and local Lombard veal dishes such as *cotoletta* and *ossobuco*. Fresh pizza from the wood-fired oven.

BRIENNO: Crotto dei Platani €€
Italian
Via Regina 73, 22010
Tel *031 81 40 38*
A water's edge terrace with a canopy of trees is the setting for creative dishes at this trendy restaurant. Try its lake fish with black truffles or the perch mousse ravioli. Features a 400-label cellar.

CERNOBBIO: La Sosta €€
Italian
Via Regina Cesare Battisti 7, 22012
Tel *030 51 05 08*
This eatery serves great wood-oven pizzas made with traditional or wholemeal dough, as well as home-made pasta such as *pizzoccheri* (a Valtellina speciality) and mouthwatering meat and fish dishes.

CERNOBBIO: La Terrazza Asnigo €€
Italian
Via Noseda 2, 22012
Tel *031 51 00 62* **Closed** *Tue–Sat lunch; Mon*
Good antipasti and primi piatti selection at this lakeside eatery. À la carte dishes feature mozzarella wrapped veal, and perch with sesame seeds.

CERNOBBIO: Trattoria del Vapore €€
Italian
Via Giuseppe Garibaldi 17, 22012
Tel *031 51 03 08* **Closed** *Wed*
With old sepia photos on the walls, this trattoria is a memorable place to enjoy authentic local dishes. The house special sage tortellini and risotto with carp must be tried.

CERNOBBIO: Gatto Nero €€€
Gourmet
Via Monte Santo 69, Rovenna, 22012
Tel *031 51 20 42* **Closed** *Mon–Fri lunch*
The "Black Cat" has an elegant, cottage-like feel and a dining terrace with lake views. Top-quality ingredients are used in dishes such as tagliatelle with black truffles.

CERNOBBIO: Giardino €€€
Italian
Via Regina 73, 22102
Tel *031 51 11 54*
Regional specialities are served alongside fresh home-made pizzas here. Dine inside or in its lush garden. Good wine list, too.

COMO: Locanda dell'Oca Bianca €
Italian
Via Canturina 251, 22100
Tel *031 52 56 05* **Closed** *Tue–Sat lunch; Mon*
Sautéed calamari with a radish tart and butternut squash roulade are some of the dishes served at this eatery. Superb home-made desserts as well as fine wines.

COMO: Minimalismo Livingroom €
Café & Patisserie
Via Dante Alighieri 67, 22100
Tel *031 207 38 60*
This restaurant and cocktail bar looks out over the *citta* (market) and is famous for its wines, cognacs and rums. Food is bistro-style pasta, pastries and cold cuts.

COMO: Sant Anna 1907 €€
Modern Italian
Via Filippo Turati 3, 22100
Tel *031 50 52 66* **Closed** *Sat lunch; Sun*
Aesthetically presented modern Lombardy dishes tempt at this chic restaurant. Try lobster with pineapple, crusted veal or risotto with fish and saffron.

COMO: L'Osteria a'Angolo dei Silenzio €€€
Italian
Viale Lecco 25, 22100
Tel *031 337 21 57* **Closed** *Mon*
A good mix of fish and meat dishes feature on the menu at this popular tavern in a renovated old stone building. The house special is *Costata Fiorentina* (steak).

Fresh thin-crust pizza, an all-time favourite

For more information on types of restaurants *see page 167*

The lovely terrace at La Terrazza, a gourmet Italian eatery in Tremezzo

COMO: Raimondi €€€
Goumet
Via Cernobbio 12, 22100
Tel *031 338 33*
Housed in the refined setting of
the 19th-century Villa Flori hotel,
Raimondi specializes in Lombardy
cuisine. The menu classics include
pappardelle with game ragout
and Guancialino veal stew.

DK Choice

**ISOLA COMACINA: Locanda
dell'Isola Comacina** €€€
Gourmet
Sala Comacina, 22010
Tel *0344 550 83* **Closed** *Nov–
mid-Mar*
This restaurant stands on a lush
private island in the centre of
Lake Como and is reached only
by boat. The menu, comprising
mainly fish but with chicken
dishes too, is said to have been
created in 1948 and remains
unchanged. A favourite haunt
of celebrities.

**LECCO: Antica Osteria
Casa di Lucia** €€
Italian
Via Lucia 27, 23900
Tel *0341 49 45 94* **Closed** *Sat
lunch & Sun*
Set in a 1600s palazzo, this *osteria*
has a loyal following. Top-quality
ingredients, lake fish and wines
are selected for its gourmet
menu. The nut tart is legendary.

LECCO: Al Porticciolo €€€
Gourmet
Via Fausto Valsecchi 5–7, 23900
Tel *0341 49 81 03* **Closed** *Mon &
Tue; Wed–Sat lunch*
Exquisite fish and shellfish
dishes at this classic lakeside
restaurant. Trout in a creamy
almond sauce or shrimps with
salsa are tempting options.

**MANDELLO DEL LARIO: Riva
Granda** €€
Italian
Piazza XXV Aprile 5a, 23826
Tel *0341 70 03 36* **Closed** *Tue in winter*
This welcoming place offers
local dishes with a modern twist.
Lake fish is used in dishes such
as perch stuffed ravioli. Home-
made pasta and desserts.

MOLTRASIO: Imperialino €€€
Gourmet
Via Antica Regina 26, 22010
Tel *031 34 61 11* **Closed** *Mon*
Housed in a lakeside hotel villa,
Imperialino excels in gourmet
fish dishes, plus regional
favourites such as veal in a sauce
or with an olive crust. Good
wine list as well.

**SALA COMACINA:
La Tirlindana** €€
Italian
Piazza Matteotti, 22010
Tel *0344 566 37*
Dine on dishes such as home-
made gnocchi with squid
followed by beef with gorgonzola
at this cosy restaurant overlooking
the harbour.

**SALA COMACINA:
Taverna Bleu** €€€
Gourmet
Via Puricelli 4, 22010
Tel *0344 551 07* **Closed** *Nov–Mar;
Tue*
Enjoy views over Isola Comacina
and gourmet-style Lariana cui-
sine at this boutique restaurant.
The menu includes *Missoltini*
served with home-made polenta.

SAN SIRO: Sole €€
Italian
Santa Maria Rezzonico, 22010
Tel *0344 500 89*
Set in a villa with the lake's water
a pebble-skim away, the family-
run Sole celebrates traditional

local cuisine. From the breakfast
croissants to the evening pasta,
all dishes are home-made.

TREMEZZO: Cantina Follie €€
Italian
Via Volta Alessandro 14, 22019
Tel *0344 423 11* **Closed** *Tue lunch*
Located in the heart of
Tremezzo, this restaurant-cum-
wine bar is a locals' favourite.
Upmarket wines are sold by the
glass, accompanied by Italian
buffet dishes.

TREMEZZO: La Terrazza €€€
Gourmet
*Grand Hotel Tremezzo, Via Regina 8,
22019*
Tel *0344 424 91*
This lakeside restaurant celebrates
the art of gastronomy. Start with
the gratined scallops followed by
a rack of lamb or the Lake Como
lavaret. Excellent desserts and
wine list.

VARENNA: Vecchia Varenna €
Italian
Contrada Scoscesa 10, 23828
Tel *0341 83 07 93*
Vecchia Varenna can be found
at the harbour in a 15th-century
stone building. Its kitchen offers
fish from the lake with capers,
meat in wine, pasta and desserts.

**VARENNA:
Albergo Del Sole** €€
Italian
Piazza San Giorgio 17, 23829
Tel *0341 81 52 18* **Closed** *Tue*
Whitefish and pike from the lake
and dishes such as *ossobuco*
made with veal shanks feature
on the menu of this eatery.
Picturesque dining terrace.

Lake Garda

BARDOLINO: La Formica €
Italian
Piazza Lenotti 11, 37011
Tel *045 721 17 05* **Closed** *Mon*
This landmark restaurant in the
old quarter offers pasta, fish and
meat dishes and decadent
desserts. *Vitello tonnato* (veal in
tuna sauce) is a speciality.

BARDOLINO: Bardolino €€
Italian
Via Gardesana dell'Acqua 10, 37011
Tel *045 621 40 11* **Closed** *Nov–Mar*
A contemporary restaurant with
almost floor-to-ceiling windows,
Bardolino offers panoramic lake
views, along with fine cuisine.
Meat and fish in traditional
sauces, plus pizza and wines,
feature on the menu.

COSTERMANO:
Tre Camini €€
Italian
Via Murlongo 82, 37010
Tel *045 720 03 42* **Closed** *Mon*
Housed in a 15th-century farm-house, this restaurant excels in à la carte fare. Try the gnocchi with truffle, followed by beef tartare with chives or *foie gras* escalopes. Good Italian wine cellar.

DK Choice

DESENZANO DEL GARDA:
Gelateria la Romana €
Café & Patisserie
Piazza Duomo 25, 25015
Tel *030 687 2057*
One of the patisseries and ice cream parlours in the Romana chain, founded in 1947, this bright eatery tempts with fabulous creations. Cakes, pastries and ice creams are made on the premises daily. Try the Piedmont hazelnut or Marsala flavoured ice cream.

DESENZANO DEL GARDA:
Antica Hostaria Cavallino €€€
Gourmet
Via Murachette 29, 25015
Tel *030 912 02 17* **Closed** *Sun dinner & Mon*
An intimate restaurant, complete with a courtyard by the lake, Cavallino serves gourmet fish dishes. Go for the caviar risotto flavoured with Franciacorta wine.

DESENZANO DEL GARDA:
Esplanade €€€
Gourmet
Via Lario 3, 25015
Tel *030 914 33 61* **Closed** *Wed*
Beautifully presented meat and fish dishes are created in the kitchen of award-winning chef Massimo Fezzardi. Choose from the excellent wine list and enjoy the lovely lakeside location.

GARDA: Giardino delle Rane €€
Italian
Via Lungolago Regina Adelaide, 37016
Tel *045 725 52 78*
Classic Italian and Mediterranean cuisine is the theme at this lively family-friendly lakeside eatery. Pizza and pasta feature strongly on the menu.

GARDONE:
Locanda Agli Angeli €€
Italian
Via Dosso 7, 25083
Tel *0365 209 91* **Closed** *Oct–mid-July: Tue; Mon–Fri lunch*
This charming restaurant can be found in a property full of beams and arches. The cuisine is homely Italian and their risotto with lake trout is a speciality.

GARDONE: Villa Fiordaliso €€€
Gourmet
Corso Zanardelli 150, 25083
Tel *0365 201 58* **Closed** *Mon*
Lying on the water's edge, this is a welcoming restaurant. High quality ingredients, many organic, are used to produce gourmet meat, fish and pasta dishes.

GARGNANO: Tortuga €€€
Italian
Via XXIV Maggio 5
Tel *0365 712 51* **Closed** *Tue*
A local favourite, Tortuga is a lakeside restaurant with a menu of light, imaginative dishes and an excellent wine list. Meat and fish is often paired with the *madernina* and *cedro di Salò* lemons that are grown in the grounds.

MANERBA: Capriccio €€€
Gourmet
Piazza San Bernardo 6, 25080
Tel *0365 55 11 24* **Closed** *Tue*
A romantic restaurant with a sophisticated menu and an 800-label wine cellar to match. The artfully presented dishes include sea bass with scallops, fennel cream and grapefruit.

Classy interiors of Esplanade, Desenzano del Garda

PESCHIERA DEL GARDA:
Ai Capitani €€
Italian
Via Castelletto 4, 37019
Tel *045 64 00 162*
A contemporarily restored fisherman's house-turned-restaurant is the setting for Ai Capitani. The menu comprises Italian and Mediterranean cuisine, focusing on fish.

PESCHIERA DEL GARDA:
L'Osteria €€
Italian
Via Cavallotti 7, 37019
Tel *045 755 05 45*
Authentic Venetian dishes feature on the menu of this cosy, rustic restaurant on the promenade. Baby octopus with polenta followed by tagliatelle with pheasant as well as fondue with truffles are tempting.

PESCHIERA DEL GARDA:
Trattoria al Combattente €€
Italian
Strada Bergamini 60, 37019
Tel *045 755 04 10* **Closed** *Mon*
Antipasti dishes of tuna-trout mousse and pike in sardine sauce, followed by pumpkin tortilla and chargrilled fish, has put this trattoria on the culinary map. Welcoming staff and an elegant ambience.

PESCHIERA DEL GARDA:
Piccolo Mondo €€€
Gourmet
Via Riviera Carducci 6, 37019
Tel *045 755 00 25* **Closed** *Mon*
Bright by day, intimate by night, the sophisticated Piccolo Mondo overlooks the lake and serves delicious gourmet cuisine. Go for the specials: tagliatelle with lobster or trout with almonds, plated with flair.

The dining room at Tortuga done up in various shades of red, Gargnano

For more information on types of restaurants *see page 167*

Diners enjoying a meal at the waterside Locanda San Vigilio, San Vigilio

RIVA DEL GARDA:
Gelateria Flora €
Café & Patisserie
Viale Rovereto 54, 38066
Tel *0464 55 16 71*
Gelateria Flora is open until late serving hearty breakfasts, morning coffee, lunches of pizza and salads and late-night pasta suppers and cocktails. Bright and modern decor.

SALÒ: Osteria dell'Orologio €€
Italian
Via Butturini 26, 25087
Tel *0365 29 01 58* **Closed** *Wed*
Housed in a gorgeous restored inn, this tavern is popular for the chef's hearty dishes. Partridge with pappardelle sauce is a speciality. Wines by the glass.

SALÒ: Antica Trattoria alle Rose €€€
Italian
Via Gasparo da Salò 33, 25087
Tel *0365 432 20* **Closed** *Wed*
Eclectic colours, sparkling glassware, fine wines and an innovative menu await at this trattoria. Menu classics include pheasant terrine and pappardelle with duck, plus fish from the lake.

SALÒ: Villa Arcadio €€€
Italian
Via Palazzina 2, 25087
Tel *0365 422 81* **Closed** *Nov–Mar*
The restaurant of Villa Arcadio offers a mouthwatering selection of Italian classics. *Trota Ripiena* (stuffed trout poached in red wine) is a speciality here.

SAN FELICE: Dream €€€
Gourmet
Via Porto 41, 25010
Tel *036 56 21 02* **Closed** *Nov–Mar*
Dream tempts with local dishes such as seafood skewer au gratin, goose with fennel, plus meat and pasta dishes. Located in Hotel Sogno.

SAN VIGILIO: Locanda San Vigilio €€€
Gourmet
Punta San Vigilio, 37016
Tel *045 725 66 88* **Closed** *Nov–Mar*
Set on a peninsula, this tavern-style restaurant offers a gourmet seasonal menu. Try its home-made risotto with Amarone, vegetable soufflé and *îles flottantes*. Fine wine list.

SIRMIONE: Al Porticciolo €
Italian
Porto Galeazzi, Via XXV Aprile 83, 25019
Tel *030 919 61 61*
Al Porticciolo is a landmark orange-washed trattoria located right beside the water. Serves innovative pizza and pasta, plus seafood and fish dishes.

SIRMIONE: Trattoria Clementina €€
Italian
Piazza Rovizzi 13, 25019
Tel *030 919 66 63* **Closed** *Mon–Sat lunch; Tue*
This lakeside trattoria has a creative menu of pasta dishes. Go for their specials – pasta with marinated smoked salmon or squid and spinach is a must-try.

SIRMIONE: La Rucola €€€
Gourmet
Via Strentelle 3, 25019
Tel *030 91 63 26* **Closed** *Thu; Jan*
Tagliatelle with trout and almonds, salmon with salsa, and delicate home-made pastries are a crowd favourite at this elegant restaurant, housed in a centuries-old stone property.

SIRMIONE: Signori €€€
Italian
Via Romagnoli 17, 25019
Tel *030 91 60 17*
An elegant restaurant with white drapes, crisp linens and rattan terrace furniture, Signori has a menu of mainly fish dishes. Wonderful lake views.

SIRMIONE: Trattoria La Speranzina €€€
Italian
Via Dante 16
Tel *030 990 62 92* **Closed** *Nov–Mar*
The freshest local fish, meat, game and produce is turned into imaginative dishes at this chic trattoria with a 1,900-label cellar.

SOIANO DEL LAGO: Villa Aurora €€
Italian
Via Ciucani 1, 25080
Tel *0365 67 41 01* **Closed** *Wed*
Aurora can be found in the hills, in a beautifully restored villa. The menu is Italian with dishes such as crusted sea bass with shellfish sauce, or guinea fowl with truffle and pastries.

Lago d'Iseo

CARZANO: Ristorante Vittoria €€
Italian
Monteisola, loc. Sensole 22, 25050
Tel *030 988 62 22* **Closed** *dinner Oct–Mar*
This family-run kitchen offers tasty dishes prepared with fish from the lake. Wine comes from the nearby Franciacorta region. A terrace with lake views overlooks the romantic island of San Paolo.

ERBUSCO: Gualtiero Marchesi €€€
Gourmet
Via Vittorio Emanuele II 23, 25030
Tel *030 776 05 62* **Closed** *Sun lunch & Mon*
Run by one of Italy's most celebrated chefs, Gualtiero Marchesi, this stylish restaurant has a fitting gastronomic menu and wines from its own vineyards.

ERBUSCO: Osteria San Clemente €€€
Italian
Via Rovato 12, 25030
Tel *030 77 60 088* **Closed** *Sun dinner; Mon*
Exquisite food featuring creative starters such as octopus with tomatoes on cream of potatoes and vegetarian tart with *robiola* and *mortadella*. Mains include pasta and gnocchi with delicate sauces.

ISEO: I Due Roccoli €€
Italian
Via Silvio Bonomelli, 25049
Tel *030 982 29 77* **Closed** *Nov–Mar*
The use of top-quality seasonal produce ensures a constantly changing menu of meat and pasta dishes at I Due Roccoli. Dine inside the farmhouse or on the lovely garden terrace.

ISEO: Osteria Il Paiolo €€
Italian
Piazza Mazzini 9, 25049
Tel *030 982 1074* **Closed** *Tue*
This traditional *osteria* lies in the historic quarter of Iseo. The menu comprises Lombardy classics. Try Florentine steak or home-made pasta with pigeon sauce.

ISEO: Osteria Il Volto €€
Italian
Via Mirolte 33, 25049
Tel *030 98 14 62* **Closed** *Wed*
Il Volto is perhaps one of the area's best-kept culinary secrets and popular with locals in the know. The finest ingredients are turned into wonderful local dishes. Try the lake-fish ragout.

ISEO: Il Conte di Carmagnola €€€
Gourmet
Via Mirabella 34, Frazione Clusane, 25049
Tel *030 989 80 51* **Closed** *Nov–Mar*
Housed in the Relais Mirabella and overlooking Lake Iseo, this restaurant serves Lombardy classics with Franciacorta wine vintages. The signature dish is oven-baked tench with polenta.

DK Choice

MONTE ISOLA: La Foresta €€
Italian
Via Peschiera Maraglio 174, 25050
Tel *030 988 62 10* **Closed** *Wed; 20 Dec–Feb*
La Foresta is legendary for fish dishes such as smoked chub from the lake, marinated sardines with polenta or trout cooked over wood. Run by two brothers: Sandro, a fisherman, and chef Silvano. Good wine cellar.

SARNICO: Il Chiostro €€
Italian
Piazza Besenzoni 1, 24067
Tel *035 91 11 90* **Closed** *Tue*
Savour delicious pasta dishes and a variety of seafood and fish. Il Chiostro also offers a good selection of pizzas. Al fresco tables during the summer allow you to enjoy views of the lake, and there is a cosy conservatory for winter.

Lago d'Orta

DK Choice

ORTA SAN GIULIO: Ai Due Santi €€
Italian
Piazza Motta 18, 28016
Tel *0322 901 92* **Closed** *Wed; Nov*
Exquisite decor, an outside dining terrace and a creative menu give this restaurant an edge over others. *Capesante dorate* or scallops topped with bacon and beef tartare are specials, while its wine list carries more than 200 labels. Located in the main square of Orta San Giulio, looking out towards San Giulio island.

ORTA SAN GIULIO: Ristorante San Giulio €€
Italian
Via Basilica 4, 28016 Orta San Giulio
Tel *0322 902 34* **Closed** *Tue*
Rabbit salad with beer, perch risotto and Piedmontese anchovy crostini, plus desserts, are just some of the dishes served at this popular eatery housed in one of the island's oldest properties.

ORTA SAN GIULIO: San Rocco €€
Italian
Via Gippini 11, 28016
Tel *0322 91 19 77*
The San Rocco has a panoramic view from its dining hall and terrace. Piedmontese-inspired dishes typically begin with quail, move on to pork pasta parcels and culminate with veal filet. Fine wine cellar.

ORTA SAN GIULIO: Villa Crespi Restaurant €€€
Gourmet
Via Fava 18, 28016
Tel *0322 91 19 02* **Closed** *Mon & Tues lunch*
The Michelin-starred restaurant of Villa Crespi excels in Piedmontese gourmet cuisine. Try lobster medallions or sea urchins with apples. Fabulous wine cellar.

PETTENASCO: Giardinetto €€
Italian
Via Provinciale 1
Tel *0323 891 18* **Closed** *Nov–Mar*
The restaurant of the Hotel Giardinetto has a waterside dining terrace where appetizers such as Piedmontese steak tartare and mains of smoked salmon can be enjoyed.

DK Choice

SORISO: Al Soriso €€€
Gourmet
Via Roma 18, 28010
Tel *0322 98 32 28* **Closed** *Mon & Tue*
Fresh, seasonal ingredients cleverly transformed into gourmet dishes has put Al Soriso on the map. Specials might feature venison with junipers and white truffles with gratin.

The plush winery in Al Soriso, Soriso

For more information on types of restaurants *see page 167*

BARS AND CAFÉS

In general, Milanese bars and cafés are places to go for lunch or an aperitif. Breakfast for most Milanese office workers tends to consist of a cappuccino with a croissant, usually consumed at the bar counter. In the Brera quarter, cafés are lively and full of atmosphere. In the early evening they are popular places to relax in with colleagues and friends. Fashions come and go and a café that is "in" one month may be suddenly empty a few months later. To counteract such swings, many Milanese bars have initiated a "happy hour", when drinks are cheaper. Cafés are usually more crowded during the lunch break, when office workers stop for a quick salad or panino. As well as cafés, Milan also has excellent cake shops or *pasticcerie*, where you can sample pastries and cakes. For a more formal afternoon tea there are tea rooms (*sala da thé*), which are also packed at lunchtime. Many are historic places with period furniture. At the lakes, some of the more enterprising bars and cafés offer entertainment in the evening, either with a piano bar area or a small band.

Where to Look

In Milan, there are plenty of places to choose from, whether you are going out for an aperitif or to eat snacks, and the choice will vary from area to area. In the atmospheric Brera quarter the bars usually have tables outside in summer. These places are popular with the fashion set and art students. **Jamaica** (*see p185*) is one established institution, an ideal place for a cocktail before dinner as well as for a chicken salad for lunch or an after-dinner drink. **Le Rosse** (*see p185*) is equally popular. This small bistrot offers a terrific selection of cold cuts and delicious wines. In the mild season you can sit outside.

Around the Navigli, which is a pedestrian precinct, from 8pm in summer all the bars and cafés have tables set out outside, and it is possible to forget that Milan is a bustling commercial city altogether.

Luini, a snack bar famous for its *panzerotti*, filled pastry pockets (*see p185*)

The Conca del Naviglio area is always busy. There are numerous places to try such as the **Caffè della Pusterla** (*see p185*), located in the renovated medieval walls of the city, **California Bakery** (*see p184*), which is a good place to try for Sunday brunch, and **Pasticceria Cucchi** (*see p184*), deservedly famous for its aperitifs.

In the Ticinese quarter **Coquetel** (*see p184*) is a popular place, especially during happy hour, when the young Milanese get together for an early evening drink.

For those with a sweet tooth who like croissants and pastries for breakfast, the place to go is **Angela** (*see p184*), near Fieramilanocity, or **Sissi** (*see p184*), where you can enjoy cream pastries. If you like brunch, a habit that is increasingly popular in Milan, you can choose from among **Refeel** (*see p184*), an American bar that looks like a living room, **Take Away** (*see p184*), which also serves good salads, and **Fioraio Bianchi Caffè** (*see p184*), with its appealingly old-fashioned look.

Historic Cafés and Bars

Some of Milan's most frequented cafés and pastry shops have a long tradition, and are housed in old palazzi with fine interiors. One interesting historic pasticceria is **Sant'Ambroeus** (*see p185*), famous for its traditional panettone. Another ornate setting for breakfast and an aperitif is **Taveggia** (*see p185*), which has been a favourite with the Milanese since 1910. Don't miss **Zucca in Galleria** (*see p185*), (formerly Camparino), a historic, old-fashioned bar and the place where the

Watching life go by at a café in Piazza del Duomo

Assortment of cakes and pastries typical of a Milanese patisserie

be surrounded by scooters, motorbikes and cars. Most bars and cafés operate two price tariffs, with higher prices charged for sitting down at a table. Ordering and consuming at the bar counter is the most economical option, but you may prefer to linger and "people-watch".

Many bars operate a "happy hour" from 6:30 to 9:30pm, when drinks such as cocktails are sold at half-price. As a result these places become extremely crowded. At bars attracting younger people the music can be very loud, so if peace and quiet are needed, "happy hour" may not suit.

world-famous Campari drink was invented. Another must is **Cova** *(see p185)*, a café-pastry shop in Via Montenapoleone in business since 1817; in the heart of the fashion district, it is perfect for a cup of mid-afternoon hot chocolate or an evening aperitif. Lastly, the **Bar Magenta** *(see p184)* has been popular year in and year out and is now an evening haunt for the young Milanese crowd.

What to Order

A vast selection of beers, wines, aperitifs, excellent cocktails and non-alcoholic drinks is served in Milanese bars. A wide range of international beers is available as well as the Italian brands Peroni and Moretti. The current fashion is for Latin-American cocktails, which are gradually replacing classics like the Alexander and Bloody Mary. Almost every bar produces its own house aperitif.

Italy is a wine-producing country and the regions of Piedmont, Lombardy and the Veneto all have extensive areas under vine. Piedmont is best known for its red wines, Barolo and Barbaresco, and the more affordable Barbera and Dolcetto. Good reds are also made in Franciacorta in Lombardy, in the Valtellina and near Verona, where Bardolino and Valpolicella are made.

These regions' white wines include Gavi, Soave, Bianco di Custoza and Lugana, and there are some very good sparkling wines. Most bars provide snacks to go with early evening drinks. These may be simple, such as peanuts, or more elaborate. For generous snacks, try **Honky Tonks** *(see p184)*, where they serve Ascoli olives and pasta salad, as well as the classic *pinzimoni* dips with raw vegetables and canapés, during happy hour.

Useful Hints

It is best to get around by public transport as parking is notoriously difficult in Milan and popular bars are likely to

Bars in Hotels

Unlike the other bars in town, those in the large hotels are mostly used as venues for business meetings. Splendidly furnished and usually quiet, they exude discretion and privacy, creating the ideal conditions for discussing business matters.

Among the most distin-guished are the Lounge Bar in the Westin Palace which hosts art exhibitions, and the Foyer, in the Hotel Four Seasons. The latter is decorated with theatre set designs. Extra charm is added by an antique fireplace, recreating the plush atmos-phere of old Milanese palazzi.

The Foyer in the Hotel Four Seasons

Happy Hour

Bar Magenta

Via Carducci 13. **Map** 3 A5 & 7 A1. **Tel** 02-805 38 08. **Open** 7am–3am Tue–Sun.

This historic café is ideal for a light lunch snack or a beer in the evening. Try an aperitif at the counter with delicious savouries and *bruschetta*. The atmosphere attracts smart young Milanese, as well as students from the Università Cattolica and the San Carlo secondary school, both of which are nearby. Live music on Thursdays.

Coquetel

Via Vetere 14. **Map** 7 B3. **Tel** 02-39 54 85 01. **Open** 8am–2am Mon–Sat; 6pm–2am Sun.

For years this establishment has been popular with young Milanese. It is especially busy in the summer, when people stroll around the grassy stretches of the adjacent Piazza della Vetra, and drop in for a beer and a chat. The cocktails are very good. Happy hour is from 6:30 to 8:30pm.

Honky Tonks

Via Fratelli Induno, corner of Via Lomazzo. **Map** 2 F1. **Tel** 02-345 25 62. **Open** 6pm–2am daily.

This establishment in a converted garage is famous for the variety and sheer quantity of the snacks offered during happy hour. The counter is laden with heaps of Ascoli olives, croquettes, stuffed *focaccia* (flat bread) and cured meats of every kind. A good choice of traditional and Caribbean cocktails.

Makia

Corso Sempione 28. **Map** 2 E2. **Tel** 02-33 60 40 12. **Open** 8am–3pm, 6pm–2am Mon–Sat. **Closed** Aug.

This chic cocktail bar-restaurant offers tasty Italian/European dishes at lunch, dinner and Sunday brunch. There are also a great selection of snacks served at your table so you avoid the crush at the bar during cocktail hour.

Pasticceria Cucchi

Corso Genova 1. **Map** 7 A2. **Tel** 02-89 40 97 93. **Open** 7am–10pm Tue–Sun.

Home-made panettone, pastries and pies are served in an elegant 1940s building with marble finishes. This café is very popular for its aperitifs and also offers a wide range of delicious snacks.

Brunch

California Bakery

Piazza Sant'Eustorgio 4. **Map** 7 B3. **Tel** 02-39 81 17 50. **Open** 8am–midnight daily.

Great atmosphere and excellent service await at this American pastry shop-restaurant. The interior is done out in stylish country decor and the cuisine is typical North American. On Sundays you can enjoy brunch al fresco in front of the Basilica di Sant'Eustorgio.

Fioraio Bianchi Caffè

Via Montebello 7. **Map** 3 C3. **Tel** 02-29 01 43 90. **Open** 8am–midnight Mon–Sat.

The decor, atmosphere and service here are all reminiscent of the former flower shop. Enjoy French food in one of the most charming cafés in town. Not to be missed.

Refeel

Viale Sabotino 20. **Map** 8 E4. **Tel** 02-58 32 42 27. **Open** 7am–2am Mon–Sat, noon–4pm Sun (for brunch).

🌐 refeel.it

This American bar looks like a living room, with leather sofas and pot plants. A great brunch is served between noon and 4pm on Saturdays and Sundays. There's live jazz on Tuesday evenings.

Take Away Bistrot

Via San Marco 33. **Map** 3 C3. **Tel** 02-655 22 04. **Open** 8am–2am daily.

This nice bistrot in the Brera quarter offers a good selection of salads, plus cocktails, in a local atmosphere.

Breakfast

Angela

Via Ruggero di Lauria 15. **Map** 2 D1. **Tel** 02-34 28 59. **Open** 8am–7:30pm Tue–Fri; 8:30am– 1.30pm, 3–7pm Sat & Sun.

This small pastry shop near the Fiera has a counter where you can pause and enjoy breakfast. Go for the pastries with custard or whipped cream, the warm puff pastry with ricotta cheese and the fresh croissants with hot custard.

De Cherubini

Via Trincea delle Frasche 2. **Map** 7 B3 & B4. **Tel** 02-54 10 74 86. **Open** 6:45am–11pm daily.

On the south side of Piazza XXIV Maggio, under a colonnade, lies this lovely café-cum-pastry shop. Good dishes at lunchtime, snacks with pre-dinner drinks and excellent croissants. Grab an outside table in good weather.

Leonardo

Via Aurelio Saffi 7. **Map** 2 F5. **Tel** 02-439 03 02. **Open** 7:30am–9pm daily.

This ice cream parlour and pastry shop is famous for its crème patissière. The pastry rolls and cream puffs are delicious. Try the home-made yogurt or vanilla ice cream.

Marchesi

Via Santa Maria alla Porta 11a. **Map** 7 B1. **Tel** 02-87 67 30. **Open** 7:30am–8pm Tue–Sat; 8:30am–1pm Sun.

This historic pastry shop, in the centre between Via Meravigli and Piazza Cordusio, offers croissants, savouries, salads, a vast assortment of cakes and delicious tartlets.

San Carlo

Via Matteo Bandello 1, corner of Corso Magenta. **Map** 7 A2. **Tel** 02-48 12 227. **Open** 6:30am–8:30pm daily.

A stone's throw from Santa Maria delle Grazie, this pastry shop features delicious chocolate-based delicacies and irresistible cream-filled pastries.

Sissi

Piazza Risorgimento 6. **Map** 4 F5 & 8 F1. **Tel** 02-76 01 46 64. **Open** 6:30am–noon Mon, 6:30am–8pm Wed–Sun.

A small pastry shop featuring a host of tempting morsels, including custard-filled croissants or raw ham savouries. The pretty courtyard with its pergola is ideal for Sunday afternoon tea.

Snacks

Coin – The Globe

Piazza Cinque Giornate 1a. Coin department store, 8th floor. **Tel** 02-55 18 19 69. **Open** 11:30am–9:30pm Mon; 11:30am–2am Tue–Sat, noon–4pm (brunch), 6:30pm–1am Sun.

This restaurant, bar and food market, on the top floor of the Coin department store, is similar to those in Harrod's or Macy's. The restaurant offers light lunches and traditional dinners, both high quality. The bar offers fine aperitifs, and you will find delectable delicatessen specialities in the food market.

De Santis

Corso Magenta 9. **Map** 3 A5 & 6 F1. **Tel** 02-87 59 68. **Open** noon–4pm, 7pm–12:30am daily. **Closed** Christmas.

This compact place specializes in filled rolls. On the walls are bank-notes from all over the world and signed photographs of celebrities who have enjoyed choosing from 150 types of sandwich, made with fresh, tasty ingredients.

El Tombon de San Marc

Via San Marco 20. **Map** 3 C3. **Tel** 02-659 95 07. **Open** 7am–3pm, 7pm–2am Mon–Sat. **Closed** Mon am, Aug.

A historic establishment that has resisted passing fashions since the 1930s. A warm, intimate atmosphere. Sandwiches and salads as well as excellent soups and various hot and cold dishes.

Latteria di Via Unione

Via dell'Unione 6. **Map** 7 C1. **Tel** 02-87 44 01. **Open** noon–4pm Mon–Sat. **Closed** Aug.

This dairy in the heart of town offers good vegetarian dishes. Get there early, because it is small and usually quite crowded.

Luini

Via Santa Radegonda 16. **Map** 7 C1. **Tel** 02-86 46 19 17. **Open** 10am–3pm Mon, 10am–8pm Tue–Sat.

Since 1949 this baker's has featured Puglian *panzerotti* (ravioli) filled with tomatoes and mozzarella.

Salumeria Armandola

Via della Spiga 50. **Map** 4 D4. **Tel** 02-76 02 16 57. **Open** 8:30am–7:30pm Mon–Sat (to 10:30pm Thu & Fri). **Closed** 2 wks mid-Aug.

People drop in here for a quick bite at the counter. The chef's specialities include baked pasta, roasted meat and a range of vegetable and side dishes.

Bars and Cafés

Biffi

Corso Magenta 87. **Map** 3 A5 & 6 F1. **Tel** 02-48 00 67 02. **Open** 6:30am–8:30pm daily.

This historic bar-pastry shop dates from the end of the 19th century. Biffi is famous for its milk rolls with cured ham or butter and anchovies. The home-made *panettone*, made every year, is one of the best in Milan.

Caffè della Pusterla

Via De Amicis 22. **Map** 7 A2. **Tel** 02-89 40 21 46. **Open** 7am–2am Mon–Sat; 9am–2am Sun.

This charming café is located in the former Pusterla, or minor gate, in Milan's medieval walls. A wide range of cocktails and a fine wine list too. The savouries served with the aperitifs are also very good.

Cova

Via Montenapoleone 8. **Map** 4 D5. **Tel** 02-76 00 05 78. **Open** 8am–8:30pm Mon–Sat. **Closed** Aug.

Founded in 1817, this elegant pastry shop is right in the heart of the fashion district and is an ideal place for a pause during your shopping spree. Cova is well-known for its chocolates and stuffed *panettone*.

Jamaica

Via Brera 32. **Map** 3 C4. **Tel** 02-87 67 23. **Open** 9am–2am daily (to 9pm Mon, to 1:30am Sun). **Closed** 2 wks Aug.

This historic Milanese café is the haunt of artists and intellectuals, who flock to this fascinating corner of the Brera quarter. Busy at all hours. Drinks as well as good huge salads.

Le Rosse

Corso Garibaldi 79. **Map** 3 B3. **Tel** 02-92 87 04 16. **Open** 12:30–3pm & 6:30–midnight Mon–Sat.

A small bistrot much loved by locals, Le Rosse offers a terrific selection of cold cuts and delicious wines. There is also outdoor seating to enjoy the bustling semi-pedestrian Corso Garibaldi.

Sant'Ambroeus

Corso Matteotti 7. **Map** 4 D5. **Tel** 02-76 00 05 40. **Open** 7:45am–8:30pm daily. **Closed** Aug.

The atmosphere in what is probably Milan's most elegant pastry shop is plush, with sumptuous window displays and slick service. The tarts, pralines and cakes are famous. There is a lovely tearoom inside and tables outside under the arcade opposite.

Taveggia

Via Visconti di Modrone 2. **Map** 8 E1. **Tel** 02-76 28 08 56. **Open** 7am–9pm Mon–Sat, 7:30am–8pm Sun. **Closed** last 3 wks Aug.

Another historic Milanese pastry shop, inaugurated in 1910. Great rice pudding, many different types of croissants and various delicacies. Taveggia is also popular for its aperitifs.

Victoria Café

Via Clerici 1. **Map** 3 C5. **Tel** 02-805 35 98. **Open** 7:30am–2am Mon–Fri; 9am–2am Sat, 5–10pm Sun.

Behind Piazza della Scala is this Parisian-style *fin de siècle café* with red lamps on the tables, lace curtains and red leather seats. Popular for aperitifs and after dinners.

Zucca in Galleria

Piazza del Duomo 21. **Map** 7 C1. **Tel** 02-86 46 44 35. **Open** 7:15am–8:40pm Tue–Sun.

This famous bar (formerly Camparino) in the Galleria has period decor and tables outside. The world-famous Campari drink was created here in the late 1800s.

Lake Bars & Cafés

Matella (Lake Maggiore)

Via Ruga 1, Pallanza. **Tel** 0323-50 19 88. **Open** 7:30am–8pm Wed–Mon (to midnight in summer). **Closed** mid-Oct–mid-Nov.

Bar-pasticceria shop in the 19th-century arcades of Palazzo Municipale featuring *amaretti* (macaroons). Nice tables for a drink outside.

Mimosa (Lake Garda)

Via RV Cornicello 1, Bardolino. **Tel** 045-621 24 72. **Open** 3–10pm daily. **Closed** mid-Oct–May.

The barman at Mimosa is a true cocktail "magician". There is also a garden where you can listen to the music while sipping your drink or enjoying good home-made ice cream.

Monti (Lake Como)

Piazza Cavour 21, Como. **Tel** 031-30 11 65. **Open** 7am–midnight Wed–Mon. **Closed** Tue.

Bar-pastry shop in lovely Piazza Cavour, with tables outside and a view of the lake. Perfect for sipping tea and tasting pastries in tranquil surroundings.

Vassalli (Lake Garda)

Via San Carlo 84, Salò. **Tel** 0365-207 52. **Open** 8am–9pm Wed–Mon (Jun–Sep: to 11pm daily).

This historic bar-pastry shop in Salò has been popular for over a century. The aperitifs and cocktails are good, but Vassalli is most well-known for its desserts, such as the exquisite *bacetti di Salò* chocolates and the lemon mousse.

SHOPS AND MARKETS

Whether buying or just looking, shopping is a real pleasure in Milan. As well as the window displays of the leading national and international fashion designers – whose outlets are all within the area between Via Manzoni, Via Montenapoleone, Via della Spiga and Via Sant'Andrea, the so-called "quadrilateral" – you can find small shops and stores throughout the city. Shops are generally smart and stylish, especially in the city centre, as good design is highly regarded in Italy, and Milan is one of the most affluent cities. For those who are interested in interior design there is plenty of choice among the specialist shops, while lovers of antiques will love the Brera and Navigli quarters, where regular outdoor antique markets are held. Milan also has some excellent *pasticcerie*, where you can purchase authentic delicacies and traditional Milanese confectionery. At the lakes the choice is widest in the bigger towns, and includes clothes shops, craft shops and wine shops selling local produce.

Opening Hours

Shops in Milan are usually open from 9:30am to 1pm and then from 3:30 to 7:30pm. However, many shops in the city centre and the department stores stay open all day, without a break, and major bookshops stay open until 11pm.

Shops are closed on Sunday and Monday mornings, except over Christmas, when they are usually open every day of the week. Food shops, on the other hand, close on Monday afternoon, with the exception of supermarkets.

During the summer holiday period, shops generally close for most of August, apart from the department stores and shopping centres which remain open as normal, even during this rather inactive month.

The Coin department store in Piazza Cinque Giornate

Department Stores

There are not many department stores in Milan. One of the most central is **La Rinascente**, which is open seven days a week and stays open until 10pm. Opposite the Duomo, it is perhaps the most prestigious department store in the city, selling everything from clothing, perfumes, toys and stationery to food, over eight floors. The restaurant has a view of the Duomo and an exhibition space.

In Piazza Cinque Giornate is the **Coin**, with quality products at medium-range prices, including clothes and household goods. **Oviesse**, in Via Spadari, is more downmarket and sells clothes and other articles at reasonable prices. **Excelsior Milano** is a former movie theatre now transformed into a concept store by the architect Jean Nouvel, with four floors of fashion, food and design. Lastly, there is **Il Portello**, a shopping centre with shops, boutiques and a large supermarket.

Markets

Italy's outdoor markets are always fun and Milan has some good specialist markets. The Mercatone dell'Antiquariato, held on the last Sunday of the month at the Alzaia Naviglio Grande, is an extensive antiques market with more than four hundred exhibitors offering antique objects and bric-a-brac. Every Saturday at the Darsena on Viale d'Annunzio there is the Fiera di Sinigaglia, where you can find almost anything, from clothing to records and ethnic handicrafts.

The Mercato dell'Antiquariato in the Brera area, between Via Fiori Chiari and Via Madonnina, is also worth a visit. Every third Saturday of the month antiques, books, postcards and jewellery go on sale here. Lastly, don't miss the Mercato del Sabato on Viale Papiniano, which offers, great designer-label bargains, clothes, shoes and bags.

Window shopping in fashionable Via Montenapoleone

The Fiera di Sinigaglia along the Darsena

Food Shops

Gourmets will appreciate the well-stocked Milanese delicatessens and food shops. Perhaps the most famous is **Peck**, which since 1883 has been synonymous with fine food and delicacies. Besides the main delicatessen in Via Spadari, selling hams, salami and cheeses of all kinds, there is also a popular Peck *rosticceria* in Via Cantù where you can buy the best ready-made dishes in Milan. The latest temple of Italian gastronomy is **Eataly**, which houses numerous bistros and restaurants, as well as showcasing the finest Italian food at evening shows and demonstrations.

Another top-quality establishment is **Il Salumaio** near Via Montenapoleone, which is both a delicatessen and a restaurant. The top floor of **La Rinascente** department store has an array of eateries

and a terrace with spectacular views of the Duomo.

N'Ombra de Vin is one of Milan's most famous *enoteche*, where you'll find the best Italian wines. For those who love chocolate, **Neuhaus Maitre Chocolatier** is paradise.

Garbagnati is the best-known baker in town, and is especially known for *panettone*. Garbagnati has been making this traditional Milanese cake with a natural leavening process since 1937.

Fabbrica di Marroni Giovanni Galli has been making the best *marrons glacés* in Milan since 1898. Equally famous is **L'Angolo di Marco**, in the Brera quarter, a delightful *pasticceria* (pastry shop) offering delectable treats of all kinds. At **Ranieri** they make a *panettone* with pineapple, and sweets and pastries with fresh fruit. Last but not least, **Marchesi** is the best place to go for meltingly good chocolates, both milk and dark.

Sales

In Milan, sales *(saldi)* are held twice a year: in early July and then in January, immediately after Epiphany. Discounts may be as much as 70 per cent, but check goods carefully before you buy, especially if the discount looks overgenerous. Shop-owners may use the sales as an excuse to get rid of old stock or defective clothing. For all-year-round bargains, try the numerous outlet shops: Il Salvagente at Via Bronzetti 16 or Diffusione Tessile in Galleria San Carlo.

Corso Vittorio Emanuele, a popular street for shopping

DIRECTORY

Department Stores

Coin
Piazza Cinque Giornate 1.
Map 8 F1. **Tel** 02-55 19 20 83.

Excelsior Milano
Galleria del Corso 4. **Map** 8 D1.
Tel 02-86 99 83 40.
w excelsiormilano.com

Oviesse
Via Spadari 2. **Map** 7 C1.
Tel 02-89 01 07 50.

Il Portello
Piazzale Accursio.
Tel 02-39 25 91.

La Rinascente
Piazza del Duomo. **Map** 7 C1.
Tel 02-88 521.

Food Shops

L'Angolo di Marco
Piazza del Carmine 6. **Map** 3 B4.
Tel 02-87 43 60.

Eataly
Piazza XXV Aprile 10.
Map 3 C2. **Tel** 02-49 49 73 01.

Fabbrica di Marroni Giovanni Galli
Corso di Porta Romana 2.
Map 7 C2. **Tel** 02-86 45 31 12.
Via Hugo. **Tel** 02-86 46 48 33.

Garbagnati
Via Veglia 57. **Tel** 02-86 09 05.

Marchesi
Via Santa Maria alla Porta 13.
Map 7 B1.
Tel 02-87 67 30.

Neuhaus Maitre Chocolatier
Via San Vittore 6. **Map** 6 E1.
Tel 02-72 00 00 96.

N'Ombra de Vin
Via San Marco 2.
Map 3 C3.
Tel 02-659 96 50.
w nombradevin.it

Peck
Via Spadari 9. **Map** 7 C1.
Tel 02-802 31 61.
Via Cantù 3 (restaurant/bar).
Map 7 C1.
Tel 02-869 30 17.
w peck.it

Ranieri
Via della Moscova 7. **Map** 3 B3.
Tel 02-659 53 08.

Il Salumaio
Via Santo Spirito 10. **Map** 4 D5.
Tel 02-76 00 11 23.

Clothing and Accessories

The clothes shops of milan are known all over the world because of their associations with famous Italian fashion designers. The city centre fashion district is stormed each year by Italians and foreigners alike in search of the latest top fashion items. However, Milan is not just about expensively priced goods, and the true secret of pleasurable shopping can lie in discovering the less well-known shops which offer good prices and still work to high standards of quality.

Classic Clothing

Women in search of impeccable classic clothing for themselves and their children should seek out the **Pupi Solari** shop, which also makes wedding dresses to order. Lovers of colourful sports clothes, on the other hand, will be more than satisfied at **Tommy Hilfiger**. Elegant children's apparel and shoes can be found at **Gusella**, while **Host** features men's sports and informal clothes. Elegant, stylish clothes for men can also be found at **Bardelli** or **Gemelli**, and **Ravizza** is an ideal shop for those who prefer classic wear with a casual touch. **Ermenegildo Zegna** is the place to go for stylish men's classic clothing made of the best quality fabrics. **Brian & Barry** offers both classic and sports clothes at reasonable prices. Lastly, **Neglia** has two floors filled with fashionable menswear, from clothing to accessories.

Designer Wear

Almost all the shops that feature the latest in top designer clothes are in or near the city centre (see pp108–9). **Hugo Boss** is a recently opened shop of some size, selling elegant clothes for men. **Giò Moretti**, an institution in Via della Spiga, features articles by the top names as well as pieces by up-and-coming fashion designers. **Marisa** is a shop specializing in Italian and foreign designers and there is always something new and interesting, while **Fay** has clothes for the young and sophisticated. **Biffi** is famous for its wide-ranging selection of top designer clothes.

Among non-Italian fashion designers **Jil Sander** is growing more and more popular. **Guess**, the well-known New York designer, is represented in the city and offers the latest lines.

The diffusion lines of the most famous designers can be found in the fashion district, where the main names have their own branches, from **Miu Miu** to **D&G** and **Emporio Armani**. Armani's Via Manzoni store also houses an art gallery and Nobu sushi bar. Lastly, **Antonio Fusco** attracts an enthusiastic clientele.

Accessories

For good quality sports shoes there is **Tod's**. Less well-known but equally good is the **Stivaleria Savoia**, which features classic styles that can also be made to measure. **Gallo** is proud of its stylish high-quality hosiery.

Ferragamo, the Italian designer known all over the world for his top fashion styles, offers elegant classic shoes. More bizarre and unconventional articles can be found at **La Vetrina di Beryl**, while **Camper** features original shoes known for their fine workmanship. **Garlando** offers a vast range of styles and colours that aim at a younger market.

Crocodile, ostrich and leather handbags can be found at **Colombo**, while **Valextra** features high-quality suitcases and briefcases. For something original head for the **Atelier Anne Backhaus**, where they make handbags and accessories using different materials.

Size Chart

Children's clothing
Italian	2–3	4–5	6–7	8–9	10–11	12	14	14+	(age)
British	2–3	4–5	6–7	8–9	10–11	12	14	14+	(age)
American	2–3	4–5	6–6X	7–8	10		12	14	16	(size)

Children's shoes
Italian	24	25½	27	28	29		30	32	33	34
British	7½	8	9	10	11		12	13	1	2
American	7½	8½	9½	10½	11½		12½	13½	1½	2½

Women's dresses, coats and skirts
Italian	38	40	42	44	46		48	50	52
British	6	8	10	12	14		16	18	20
American	4	6	8	10	12		14	16	18

Women's blouses and sweaters
Italian	40	42	44	46	48		50	52
British	30	32	34	36	38		40	42
American	6	8	10	12	14		16	18

Women's shoes
Italian	36	37	38	39	40	41
British	3	4	5	6	7	8
American	5	6	7	8	9	10

Men's clothing
Italian	44	46	48	50	52		54	56	58
British	34	36	38	40	42		44	46	48
American	34	36	38	40	42		44	46	48

Men's shirts
Italian	36	38	39	41	42		43	44	45
British	14	15	15½	16	16½		17	17½	18
American	14	15	15½	16	16½		17	17½	18

Men's shoes
Italian	40	41	42	43	44		45	46
British	7	7½	8	9	10		11	12
American	7½	8	8½	9½	10½		11	11½

The **Mandarina Duck** shops have stylish sports bags, luggage, casual handbags and knapsacks. **Borsalino** is the place to go for top-quality classic hats. **Giusy Bresciani** has more original designs, as well as gloves and other highly stylish accessories. **Cappelleria Melegari** deals in hats imported from all over the world and they can do hat alterations in their workshop if a customer requires. A wide range of ties can be found at **Andrew's Ties** and **Fedeli**, which also holds a good selection of knitwear and gloves.

Jewellery

Elegant, classic jewellery is featured at **Rocca 1872**, which has designed jewels for smart Milanese women since 1840, and **Cusi**, which has been in business since 1885. **Tiffany & Co** is known for high-class jewellery, while Mario Buccellati has gold and silver pieces of elegant workmanship. Another historic shop is **Bulgari**, known for its beautiful jewellery and watches. **Mereú** features original and modern hand-crafted jewels. Jewellery dating from the 19th century to 1950 is to be found at **Mirella Denti**. For modern costume jewellery, you will find a good collection at **Donatella Pellini**, and **Anaconda** also has a good choice of the latest costume jewellery and jewellery styles, made of original materials.

DIRECTORY

Classic Clothing

Bardelli
Corso Magenta 13. **Map** 3 A5. **Tel** 02-86 45 07 34.

Brian & Barry
Via Durini 28. **Map** 8 D1. **Tel** 02-76 00 55 82.

Ermenegildo Zegna
Via Montenapoleone 27. **Map** 4 D5. **Tel** 02-76 00 64 37.

Gemelli
Corso Vercelli 16. **Map** 2 D5. **Tel** 02-48 00 46 89.

Gusella
Via della Spiga 31. **Map** 4 D4. **Tel** 02-76 34 07 78.

Host
Piazza Tommaseo 2. **Map** 2 E5. **Tel** 02-43 60 85.

Neglia
Via Noe 23. **Tel** 02-23 62 514.

Pupi Solari
Piazza Tommaseo 2. **Map** 2 E5. **Tel** 02-46 33 25.

Ravizza
Via Hoepli 3. **Map** 4 D5. **Tel** 02-869 38 53.

Tommy Hilfiger
Piazza G. Oberdan 2a. **Map** 4 F4. **Tel** 02-20 24 15 73.

Designer Wear

Antonio Fusco
Via Sant'Andrea 11. **Map** 4 D5. **Tel** 02-76 00 18 88.

Biffi
Corso Genova 6. **Map** 7 A2. **Tel** 02-831 16 01.

D&G
Corso Venezia 7. **Map** 4 E4. **Tel** 02-76 00 40 91.

Emporio Armani
Via Manzoni 31. **Map** 3 C5. **Tel** 02-72 31 86 00.
Ⓦ armanivia
manzoni31.com

Fay
Via della Spiga 15. **Map** 4 D4. **Tel** 02-76 01 75 97.

Giò Moretti
Via della Spiga 4. **Map** 4 D4. **Tel** 02-76 00 31 86.

Guess
Piazza San Babila 4b. **Map** 4 D5. **Tel** 02-76 39 20 70.

Hugo Boss
Corso Matteotti 11. **Map** 4 D5. **Tel** 02-76 39 46 67.

Jil Sander
Via P Verri 6. **Map** 4 D5. **Tel** 02-777 29 91.

Marisa
Via della Spiga 52. **Map** 4 D4. **Tel** 02-76 00 20 82.

Miu Miu
Via Sant'Andrea 21. **Map** 4 D5. **Tel** 02-76 00 17 99.

Accessories

Andrew's Ties
Galleria Vittorio
Emanuele II. **Map** 7 C1.
Tel 02-86 09 35.

Atelier Anne Backhaus
Corso di Porta Vigentina 10. **Map** 8 D3. **Tel** 02-58 30 27 93.

Borsalino
Galleria Vittorio Emanuele II. **Map** 7 C1. **Tel** 02-89 01 54 36.

Camper
Via Torino 15. **Map** 7 B1. **Tel** 02-805 71 85.

Cappelleria Melegari
Via P Sarpi 19. **Map** 3 A2. **Tel** 02-31 20 94.

Colombo
Via della Spiga 9. **Map** 4 D4. **Tel** 02-76 02 35 87.

Fedeli
Via Montenapoleone 8. **Map** 4 D5. **Tel** 02-76 02 33 92.

Ferragamo
Via Montenapoleone 3. **Map** 4 D5. **Tel** 02-76 00 00 54.

Gallo
Via Durini 26. **Map** 8 D1. **Tel** 02-76 00 20 23.

Garlando
Via Madonnina 1. **Map** 3 B4. **Tel** 02-87 46 65.

Giusy Bresciani
Via del Carmine 9. **Map** 3 C4. **Tel** 02-89 01 35 05.

Mandarina Duck
Corso Buenos Aires 16/18. **Map** 4 F3. **Tel** 02-29 52 27 99.

Stivaleria Savoia
Via Petrarca 7. **Map** 2 E4. **Tel** 02-46 34 24.

Tod's
Via della Spiga 22. **Map** 4 D4. **Tel** 02-76 00 24 23.

Valextra
Via Manzoni 3. **Map** 4 D5. **Tel** 02-99 78 60 60.

La Vetrina di Beryl
Via Statuto 4. **Map** 3 B3. **Tel** 02-65 42 78.

Jewellery

Anaconda
Via Bergamini 7. **Map** 8 D1. **Tel** 02-58 32 56 84.

Bulgari
Via Montenapoleone 2. **Map** 4 D4. **Tel** 02-77 70 01.

Cusi
Corso Monforte 23. **Map** 4 E5. **Tel** 02-76 28 12 93.

Donatella Pellini
Corso Magenta 11. **Map** 3 A5. **Tel** 02-72 01 05 69.

Mario Buccellati
Via Montenapoleone 23. **Map** 4 D5. **Tel** 02-76 00 21 53.

Mereú
Via Solferino 22. **Map** 3 C3. **Tel** 02-86 46 07 00.

Mirella Denti
Via Montenapoleone 23. **Map** 4 D5. **Tel** 02-76 02 25 44.

Rocca 1872
Piazza Duomo 25. **Map** 7 C1. **Tel** 02-805 74 47.

Tiffany & Co
Via della Spiga 19a. **Map** 4 D4. **Tel** 02-76 02 23 21.

Design and Antiques

Milan is the acknowledged capital of modern design and a paradise for enthusiasts, who can spend their free time browsing in the numerous shops and showrooms throughout the city. Every spring the Salone del Mobile, the famous Milan furniture fair, attracts all the top designers and trade buyers. During the fair, many of Milan's interior design shops extend their opening hours and put on various events for trade experts and visitors.

Interior and Industrial Design

At **De Padova**, elegant, studiously avant-garde objects for the home, including furniture, are made of the finest materials. For stylish lighting there is **Artemide**, which is known for its superb modern designs, created by well-known names, and **Flos**, in Corso Monforte, which features sleek ultra-modern lighting of all kinds.

Fontana Arte is a kind of gallery and a leading light in the field of interior design. Founded in 1933, its displays include splendid lamps, mostly crystal.

Zanotta is a bright, dynamic store where design lovers can buy high-quality interior design products by top Italian designers. **Galleria Colombari**, on the other hand, offers modern antiques as well as a range of contemporary design objects.

Cappellini is a showroom for informal and elegant furniture, while **Blitz Bovisa** is a large outlet that features a wide range of interior design and vintage home accessories along with furniture pieces.

Kartell stocks various articles for the home and the office. **Venini** is an institution in the production of blown Venetian glass vases, while **Barovier & Toso** offers extremely high-quality chandeliers and vases, and **Cassina** features products by leading designers.

Spazio 900 has fabulous furniture and interior objects by top designers from the 1950s to the 1980s, as well as vintage and end-of-line pieces at discount prices.

Alessi, in Via Manzoni, specializes in interior design pieces and kitchenware in stainless steel and colourful plastic. **Kitchen** has everything a cook could need, including top quality utensils and a cookery school for those looking to expand their repertoire of dishes.

Those who love stylish period furniture should stop by **Il Valore Aggiunto**, which offers decor objects, lamps and chandeliers dating from AD 700 to 1950.

Since 1955, **Arform** has been selling a wide range of household items as well as furniture and clothing chosen by the founding family. The store proudly boasts an independent selection from the usual fashion trends found on the high street. The store specializes in contemporary Scandinavian design.

Megastores

The megastore, where you can purchase almost anything under the sun, from the tiniest household article to a large piece of furniture, is now becoming the rage in Milan as well as in other Italian cities. These large establishments (empori) are usually open late in the evening and on Sunday and are frequently able to offer their customers various additional services.

High Tech was one of the first to offer this new mode of shopping. Come here for exotic furniture, fabrics and wallpaper for the home, kitchenware, perfume and accessories imported from all over the world.

Visit **Cargo Hightech's** warehouse store for beautiful Chinese laquered chests or ultra-modern Italian design lighting. Alternatively, browse their clothing in glorious fabrics from India and bamboo furniture from the Philippines.

10 Corso Como is an unusual place featuring designer articles and objects from the Middle and Far East. It has a gallery and an interesting café/bar.

The ultra-modern and unconventional **Moroni Gomma** offers boots, raincoats, kitchenware and interior design and household articles, all made of plastic or rubber (gomma).

Fabrics and Linen for the Home

For elegance and high-class interior design, Milan cannot be beaten. There are many shops that specialize in fabrics and linen which can be made to order.

Etro, in Via Montenapoleone, is famous for its fabrics and stylish accessories. In the Brera area **KA International** is a sales outlet for a Spanish chain of fabric shops, offering excellent value for money. Among the many other articles, **Lisa Corti** features original Indian cotton and cheesecloth fabrics with floral and stripe patterns. **Bellora** has been specializing in high-quality linen since 1883 and **Castellini & C** is known mostly for its linen products.

Original and exclusive fabrics can be found at **Fede Cheti**. Among the shops featuring household linen, **Pratesi**, in the heart of the fashion district, is known for its classic and elegant ranges. **Society Limonta** is a very well-known name in Italy for beautifully made fabrics.

Bed linen and table linen in both modern and practical styles are featured at **Mirabello**. Since 1860 **Frette** has been a guarantee of high-quality bed linen, table linen and articles for the bathroom such as towels and bathrobes. They also offer delivery throughout the world as well as advice and help from an interior designer.

Antiques

Milan has numerous antique shops and workshops. Subert, in Via della Spiga, specializes in 18th-century furniture and scientific instruments. In the same street is **Mauro Brucoli**, where they specialize in 19th-century furniture and objects as well as splendid jewellery dating from the same period.

At Franco Sabatelli, which is also a furniture restorers, you can find picture frames of all periods, some even dating from the 16th century.

Lovers of 18th- and 19th-century British furniture must head for Old English Furniture, which also has a fine stock of medical and scientific instruments. If you prefer the unusual or even bizarre object, try **L'Oro dei Farlocchi**, a historic antique gallery in the Brera area. **Galleria Blanchaert** is one of Milan's

best-known shops for antique glass, with Murano chandeliers and Venini vases.

At **Antichità Caiati** you will find stunning 17th- and 18th-century Italian paintings. Valuable canvases are also sold at **Walter Padovani** as well as decorative art, sculpture and precious stones. **Carlo Orsi** has exclusive antiques, including bronze sculpture, splendid paintings, fine furniture, delicate ivory pieces and precious stones.

DIRECTORY

Interior and Industrial Design

Alessi
Via Manzoni 14/16.
Map 4 D4.
Tel 02-79 57 26.

Arform
Via della Moscova 22.
Map 4 D3.
Tel 02-655 46 91.
🅦 arform.it

Artemide
Corso Monforte 19.
Map 4 E5.
Tel 02-76 00 69 30.

Barovier & Toso
Via Durini 5. **Map** 8 E1.
Tel 02-76 00 09 06.

Blitz Bovisa
Via Cosenz 44.
Tel 02-37 60 990.
🅦 blitzbovisa.com

Cappellini
Via S Cecilia 4.
Tel 02-76 00 38 89.

Cassina
Via Durini 16.
Map 8 D1.
Tel 02-76 02 07 58.

De Padova
Via Santa Cecilia 4.
Map 4 E5.
Tel 02-77 72 01.
🅦 depadova.it

Flos
Corso Monforte 9. **Map** 4 E5. **Tel** 02-76 00 36 39.

Fontana Arte
Corso Monforte 13.
Map 4 E5.
Tel 02-87 21 38 72.

Galleria Colombari
Via Maroncelli 10.
Map 3 B1.
Tel 02-29 00 15 51.

Kartell
Via Turati (corner of Via Porta 1). **Map** 4 D3.
Tel 02-659 79 16.

Kitchen
Via de Amicis 45.
Map 7 A2.
Tel 02-58 10 28 49.

Spazio 900
Corso Garibaldi 42.
Map 3 B2.
Tel 02-72 00 17 75.
Viale Campania 51.
Tel 02-70 12 57 37.
🅦 spazio900.com

Il Valore Aggiunto
Via Goffredo Mameli 3.
Map 8 F1.
Tel 02-74 40 76.
🅦 ilvaloreaggiunto.it

Venini
Via Montenapoleone 9.
Map 4 D5.
Tel 02-76 00 05 39.

Zanotta
Piazza del Tricolore 2.
Map 4 F5.
Tel 02-76 02 57 62.
🅦 zanotta.it

Megastores

10 Corso Como
Corso Como 10. **Map** 3 C2. **Tel** 02-29 00 26 74.

Cargo Hightech
Via Meucci 39.
Tel 02-272 21 31.
🅦 cargomilano.it

High Tech
Piazza XXV Aprile 12.
Tel 02-624 11 01.

Moroni Gomma
Corso Matteotti 14.
Map 4 D5.
Tel 02-76 00 68 21.

Fabrics and Linen for the Home

Bellora
Via V Monti 27.
Map 3 A5.
Tel 02-43 90 092.

Castellini & C
Via B Zenale. **Map** 6 F1.
Tel 02-48 01 50 69.

Etro
Via Montenapoleone 5.
Map 4 D5.
Via Bigli 2. **Map** 4 D5.
Tel 02-76 00 50 49.

Fede Cheti
Via Manzoni 23.
Map 3 C5.
Tel 02-86 46 40 05.

Frette
Via della Spiga 31.
Map 4 D4.
Tel 02-84 25 40 21.
Via Manzoni 11.
Map 3 C5.
Tel 02-86 44 43.

KA International
Via dell'Orso 1. **Map** 3 C5.
Tel 02-36 59 81 19.
🅦 kamilano.com

Lisa Corti
Via Lecco 2. **Map** 4 E3.
Tel 02-29 40 55 89.

Mirabello
Via Balzan (corner of Via San Marco). **Map** 3 C3.
Tel 02-65 48 87.

Pratesi
Via A. Manzoni 1.
Map 3 C5.
Tel 02-89 09 51 35.

Society Limonta
Via Palermo 1.
Map 3 C3.
Tel 02-72 08 04 53.
🅦 societylimonta.com

Antiques

Antichità Caiati
Via Gesù 17.
Map 4 D5.
Tel 02-79 48 66.

Carlo Orsi
Via Bagutta 14.
Tel 02-76 00 22 14.

Galleria Blanchaert
Piazza Sant'Ambrogio 4.
Map 7 A1.
Tel 02-86 45 17 00.

Mauro Brucoli
Via della Spiga 17.
Map 4 D4.
Tel 02-76 02 37 67.

L'Oro dei Farlocchi
Via Madonnina, opposite No. 5.
Map 3 B4.
Tel 02-86 05 89.

Walter Padovani
Via Santo Spirito 25.
Map 4 D4.
Tel 02-76 31 89 07.

Books and Gifts

Milan is well supplied with good bookshops, many offering foreign-language publications as well as books in Italian. The larger bookstores in the centre are usually open late in the evening and also on Sundays. They have plenty of space where you can quietly browse through the books on display at your leisure. In addition there are plenty of small bookshops, many stocking rare or out-of-print books. Around the University there are many specialist bookshops. Music fans can head for the megastores and the many music shops in town, while the specialist gift shops will help those interested in buying presents to take home.

Bookshops

The **Mondadori Multicenter** is centrally located and open daily until 11pm. It stocks newspapers and periodicals (including international ones) along with new releases, both fiction and non-fiction, for visitors who read Italian. It also has a café on the first floor, Puro Gusto.

Computer buffs should head for **Mondadori Informatica**, which is a paradise for anyone who is interested in IT.

Another large, well-stocked and very popular bookstore is **Rizzoli** in the Galleria Vittorio Emanuele, which has a fine arts section.

Feltrinelli has six bookshops in Milan, which are open every day including Sunday. The main bookshop in Piazza del Duomo, almost 500 sq m (5,380 sq ft) in size, has more than 60,000 books and offers various services, such as wedding lists, to its customers.

Five-floor **Hoepli** is a serious bookstore steeped in tradition. It specializes in scientific publications and subscriptions to foreign periodicals. The **American Bookstore** specializes in English-language literature and the **Il Libro** has a good selection of publications in French.

For second-hand books, go to **Il Libraccio**, which has a number of branches. Besides school textbooks, it has various books, comic books and even CDs.

A small shop where opera fans can find interesting publications is **Il Trovatore**. Out-of-print editions, scores and libretti are offered together with valuable rarities such as facsimiles of scores by Donizetti or Verdi with the composers' signatures. This music store also provides a catalogue of its publications.

Books Import specializes in books on art, architecture, design and photography, almost all of which are published abroad. Their section on hobbies is particularly good. **Bookshop Armani**, on the first floor of the Armani complex in Via Manzoni, specializes in books on fashion, travel and hotels, and the arts.

L'Archivolto, which specializes mostly in architecture and design, also has a section on antiques with books from the 1500s to the present. This shop also has modern design objects on display. The **Libreria della Triennale** also deals mainly in books on architecture and design, but has a well-stocked children's book section as well.

Art lovers will also enjoy the **Libreria Bocca**, in the Galleria Vittorio Emanuele. The **Libreria dei Ragazzi** is the only bookshop in town entirely given over to children's books, with games and educational books. The **Libreria del Mare**, as its name suggests, offers a wide range of prints and books on the sea (il mare), while the **Libreria Milanese** has books (including photographic ones), prints, posters and gadgets concerning Milan. The **Libreria del Touring Club**

Italiano offers travel guides and maps. **Luoghi e Libri** specializes in travel books, novels, non-fiction and original language books. Comic-book fans should visit **La Borsa del Fumetto**, which also has rare and old editions.

Besides travel guides, the **Libreria dell'Automobile** stocks handbooks and illustrated books on cars and motorcycles. **Libreria dello Sport** features books and videos on all kinds of sport, and **Libreria dello Spettacolo** specializes in theatre and biographies of famous actors and actresses. **Libreria della Natura** is another great option for a wide variety of books specializing in botanic and garden design, zoology and trekking.

Music, CDs & Records

A good music shop in the city is the **Ricordi Media Store**, which has parts and scores as well as books on composers and their works. It is open even on Sundays (until 8pm), offers discounts on items at least once a month and also has a ticket office for concerts. Another good destination for music lovers is **Mondadori**. Located over three floors, it boasts a vast range of records, tapes and CDs, as well as a well-stocked section with books on music in various foreign languages.

The **Bottega Discantica** is a paradise for lovers of opera and church and symphonic music, while **Serendipity** is a shop with a British flavour: besides the latest trends in music, there are records that are almost impossible to find elsewhere and a wide range of Italian and foreign periodicals as well as rare music-themed T-shirts. **Buscemi Dischi** is one of the best-stocked and low-priced music shops and is especially recommended for jazz lovers.

Trony, on Via Torino, has a large assortment of music, computers and phones, as well as a coffee shop and a ticket office for events.

Gifts

Visitors in search of gifts would do well to try **D-Mail** that offers quirky and original gift items or **Fabriano**, which specializes in paper and writing products. For something special try **Natura è**. If circumstances call for a more sophisticated gift, head for **Ca' Albrizzi**, a famous book-binder's dealing in quality notebooks, albums and other handcrafted articles. Another good alternative in this field is **Tra le Pagine**, where visitors will find excellent handcrafted stationery, including writing paper and cardboard articles.

Smokers will love **Noli Tabacchi**, a certified *bottega storica* (historical shop) with a vast collectiion of high-quality pipes, cigars and tobacco, as well as a private collection of pipes. Again for the smoker, **Savinelli** is an institution in Milan. Since 1876 it has sold pipes of all kinds, at all prices, up to unique and extremely expensive ones.

For toys or games, try the **Città del Sole**, which stocks Milan's largest assortment of traditional wooden toys, educational games and board games for both children and adults. **Milan Model**, in business since 1932, is the domain of model-making enthusiasts, while Pergioco specializes in more modern pursuits such as video games and DVDs, as well as computer games.

DIRECTORY

Bookshops

American Bookstore
Via Camperio 16.
Map 3 B5. **Tel** 02-87 89 20.

L'Archivolto
Via Marsala 3. **Map** 3 C3.
Tel 02-659 08 42.

Books Import
Via Maiocchi 11.
Tel 02-29 40 04 78.

Bookshop Armani
Via Manzoni 37. **Map** 3 C5. **Tel** 02-72 31 86 75.

La Borsa del Fumetto
Via Lecco 16. **Map** 4 E3.
Tel 02-29 51 38 83.

Feltrinelli
Branches across Milan.
Megastore: Piazza Piemonte 2. **Map** 1 C5.
Tel 02-43 35 41.
Via Manzoni 12.
Map 3 C5.
Tel 02-76 00 03 86.
Via Foscolo 1–3.
Tel 02-86 99 68 97.
Corso Buenos Aires 33.
Map 4 F3.
Tel 02-20 23 361.
Via MV Traiano 79
(Il Portello).
Tel 02-392 71 53.

Hoepli
Via Hoepli 5. **Map** 4 D5.
Tel 02-86 48 71.
W hoepli.it

Il Libraccio
Via Arconati 16.
Tel 02-55 19 06 71.
Via Corsico 9. **Map** 6 F3.
Tel 02-837 23 98.
Via Santatecla 5.
Tel 02-87 83 99.

Viale Vittorio Veneto 22.
Map 4 E3.
Tel 02-655 56 81.
Via Romolo 9. **Map** 6 E5.
Tel 02-89 41 01 86.

Libreria dell'Automobile
Corso Venezia 43. **Map** 4 E4. **Tel** 02-76 00 66 24.

Libreria Bocca
Galleria Vittorio Emanuele II 12. **Map** 7 C1.
Tel 02-86 46 23 21.

Libreria del Mare
Via Broletto 28. **Map** 3 B5.
Tel 02-89 01 02 28.

Libreria Milanese
Via Meravigli 18. **Map** 3 B5. **Tel** 02-86 45 31 54.

Libreria della Natura
Corso Magenta 48. **Map** 6 F1. **Tel** 02-48 00 31 59.

Libreria dei Ragazzi
Via Tadino 53. **Map** 4 F2.
Tel 02-29 53 35 55.

Libreria dello Spettacolo
Via Terraggio 11. **Map** 7 A1. **Tel** 02-86 45 17 30.

Libreria dello Sport
Via Carducci 9. **Map** 3 A5.
Tel 02-805 53 55.

Libreria del Touring Club Italiano
Corso Italia 10. **Map** 7 C2.
Tel 02-85 26 304.

Libreria della Triennale
Viale Alemagna 6. **Map** 2 F3. **Tel** 02-72 01 81 28.

Libro
Via Ozanam 11. **Tel** 02-20 49 022. W il-libro.it

Luoghi e Libri
Via Vettabbia 3. **Map** 4 F5.
Tel 02-58 31 07 13.
W luoghielibri.it

Mondadori Informatica
Via Marghera 28.
Map 1 C5. **Tel** 02-48 04 71.

Mondadori Multicenter
Piazza Duomo.**Map** 7 C1.
Tel 02-454 41 10.
Corso Vittorio Emanuele II 34. **Map** 8 D1.
Tel 02-76 05 51.

Rizzoli
Galleria Vittorio Emanuele II 79. **Map** 7 C1.
Tel 02-86 46 10 71.

Il Trovatore
Via Carlo Poerio 3.
Tel 02-76 00 16 56.

Music

La Bottega Discantica
Via Nirone 5. **Map** 7 A1.
Tel 02-86 29 66.

Buscemi Dischi
Via Terraggio. **Map** 7 A1.
Tel 02-80 41 03.

Mondadori
Galleria del Corso 2.
Tel 02-76 05 54 31.

Ricordi Media Store
Galleria Vittorio Emanuele II. **Map** 7 C1.
Tel 02-86 46 02 72.

Serendipity
Corso di Porta Ticinese 100.
Map 7 B2.
Tel 02-89 40 04 20.

Trony
Via della Palla 2 (corner of Via Torino). **Map** 7 B2.
Tel 02-84 25 90 30.

Gifts

Ca' Albrizzi
Corso Venezia 29.
Map 4 E4.
Tel 02-76 00 44 39.

Città del Sole
Via Orefici 13. **Map** 7 C1.
Tel 02-86 46 16 83.

D-Mail
Via San Paolo 15.
Map 4 D5.
Tel 02-86 98 41 10.

Fabriano
Via Ponte Vetero 17.
Map 3 B5.
Tel 02-76 31 87 54.
W fabrianoboutique. com

Milan Model
Via C Imbonati 78.
Tel 02-68 08 07.
W modellismomilano.it

Natura è
Corso Garibaldi 73.
Map 3 B2.
Tel 02-86 46 50 56.
W natura-e.com

Noli Tabacchi
Galleria Vittorio Emanuele 82. **Map** 7 C1.
Tel 02-87 56 58.
W nolitabacchi.it

Savinelli
Via Orefici 2. **Map** 7 C1.
Tel 02-87 66 60.

Tra le Pagine
Via Palermo 11. **Map** 3 B3.
Tel 02-86 11 13.

ENTERTAINMENT IN MILAN

The entertainment scene is lively in Milan and there is plenty of choice for those who love night life, given the hundreds of clubs that animate the Brera and Navigli quarters in particular. Pubs, discos and nightclubs with live music, as well as late-night bistros, are filled every evening with people who come from all corners of Italy. The theatres offer the public a rich and varied programme: La Scala represents the best in opera and ballet. Major music concerts are usually held in the Palavobis arena (formerly PalaTrussardi) or at the

Mediolanum Forum at Assago. Milan is equally generous to sports lovers. Every Sunday from September to May the San Siro stadium plays host to the matches of local football teams Inter and AC Milan. It also stages national and international championship matches. Sometimes matches are also scheduled during the week. Horse racing takes place all year round at the Ippodromo racecourse. Finally, Milan's many sports and leisure clubs cater to those who like to play as well as watch sports.

Information

In order to find out the latest information on the many evening events in Milan, check the listings in *ViviMilano*, a Wednesday supplement to the newspaper *Corriere della Sera*. Every Thursday the daily paper *La Repubblica* publishes *Tutto Milano*, which is also full of useful information.

The IAT tourist offices in Piazza Castello and the Stazione Centrale (main railway station) provide free copies of the brochure *Milano Mese*, containing information on art shows, light and classical music concerts, jazz and other cultural events. Alternatively, pick up a copy of *Easy Milano*. You can also log on to the *Inmilano* or *Easy Milano* web-sites: (www.inmilano.it or

www.easymilano.it) for information on Milanese nightlife, exhibitions, plays and other forms of entertainment.

Buying Tickets

Tickets for the theatre and various concerts can be purchased in specialist booking offices such as **Ricordi Box Office**, **Ticket It** (telephone reservations and online www.ticket.it) or **Ticket One**. However, note that for performances at La Scala, you have to go in person to the box office in the Duomo metro station or book through the theatre's website (www.teatroallascala.org).

Tickets for football (soccer) matches can be purchased directly from the stadium box

Alcatraz, one of the trendiest discos in Milan *(see p196)*

offices. Alternatively tickets for Inter matches can be bought from the Banca Popolare di Milano, Banca Briantea, Banca Agricola Milanese and Ticket One. Tickets for AC Milan matches are sold by Cariplo bank, various businesses (40 bars and shops) and Milan Point, whose listings are shown at the Milan Club.

Tickets for the annual Formula 1 Grand Prix, held in September at the Autodromo Nazionale in Monza, are sold at the **Automobile Club Milano**, **Acitour Lombardia** and AC Promotion. The Monza race track is usually open to visitors at weekends when there are no other events going on. Cars and motorbikes can be driven on the track when it is free. For more information, enquire at the **Autodromo Nazionale**.

The auditorium of La Scala, Milan's premier theatre

The Mediolanum Forum at Assago is a sports arena which is also used for concerts *(see p197)*

Children

Milan does not have extensive specialist entertainment available for children. However, some of the museums and galleries are quite child-friendly. To stimulate the young imagination and provide lots of interesting educational material, there are the Planetarium *(see p122)* and the Science and Technology Museum *(see p90)*, as well as the Civic Aquarium *(see p70)*. **MUBA** is the first museum entirely dedicated to children. It has interactive exhibitions, games, events and workshops to encourage creative thinking and learning through play.

The **Teatro delle Marionette** is a popular children's puppet theatre that performs classic plays and famous novels. For pure entertainment, the amusement park at the **Idroscalo** is a good choice.

In the summer months (Jun–Sep), **Gardaland Water Park** is a popular place with slides, pools and shows that will entertain youngsters and adults alike.

Children over the age of 12 who are keen on video games can try out one of the numerous amusement arcades in the city.

A good place for entertaining smaller children is **Play Planet**, a recreation centre where kids can let off some steam or become involved in some of the creative workshops on offer. Play Planet is open all year round, and there are also two rooms in which birthday parties can be held.

In sunny weather, head to a local public park. The most suitable parks for children are the ones at Porta Venezia and Via Palestro, where theoretically no one is allowed to enter unless they are accompanied by a child. There is also a large play area with an electric train in Parco Sempione (between Piazza Castello and Piazza Sempione), near the Arco della Pace. **Fun & Fun** is the biggest covered playground in the city. Created in collaboration with an expert in educational psychology, it offers numerous play areas arranged by age, and there are comfortable and colourful sofas for the adults to relax.

Inside children's museum MUBA

DIRECTORY

Ticket Agencies

Acitour Lombardia
Corso Venezia 43.
Map 4 E4.
Tel 02-76 00 63 50.

ACP & Partners
Piazza E Duse 1.
Map 4 F4.
Tel 02-76 00 25 74.

Autodromo Nazionale
Parco di Monza.
Tel 039-248 21.
Ⓦ monzanet.it

Automobile Club Milano
Corso Venezia 43.
Map 4 E4.
Tel 02-76 00 34 47.

Ricordi Box Office
Galleria Vittorio Emanuele II.
Map 7 C1.
Tel 02-72 00 70 31.

La Scala Box Office
Galleria del Sagrato (inside Duomo metro station)
Tel 02-72 00 37 44.
Ⓦ teatroallascala.org

Ticket It
Tel 02-542 71.
Ⓦ ticket.it

Ticket One
Tel 892 101.
Ⓦ ticketone.it

Children

Fun & Fun
Via Beroldo 2.
Tel 02-26 14 42 94.
Ⓦ funefun.it

Gardaland Water Park
Via G Airaghi 61.
Tel 02-48 20 01 34.
Ⓦ gardalandwaterpark.it

Idroscalo (Fun Park)
Via Rivoltana 64.
Tel 02-70 20 10 39.
Ⓦ lunaeuropark.it

MUBA (Children's Museum)
Via Besana 12.
Tel 02-43 98 04 02.
Ⓦ muba.it

Play Planet
Via Airolo 4.
Tel 02-668 88 38.
Ⓦ playplanet.it

Teatro delle Marionette
Via Oglio 18.
Tel 02-55 21 13 00.

Nightlife

One of the characteristics that distinguishes Milan from other Italian cities is the way in which the city really comes alive at night. From Tuesday to Saturday the city's pubs, bars, restaurants, cafés and discotheques are generally packed, though there are fewer Milanese and more people from outside the city on Saturdays. Monday and, to a certain extent, Sunday, are the quiet days, offering only rare occasions for entertainment. During the week clubs and discos organize theme evenings, and some of them operate a strict door policy. Places offering live music are also very popular; they often feature promising new performers. The majority are located in the Navigli district, one of Milan's most vibrant areas.

Discos and Clubs

For the energetic on the lookout for new trends in music and dance, Milan is a great place to be. The many discos and clubs in town offer different types of music and are so popular that they attract young people from all over Italy. The scene is quite volatile and with rare exceptions – some places have become positive institutions – Milan discos change their name, management and style periodically. It is quite common for a wildly popular club to fall out of favour, only to return to popularity once again some time later.

Some places charge an entrance fee; others are free but you are obliged to pay for drinks. Prices vary quite a lot; the so-called drinkcard system, whereby you pay for your drinks at the entrance, is fairly common.

One disco that has adopted this method is **Alcatraz**, a former factory converted into a multi-purpose venue for concerts, fashion shows and even conventions. Friday is given over to 1970s and 1980s revival dance music.

La Banque attracts a chic crowd to its good restaurant. The clientele stay on to dance to music mixed by hip DJs. Situated right beside the Porta Ticinese, **Le Trottoir alla Darsena**, offers live music almost every evening.

Currently drawing in the fashion crowd is **Hollywood**. This is the place to go if you fancy celebrity spotting. The **Magazzini Generali**, which is also used for concerts and exhibitions, attracts a mixed crowd. The week opens on Wednesday and themed evenings include new musical trends and popular DJs. Friday is usually international night, with the latest music from around the world. Saturdays focus on the best of new dance, rock and contemporary pop music.

The **Shocking Club** is crowded every night from Monday to Saturday, and has become a Milanese institution just like **Nepentha**. There is a strict door policy. A trendy multi-purpose disco is the **Circolo Magnolia**, which hosts many live music acts. **Fabrique** is a futuristic architectural structure putting on top live entertainment.

The **Old Fashion**, inside the Triennale, is a disco with popular theme evenings. (The restaurant is also a big draw, especially for Sunday brunch.)

One of the largest discos in Milan is **Limelight**. The place is also used for television programmes and for holding music concerts.

The **Black Hole** opens up its huge summer garden for dancing from May through September. It has students' night on Thursdays and gay nights on Fridays. **Il Ragno**

d'Oro, near the Spanish walls overlooking Porta Romana, is jam-packed in the summer.

Nightspots with Live Music

Listening to live music is a popular activity in the city and the choice of venues is wide. **Blue Note** is one of the city's historic nightspots. It is the place to go for live jazz, but recently has been offering a wider selection of blues and ethnic music. The place gets very crowded and it can be difficult to find a table unless you book in advance.

In the Navigli area, **Rocket** is worth checking out for up-and-coming bands. **Ittolittos** is the place to hear jazz and blues. There is also a restaurant here.

Nidaba is small, dark and smoky, but people love the atmosphere and it is always full. Promising young bands often perform here.

Lastly, concerts of current music are held at the **Tunnel**, a converted warehouse under the Stazione Centrale (main railway station). Tunnel also functions as a cultural centre, hosting shows and exhibitions as well as book launches for new publications.

Discopubs

For those who want to dance without going to a disco there are so-called discopubs. In the early evening, these places are ideal for a relaxing drink and quiet conversation. Later in the evening, the atmosphere livens up considerably. **Loolapaloosa**, for example, is an Irish pub with a happy hour extending from 5 to 9pm. Late at night it transforms into a totally different creature: the volume is turned up and every available spot is used for dancing, including the tables and the counter.

B Space, in the Isola quarter, is another great place to enjoy a long happy hour followed by dancing to live music or a DJ set in its basement.

Situated in a historic building a few steps from Corso Como, is **11 Clubroom**, an elegant lounge-bar that offers great cocktails and a different music entertainment every evening. Happy hour extends from 6:30 to 9pm.

Shu Club is a bar and disco on two floor levels, inspired by Celtic culture. It is popular for theme evenings, live music and Latin-American dance courses. Happy hour extends from 6 to 10:30pm.

Latin-American

Latin-American dance is very popular in Milan. The place to go for uninhibited dancing is the **Tropicana**. It attracts mostly the over-thirty crowd and the best evenings to go are Thursday, Friday and Saturday.

If you find Cuban atmosphere intriguing and feel like trying out some Creole cuisine, the place to go is **Bodeguita del Medio**. Live music is on offer late at night and you can try salsa and merengue dancing.

A disco with Latin-American music only is Etoile, where entry is free but drinks are obligatory.

Oficina do Sabor, on the other hand, alternates rock and blues evenings with nights entirely given over to Latin-American music. They also offer courses in salsa-merengue dancing, and anyone who wants to celebrate a special occasion can rent the club.

Mas Que Nada is a great place to try Mexican food in a re-created Mayan temple while listening to music and dancing. There's an all-you-can-eat hamburgers on Thursdays.

Major Concert Venues

Milan's largest concerts are sometimes performed in places normally associated with football. The stadium San Siro *(see p200)* is sometimes used for world-famous acts, like Bruce Springsteen and Beyoncé, but the usual venue is the **Mediolanum Forum**, an ultra-modern sports arena with a seating capacity of 12,000. Other venues include the **Palasharp**, the former Palavobis, which can hold as many as 9,000 people, and the **Palalido**, with 5,000 seats. Although space is limited at the **Leoncavallo** social centre, interesting concerts are put on. In the summer, concerts are also held at the Idroscalo or under the Arco della Pace. Sponsored by the Milan city council, entry to these events is usually free.

DIRECTORY

Opera, Theatre and Cinema

The theatre season in Milan is undoubtedly one of the best and most varied in Italy. Visitors interested in a specific performance (especially if it is being put on in a well-known theatre such as the Scala or the Piccolo) should book well in advance, either directly through the theatre box office or by contacting one of the booking agencies in the city centre (see p195).

For those who prefer films to the stage, Milan has a great number of cinemas. A bonus is that new releases are shown in Milan ahead of most other Italian cities. Many of the cinemas are multiplexes with plenty of screens, and the majority are concentrated in the city centre. Foreign-language films are also screened at some cinemas on specific days of the week.

Opera, Ballet & Theatre

It would be a shame to leave Milan without having seen an opera at **La Scala** (see pp54–5). The opera season begins on 7 December, the feast day of Sant'Ambrogio, the city's patron saint. Lovers of ballet and classical music can also enjoy performances of the highest level from the theatre's ballet company and Filarmonica orchestra. It is important to book as far ahead of performances as possible, because, inevitably, there is much competition for seats at one of the world's most famous opera houses.

Another prestigious theatre venue is the **Piccolo Teatro Grassi**. Founded just after World War II by Giorgio Strehler as "an arts theatre for everyone", its productions are known for their excellence. The **Piccolo Teatro Strehler**, opened in 1998, was dedicated to the maestro, who had planned a state-of-the-art theatre worthy of his company's quality productions for over 40 years. The theatre, with a seating capacity of 974, hosts the major Piccolo Teatro productions.

The **Piccolo Teatro Studio** was originally meant to be a rehearsal hall for the Piccolo Teatro, but later became an independent company. Though interesting from an architectural standpoint, it is not all that comfortable.

The **Manzoni**, a favourite with the Milanese, presents a very eclectic programme, ranging from musicals to drama and comedy, that always attracts top-level directors and actors.

Another historic theatre is the **Carcano**, first opened in 1803. It was restructured in the 1980s and has a capacity of 990 people. Its repertoire is classical, and dance is sometimes offered as well. For comedy, head for the **Ciak**, which usually stars leading comic actors.

For lovers of experimental and avant-garde theatre there are the **Teatro Elfo Puccini** and **Teatro Leonardo** theatres, which are dedicated to performing original works that are always fascinating and thought-provoking, and may sometimes shock. The **Out Off** is also dedicated to avant-garde productions.

Milanese experimental theatre is performed at the **CRT Teatro dell'Arte**, which has a seating capacity of 800.

The **San Babila** theatre offers a programme of more traditional theatre. Here the fame of the directors and actors attracts a large number of spectators, so that getting hold of a ticket may be difficult.

One of the largest theatres in Milan is the **Teatro Arcimboldi**, which can seat 2,346 people. Besides famous musicals, it plays host to dance performances, straight theatre and concerts.

The **Teatro Nazionale** always features famous actors and has been concentrating more and more in recent years on dance and operettas.

The **Litta**, in Corso Magenta, is an elegant theatre that usually presents classic 20th-century plays. Another fascinating theatre is the **Teatro Franco Parenti**, which has a seating capacity of 500. The programme is quite varied, with particular attention being paid to new international works and music.

The small, intimate **Filodrammatici**, next to La Scala, presents a repertoire of classical works that also includes contemporary plays. The **Nuovo**, with its 1,020 seats, presents different kinds of theatrical productions, including musicals, comedies and dance, usually with famous actors. The **Teatro Dal Verme** is also worth checking out.

Cinemas

Most of the leading cinemas in Milan are concentrated in the city centre, around Corso Vittorio Emanuele II. Most of these are multiplexes, which means there is plenty of choice. Ticket prices are reduced on Wednesday evening and in almost all cinemas on weekday afternoons as well. When popular new films are being shown there are always long queues, so be sure to go early.

Most non-Italian films are dubbed into Italian and presented without subtitles, so they will be difficult to follow for anyone unfamiliar with the language. Visitors who want to see a film with the soundtrack in the original language (in lingua originale) can try **Anteo Spazio Cinema** on Mondays, or **Arcobaleno** on Tuesdays, **Mexico** on Thursdays or the **Odeon The Space Cinema**, where they have all-day showings of films in the original language on Mondays.

The **Teatro alle Colonne**, with 170 seats, promotes various cultural events and programmes, such as the African Cinema Festival. The **Auditorium San Fedele** is the home of three film clubs which offer different screening schedules and subject matter. The **Odeon The Space Cinema**, a multiplex, is the largest cinema in Milan, with ten screens. Near Corso Vittorio Emanuele II there is **Apollo Spazio Cinema**, with five screens. Another centrally located option is the **Eliseo Multisala**, which shows lesser-known films that do not benefit from high-budget publicity campaigns.

Another popular venue is the **Arlecchino** on Via San Pietro all'Orto. The **Anteo Spazio Cinema** houses three theatres and also presents children's films.

The **Plinius Multisala**, in Viale Abruzzi, is a multiplex with six screens, while the **Colosseo** has five theatres. The **Ducale**, in Piazza Napoli, is an old cinema that has been converted into a multiplex with four theatres. The **Orfeo Multisala**, near Porta Genova, features state-of-the art screening and sound equipment in a setting decorated with drawings of both Hollywood and Italian film stars.

The **UCI Bicocca**, in the Bicocca Village shopping centre has 18 screens, as well as shops, restaurants and a Wi-Fi zone.

The renovated **Gloria Multisala** has two theatres (Garbo and Marilyn), huge screens and a good audio system. Fans of arthouse films can head for the **Ariosto** or the **Cinema Centrale**, which also shows foreign-language films. At the **Cinema Beltrade**, Milan city council organizes themed seasons of films, debates and film club showings. The **Spazio Oberdan** hosts film fetivals, conferences and lectures about cinema.

Every year the Milan city council organizes cinema festivals, one of the best of which is the Panoramica di Venezia, held in September, when previews of the films competing in the Venice Film Festival are shown.

Many cinemas in Milan provide wheelchair access, but it is always a good idea to telephone beforehand for advice.

DIRECTORY

Theatres

Carcano
Corso di Porta Romana 65. **Map** 8 E3.
Tel 02-55 18 13 77.
W teatrocarcano.com

Ciak
Via Procaccini Giulio 4.
Tel 02-76 11 00 93.
W teatrociak.it

CRT Teatro dell'Arte
Viale Alemagna 6. **Map** 2 F3. **Tel** 02-89 01 16 44.
W teatrocrt.org

Filodrammatici
Via Filodrammatici 1.
Map 3 C5.
Tel 02-36 72 75 50.
W teatrofilo
drammatici.it

Litta
Corso Magenta 24.
Map 3 A5.
Tel 02-86 45 45 45.
W teatrolitta.it

Manzoni
Via Manzoni 42. **Map** 4 D4. **Tel** 02-76 36 901.
W teatromanzoni.it

Nuovo
Piazza San Babila 37.
Map 4 D5.
Tel 02-76 00 00 86.
W teatronuovo.it

Out Off
Via MacMahon 16.
Tel 02-34 53 21 40.
W teatrooutoff.it

Piccolo Teatro Grassi
Via Rovello 2. **Map** 3 B5.
Tel 02-848 80 03 04.
W piccoloteatro.org

Piccolo Teatro Strehler
Largo Greppi 1.
Tel 02-848 80 03 04.

Piccolo Teatro Studio
Via Rivoli 6. **Map** 3 B4.
Tel 02-848 80 03 04.

San Babila
Corso Venezia 2/a.
Map 4 E4.
Tel 02-79 54 69.
W teatrosanbabila.it

Teatro Arcimboldi
Via dell'Innovazione 10.
Tel 02-64 11 42 200.
W teatroarcimboldi.it

Teatro Dal Verme
Via San Giovanni sul Muro. **Map** 3 B5.
Tel 02-87 905.
W dalverme.org

Teatro Elfo Puccini
Corso Buenos Aires 33.
Map 4 F3.
Tel 02-00 66 06 06.
W elfo.org

Teatro Franco Parenti
Via Pier Lombardo 14.
Tel 02-59 99 52 06.

Teatro Leonardo
Via Ampere 1. **Map** 7 C2.
Tel 02-26 68 11 66.
W teatroleonardo.org

Teatro Nazionale
Piazza Piemonte 12. **Map** 1 C5. **Tel** 02-848 44 88 00.

Teatro alla Scala
Via Filodrammatici 2.
Tel 02-86 07 75
(automatic booking service).
Tel 02-72 00 37 44
(information).
W teatroallascala.org

Cinemas

Anteo Spazio Cinema
Via Milazzo 9. **Map** 3 C2.
Tel 02-659 77 32.

Apollo Spazio Cinema
Galleria de Cristoforis 3.
Map 8 D1.
Tel 02-78 03 90.

Arcobaleno
Viale Tunisia 11. **Map** 4 E2.
Tel 29 40 60 54.

Ariosto
Via Ariosto 16. **Map** 2 E4.
Tel 02-48 00 39 01.

Arlecchino
Via San Pietro all'Orto 9.
Map 4 D5.
Tel 02-76 00 12 14.

Auditorium S Fedele
Via Hoepli 3b. **Map** 4 D5.
Tel 02-86 35 22 31.

Cinema Beltrade
Via N. Oxilia 10.
Tel 02-26 82 05 92.

Cinema Centrale
Via Torino 30–32. **Map** 7 B1. **Tel** 02-87 48 26.

Colosseo
Viale Montenero 84.
Tel 02-59 90 13 61.

Ducale
Piazza Napoli 27. **Map** 5 C3. **Tel** 02-899 39 98 16.

Eliseo Multisala
Via Torino 64. **Map** 7 B2.
Tel 02-72 00 82 19.

Gloria Multisala
Corso Vercelli 18. **Map** 2 D5. **Tel** 02-48 00 89 08.

Mexico
Via Savona 57. **Map** 5 B3.
Tel 02-48 95 18 02.

Odeon The Space Cinema
Via Santa Radegonda 8.
Tel 02-89 21 11.

Orfeo Multisala
Viale Coni Zugna 50.
Map 6 E2.
Tel 02-89 40 30 39.

Plinius Multisala
Viale Abruzzi 28–30.
Tel 02-29 53 11 03.

Spazio Oberdan
Viale Vittorio Veneto 2.
Map 4 F3.
Tel 02-77 40 63 16.

Teatro alle Colonne
Corso di Porta Ticinese 45.
Map 7 B2.
Tel 02-58 11 31 61.

UCI Cinemas Bicocca
Viale Sarca 336. **Tel** 02-89 29 60. W ucicinemas.it

Sports and Outdoor Activities

Visitors to Milan who want to continue with a sports or exercise routine will find plenty of facilities in the city, including health clubs and gymnasiums, that are more than suitable. These centres often offer a range of activities under one roof so that you can make the most of your free time. Visitors preferring to spectate rather than participate can go and see the local football (soccer), basketball and hockey teams. All are in the first division and offer top-quality sport.

Spectator Sports

Football (soccer) fans should go to a match at the **Meazza** (or **San Siro**) **Stadium** (see p201) at least once in their lifetime. Called the "Scala of football", this stadium has a seating capacity of over 80,000. One particularly popular competition from both the sporting and the theatrical point of view is the local derby between the city's two teams, Inter and AC Milan. However, it is best to plan attendance in advance as tickets sell out pretty quickly.

For horse-racing fans there is the **Ippodromo**, where races are held all year long, except for December. Night races are held from June to September.

The Mediolanum Forum arena at Assago (see p197) is the home of the local basketball (Pallacanestro Olimpia) and volleyball (Gonzaga) teams. The arena also plays host to various tennis tournaments, first and foremost the Internazionale di Milano, which takes place in spring.

Ice-hockey buffs can follow the matches of the Vipers, who play at the **PalAgorà** arena. They have won the Italian championship for the last four years.

Five-a-Side Football

One of the most popular sports at the moment in Milan is calcetto – five-a-side football (soccer). Those wishing to play should go to the **Centro Peppino Vismara**, where they play 11-, 7- and 5-a-side games. Another good leisure facility is the **Palauno**, where there are five pitches.

Golf

There are several golf courses in the Milan area. The closest one to the city is **Le Rovedine Golf Club – Sporting Mirasole**, which is about 7 km (4 miles) from the city centre. There is also a restaurant for the use of players at the club.

Swimming

For a relaxing swim, one good swimming pool is the **Piscina Solari**, which has five lanes. A good alternative is the **Piscina Giovanni da Procida**, which boasts a half-size Olympic pool with six lanes. There is also a gym at this site which is ideal for warming up.

The **Lido** is the city's most popular outdoor swimming pool. Visitors who are not daunted by large crowds and enjoy slides can come here to swim during the heat of the Milanese summer.

Skating

Those keen on roller skating will enjoy themselves at the multi-purpose **Quanta Village**, which has rinks for roller-skating, roller-hockey and aerobic roller-skating. They also offer facilities for many other sporting activities, including tennis, basketball, swimming and mountain biking. Ice-skaters can go to the **PalAgorà**, which has an indoor rink where people can skate at their leisure on Friday and Saturday nights (9:30pm–12:30am, from 10:30pm Sat) and Sunday mornings (10am–noon). It is also open in the afternoon at the weekends from 3 to 6pm.

All the rinks have skates for rent. During the Christmas season (24 Dec–8 Jan) an ice-skating rink is usually set up near the Giardini Pubblica enabling people to skate by starlight. From 2–8pm performances, which range from ice hockey to figure skating, take place.

Squash

This sport is ideal for fitness, and players usually head to the **Mediolanum Forum Club**, where there are nine courts. Private and group lessons are available, and equipment can be hired. The centre is open every day, including the evening. Although this is a private club, visitors are welcome.

Tennis

Tennis players can play in an ideal setting at the **Associazione Sporting Club Corvetto**. The Club does not operate a membership card scheme, and there are 13 indoor courts as well as a gymnasium, bar and restaurant and parking space reserved for customers.

The **Centro Sportivo Mario Saini** has 12 courts, either covered or open to the air, depending on the season. It is best to book ahead by telephone. Another place where it is possible to play in peace and quiet, in a sporting club reserved exclusively for this sport, is the **Tennis Club 5 Pioppi**, in Fieramilanocity. There are four courts that can be used both in summer and winter.

Jogging

The best and healthiest place for running is the Monte Stella park (also known as the "Montagnetta"), near the San Siro Stadium. This large area of greenery is a good place to jog, following marked paths, or even for cycling around on mountain bikes. In the summer the park is often filled with numbers of apartment-dwelling Milanese, catching some sun.

DIRECTORY

Sports Facilities

Ippodromo
Via Piccolomini 2.
Tel 02-48 21 61.
[w] trenno.it

Meazza Stadium (San Siro)
Piazzale A Moratti.
Tel 02-48 79 82 02.
[w] sansiro.net

Five-a-Side Football

Centro Peppino Vismara
Via dei Missaglia 117.
Tel 02-826 58 23.

Palauno
Largo Balestra 5.
Tel 02-423 54 48.
[w] palauno.it

Golf

Le Rovedine Golf Club – Sporting Mirasole
Via K Marx 16,
Noverasco di Opera.
Tel 02-57 60 64 20.
[w] rovedine.com

Swimming

Lido
Piazzale Lotto 15.
Tel 02-39 27 91.

Piscina Giovanni da Procida
Via Giovanni da Procida
20. **Map** 2 D2.
Tel 02-33 10 49 70.

Piscina Solari
Via Montevideo 20.
Map 6 E2.
Tel 02-469 52 78.

Skating

PalAgorà
Via dei Ciclamini 23.
Tel 02-48 30 09 46.

Quanta Village
Via Assietta 19.
Tel 02-662 16 11.
[w] quantavillage.com

Squash

Mediolanum Forum Club
Via G Di Vittorio 6, Assago.
Tel 02-48 85 72 20.

Tennis

Associazione Sporting Club Corvetto
Via Fabio Massimo 15/4.
Tel 02-53 14 36.

Centro Sportivo Mario Saini
Via Corelli 136.
Tel 02-756 27 41.

Tennis Club 5 Pioppi
Via Marostica 4. **Map** 5 A1.
Tel 02-404 85 93.

San Siro Stadium Seating Plan

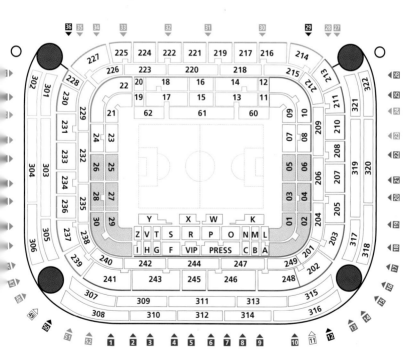

Key

○ Ticket office
▓ Stadium entrances
▓ Area for AC Milan guests
▓ Area for Inter guests

— Block of seats
— Block of seats
— Block of seats
--- Block of seats

Getting There

Avoid going by car, since parking space is very hard to find. The best way to get there is to take line 5 of the metro to the San Siro Stadio stop. At the end of the match the No. 16 trams (under the blue area) go to the city centre.

ENTERTAINMENT AT THE LAKES

At the lakes it is possible to devote a considerable amount of leisure time to entertainment and sport. At Lake Garda in particular, you will be able to practise any type of aquatic sport, have a go at trekking in the hinterland and dance the night away at the discos. Of the lakes, Garda also has the liveliest nightlife and is the most popular with young people. Lake Como, Lake Maggiore and the smaller lakes still offer a variety of opportunities for entertainment. In recent years the enterprising local IAT tourist offices, sponsored by the town administrations, have been quite successful in promoting initiatives aimed at making holidays more interesting for visitors. Outdoor markets, feasts, festivals and other events have therefore become more and more frequent. The lakes offer breathtaking scenery, an entertainment in itself, and every year there are programmes of cultural events. In addition there are fine architectural and artistic works to be seen, lovely gardens to explore, and nature reserves to wander through.

Sports

If keeping in top physical shape is a priority, there are plenty of activities that serve the purpose at the lakes. Lake Garda is the domain of windsurfing; Torbole and Riva in particular are the most popular places for surfers both in summer and winter. Sailing fans will enjoy the Centomiglia, an annual regatta organized by the Circolo Vela Gargnano sailing club and held on the second weekend of September. For a more relaxing time, there are also opportunities to go fishing.

In the Garda hinterland, hiking has become very popular, and touring the area on a mountain bike is the most recent vogue. More adventurous souls can take lessons in paragliding. Lake Maggiore offers not only many aquatic sports but is quite popular with golf enthusiasts. There are state-of-the-art golf courses in lovely natural settings that are enjoyed by Italian and foreign golfers alike.

The hills and valleys around the lake are ideal places for horse riding, hiking, mountaineering, free climbing, hang-gliding and paragliding and, in the winter, when snow covers the high ground, skiing and snowboarding.

The most popular sports at Lake Como are sailing and water-skiing. Lessons are available from qualified instructors, whatever your age and experience.

Another enjoyable activity is canoeing. All the lakes have clubs where you can rent canoes and equipment. For the more sedentary, there are many spas (terme) at the lakes or in the vicinity. These centres offer a variety of treatments.

A water-skiing instructor and his pupil at Lake Como

Other Activities

Visitors to Lake Garda, especially families with children, might want to visit the Gardaland amusement park (see pp154–5). It is recommended for children and adults alike, an ideal place to spend a day as a family and even experience the occasional thrill. However, in peak season, be prepared for a long wait at the most interesting attractions.

About 2 km (1 mile) from Gardaland is **Caneva**, the largest water amusement park in Italy. Shows, water games and other displays, plus an area reserved for small children, make this a big aquatic attraction.

To take a closer look at some rare and endangered animal species, visit the **Parco Natura**

A group of windsurfers in action on Lake Garda

Camels in the Natura Viva zoological park, at Bussolengo-Pastrengo near Lake Garda

Viva, a zoo located at Bussolengo-Pastrengo. A pleasant walk among ancient oak trees and plants takes visitors around the home of the 1,000 specimens in this lovely park. Cars are also allowed into the safari park, where a 6-km (4-mile) tour brings you into closer contact with some of the wild animals of the savannah.

Another popular place for lovers of interesting plants is the **Giardino Botanico della Fondazione André Heller** at Gardone Riviera: 1.5 ha (3.7 acres) of land with over 8,000 plants from every climatic zone in the world. The **Parco Giardino Sigurtà** lies 8 km (5 miles) from Peschiera. This 50-ha (123-acre) garden is a temple to ecology.

At Lake Maggiore the Villa Pallavicino park *(see p139)* has a lovely 20-ha (49-acre) botanical garden with 40 different species of animals.

Logo of the Natura Viva zoological park

Nightlife

The best area for nightlife is Lake Garda, which boasts internationally known nightspots. Desenzano, in particular, has a number of pubs and other spots for evening entertainment, while in the outskirts are some of the largest discotheques in Italy. The undisputed king is **Coco Beach Club**, a gigantic and extremely popular place, especially in the summer. Another famous and very popular nightspot is **Noname**, a multimedia disco where theme evenings feature. On Friday there is funk, soul and "rare groove" music, while the other evening (and night) programmes are more unconventional. At Lake Como, a popular spot for dinner and drinks with music is **Vintage Jazz Café**, which caters to a young and trendy crowd. For more live music, go to **L'Ultimo Caffè**.

At Lake Maggiore, do not miss **La Rocca**, a lively disco situated on a steamer boat with a floating dock, and **Il Battello**.

At Verbania, go to **Tony's Diner Café**; **Beba**, at Ornavasso, is another lively spot.

DIRECTORY

Activities

Caneva
Località Fossalta 58, Lazise.
Tel 045-69 69 900.
W canevaworld.it

Giardino Botanico della Fondazione André Heller
Via Roma, Gardone Riviera.
Tel 033-64 10 877.
W hellergarden.com

Parco Giardino Sigurtà
Via Cavour 1, Valeggio sul Mincio.
Tel 045-637 10 33.
W sigurta.it

Parco Natura Viva
Località Figara 40, Bussolengo-Pastrengo, Varenna.
Tel 045-717 01 13.
W parconaturaviva.it

Nightlife

Il Battello
Corso Repubblica, Arona.
Tel 338-91 68 438.
W battelloarona.it

Beba
Via A. Di Dio 46, Ornavasso (Verbania).
Tel 0323-837 137.
W bebadiscobar.it

Coco Beach
Via Catullo 5, Lonato.
Tel 030-207 77 57.
W cocobeachclub.com

Noname
Via Lavagnone 13, Lonato.
Tel 340 767 5118.
W nonameclub.it

La Rocca
Via Verbano 1, Arona.
Tel 0322-48 051.

Tony's Diner Café
Piazza Flaim 16, Verbania.
Tel 0323-40 321.

L'Ultimo Caffè
Via Giulini 32, Como.
Tel 031-27 30 98.

Vintage Jazz Café
Via Oliginati 14, Como.
Tel 031-414 13 46.
W vintagejazzcomo.it

Beautiful water lilies in a pond at Parco Giardino Sigurtà

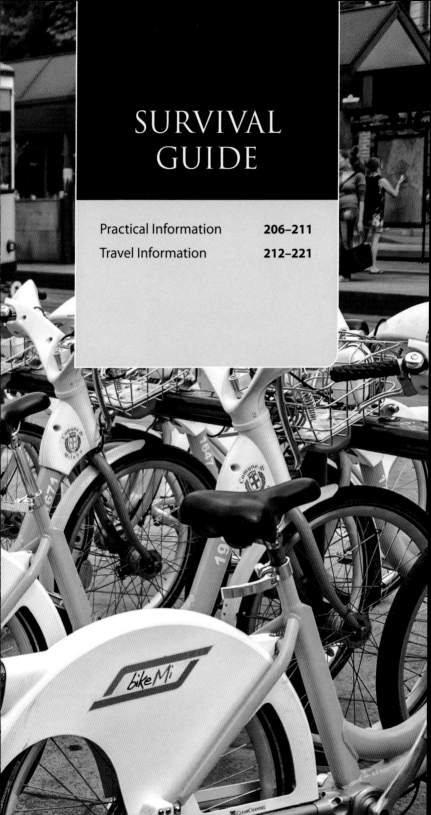

SURVIVAL GUIDE

PRACTICAL INFORMATION

Milan is one of Italy's most efficient and business-like cities, with an excellent public transport network and good public services. In the capital of fashion, appearances do matter, and you are likely to receive better service and attention if you are smartly dressed. Milan has its share of petty crime, and it is advisable to take some basic precautions in order to enjoy your stay to the full. Keep bags and cameras close to you at all times, and take extra care travelling on public transport, where pickpockets may be operating. The public transport system is, however, the best way to get around the city. Pedestrians should stay alert in the chaotic traffic, and take particular care crossing streets. Tourist offices are the best places to go for practical information, including maps. At the lakes, brochures are available from IAT offices, with information on local festivals and other entertainment. Information can also be obtained ahead of your visit from the Italian tourist office (ENIT) in your home country.

Visitors on the roof of the Gothic Duomo

When to Go

Although Milan is great to visit year-round, the mild climate in June makes it one of the best months to go. The balmy spring months are also pleasant with cool breezes. Milan in August can be brutally hot and many shops and restaurants are closed. Most tourist attractions remain open, however. Winter in Milan can be very cold. The lakes are best visited from April to October, but they are packed in July and August.

Visas and Passports

Italy is part of the Schengen Agreement, whereby travellers moving from one Shengen country to another are not subject to border controls, although there are spot checks.

Other EU nationals and citizens of the US, Canada, Australia and New Zealand do not need visas for stays of up to three months.

All visitors to Italy must register with the police within eight working days of arrival. If you are staying in a hotel, this will be done for you. Otherwise, contact the local *questura* (police station).

Anyone wishing to stay for more than three months (eight working days for citizens from countries other than those mentioned above) will have to obtain a *permesso di soggiorno* (permit to stay). EU citizens can apply for a permit at any main police station. Non-EU citizens must apply in advance in their home country.

If you lose your passport contact your embassy.

Travel Safety Advice

Visitors can get up-to-date travel safety information from the **Foreign and Commonwealth Office** in the UK, the **State Department** in the US and the **Department of Foreign Affairs and Trade** in Australia.

Tourist Information

Information on hotels and local amenities is available from the Italian tourist board, **ENIT (Ente Nazionale Italiano per il Turismo)**, which has offices in many major cities, including London and New York. In Milan, **IAT (Informazione e Accoglienza Turistica)** offices have information on the city, including free lists of hotels and restaurants, and details of cultural events.

At the lakes, look for IAT offices in larger towns, and Pro Loco tourist offices in smaller towns and villages; these are usually located in the town hall (*comune*) and are sometimes open only during the tourist season.|

Opening Hours and Admission Prices

Most state-owned museums are open from Tuesday to Sunday, while privately owned museums operate their own timetables. Churches are open daily but some close for lunch from 12:30 to 2pm. Church services held on Saturday afternoons are listed as pre-hols in the guide.

EU residents aged under 18 and over 65 benefit from discounts in most state-run places, though proof is required. The Milano Card gives free public transport and reduced entry to several museums and galleries. A three-day card, available from www.milanocard.it, is €13 plus postage costs if sent to your hotel on arrival.

◀ Bicycles for hire neatly lined up on a street in Milan

Disabled Travellers

Milan is a challenging city for disabled travellers. Pavements can be uneven or blocked by parked cars, and tram lines can make crossing the road difficult. However, the majority of Milan's metro system is wheelchair-accessible, as are the green, low-level trams. An excellent source of information for disabled travellers is the **AIAS MILANO Onlus** website.

International Student Identity Card

Student Travellers

The **Centro Turistico Studentesco (CTS)** issues the **International Student Identity Card (ISIC)** and discount tickets to people under 26; these can be used for travel not only in Milan, but also in the rest of Italy and Europe.

There are two youth hostels in Milan: the **Ostello della Gioventù P Rotta**, where you need an annual membership card (which can be bought at the hostel), and **La Cordata (Casa Scout)**. For information on youth hostels around the lakes, contact the **Associazione Italiana Alberghi per la Gioventù** (Italian Youth Hostelling Association).

Italian Time

Milan is 1 hour ahead of Greenwich Mean Time. This means New York and Los Angeles are 6 and 9 hours behind Italian time, and Moscow is 2 hours ahead. Tokyo and Sydney are 8 and 9 hours ahead respectively.

Responsible Travel

Milan doesn't immediately impress the eco-conscious visitor. Things are greener beneath the surface, however, particularly when it comes to food. Piazza Gramsci, in the Sempione district, has a small organic market on the first Sunday of each month, while Via F Confalonieri, in the Garibaldi area, hosts a similar market on the second Sunday of each month. **Simply SMA** is the city's first eco-supermarket. **Natura Si** and **Bio c' Bon** are chains selling organic and natural products.

Recycling bins are everywhere, while in metro stations, the *salvagiornali* bins are a response to the nuisance of free newspapers.

Agriturismi Bio lists farm or country holidays considered fully or partly organic.

Colourful produce at one of Milan's organic markets

DIRECTORY

Consulates

UK
Via San Paolo 7.
Map 4 D5. **Tel** 02-72 30 01.

US
Via Principe Amedeo 2/10.
Map 4 D3. **Tel** 02-29 03 51.

Travel Safety Advice

Foreign and Commonwealth Office (UK)
w gov.uk/foreign-travel-advice

US Department of State
w travel.state.gov/

Department of Foreign Affairs and Trade (Australia)
w dfat.gov.au/smartraveller.gov.au/

Tourist Information

Enit UK
1 Princes Street, London W1B 2AY. w italian touristboard.co.uk

Enit US
630 Fifth Avenue, Suite 1565, NY 10111.
w italiantourism.com

IAT OFFICES

MILAN
Piazza Castello. **Map** 3 A4.
w visitamilano.it

LAKE COMO
IAT di Bellagio
Piazza G Mazzini 12.
w bellagiolakecomo.com

IAT di Cernobbio
Via Regina 33.
Tel 031-51 01 98.

IAT di Como
Piazza Cavour 17.
w lakecomo.org

IAT di Lecco
Piazza XX Settembre 23.
w provincia.lecco.it

IAT di Tremezzo
Via Regina 3. **Tel** 0344-404 93. (Seasonal opening).

LAKE GARDA
IAT di Desenzano
Via Porto Vecchio 34.
Tel 030-374 87 26.

IAT di Gardone
Corso Repubblica 8.
Tel 0365-203 47 or 30 37 48 736.

IAT di Sirmione
Viale Marconi 8.
w comune.sirmione.bs.it

IAT di Toscolano Maderno
Via Sacerdoti 1.
Tel 0365-64 13 30.

LAKE ISEO
IAT d'Iseo
Lungolago Marconi 2.
Tel 030-98 02 09.

LAKE MAGGIORE
IAT di Laveno
Piazza Italia 2.
Tel 0332-66 87 85.

IAT di Varese
Via Romagnosi 9.
w vareseland oftourism.it

Disabled Travellers

AIAS Milano Onlus
w milanopertutti.it

Student Travellers

Associazione Italiana Alberghi per la Gioventù
w aighostels.it

Centro Turistico Studentesco
w cts.it

La Cordata
Via Burigozzo 11. **Map** 7 B3. w lacordata.it

ISIC
w isic.org

Ostello della Gioventù P Rotta
Via Martino Bassi 2. **Map** 1 A1. w hostelmilan.org

Responsible Travel

Agriturismi Bio
w agriturismibio.it

Bio c' Bon
w bio-c-bon.eu/it

Natura Si
w naturasi.it

Simply SMA
Via Novara 15.

Personal Security and Health

In Milan, there is widespread petty crime, a problem common to all large cities. Stay wary, particularly in crowded areas, and keep a close eye on personal property such as bags and cameras, especially in the evening. The towns and villages around the lakes are very safe areas, however, and there should be no cause for concern. Should you fall ill during your stay, Italian pharmacists can advise on minor ailments.

A municipal policewoman directing traffic in Milan

Police and Emergencies

There are several police forces in Italy. The *polizia* (state police) deal with all kinds of criminal offences and issue *permessi di soggiorno* (residence permits) to foreigners and passports to Italian citizens.

The *vigili urbani* (municipal police) wear blue-and-white uniforms in winter and white ones in summer; they regulate traffic and parking offences.

The *carabinieri* (military police) deal with everything from speeding offences to drug-related crimes.

Police stations *(questura)* and hospitals *(ospedale)* with a casualty unit/emergency room *(pronto soccorso)* are shown on the Street Finder maps *(see pp222–35)*.

For urgent medical attention see *Hospitals and Pharmacies*. Emergency phone numbers are listed in the Directory.

What to be Aware of

Pay attention when walking alone at night in poorly lit streets away from the city centre. Unaccompanied women should take particular care. Petty theft is a perennial problem, so keep a tight grip on your bag, especially in trams and on the metro. Pickpockets are common and well organized. Keep your handbag closed and do not carry backpacks or shoulder bags on your back. Keep valuables such as your wallet or purse, camera and mobile phone well out of sight. When walking along the street, keep handbags on the inside, away from the road.

Visitors with cars should take all the usual precautions appropriate in a big city. Do not leave personal belongings or car radios visible inside the car. Whenever possible, leave your car in an attended parking space *(parcheggio custodito)*.

Lost Property

If you lose documents or other personal property, report the loss immediately at the nearest police station. An official report will be needed for insurance claims. It may also be worth contacting the city's **Ufficio Oggetti Smarriti** (Lost Property Office, c/o Railway Police). If you lose something on a train or in a station, contact the lost property office on the ground floor of the **Stazione Centrale**.

Should an interpreter be needed, ask at your hotel or try the Yellow Pages (*Pagine Gialle; www.paginegialle.it*). where agencies will be listed. The **Associazione Italiana di Traduttori e Interpreti (AITI)** also has a list of qualified translators and interpreters. Your consulate should be able to provide interpreters too.

It is advisable to take photocopies of all important documents, including passport pages, before travelling.

Hospitals and Pharmacies

Milan has state-of-the-art health facilities should you become ill during your stay. If the ailment is minor, go to a pharmacy *(farmacia)* first. Italian pharmacists are well trained to deal with routine problems. Pharmacies can be identified by a neon green cross over the door. A list of pharmacies open at night *(servizio notturno)* and on public

Milanese police at a road block

Fire engine

Ambulance

Police car

holidays will be on display. A useful chemist is the **Farmacia della Stazione Centrale**, at the main railway station, open 24 hours a day.

Pronto Farmacia is a free emergency service that will deliver urgent medicines. The 24-hour service also gives advice and information on pharmacies that are open at night and on Sundays.

If you need urgent medical assistance, call the **Emergenza Sanitaria/Ambulanze** (Health Emergencies/Ambulance) or go straight to the Pronto Soccorso (Casualty Department/Emergency Room) at the nearest hospital.

If you should need a doctor at your hotel, contact the **Guardia Medica** (Night Duty Physician). In the event of dental problems, go to the emergency dentist **Pronto Soccorso Odontoiatrico**.

Minor Hazards

Mosquitoes (zanzare), which appear at the first sign of warm weather, can be a real pest. Despite the various anti-mosquito devices such as burning coils and plug-ins, it is difficult to fend them off altogether, especially when sitting at outdoor cafés at the lakes (the Navigli quarter in the city is also particularly bad). Always remember to apply insect repellent cream or spray.

Tap water is safe to drink in Italy, but many people prefer to drink bottled water (acqua minerale), which may be either fizzy (frizzante or con gas) or still (naturale).

Milan's pollution and its notorious smog, which is particularly prevalent in winter, can be problematic for people with breathing difficulties who should consider wearing anti-pollution masks.

Travel and Health Insurance

All EU citizens should travel with the European Health Insurance Card (EHIC), available from the UK Department of Health (www.dh.gov.uk) or a post office. The card entitles the holder to receive healthcare at reduced cost or sometimes for free, and reciprocal health care in Italy. It is wise, however, for visitors to have additional health insurance.

Always take out adequate travel insurance before leaving for Italy, and report any loss or theft at a local police station.

Safety Outdoors

Aside from the high levels of pollution and strong sun in summer, Milan poses little environmental danger. Visitors to the lakes are unlikely to experience anything more alarming than the odd mosquito. Those keen to practise water-sports should follow certain guidelines. At Lakes Maggiore and Como, cold water and strong currents challenge even experienced swimmers. On Lake Garda, windsurfers may be taken by surprise by sudden gusts of wind, particularly in the areas around Torbole and Riva (the northern part of the lake).

DIRECTORY

Police and Emergencies

Emergenza Sanitaria/ Ambulanze (Health Emergencies/Ambulance)
Tel 118.

General Emergencies
Tel 112.

Fire
Tel 115.

Police
Tel 113 (Carabinieri).
Tel 02-77 27 01 00 (Vigili Urbani).

Lost Property

Associazione Italiana di Traduttori e Interpreti
w aiti.org

Stazione Centrale
Piazza Duca d'Aosta (Platform 21).
Map 4 E1.
Tel 02-63 71 24 28.
Open 24 hours.

Ufficio Oggetti Smarriti
Via Friuli 30. Map 8 F4.
Tel 02-88 45 39 00.
Open 8:30am–4pm Mon–Fri.

Hospitals and Pharmacies

Farmacia della Stazione Centrale
Map 4 F1. Tel 02-669 07 35.

Guardia Medica
Tel 02-345 67.

Pronto Farmacia
Tel 800-80 11 85 (free).

Pronto Soccorso Odontoiatrico
Via della Commenda 10.
Map 8 E2.
Tel 02-55 03 25 14.

Canoeing, a popular outdoor activity in the lakes in Lombardy

Banking and Currency

Milan has very good public services. There is a bank on almost every street corner, and most of them have automatic cash dispensers. In the smaller villages around the lakes, banks with cash dispensers are less easy to find, so plan ahead and take some cash with you. Credit cards are widely accepted by all but the smallest of businesses. Currency can be exchanged at post offices, banks, bureaux de change and, at a less competitive rate, some hotels. Always compare rates to find the most favourable one.

Main branch of the UniCredit bank, in Piazza Cordusio

Banks

Milanese banks are open 8:30am–1:30pm and 2:30–4pm Monday to Friday and some open on Saturday mornings; opening times may vary by about a quarter of an hour from bank to bank. Most banks have ATMs, which take all major credit cards, including American Express and Visa.

Currency Exchange

It is a good idea to bring some euros with you to avoid poor exchange rates and/or high charges, but it is possible to change money at the airports.
 Forexchange Linate in the arrival lounge of Linate airport, is open 7am–midnight daily; the office in the departure lounge is open 6am–10pm.
Forexchange Malpensa, in Malpensa airport departures, is open 7am–11pm daily.
 Larger post offices and banks also offer exchange services at attractive rates;

however, using an ATM to withdraw cash can often be a more economical option.

ATMs

ATMs *(bancomat)* are ubiquitous in Milan. Be aware, though, that some of the smaller villages around the lakes may not have either a bank or an ATM. The majority of ATMs have instructions in English and other European languages. Always use caution when withdrawing cash and avoid any machine you are unsure about.

Credit Cards and Traveller's Cheques

Both in Milan and at the lakes, most businesses accept **MasterCard** and **Visa**, while **American Express** and **Diners Club** are less frequently accepted. However, some restaurants, cafés and shops may require a minimum expenditure to accept credit card payment. Always make sure you have some cash in case your credit card is not accepted. Note that petrol stations do not take credit cards, only cash.
 To avoid problems using your card while abroad, inform your credit card company before travelling. In the event of the loss or theft of your credit card, contact the numbers listed in the Directory immediately.
 Traveller's cheques are not as popular as they used to be and tourists are finding it increasingly hard to cash or spend them. If you decide to use them, choose a well-known name such as American Express.

Currency

Italy's currency is the euro. Euro banknotes have seven denominations. The €5 note (grey) is the smallest, followed by the €10 note (pink), €20 note (blue), €50 note (orange), €100 note (green), €200 note (yellow) and the €500 note (purple). The euro has eight coin denominations: the €1 and €2 coins are both silver and gold in colour; the 50-, 20- and 10-cent coins are gold; and the 5-, 2- and 1-cent coins are bronze.
 Do not carry large amounts of cash on you, and never underestimate the need for coins and small notes in Italy. Taxis and smaller shops and museums can rarely change large notes.

DIRECTORY

Banks

Banca Popolare di Milano
Piazza Filippo Meda 4.
Map 4 D5. **Tel** 02-770 01.

Banca Popolare di Lodi
Piazza dei Mercanti 5.
Map 7 C1. **Tel** 02-850 81.

Intensa San Paolo
Via Verdi 8. **Map** 7 C1.
Tel 02-88 621.

UniCredit
Piazza Cordusio.
Map 7 C1. **Tel** 02-88 621.

Currency Exchange

Forexchange Linate
International arrivals.
Tel 800-30 53 57.
w forexchange.it

Forexchange Malpensa
International departures T2.
Tel 800-30 53 57.
w forexchange.it

Lost and Stolen Credit Cards

American Express
Tel 06-72 90 03 47 or 800-87 43 33 (toll free).

Diners Club
Tel 800-39 39 39 (toll free).

MasterCard
Tel 800-87 08 66 (toll free).

Visa
Tel 800-87 72 32 (toll free).

Communications and Media

Public phones are increasingly hard to find in Milan, as access to Internet services and the use of mobile phones have increased. Mobile phone users should consider purchasing a SIM card for use in Italy before they travel, or a prepaid phone on arrival. In addition to Internet cafés, Wi-Fi hotspots are ever more common in bars, restaurants and hotels. News-stands carry a huge range of publications, and many sell English-language newspapers too. The postal service in Italy, once notoriously slow, is much improved.

International and Local Telephone Calls

The area code *(prefisso)* for Milan is 02. Be aware that it is necessary to dial telephone numbers in full, including the area code, even for local calls. For information in English concerning international calls, dial 4176. To make an international reverse charge (collect) call, the number to dial is 170. For Italian directory enquiries, dial 1254.

Mobile Phones

GSM mobile phones work in Italy, but North American phones may not work abroad if they are locked or will not accept other SIM cards. If you know that your handset will function and is unlocked, consider buying an Italian SIM on arrival. Most offer free incoming calls and low outgoing call rates.

If your phone is locked, you could buy a prepaid phone once in Italy, though all shops will ask for a tax code, which you won't be able to provide. You can find shops for Milan's mobile providers (**Vodafone**, **Negozio TIM** and **Negozio Wind**) all over the city.

Public Telephones

Most telephone booths in Milan are scheduled to disappear by 2015; around the lakes they are still quite commonplace. Public phones usually operate with telephone cards *(schede telefoniche)*, sold at Internet shops, tobacconists and newsstands. An international card *(scheda telefonica internazionale)* is the cheapest way of calling home.

Internet café in Milan

Internet Access

There are Internet cafés all over Milan, including **Internet Point Duomo** and **Mondadori**, and in the main lake towns. Wi-Fi is common in bars, restaurants and hotels. It can also be accessed both inside and outside public buildings such as libraries, schools, museums and more.

Postal Services

Post offices are usually open 8am–7pm on weekdays and 8:30am–12:30pm on Saturday. The **Ufficio Centrale** offers a poste restante *(Fermo Posta)* service and it is possible to change money there.

You can buy stamps *(francobolli)* from post offices and any tobacconist with the black-and-white T sign.

Newspapers and Magazines

Milan dailies, such as *Il Corriere della Sera*, have local news sections and entertainment listings. The free *Milano Mese* (available at IAT offices) has listings of cultural events.

Websites such as www. tuttomilano.it, www.about milan.com and http://ciao milano.it have information on cultural activities.

DIRECTORY

Mobile Phones

Negozio TIM
Tel 02-80 92 32.

Negozio Wind
Tel 02-67 48 18 56.

Vodafone
Tel 02-34 22 08.

Internet Cafés

Internet Point Duomo
Inside the Duomo metro station.
Map 7 C1.
Tel 02-36 52 17 21.

Mondadori
Via Marghera 28.
Map 1 C5.
Tel 02-48 04 71. Piazza del Duomo 1.
Map 7 C1.
Tel 02-454 41 10.

Postal Services

Ufficio Centrale
Via Cordusio 4.
Map 7 B1.
Tel 02-87 91 44 46.
w poste.it

Other Post Offices
Via Sammartini 2, off Piazza Duca d'Aosta (Stazione Centrale, ground floor).

Newsagent selling national and international publications

Television

There are three state-owned television channels in Italy (RAI 1, RAI 2 and RAI 3) and many private channels, some of which are owned by Mediaset (Retequattro, Canale Cinque, and Italia Uno). There are also many local channels. Most hotels 3-stars and above have satellite TV with BBC and CNN news in English, as well as German and French channels.

TRAVEL INFORMATION

Three airports link Milan with the rest of the world. Linate airport is only a few kilometres from the city centre and connects the capital of Lombardy with the main Italian and European cities. Malpensa is an intercontinental airport about 50 km (30 miles) from Milan, while Orio al Serio, which handles many European budget flights, is located 45 km (27 miles) away, near Bergamo. There are car rental offices at all the airports, though it is usually cheaper to book a fly-drive deal ahead rather than

arrange hire on arrival. There are excellent train links between Milan and other cities in Italy. The city is also well connected to the rest of Europe, with fast, easy routes to France and Switzerland, and to Austria and Germany via Verona. Visitors arriving by car will use the excellent road and motorway networks. Exits from the ring road around Milan are clearly marked. However, these roads are often congested with traffic, particularly at rush hour, so journey times can be slow.

Linate Airport, located within easy reach of the city centre

Arriving by Air

Visitors from outside Italy arriving in Milan by air are likely to fly into either Malpensa or Orio al Serio airports (the latter is often referred to as Bergamo airport). Linate airport handles more domestic than international flights. Frequent flights between London and Milan are operated by **Alitalia**, **British Airways** and **easyJet**. The majority of low-cost airlines, such as **Ryanair**, fly to Orio al Serio in Bergamo.

British Airways and **Lufthansa** offer a good choice of direct flights from the United States, linking Milan with Boston, New York, Chicago, Miami and Los Angeles. Alitalia also has good connections from Toronto, Vancouver and Sydney; however, many of its flights from the US go via Rome, necessitating a connection to Milan.

Linate Airport

Linate handles a small number of European flights with airlines such as Alitalia, **Air France**, British Airways, **BMI**, Lufthansa and **KLM**, and domestic flights with carriers such as **Meridiana**.

The airport has left luggage facilities, car rental offices including Avis and Hertz *(see pp220–21)*, and plenty of car parking space.

Getting from Linate to the centre of Milan is easy. Taxis take around 20 minutes (longer in rush hour) and cost about €15–€25. A taxi stand is situated right in front of the airport exit.

ATM bus No.73 runs every 10 minutes from 5:35am to 0:35am daily, linking the airport with the city centre, going as far as Piazza San Babila. There are two services – a regular service and a non-stop one. Tickets (€1.50) are sold at the vending machine near the bus stop. They can also be bought on the non-stop bus. The **Starfly** bus runs every

30 minutes between 5:30am and 11:45pm, connecting Linate and Milan's central station. Tickets cost €5 and can be bought on board.

Malpensa Airport

Located 50 km (30 miles) from the city, Malpensa is the largest of the Milan airports, with two terminals.

The **Malpensa Express** rail service links Terminal 1 with Stazione Nord in Piazza Cadorna, Stazione Centrale and Stazione Garibaldi. Journey times vary from 29 to 43 minutes, with trains leaving the airport every 30 minutes between 5:26am and 0:29am. The last coach to Cadorna is at 1:30am. Trains from Milan depart from 4:28am to 0:28am. A one-way ticket costs €12 (€6 children); the only returns available are day returns.

Two coach lines also offer a good airport service. The

Interior of Malpensa airport, the largest in Milan

A highway congested with traffic heading into Milan

Malpensa Shuttle runs every 20 minutes, starting at 5am from the Stazione Centrale (there is an earlier coach at 4:15am), and 5:30am from Malpensa (T1 and T2); the last coach from the airport leaves at 1:20am. The journey time is about 1 hour; tickets cost €10 for a single or €16 for a return.

The **Malpensa Bus Express**, operated by Autostradale, runs approximately every 20 minutes starting at 4am from the Stazione Centrale and 6am from Malpensa (T1 and T2). A single journey costs €10. An **Airpullman** bus links Malpensa and Linate every 90 minutes, starting from 9:30am; the last coach leaves Linate at 4:30pm and Malpensa at 6:20pm. The journey time is 70 minutes and tickets cost €13.

A taxi from Malpensa takes around an hour (more in rush hour) and costs €90 to Milan.

Orio Al Serio Airport

Used by several European carriers (including many low-cost airlines), Orio al Serio has only one terminal, meaning that crowds and queues are commonplace.

Autostradale runs an efficient bus service between the airport and Milan's Stazione Centrale, leaving every 30 minutes during the day. The journey time is about 1 hour, and a round-trip ticket costs €9.

An urban bus route links the airport to Bergamo train station every 20–30 minutes (6:05am–0:15am Mon–Sat; service is less frequent on Sundays); tickets cost €2.10.

A taxi to Milan takes 60 minutes and costs about €100.

Arriving by Car

Visitors arriving from the *autostrada* (motorway) will approach Milan via the ring roads, *tangenziale est* (east) and *tangenziale ovest* (west), which are often congested with traffic. Approaching the centre, look for an official car park *(see p217)*, then use public transport. The alternative is to use the ATM parking areas *(see chart below)* that are on the outskirts but well served by the metro. Fees vary from €1 for half a day to €2 for up to 8 hours. Some ATM parking is free after 8pm.

Car parks closer to the city centre are more expensive.

Arriving from	Motorway Exits	Car Park	Number of Cars	Metro and Bus	Distance from City Centre
	Cavenago/Cambiago	Gessate	500	Ⓜ 2 (30/ 35 min.)	23 km (14 miles)
Trieste	Sesto San Giovanni/V.le Zara	Sesto Marelli	250	Ⓜ 1 (20 min.)	8 km (5 miles)
Venice **Verona**	Tang. est/Cologno Monzese	Cologno Nord	500	Ⓜ 2 (30 min.)	9 km (5.5 miles)
Brescia	Tang. est/Viale Palmanova Crescenzago	Cascina Gobba/ 600	800	Ⓜ 2 (20 min.)	6 km (4 miles)
	Tang. est/ Viale Forlanini	Forlanini	650	🚊 12 🚌 73	6 km (4 miles)
Turin **Aosta**	Viale Certosa	Lampugnano	2,000	Ⓜ 1 (20 min.)	5 km (3 miles)
Como **Chiasso** **Varese**	Pero	Molino Dorino	1,600	Ⓜ 1 (25 min.)	8.5 km (5 miles)
Gravellona	Tang. ovest/Milano Baggio	Bisceglie	900	Ⓜ 1 (20/ 25 min.)	6 km (4 miles)
Ventimiglia **Genoa**	Viale Liguria/Centro Città/ Filaforum	Romolo/ Famagosta	250 560	Ⓜ 2 (20 min.)	4–5 km (2.5–3 miles)
Naples **Rome** **Florence** **Bologna**	Milano/Piazzale Corvetto	Rogoredo/ San Donato	350 2,400	Ⓜ 3 (20 min.)	5–7 km (3–4 miles)

An ETR Eurostar train at the Stazione Centrale in Milan

Arriving by Rail

The main railway station in Milan is the **Stazione Centrale**, where all the major domestic and international trains arrive. Connections with your destination in town can be made by taxi, metro (underground) lines 2 and 3, and many trams and buses, all of which are just outside the entrance. **Porta Garibaldi**, in the Centro Direzionale area, and Milano Lambrate (near Città Studi) are much smaller railway stations. Both can be reached via metro line 2. Metro line 3 links **Rogoredo** station, near San Donato Milanese, with central Milan.

A regional train service run by the **Ferrovie Nord Milano** connects the city with Como, Varese and the Brianza region. Trains depart from Piazzale Cadorna, where metro lines 1 and 2 converge.

The Passante Ferroviario (see p219) is a suburban railway link network that connects various metro lines with the Porta Garibaldi station, run by the **Ferrovie dello Stato** (state railway), and with the Milano–Bovisa station, run by Ferrovie Nord.

A number of different types of train operate on Italy's railways. The fastest trains linking Milan and the main national and international cities are the ETR Eurostar trains (le frecce). The ticket price includes a supplement and obligatory seat reservation. International Eurocity trains also offer fast links to major European cities such as Zurich, Paris and Barcelona. Intercity trains link Milan and the main cities within Italy, such as Florence and Rome. On both Eurocity and Intercity services, tickets should be booked ahead. A supplement is charged.

The other types of train are slower, but the fares are very reasonable and calculated by the kilometre. *Espresso* trains stop only at main stations, *Diretto* trains stop at most stations and the *Locale* ones stop at every single station along the route.

There are also trains with sleeping cars for people travelling at night. It is possible to reserve a *cuccetta* (bunk bed) in a compartment holding four to six beds. A more expensive but more private and comfortable alternative are the Wagons-Lits carriages (*vagoni letto*).

These compartments have washing facilities, and breakfast is provided. A first-class ticket is obligatory to secure a one-bed cabin.

Rail Tickets

Train tickets can be purchased online on the Trenitalia website (www.trenitalia.com), at railway stations or in travel agencies. E-tickets and ticketless purchases sent to your mobile phone are also available. Standard tickets must be validated before departure by date-stamping them at the small yellow stamping machine at the entrance to each platform (*binario*).

Tickets are valid for two months from the time of purchase; however, once date-stamped, they must be used within 24 hours. If you are adversely affected by a railway strike, tickets for travel should be stamped by a ticket inspector or cashier in order to claim a refund. Online re-imbursements are also possible for those with ticketless purchases.

Should you need to amend a booking, Trenitalia offers a range of possibilities – and restrictions. Full details are available online.

FERROVIE DELLO STATO

The Ferrovie dello Stato logo

Arriving by Coach

Coaches (in Italian, *pullman*) arriving in Milan end their journey at the coach terminus at Lampugnano, next to the metro stop of the same name

The concourse at Milan's Stazione Centrale

Autostradale coaches parked at a terminus in Milan

service connecting Milan with Rome, Venice and Florence.

Long-distance coaches are comfortable, with reclining seats, air conditioning, toilets and television. They make regular stops at motorway service stations.

Coach Tickets and Fares

Tickets for coach travel can be purchased directly at the bus terminal in Lampugnano or online at **Bus Italia**. There are also Autostradale offices in Piazza Castello and at Orio al Serio. Timetables and rates vary according to the length of the journey and the season. Reductions are often available for children aged 2–14 and people over 60.

(line 1). The most important coach carrier connecting Milan with the rest of Italy, including Sicily, is **Autostradale Viaggi**; the company also run airport buses that can be booked online. **SAFduemila** links Milan to Lake Maggiore, going to Arona, Stresa and Verbania. It also has a service that connects Malpensa airport to Stresa, Arona and Intra. Reserve tickets the day before travelling before 11am.

For destinations in the rest of Europe, the main firm is **Eurolines**, which also offers a

DIRECTORY

Arriving by Air

Air France
Tel 0871-663 37 77.
W airfrance.co.uk

Alitalia
Tel 06-656 49.
W alitalia.it

BMI
W flybmi.com

British Airways
Tel 199-71 22 66.
W ba.com

Easyjet
Tel 199 291 840.
W easyjet.com

KLM
W klm.com

Lufthansa
Tel 199-400 044.
W lufthansa.it

Meridiana
Tel 89 29 88.
W meridiana.it

Ryanair
Tel 895 895 89 89.
W ryanair.com

Linate Airport

ATM
Tel 02-48 60 76 07
W atm.it

First Aid
Tel 02-74 85 22 22.

Information
Tel 02-23 23 23 (call centre).
W sea-aeroport imilano.it

Left Luggage
Tel 02-58 58 12 85.

Lost Property
W sea-aeroporti milano.it/en/pdf/lost_ property_form.pdf

Starfly
Tel 02-58 58 72 88.
W starfly.net

Malpensa Airport

Airpullman Linate – Malpensa
Tel 02-58 58 31 85.
W airpullman.com

First Aid
Tel 02-74 85 44 44 (T2).

Information
Tel 02-23 23 23 (call centre). W sea-aeroportimilano.it

Left Luggage
Tel 02-58 58 12 85 (T1).

Lost Property
W sea-aeroportimilano .it/en/pdf/lost_ property_form.pdf

Malpensa Bus Express
Tel 02-33 91 07 94.
W stie.it

Malpensa Express (train)
Tel 02-72 49 49 49.
W malpensaexpress.it

Malpensa Shuttle
Tel 02-58 58 31 85.
W malpensashuttle.com

Orio Al Serio Airport

Autostradale
Tel 02-33 91 07 94 or 035-31 84 72.
W autostradale.it

Information
Tel 035-32 63 23.
W sacbo.it

Arriving by Rail

Ferrovie dello Stato
Tel 89-20 21.
W trenitalia.it

Ferrovie Nord Milano (Cadorna)
Piazzale Cadorna 14.
Map 3 A5.
Tel 02-72 49 49 49.
W trenord.it

Porta Garibaldi
Map 3 C1.
Tel 02-89 20 20 (information).

Rogoredo
Tel 89-20 21.

Stazione Centrale
Map 4 F1. Tel 89-20 21 (state railway call centre).
Tel 02-77 40 43 18 (tourist information).
Tel 02-63 71 22 12 (left luggage).
Tel 02-63 71 24 28 (railway police).

Arriving by Coach

Autostradale Viaggi
Lampugnano.
Tel 02-30 08 91.
W autostradale.it

Eurolines
c/o Autostradale Viaggi, Lampugnano.
Tel 02-30 08 91, 0861 199 19 00 (main office).
W eurolines.com

SAFduemila
Tel 0323-55 21 72.
W safduemila.com

Coach Tickets and Fares

Bus Italia
W busitalia.it

Getting Around Milan

Although there are some traffic-free areas, such as Brera and the historic centre, Milan is not very pedestrian-friendly. Traffic is heavy and chaotic, and parking space is hard to find. Public transport *(see pp218–19)* is the best way of getting around. The tram, bus and metro network is efficient, and a flat fare operates in the city centre. One- and two-day passes offer good value. All tickets, including the passes, must be date-stamped before use. Fines are imposed on anyone caught having a "free ride".

Green Travel

The biggest problems facing Milan are traffic and the lack of parking space. However, the public transport system is well used and represents good value, with tickets valid on all forms of transport.

The **Area C** *(see Driving Around Milan)*, is the city council's attempt to curb traffic entering the city. All cars pay a €5 fee to access the city centre. Tickets are available from tobacconists, newsagents and some Banca Intesa San Paolo ATMs. Profits from this scheme are reinvested in more sustainable transport.

Milan's public transport authority, ATM *(see p219)*, is replacing traditional buses with hydrogen-powered and hybrid vehicles. Since 2008, around 250 "clean" forms of transport have been introduced in the city.

ATM also operate a bike-sharing scheme for residents and visitors, **BikeMi**. This popular initiative allows you to pick up a bike and return it to a designated place elsewhere in the city.

Walking in Milan

Some areas of Milan are very pleasant to walk around. Strolling around the fashion district window shopping, for example, is always an enjoyable aspect of the city. Pedestrianized areas in Milan can be found around Corso Vittorio Emanuele, Via dei Mercanti, Piazza San Babila, Via Dante, Via della Spiga and the Brera quarter. The Navigli quarter is a pedestrian zone after 8pm in summer.

However, outside of oases like these, the pedestrians' lot is by no means an easy one. The main problem is the heavy traffic. Drivers tend to treat the streets as race tracks, and even where people crossing the streets are using the zebra crossings, the road markings may be ignored by motorists. An additional problem is that the chronic lack of parking space means that cars are usually parked on the pavements, leaving pedestrians very little room to manoeuvre. This is a particular problem for those trying to get around with prams or push-chairs and for those who are wheelchair-bound.

Street Crossings

Theoretically, pedestrians have right of way at crossings when the green *avanti* sign is lit up; however, you won't have long to get across, so be alert. The red *alt* sign means that you must wait. Underground crossings are indicated by a sign reading *sottopassaggio*.

Driving Around Milan

Heavy traffic and no-entry areas, known as the ZTL *(zona a traffico limitato)* for taxis, buses and emergency vehicles only, make driving in Milan difficult. On-street parking (indicated by blue lines) is allowed for up to 2 hours 8am–1pm (suburbs), 8am–7pm (central Milan) and 8am–midnight (Area C). Check the area you are parking in and pay at a pay station or by using a Sosta Milano card, a pre-pay parking ticket sold at authorized ATM sales points (tobacconists, newsstands and bars). Areas marked with yellow lines are for residents only, while white lines indicate free parking. Disabled drivers displaying a badge can park for free in designated areas. Alternatively, use the Private Car parking in the centre of Milan *(see chart opposite)* or the ATM parking areas on the outskirts of the city, which are well served by the metro *(see p213)*.

Cars entering central Milan 7:30am–7:30pm Mon–Fri (till 6pm Thu) have to pay a €5 eco tax in Area C. This zone is clearly signposted; there is no access for diesel vehicles. You have until midnight the following day to pay the charge. A multiple Area C ticket (worth €30, €60 or €100) entitles you to enter central Milan on different days, without having to pay on a daily basis. Most hotels will assist visitors with fulfilling the Area C requirements. For rental cars, it is best to check with the car hire company.

By registering with **car2go** and **Enjoy**, you can hire a car for use in and around the city. This car-sharing scheme has free parking everywhere (no charge for Area C), and petrol is included in the rental fee.

Traffic on a busy thoroughfare in Milan

Motorbikes and scooters parked in Piazza Cordusio

Scooters, Mopeds and Bicycles

Scooters and mopeds *(moto)* are good means of getting around Milan and avoiding traffic jams. Bicycles *(biciclette)* can also provide an alternative, provided you are confident and keep your wits about you. The tram tracks can be a nuisance for bicycle wheels.

Companies that offer moped or bicycle hire (rent) include **AWS** (bicycles) and **Bianco Blu** (scooters).

Taxis

Official taxis are generally white, but you may see yellow ones or taxis with the livery of their sponsors. Taxi stands are located throughout the city; all taxis have telephones, and the numbers are listed in the telephone directory. At the beginning of the ride the meter should read €3.20 for daytime weekday rides, €5.20 on Sundays and holidays, and €6.20 at night. To call a taxi, ring the **Radio Taxi** service. Taxis leaving from the airport charge a minimum of €12.50.

DIRECTORY

Green Travel

Area C
W areac.it

BikeMi
W bikemi.com

car2go
W car2go.com/en/milano

Enjoy
W enjoy.eni.com

Scooters, Mopeds and Bicycles

AWS
Via Ponte Seveso 33.
W awsbici.com

Bianco Blu
Via Gallarate 33.
W biancoblu.com

Taxis

Radio Taxi
Tel 02-85 85; 02-40 40; 02-69 69.

Car Parks in the City Centre

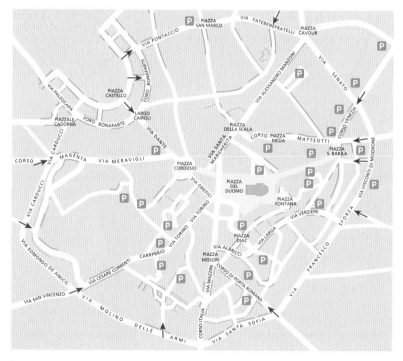

Key

— Pay on-street parking

⇥ Area C zone

---- Resident parking

For keys to symbols *see back flap*

Travelling by Public Transport

To avoid stress and parking problems, the best and least expensive way to get around town is to use public transport. Milan has a very efficient city transport system, run by the Azienda Trasporti Milanesi (ATM), which comprises trams, buses, trolleybuses and the three lines of the underground railway *(metropolitana)*.

A tramcar going through the Navigli quarter

Trams and Buses

Trams, buses and trolleybuses in Milan are efficient and serve virtually the entire city. They are always crowded, especially at rush hour, and generally pass by every 5–7 minutes.

Bus and tram stops are easy to recognize. Each has a yellow sign displaying the route taken. Stops are often located on islands in the road, with seats for waiting passengers.

The yellow signs also have a timetable, but be careful to distinguish the summer *(estate)* from the winter *(inverno)* schedules, as they are posted side by side. Italian timetables always use the 24-hour clock.

On most buses and trams you can use any door to get on or get off. A few vehicles have signs indicating which door must be used to enter *(entrare)* and exit *(uscita)*.

Tickets must be bought before you get on from a nearby newsstand or bar, and date-stamped on the bus or tram. There is a small machine to validate *(convalidare)* your ticket; it is usually at the front, behind the driver, but on longer vehicles there are at least two, one in the front and one at the back.

When you want to get off, press the red button. A sign saying *"fermata prenotata"* will flash until the next stop is reached. The driver will open the doors when the tram or bus reaches the stop; if not press the button next to the doors.

The **ATM** runs a night bus called **District Radiobus**. Call ahead to book a pick-up at your nearest stop. It costs €4 a ride.

Always keep a close eye on your personal belongings, including luggage, particularly on a crowded bus or tram. Pickpockets – including children – are on the look-out for handbags, mobile phones and wallets, and you must be wary.

Families travelling with prams and people in wheelchairs will find the newer, green trams easier to board.

Useful Bus and Tram Routes

This map shows the best bus and tram routes for sightseeing in Milan. The locations of major sights are marked, as well as the nearest useful stop. Sights should then only be a short walk away.

Corso Sempione
Piazza Bausan
Porta Volta
Stazione Centrale
Arco della Pace
Piazza L. Lombarda
Piazza VI Febbraio
Lanza
Pinacoteca di Brera
Piazza Cavour
Castello Sforzesco
Teatro alla Scala
Piazza Virgilio
Cadorna
Teatro alla Scala
Santa Maria delle Grazie
Duomo
Piazza Sant'Ambrogio Via Carducci
Duomo
Largo Augusto
Sant'Ambrogio
Pinacoteca Ambrosiana
Viale Ungheria
Piazza Resistenza Partigiana
Colonne di San Lorenzo
Corso P.ta Romana Via S. Sofia
Piazzale Negrelli
Gratosoglio

Key

Major sight
Tram route
Bus route
O Stop

The Metro

There are four metro lines: number 1 (red), 2 (green), 3 (yellow) and 5 (purple). One further line is being planned or constructed, with the proposed Line 4 connecting Linate airport to the city. Stations all have escalators and many have lifts for disabled passengers *(see Back Endpaper)*, and they are usually located close to tram and bus stops. The trains run approximately every 2 minutes during rush hour and are often crowded. They run every 5 minutes at other times of the day. Once stamped, tickets can also be used for other means of public transport within 90 minutes.

Passante Ferroviario

This commuter train service links the northwest of Milan with the metro. The line goes from Porta Vittoria to Bovisa, with intermediate stops at Porta Venezia, Piazza della Repubblica, Stazione Garibaldi and Via Lancetti.

Tickets and Timetables

All tickets and travelcards can be used for above-ground transport, the metro and the Passante Ferroviario. Tickets are valid for 90 minutes on all lines but they cannot be used twice on the metro and Passante Ferroviario.

Tickets and electronic travelcards must be bought in advance from newsstands, tobacconists and automatic vending machines in metro stations, which operate with coins, banknotes and credit cards. It is also possible to buy them via SMS (see www.atm.it).

Tourist tickets are good value. They cost from €4.50/8.25 and are valid for 24/48 hours. Weekly and monthly passes *(abbonamenti)* are also available. The Milano Card, also available for tourists, gives free public transport for three days *(see p206)*.

Milanese public transport usually operates from 6am to 12:30am, but some buses and trams run until 2am.

Ticket for the metro

Guided Tours

A unique way of touring Milan is on an antique tram made into an Orient Express-style restaurant. Called **ATMosfera**, the tram, which offers dinner (and lunch, if you book the entire tram), leaves from Piazza Castello, on the corner of Via Beltrami, Tuesday to Sunday; the tour lasts around 2 hours. Reservations must be made by 7pm the day before.

Zani Grand Tour leaves twice daily (9:30am and 2:30pm) from Foro Bonaparte. From Tuesday to Sunday, this 3½-hour bus tour includes visits to Teatro alla Scala and its Museum, the Duomo and *The Last Supper*. Zani also runs two daily hop-on, hop-off open-topped buses, City Sightseeing, from Piazza Castello. Tickets are available

DIRECTORY

Trams and Buses

ATM
Tel 02-48 60 76 07.
🌐 atm-mi.it
For season tickets and travel passes: Duomo, Cadorna, Centrale FS, Garibaldi FS, Loreto and Romolo stations.
Open 7:45am–7:15pm Mon–Sat.

District Radiobus
Tel 02-48 03 48 03 (1pm–2am) to book time and route (service runs 10pm–2am).

Guided Tours

ALGAT
Via Giovanni Aurispa 2.
Map 7 B3. Tel 02-55 21 04 77.
🌐 guideturistichemilano.it

ATMosfera Restaurant Tram
Tel 02-48 60 76 07.
🌐 atm-mi.it

Autostradale
Passaggio Duomo 2.
Map 7 C1. Tel 02-33 91 07 94.
🌐 autostradale.it

Centro Guide Milano
Via Pietro Calvi 5.
Map 4 F5. Tel 02-86 45 04 33.
🌐 centroguidemilano.net

Ordine Architetti
🌐 ordinearchitetti.mi.it/en/mappe/itinerari/repertorio

Zani Viaggi
Foro Bonaparte 76. Map 3 B5.
Tel 02-86 71 31. 🌐 zaniviaggi.it

online, at their office and on board (sightseeing tours only).

Autostradale offers two daily tours leaving from Passaggio Duomo at 9:30am and 11am, both with a visit to *The Last Supper*. Buy tickets online or at the office. They also organize walking tours from April to July and September to October.

ALGAT (Association of Lombard Guides) organizes private walking tours and museum visits. **Centro Guide Milano** offers customized history- and culture-themed tours of the city, while the **Ordine Architetti** organizes themed itineraries that take in some of Milan's most iconic modern buildings.

Milan's antique ATMosfera tourist tram

Getting to and Around the Lakes

The lakes are easily accessible from Milan, both by car and by train. Visitors arriving by car will take the Autostrada dei Laghi motorway or the Valassina *superstrada*. There are good train links with all the lakes using either the Ferrovie dello Stato (FS) or the Ferrovie Nord Milano (FNM) railways. Both offer frequent services. Bus services link the various towns and villages around the lakes, or you may well prefer to use the hydrofoils or ferries in order to avoid traffic jams on the crowded roads, especially at weekends. Be advised that all lake ferry companies run a much reduced service in the winter months, generally between November and March.

A Ferrovie dello Stato regional train

Car Hire

At Malpensa, most car hire companies are located on the first floor of Terminal 1. Rental companies at the airport include **Hertz**, **Avis**, **Maggiore**, **Europcar**, **Budget** and **Sixt**. Desks are usually open from 7am to 11pm/midnight daily. At Linate, car hire firms are on the ground floor (arrivals). Opening times vary, with some desks – Europcar, for example – closed at weekends. Many car rental firms also operate from Orio al Serio. Arrange car hire before you travel for a better deal.

Lake Maggiore

To get to Lake Maggiore from Milan by car, take the A8 *autostrada* and exit at Sesto Calende. From here, take the road to Angera to go to the Lombardy side of the lake, or the road to Arona to go to the Piedmontese side.

To get to the upper part of the lake, proceed northwards, turn off at Gravellona Toce and then follow the signs for Fondotoce and Verbania.

If you go to Lake Orta, take the Borgomanero turnoff and follow the signs for Gozzano–Orta San Giulio. The A8 *autostrada* is also the easiest way to get to Lake Varese from Milan: take the Varese exit and continue to Gavirate.

Lake Maggiore is also accessible by train. Trenitalia run a regular service from Stazione Centrale to Arona and Stresa *(see p214)*; local trains go as far as Luino, via Gallarate. The Ferrovie Nord railway *(see p214)* has frequent daily train services to Laveno.

The most enjoyable way of travelling from one town to another on Lake Maggiore is to use the hydrofoils and ferries. The main towns are connected by the **Navigazione Lago Maggiore** service, which has a fleet of steamboats, motor boats and ferries. The timetables are posted at local hotels, restaurants and all the ports, and are subject to seasonal changes.

If you are travelling from outside Italy, Malpensa airport (about 50 km/30 miles from Milan; *see pp212–13*) is the closest to Lake Maggiore.

Lake Como

The shortest route from Milan to Lake Como by car is to take the A9 *autostrada* and exit at the Como Nord signs. To get to the western side of the lake, from Como take the Statale 340 road, the ancient Via Regina, which goes as far as Sorico. If, however, you are headed for the other side, go up the state road 583, which passes through Bellagio and goes as far as Lecco.

Traffic can be very heavy during the weekend, and as there is not much parking space around, the best solution may be to use a combination of car followed by one of the frequent hydrofoil or car ferry services. The hydrofoils are particularly frequent on the Como–Colico line, with intermediate stops, while the ferries stop only at Cadenabbia, Bellagio, Menaggio and Varenna. For detailed information, contact **Navigazione Lago di Como**.

The town of Como is also served by the Ferrovie dello Stato (FS) and Ferrovie Nord railways. The FS trains depart from Stazione Centrale and go to Como on the Milan–Chiasso line. The Nord trains leave from Piazzale Cadorna in Milan and arrive at Piazza Cavour.

A ferry connecting the main towns around Lake Como

If you travel by air, Malpensa *(see pp212–13)* is the closest airport to Lake Como.

Lake Garda

Verona is the nearest main town to the lake. It is on routes linking Milan with Venice, both by road and rail.

To reach Salò from the Milan–Venice A4 motorway, exit at Brescia Centro and go easwards on the *tangenziale* (ring road) until you see signs for the Salò *superstrada* (highway). Alternatively, exit at Desenzano del Garda (118 km/73 miles from Milan), cross the town and go up the Statale 572 road for 20 km (12 miles).

A few kilometres past Salò is Gardone. Sirmione can be reached from Desenzano del Garda by following the southern side of Lake Garda for 9 km (6 miles) or leaving the *autostrada* at the Sirmione–San Martino della Battaglia exit.

To get to the Veneto side of the lake, take the A22 *autostrada* to Brennero and then exit at Affi.

To get to Lake Idro from Milan, take the A4 *autostrada* to Brescia Ovest and then proceed to Lumezzane.

Those coming from the east should take the state road that goes from Salò to Barghe, and then follow the signs for Madonna di Campiglio.

Lake Garda is also well served by trains. Desenzano del Garda and Peschiera del Garda are stops on the Milan–Venice line, and coaches will take you onwards from these stations to Sirmione, Salò, Gardone and Limone. For more information, contact the **Azienda Provinciale Trasporti di Verona**.

There is a good boat service on Lake Garda, except in the winter season. The hydrofoils are the fastest means of crossing the lake, while car ferries run between Maderno and Torri del Benaco and Limone and Malcesine. Boat services are run by **Navigazione Lago di Garda (Navigarda)**; see the website for timetables.

Navigarda tickets

The nearest airport to Lake Garda is Verona-Villafranca (also known as Valerio Catullo airport). Other possibilities are Orio al Serio *(see p213)*, Linate *(see p212)* and Marco Polo in Venice.

Lake Iseo

The easiest way to get to Lake Iseo by car is to take the A4 Milan–Venice motorway. Come off at the Ponte Oglio and Palazzolo exits to get to Sarnico, and at the Rovato, Ospitaletto and Brescia Ovest exits to get to Iseo.

If you go by train, the state railway from Stazione Centrale takes you to Brescia; from there you can go on the Ferrovie Nord Brescia–Iseo–Edolo line; bicycles are allowed on board.

The best way to get to Sarnico and Lovere is by boat from Iseo. **Navigazione Lago Iseo** will provide timetables.

In spring and autumn (suspended in July and August), a steam train service, the **Treno Blu**, travels to Sarnico on the Palazzolo–Paratico–Sarnico line. It is run by the Ferrovia del Basso Sebino, which operates in the Oglio River Regional Park in cooperation with the WWF and other environmental associations. **Pro Loco Sarnico** has information.

The Ferrovie Nord railway station, in Piazzale Cadorna, Milan

DIRECTORY

Car Hire

Linate
Avis **Tel** 02-71 51 23.
Budget **Tel** 199 44 59 19.
Europcar **Tel** 02-76 11 02 58.
Hertz **Tel** 02-70 20 02 56.
Maggiore **Tel** 02-71 72 10.
Sixt **Tel** 02-70 20 02 68.

Malpensa Terminal 1
Avis **Tel** 02-585 84 81.
Budget **Tel** 02-74 86 73 47.
Europcar **Tel** 02-585 86 21.
Hertz **Tel** 02-58 58 10 81.
Maggiore **Tel** 02-58 58 11 33.
Sixt **Tel** 02-58 58 02 71.

Orio al Serio
Avis **Tel** 035-31 60 41.
Budget **Tel** 035-33 06 99.
Europcar **Tel** 035-31 86 22.
Hertz **Tel** 035-31 12 58.

Lake Maggiore

Navigazione Lago Maggiore
Tel 800-55 18 01 (toll free).
W navlaghi.it

Lake Como

Navigazione Lago di Como
Tel 800-55 18 01 (toll free).
W navlaghi.it

Lake Garda

Azienda Provinciale Trasporti di Verona
Tel 045-805 78 11.
W apt.vr.it

Navigazione Lago di Garda (Navigarda)
Tel 800-55 18 01 (toll free).
W navlaghi.it

Lake Iseo

Navigazione Lago Iseo
Via Nazionale 16, Costa Volpino.
Tel 035-97 14 83.
W navigazionelagoiseo.it

Pro Loco Sarnico
Via dei Lantieri, Sarnico.
Tel 035-91 09 00.
W prolocosarnico.it

Treno Blu
Tel 030-98 11 54.

How to Use the Maps

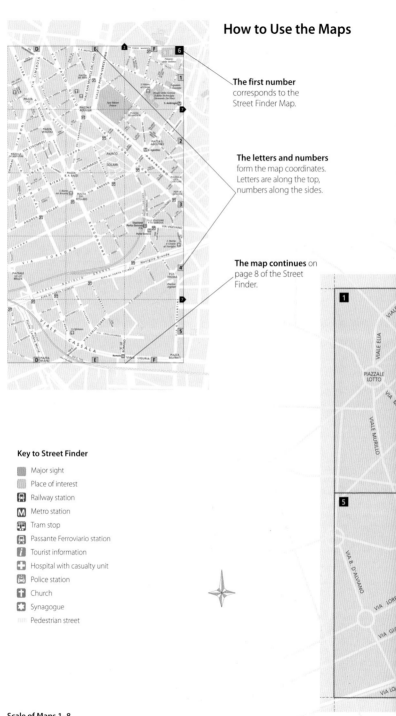

The first number corresponds to the Street Finder Map.

The letters and numbers form the map coordinates. Letters are along the top, numbers along the sides.

The map continues on page 8 of the Street Finder.

Key to Street Finder

- Major sight
- Place of interest
- Railway station
- Metro station
- Tram stop
- Passante Ferroviario station
- Tourist information
- Hospital with casualty unit
- Police station
- Church
- Synagogue
- Pedestrian street

Scale of Maps 1–8

| 0 metres | 400 |
| 0 yards | 400 |

MILAN STREET FINDER

All the map references in this guide, both in the *Milan Area by Area* and in the *Travellers' Needs* sections, refer to the maps in this *Street Finder* only. The page grid superimposed on the *Area by Area* map below shows which parts of Milan are covered by maps in this section. Besides street names, the maps provide practical information, such as metro stations, tram and bus stops, post offices, hospitals and police stations. The key on the opposite page shows the scale of the map and explains the symbols used. The main sights are shown in pink. On the inside back flap there is a map of the Milan metro system, including the Passante Ferroviario.

0 kilometres		1
0 mile		1

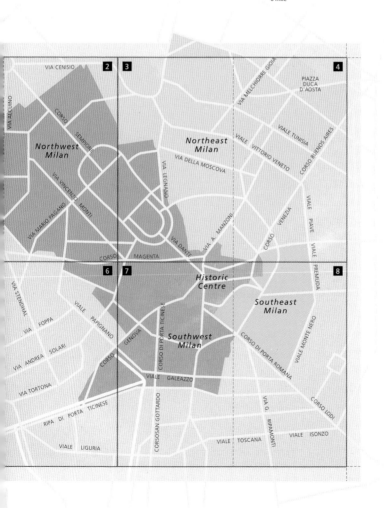

Street Finder Index

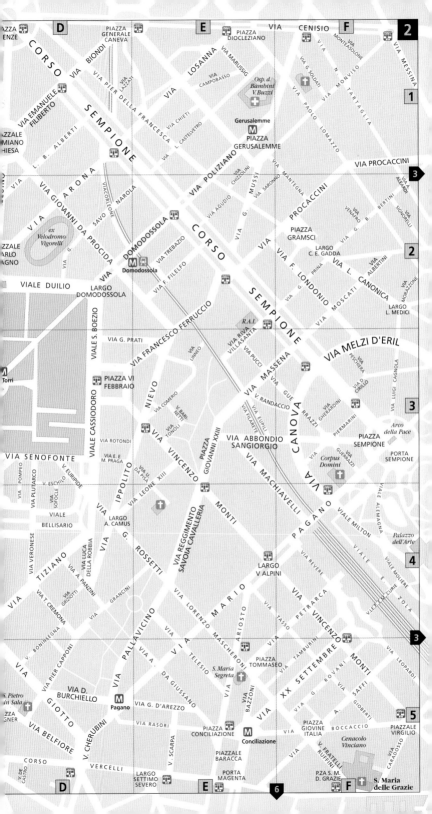

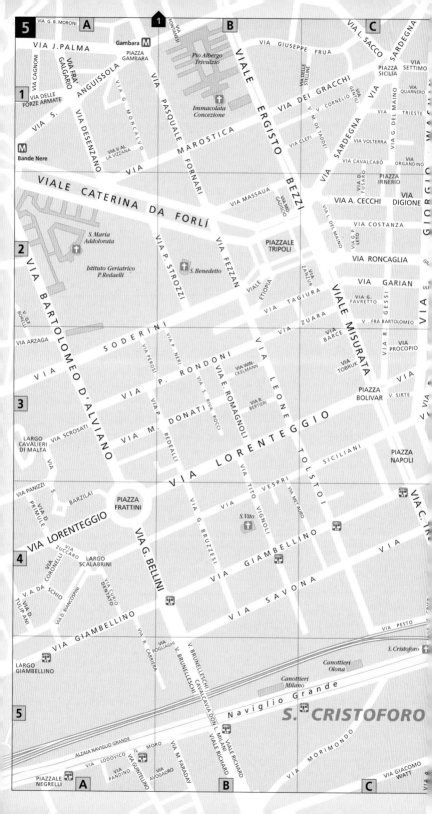

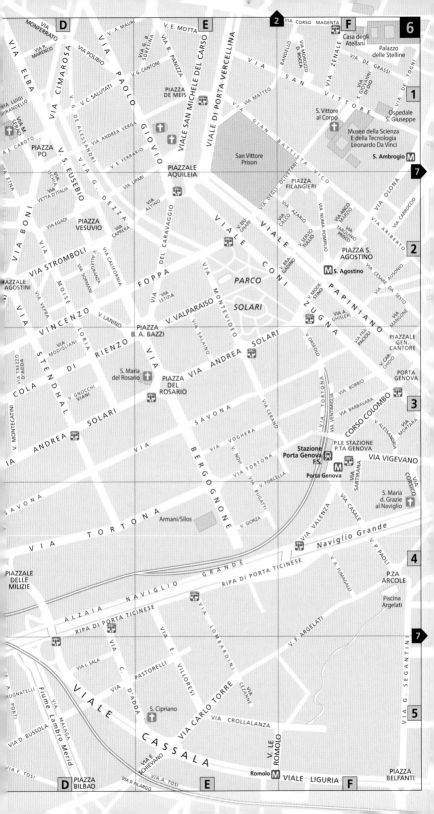

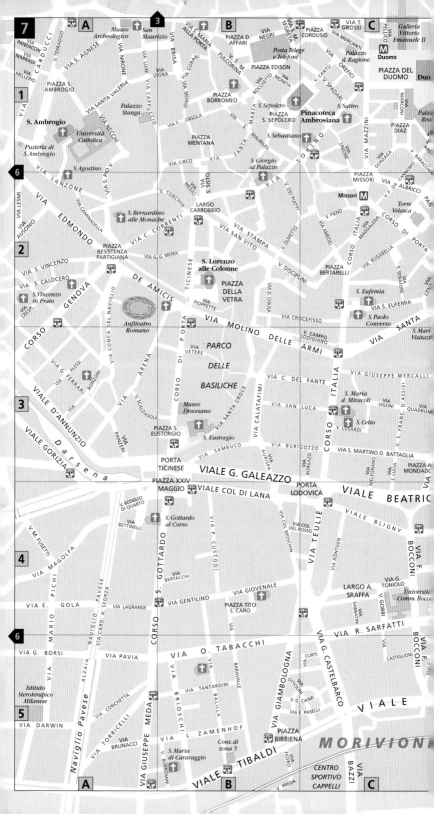

General Index

Acknowledgments

Dorling Kindersley would like to thank all the people, organizations and associations whose contributions and assistance have made the preparation of this book possible. Special thanks are due to the following organizations and individuals: APT di Como (Sig. Pisilli), Silvia Dell'Orso, Direzione Civiche Raccolte d'Arte del Castello Sforzesco (Walter Palmieri), Giorgio Facchetti, Diana Georgiacodis, Alberto Malesani (Gardaland), Enrico Pellegrini, chef of the *Locanda degli Angeli* (Gardone), Augusto Rizza, Silvia Scamperle, Carla Solari, Crisca Sommerhoff, Valentina Tralli.

Revisions and Relaunch Team

Ashwin Raju Adimari, Gillian Allan, Douglas Amrine, Hansa Babra, Marta Bescos Sanchez, Sonal Bhatt, Hilary Bird, Subhadeep Biswas, Emma Brady, Michelle Clark, Michelle Crane, Vivien Crump, Imogen Corke, Cristina Dainotto, DG Consulting s.a.s. di Julia Dunn & C, Vidushi Duggal, Conrad van Dyk, Mohammad Hassan, Annette Jacobs, Priya Kukadia, Louise Bostock Lang, Maite Lantaron, Delphine Lawrance, Jude Ledger, Hayley Maher, Cristina Minoni, Deepak Mittal, Scarlett O'Hara, Catherine Palmi, Rada Radojicic, Federica Raggio, Sands Publishing Solutions, Ellie Smith, Mary Sutherland, Vinita Venugopal.

Additional Assistance

Reid Bramblett, Sally Bloomfield, Susi Cheshire.

DK Photographers

John Heseltine, Anna Mockford, Mockford and Bonetti, **Rough Guides**: Helena Smith

Picture Credits

Key: a-above; b-below/bottom; c-centre; f-far; l-left; r-right; t-top.

Every effort has been made to trace the copyright holders. The publisher apologizes for any unintentional omissions and would be pleased, in such cases, to add an acknowledgment in future editions.

All the photographs reproduced in this book are from the Image Bank, Milan, except for the following:

123RF.com: Boris Stroujko 133b
10 Corso Como: 166cr, 173bl.
Agriturismo Villa Bissiniga: 165bl. **Aimo e Nadia:** 172tl. **Al Sorriso:** 167bl, 181br. **Alamy Images:** Agencja Fotograficzna Caro 180t; David Bagnall 177tl; Giuseppe Belluccio 64cla; Tibor Bognar 10cra; CuboImages srl/Bluered 168cl; CuboImages srl/Eddy Buttarelli 37bc, 105tl; CuboImages srl/Dario Mainetti 169cb; David Sanger photography/Sam Bloomberg-Rissman 169tl; Adam Eastland 12br, 126clb; IML Image Group Ltd 183tl; M.Flynn 111br; Chuck Pefley 207cr; SFM Italy 2 13br, 94; SFM Milano 84t; Tom Thulen 211crb; Vittorio Valletta 62; John Warburton-Lee Photography/Ian Aitken 11tr. **Archivio Fotografico del Teatro alla Scala:** 54bl, 55tl, 55crb, 55bl; Andrea Tamoni 54cl. **Archivio Fotografico Electa:** 58–9 (all the photographs), 60tr, 60c, 60bl, 61tr, 61c,148tr, 150c, 151tl, 151crb. **Armani/Silos:** Davide Lovatti 93br. **Atm S.p.A - Archivio Fotografico:** 219ca, 219bl. **Simonetta Benzi:** 38cl, 53tr, 53cl, 53cr, 70cr, 71cr, 76br, 77tr, 77cl, 80tr, 82br, 87cb, 89crb, 90cr, 90br, 92c, 92bl, 99cr, 99clb, 100c, 102tl, 102br, 103bc, 114tl, 115bl, 124cr, 124cb, 124br, 125cla, 125cl, 125crb. **Corbis:** Atlantide Phototravel/Mario Cipriani 206cl; Leemage 8-9; The Gallery Collection 74tr, 74–5c; Massimo Listri 145tr. **Corpo Nazionaledei Vigili Del Fuoco:** 209tl. **Cracco:** 167tr, 170br. **Cristina Dainotto:** 81tl.
Dorling Kindersley Photo Library: Paul Harris and Anne

Heslope 134cl, 135tl, 135bl, 211ca, 212cl; Ian O'Leary 168tr/cb/bl/br, 169bl/bc/br. **Dreamstime.com:** Fabio Alcini 39cla; Alefl04 112cl; Claudio Giovanni Colombo 72bl; Conde 57crb; Piero Cruciatti 91bl; Denise2904 39br; Dennis Dolkens 150bl; Rob Van Esch 78; Gepapix 203bl; Rostislav Glinsky 121tl; Helenlbuxton 177br; Jojjik 134bl; Kjetil Kolbjornsrud 30; Slawomir Kruz 153br; Martin Lehmann 106; Luca Lorenzelli 157br; Fabio Lotti 91cl; Lukaszimilena 153tl; Simone Matteo Giuseppe Manzoni 123br; Michelepautasso 138tl; Ohmaymay 139tr; 156tl; Matyas Rehak 216bl; Franco Ricci 42-43; 52tr; 56bl; 64br; Valeria Sangiovanni 40c; Jozef Sedmak 13tc; Moreno Soppelsa 12tl; Alena Stalmashonak 204-205; Tixtis 38br; Travelpeter 130-131, 140tr; Anibal Trejo 1c; Valentino Visentini 40bl, 220bl; Volgariver 2-3. **The Eurail Group:** 214tl, 214br. **Esplanade:** 179tr.
Fabio De Angelis: 31tl, 31cl, 34br, 35tl, 35tr, 35bl, 47br, 51tl, 51c, 82tr, 85tr, 85cl, 85br, 87tc, 87bl, 90tl, 92tr, 98c, 98br, 100br, 101tr, 104tr, 113br, 115c, 121cr, 121br, 123tc, 151bl, 186bl, 194cr. **Firenze:** Alberti 129br; Pizzi 128c. **Giovanni Francesio:** 34bl. **Gardaland:** 154–155. **Getty Images:** 209cl; Vincent Lombardo 70b; Lonely Planet 175t. **Grand Hotel Tremezzo:** 160cr, 164tr. **Grand Hotel Villa Serbelloni (Bellagio):** 147tr, 161tl. **Grandi Stazioni s.p.a:** 214cr; Archivio Marcello Mencarini/La Scala Theatre Museum, Milan Ulisse Surtini Portrait of Maria Callas 127tr; Barbara Seghezzi 126br, 128tr, 128clb, 129tc. **Highline Galleria:** 52bl. **Hotel Four Seasons (Milan):** 183br. **IAT di Como:** 146tl. **Il Baretto al Baglioni:** 174bl. **Il Dagherrotipo:** 51br. **iStockphoto.com:** Narvikk 213tl. **La Foresta:** 166bl. **La Rampolina:** 176tl. **La Terrazza:** 178tl. **Luini:** 182c.
Marka, Milan: 194bl, 221b; Roberto Benzi 127bl; Danilo Donadoni 10bl; Nevio Doz 11bl; Alessandro Villa 215bl. **MUBA – Museo dei Bambini Milano:** 195bl. **Museo Diocesano:** 92tl. **Museo Teatrale alla Scala:** 37crb.
Omega Fotocronache: 32tr, 32cl, 32bl. **Orto Botanico di Brera:** Archive – Orto Botanico di Brera dell'Università degli Studi di Milano 113cra.
Palazzo Parigi Hotel & Grand Spa Milano: 160bl, 162bl. **Photoshot:** Vittorio Valletta 44, VALTERZA 139bl.
Laura Recordati: 34cl, 56tl, 80br, 97tcl, 98tl, 100tl. **Rex by Shutterstock:** Andrea Delbo 161br. **Robert Harding Picture Library:** Age Fotostock 132; Look 158-9.
Marco Scapagnini: 148cl. **SOS Milano:** 209cla. **STA Travel Group:** 207cla. **SuperStock:** Universal Images Group 114cr. **Tortuga:** 179bl. **Trussardi alla Scala:** 171t; published with kind permission of the Università degli Studi di Milano: Paolo Sacchi 99br.
Villa Crespi: 165tc.
The Yard Milano: 163tl.

Front Endpapers: **Alamy Images:** SFM Italy 2 br, Vittorio Valletta tl. **Dreamstime.com:** Rob Van Esch cl, Martin Lehmann tr. **Robert Harding Picture Library:** Age Fotostock bl. **Photoshot:** Vittorio Valletta 44.

Sheet Map Cover: **4Corners:** Johanna Huber/SIME .

Cover: Front and spine: **4Corners:** Johanna Huber/SIME.

Special Editions of DK Travel Guides

DK Travel Guides can be purchased in bulk quantities at discounted prices for use in promotions or as premiums. We are also able to offer special editions and personalized jackets, corporate imprints, and excerpts from all of our books, tailored specifically to meet your own needs.

To find out more, please contact:
in the United States **specialsales@dk.com**
in the UK **travelguides@uk.dk.com**
in Canada DK Special Sales at **specialmarkets@ dk.com**
in Australia **penguincorporatesales@ penguinrandomhouse.com.au**

Phrase Book

In Emergency

Help!	Aiuto!	eye-**yoo**-toh
Stop!	Fermate!	fair-**mah**-teh
Call a doctor.	Chiama un medico	kee-**ah**-mah oon **meh**-dee-koh
Call an ambulance.	Chiama un' ambulanza	kee-**ah**-mah oon am-boo-**lan**-tsa
Call the police.	Chiama la polizia	kee-**ah**-mah lah pol-ee-**tsee**-ah
Call the fire brigade.	Chiama i pompieri	kee-**ah**-mah ee pom-pee-**air**-ee
Where is the telephone?	Dov'è il telefono?	dov-**eh** eel teh-**leh**-foh-noh?
The nearest hospital?	L'ospedale più vicino?	loss-peh-**dah**-leh pee-oo vee-**chee**-noh?

Communication Essentials

Yes/No	Si/No	see/noh
Please	Per favore	pair fah-**vor**-eh
Thank you	Grazie	**grah**-tsee-eh
Excuse me	Mi scusi	mee **skoo**-zee
Hello	Buon giorno	bwon jor-noh
Goodbye	Arrivederci	ah-ree-veh-**dair**-chee
Good evening	Buona sera	**bwon**-ah **sair**-ah
morning	la mattina	lah mah-**tee**-nah
afternoon	il pomeriggio	eel poh-meh-**ree**-joh
evening	la sera	lah **sair**-ah
yesterday	ieri	ee-**air**-ee
today	oggi	**oh**-jee
tomorrow	domani	doh-**mah**-nee
here	qui	kwee
there	la	lah
What?	Quale?	**kwah**-leh?
When?	Quando?	**kwan**-doh?
Why?	Perchè?	pair-**keh**?
Where?	Dove?	**doh**-veh?

Useful Phrases

How are you?	Come sta?	**koh**-meh stah?
Very well, thank you.	Molto bene, grazie.	**moll**-toh **beh**-neh **grah**-tsee-eh
Pleased to meet you.	Piacere di conoscerla.	pee-ah-**chair**-eh dee coh-noh-**shair**-lah
See you later.	A più tardi.	ah pee-**oo** tar-dee
That's fine.	Va bene.	va **beh**-neh
Where is/are…?	Dov'è/Dove sono…?	dov-**eh**/doveh **soh**-noh?
How long does it take to get to…?	Quanto tempo ci vuole per andare a…?	**kwan**-toh **tem**-poh chee voo-**oh**-leh pair an-**dar**-eh ah…?
How do I get to…?	Come faccio per arrivare a…?	**koh**-meh **fah**-choh pair arri-**var**-eh ah…?
Do you speak English?	Parla inglese?	**par**-lah een-**gleh**-zeh?
I don't understand.	Non capisco.	non ka-**pee**-skoh
Could you speak more slowly, please?	Può parlare più lentamente, per favore?	pwoh par-**lah**-reh pee-oo len-ta-**men**-teh pair fah-**vor**-eh?
I'm sorry.	Mi dispiace.	mee dee-spee-**ah**-cheh

Useful Words

big	grande	**gran**-deh
small	piccolo	**pee**-koh-loh
hot	caldo	**kal**-doh
cold	freddo	**fred**-doh
good	buono	**bwoh**-noh
bad	cattivo	**kat**-tee-voh
enough	basta	**bas**-tah
well	bene	**beh**-neh
open	aperto	ah-**pair**-toh
closed	chiuso	kee-**oo**-zoh
left	a sinistra	ah see-**nee**-strah
right	a destra	ah **dess**-trah
straight on	sempre dritto	**sem**-preh **dree**-toh
near	vicino	vee-**chee**-noh
far	lontano	lon-**tah**-noh
up	su	soo
down	giù	joo
early	presto	**press**-toh
late	tardi	**tar**-dee
entrance	entrata	en-**trah**-tah
exit	uscita	oo-**shee**-ta
toilet	il gabinetto	eel gah-bee-**net**-toh
free, unoccupied	libero	**lee**-bair-oh
free, no charge	gratuito	grah-**too**-ee-toh

Making a Telephone Call

I'd like to place a long-distance call.	Vorrei fare una interurbana.	vor-**ray far**-eh oona in-tair-oor-**bah**-nah
I'd like to make a reverse-charge call.	Vorrei fare una telefonata a carico del destinatario.	vor-**ray far**-eh oona teh-leh-fon-**ah**-tah ah **kar**-ee-koh dell dess-tee-nah-**tar**-ree-oh
I'll try again later.	Ritelefono più tardi.	ree-teh-**leh**-foh-noh pee-oo tar-dee
Can I leave a message?	Posso lasciare un messaggio?	**poss**-oh lash-**ah**-reh oon mess-**sah**-joh?
Hold on.	Un attimo, per favore	oon **ah**-tee-moh, pair fah-**vor**-eh
Could you speak up a little please?	Può parlare più forte, per favore?	pwoh par-**lah**-reh pee-oo for-teh, pair fah-**vor**-eh?
local call	telefonata locale	te-le-fon-**ah**-tah loh-cah-leh

Shopping

How much does this cost?	Quant'è, per favore?	kwan-**teh** pair fah-**vor**-eh?
I would like…	Vorrei…	vor-**ray**
Do you have…?	Avete…?	ah-**veh**-teh…?
I'm just looking.	Sto soltanto guardando.	stoh sol-**tan**-toh gwar-**dan**-doh
Do you take credit cards?	Accettate carte di credito?	ah-chet-**tah**-teh **kar**-teh dee **creh**-dee-toh?
What time do you open/close?	A che ora apre/chiude?	ah keh or-ah **ah**-preh/kee-oo-deh?
this one	questo	**kweh**-stoh
that one	quello	**kwell**-oh
expensive	caro	**kar**-oh
cheap	a buon prezzo	ah bwon **pret**-soh
size, clothes	la taglia	lah **tah**-lee-ah
size, shoes	il numero	eel **noo**-mair-oh
white	bianco	bee-**ang**-koh
black	nero	**neh**-roh
red	rosso	**ross**-oh
yellow	giallo	**jal**-loh
green	verde	**vair**-deh
blue	blu	bloo

Types of Shop

antique dealer	l'antiquario	lan-tee-**kwah**-ree-oh
bakery	il forno/ il panificio	eel **forn**-oh /eel pan-ee-**fee**-choh
bank	la banca	lah **bang**-kah
bookshop	la libreria	lah lee-breh-**ree**-ah
butcher	la macelleria	lah mah-chell-eh-**ree**-ah
cake shop	la pasticceria	lah pas-tee-chair-**ee**-ah
chemist	la farmacia	lah far-mah-**chee**-ah
delicatessen	la salumeria	lah sah-loo-meh-**ree**-ah
department store	il grande magazzino	eel **gran**-deh mag-gad-zee-noh
fishmonger	il pescivendolo	eel pesh-ee-**ven**-doh-loh
florist	il fioraio	eel fee-or-**eye**-oh
greengrocer	il fruttivendolo	eel froo-tee-**ven**-doh-loh
grocery	alimentari	ah-lee-men-**tah**-ree
hairdresser	il parrucchiere	eel par-oo-kee-**air**-eh
ice cream parlour	la gelateria	lah jel-lah-tair-**ee**-ah
market	il mercato	eel mair-**kah**-toh
newsstand	l'edicola	leh-**dee**-koh-lah
post office	l'ufficio postale	loo-**fee**-choh pos-**tah**-leh
shoe shop	il negozio di scarpe	eel neh-goh-tsioh dee **skar**-peh
supermarket	il supermercato	eel su-pair-mair-**kah**-toh
tobacconist	il tabaccaio	eel tah-bak-**eye**-oh
travel agency	l'agenzia di viaggi	lah-jen-**tsee**-ah dee vee-**ad**-jee

Sightseeing

art gallery	la pinacoteca	lah peena-koh-**teh**-kah
bus stop	la fermata dell'autobus	lah fair-**mah**-tah dell ow-toh-booss
church	la chiesa	lah kee-**eh**-zah
	la basilica	lah bah-**seel**-i-kah
closed for holidays	chiuso per le ferie	kee-oo-zoh pair leh **fair**-ee-eh
garden	il giardino	eel jar-**dee**-noh
library	la biblioteca	lah beeb-lee-oh-**teh**-kah
museum	il museo	eel moo-**zeh**-oh
railway station	la stazione	lah stah-tsee-**oh**-neh
tourist information	l'ufficio del turismo	loo-**fee**-choh del too-**ree**-smoh

Staying in a Hotel

Do you have any vacant rooms?	**Avete camere libere?**	ah-**veh**-teh **kah**-mair-eh **lee**-bair-eh?
double room	**una camera doppia**	oona **kah**-mair-ah **doh**-pee-ah
with double bed	**con letto matrimoniale**	kon **let**-toh mah-tree-moh-nee-**ah**-leh
twin room	**una camera con due letti**	oona **kah**-mair-ah kon **doo**-eh let-tee
single room	**una camera singola**	oona **kah**-mair-ah **sing**-goh-lah
room with a bath, shower	**una camera con bagno, con doccia**	oona **kah**-mair-ah kon ban-yoh, kon **dot**-chah
porter	**il facchino**	eel fah-**kee**-noh
key	**la chiave**	lah kee-**ah**-veh
I have a reservation.	**Ho fatto una prenotazione.**	oh **fat**-toh oona preh-noh-tah-tsee-**oh**-neh

Eating Out

Have you got a table for...?	**Avete un tavolo per...?**	ah-**veh**-teh oon **tah**-voh-loh pair...?
I'd like to reserve a table.	**Vorrei riservare un tavolo.**	vor-**ray** ree-sair-**vah**-reh oon **tah**-voh-loh
breakfast	**colazione**	koh-lah-tsee-**oh**-neh
lunch	**pranzo**	**pran**-tsoh
dinner	**cena**	**cheh**-nah
The bill, please.	**Il conto, per favore.**	eel **kon**-toh pair fah-**vor**-eh
I am a vegetarian.	**Sono vegetariano/a.**	**soh**-noh veh-jeh-tar-ee-**ah**-noh/nah
waitress	**cameriera**	kah-mair-ee-**air**-ah
waiter	**cameriere**	kah-mair-ee-**air**-eh
fixed price menu	**il menù a prezzo fisso**	eel meh-**noo** ah **pret**-soh **fee**-soh
dish of the day	**piatto del giorno**	pee-**ah**-toh dell **jor**-no
starter	**antipasto**	an-tee-**pass**-toh
first course	**il primo**	eel **pree**-moh
main course	**il secondo**	eel seh-**kon**-doh
vegetables	**il contorno**	eel kon-**tor**-noh
dessert	**il dolce**	eel **doll**-cheh
cover charge	**il coperto**	eel koh-**pair**-toh
wine list	**la lista dei vini**	lah **lee**-stah day **vee**-nee
rare	**al sangue**	al **sang**-gweh
medium	**al puntino**	al poon-**tee**-noh
well done	**ben cotto**	ben **kot**-toh
glass	**il bicchiere**	eel bee-kee-**air**-eh
bottle	**la bottiglia**	lah bot-**teel**-yah
knife	**il coltello**	eel kol-**tell**-oh
fork	**la forchetta**	lah for-**ket**-tah
spoon	**il cucchiaio**	eel koo-kee-**eye**-oh

Menu Decoder

l'acqua minerale gassata/naturale	**lah**-kwah mee-nair-**ah**-leh gah-zah-tah/nah-too-rah-leh	mineral water fizzy/still
l'agnello	lah-**niell**-oh	lamb
l'aceto	lah-**cheh**-oh	vinegar
l'aglio	lal-ee-oh	garlic
al forno	al **for**-noh	baked
alla griglia	ah-lah **greel**-yah	grilled
l'aragosta	lah-rah-**goss**-tah	lobster
l'arrosto	lar-**ross**-toh	roast
la birra	lah **beer**-rah	beer
la bistecca	lah bee-**stek**-kah	steak
il brodo	eel **broh**-doh	broth
il burro	eel **boor**-oh	butter
il caffè	eel kah-**feh**	coffee
i calamari	ee kah-lah-**mah**-ree	squid
i carciofi	ee kar-**choff**-ee	artichokes
la carne	la **kar**-neh	meat
carne di maiale	**kar**-neh dee mah-**yah**-leh	pork
la cipolla	la chip-**oh**-lah	onion
i contorni	ee kon-**tor**-nee	vegetables
i fagioli	ee fah-**joh**-lee	beans
il fegato	eel **fay**-gah-toh	liver
il finocchio	eel fee-**nok**-ee-oh	fennel
il formaggio	eel for-**mad**-joh	cheese
le fragole	leh **frah**-goh-leh	strawberries
il fritto misto	eel free-toh **mees**-toh	mixed fried dish
la frutta	la **froot**-tah	fruit
frutti di mare	froo-tee dee **mah**-reh	seafood
i funghi	ee **foon**-ghee	mushrooms
i gamberi	ee **gam**-bair-ee	prawns
il gelato	eel jel-**lah**-toh	ice cream
l'insalata	leen-sah-lah-tah	salad
il latte	eel **laht**-teh	milk
il lesso	eel **less**-oh	boiled
il manzo	eel **man**-tsoh	beef
la melanzana	lah meh-lan-tsah-nah	aubergine
la minestra	lah meh-**ness**-trah	soup
l'olio	loh-lee-oh	oil
il pane	eel **pah**-neh	bread
le patate	leh pah-**tah**-teh	potatoes
le patatine fritte	leh pah-tah-**teen**-eh **free**-teh	chips
il pepe	eel **peh**-peh	pepper
la pesca	lah **pess**-kah	peach
il pesce	eel **pesh**-eh	fish
il pollo	eel **poll**-oh	chicken
il pomodoro	eel pom-moh-**dor**-oh	tomato
il prosciutto cotto/crudo	eel pro-**shoo**-toh **kot**-toh/**kroo**-doh	ham cooked/cured
il riso	eel **ree**-zoh	rice
il sale	eel **sah**-leh	salt
la salsiccia	lah sal-**see**-chah	sausage
le seppie	leh **sep**-pee-eh	cuttlefish
secco	**sek**-koh	dry
la sogliola	lah **soll**-yoh-lah	sole
gli spinaci	lyee spee-**nah**-chee	spinach
succo d'arancia/ di limone	**soo**-koh dah-**ran**-chah/ dee lee-**moh**-neh	orange/lemon juice
il tè	eel **teh**	tea
la tisana	lah tee-**zah**-nah	herbal tea
il tonno	eel **ton**-noh	tuna
la torta	lah **tor**-tah	cake/tart
l'uovo	loo-oh-voh	egg
vino bianco	**vee**-noh bee-**ang**-koh	white wine
vino rosso	**vee**-noh **ross**-oh	red wine
il vitello	eel vee-**tell**-oh	veal
le vongole	leh **von**-goh-leh	clams
lo zucchero	loh zoo-kair-oh	sugar
gli zucchini	lyee dzu-**kee**-nee	courgettes
la zuppa	lah **tsoo**-pah	soup

Numbers

1	**uno**	**oo**-noh
2	**due**	**doo**-eh
3	**tre**	treh
4	**quattro**	**kwat**-roh
5	**cinque**	**ching**-kweh
6	**sei**	**say**-ee
7	**sette**	**set**-teh
8	**otto**	**ot**-toh
9	**nove**	**noh**-veh
10	**dieci**	dee-**eh**-chee
11	**undici**	**oon**-dee-chee
12	**dodici**	**doh**-dee-chee
13	**tredici**	**tray**-dee-chee
14	**quattordici**	kwat-**tor**-dee-chee
15	**quindici**	**kwin**-dee-chee
16	**sedici**	**say**-dee-chee
17	**diciassette**	dee-chah-**set**-teh
18	**diciotto**	dee-**chot**-toh
19	**diciannove**	dee-chah-**noh**-veh
20	**venti**	**ven**-tee
30	**trenta**	**tren**-tah
40	**quaranta**	kwah-**ran**-tah
50	**cinquanta**	ching-**kwan**-tah
60	**sessanta**	sess-**an**-tah
70	**settanta**	set-**tan**-tah
80	**ottanta**	ot-**tan**-tah
90	**novanta**	noh-**van**-tah
100	**cento**	**chen**-toh
1,000	**mille**	**mee**-leh
2,000	**duemila**	**doo**-eh **mee**-lah
5,000	**cinquemila**	**ching**-kweh **mee**-lah
1,000,000	**un milione**	oon meel-**yoh**-neh

Time

one minute	**un minuto**	oon mee-**noo**-toh
one hour	**un'ora**	oon **or**-ah
half an hour	**mezz'ora**	medz-**or**-ah
a day	**un giorno**	oon **jor**-noh
a week	**una settimana**	oona set-tee-**mah**-nah
Monday	**lunedì**	loo-neh-**dee**
Tuesday	**martedì**	mar-teh-**dee**
Wednesday	**mercoledì**	mair-koh-leh-**dee**
Thursday	**giovedì**	joh-veh-**dee**
Friday	**venerdì**	ven-air-**dee**
Saturday	**sabato**	**sah**-bah-toh
Sunday	**domenica**	doh-**meh**-nee-kah

Milan's Underground Network and Urban Railway System

Milan's metro runs from 6am until 12:30am daily (until 1:30am on Saturday). There are four lines: M1 (red), M2 (green), M3 (yellow) and M5 (purple). These intersect with the Passante Ferroviaria (blue) line, which connects the suburbs with the city. For more details on travelling on Milan's underground system, *see pages 218–19 and the pull-out map.*

RETE METROPOLITANA E TRATTE FERROVIAR
UNDERGROUND NETWORK AND URBAN RAILW

M1 Metropolitana linea 1
Underground line 1

M2 Metropolitana linea 2
Underground line 2

M3 Metropolitana linea 3
Underground line 3

M5 Metropolitana linea 5
Underground line 5

||| In costruzione
Under construction

Stazione accessibile
Accessible station

i ATM Point: informazioni e punto vendita
ATM Point: information and retail

Linee ferroviarie regionali
Regional railways

Interscambio con rete ferroviaria
Connection with railway system

Autobus X73 Express e 73 per Aeroporto di Linate
Bus X73 Express and 73 to Linate Airport

Autobus per Aeroporto di Linate, Malpensa e Orio al Serio
Bus service to Linate, Malpensa and Orio al Serio Airports

Treno per Aeroporto di Malpensa
Train to Malpensa Airport

Bus terminal
Bus terminal

P Parcheggio di corrispondenza ATM
ATM interchange parking areas

S Linee ferroviarie suburbane
Suburban railways

S1 Saronno - Milano Passante - Lodi

S2 Mariano Comense - Milano Passante - Milano Rogoredo

S3 Saronno - Milano Cadorna

S4 Camnago Lentate - Seveso - Milano Cadorna

S5 Varese - Milano Passante - Treviglio

S6 Novara - Milano Passante - Treviglio

S8 Lecco - Carnate - Milano P.ta Garibaldi

S9 Saronno - Milano S. Cristoforo - Albairate

S11 Chiasso - Como S. Giovanni - Milano P.ta Garibaldi

S13 Milano Bovisa - Milano Passante - Pavia